Women Political Leadership in India

Some Important Dimensions

Women Political Leadership in India

Some Important Dimensions

Archana Kumari
R. K. Verma

SERIALS PUBLICATIONS
NEW DELHI (INDIA)

First Published - 2010

ISBN: 978-81-8387-354-3

Published by

SERIALS PUBLICATIONS
4830/24, Prahlad Street, Ansari Road
Darya Ganj, New Delhi-110002 (India)
Phone : 23245225 Fax : 91-11-23272135
E-mail: serials@satyam.net.in

Contents

PART-2
MICRO LEVEL WOMEN POLITICAL LEADERSHIP

PART-3
MACRO LEVEL WOMEN POLITICAL LEADERSHIP

PART-5
VIVID DIMENSIONS OF WPL

Acknowledgements

Several politico-legal arrangements have been made by the state craft in favour of women in order to improve their situation. Besides, other non governmental agencies have also taken steps in this regard. But situation has not improved to the desired extent. It has been a predominant assumption that the position of women in our society cannot be improved unless they seek power and have say in the decision making process. Hence the issue of women political leadership becomes pertinent in present situation. The politico-legal arrangements have also not been found effective due to lack of self assertion among the common women. In order to make these arrangements effective, women themselves have to be self assertive and sensitized to play roles in social and political domain. The introduction of new Panchayat Raj Institutions (PRIs) has broadened the canvas of their political roles at grassroots level in general in India and in Bihar in particular. On the contrary, it is largely alleged that proxy leadership prevails among women. If they are not assertive they should be sensitized to play political roles and made aware and enthused to take part in the decision making process. Political parties and voluntary agencies need to come up for making women sensitized to take roles in social and political domain. A number of voluntary agencies have taken steps in this regard in Bihar. Thus, the phenomenon of women political leadership acquires significance. It is high time to take the stock of situation of women political leadership in our polity in its varied dimensions like emergence / induction, roles and functions, their situation/roles in political bodies and parties' functionaries at both macro and micro levels, their relationship with their male counterparts, social capital among them, women leadership in other spheres, the impact of voluntarism and socio-economic ecology and so on.

As such present discourse intends to provide variegated facets of views on women political leadership in context of various dimensions mainly emergence, nature, roles and women empowerment. It does also provide the impact of ICT and environmental issues on the women political leadership. The present book is an outcome of the UGC sponsored national seminar on "Dimensions of Women Political Leadership" held recently. The editors have been supported by various persons in compilation and editing of the book. Their contributions must be acknowledged.

First of all, we express our gratitude to the anonymous experts and authorities of the UGC for providing financial support for organization of the seminar and creating an opportunity to consolidate the variegated views and issues on the subject. Dr S P Sinha, Principal, R N College, Hajipur has provided all kinds of support, cooperation, encouragement and guidance at all the stages from initiating the seminar to compilation of the write up. We express our gratitude to him from the core of the heart. The Head and other faculty members of the P G Department of Political Science, R N College, Hajipur provided help to us. We are thankful to all of them. The academic guidance, tips and suggestions have been received from Prof Sushma Yadav of I I P A, Prof L N Sharma of Patna University, Dr Sanjeev Kumar Sharma of Ch Charan Singh University, Meerut, Prof Upendra Mishra of B R A Bihar University, Muzaffarpur, Dr Navanit Sinha of I I P A Bihar Regional Branch, Patna and Prof Vijay Kumar of T M Bhagalpur University, Bhagalpur. We express our gratitude to all of them. Besides Dr M S Gupta of R K D College, Patna has been of much help in encouraging us to edit the contributions in a book form. We are grateful to him.

It will be injustice to ignore the contributors of this volume without whom the discourse could not have been completed. We are thankful to all of them.

The family members and the children especially, Shreya and Shreeja (daughters of Dr Archana) and Nisha and Aditya (children of Dr Verma) have been facilitating our work (like arranging and searching the papers, operating computers etc) and enhanced our joy in academic exercises. Sometimes, they participated, with their innocent suggestions, in the discussions; but to the best of their capacity, which added our joy of work. Dr Rajesh Kumar (husband of Dr Archana) had added wits and humors during the discussions and corrections in order to make us re-energized. We owe this venture to them.

Sri Satish Sinha has done the most difficult work of computer typing and M/S Serial Publications has shown enough interest in publishing the discourse. We are thankful to both of them. However, we take the responsibility of the mistakes in the discourse, if any.

June 2009

Archana Kumari
R.K. Verma

List of Contributors

Ms. Sonal Shree, Regional Manager, HTC Uttaranchal and Eastern U.P. H.R. Galaxy.

Dr. C.D. Amar, University Department of Political Science,. B.R.A. Bihar University, Muzaffarpur.

Mahesh Kumar Paswan, Research Scholar, Patna University, Patna.

Kranti Mandal, Research Scholar, T M Bhagalpur University, Bhagalpur.

Dr. Sandhya Rani, Department of Economics, Maharaja College, (V K Singh University), Ara.

Dr. Henna Tabassum, Head, Department of Sociology, A.N. College, (Magadh University, Bodh-Gaya), Patna.

Dr. Arjun Sharma, Lecturer, Department of Political Science, S.M.D. College, Punpun (Patna).

Dr. Kumari Saroj, Lecturer in Political. Science, M.D.D. College, (B R A Bihar University), Muzaffarpur.

Dr. Rajesh Kumar, Assistant Professor, Division of Applied Sciences S.D. Institute of Technology and Management, Israna (Panipat), Hryana.

Anand Kumar, Lecturer, S.D. Institute of Technolgy and Management, Israna, Panipat, Haryana

Dr. Kumari Manju, Lecturer in Economics, R.N. College, (B R A Bihar University), Hajipur.

Ajay Kumar, Research Scholar, T. M. Bhagalpur University, Bhagalpur.

Devkant , Research Scholar, T.M.B.U. Department of Political Science, Bhagalpur.

Dr. Punam Kumari, Lecturer in Home Science, Patna Women's College, (Patna University), Patna.

Dr. Anil Kumar Singh, Lecturer in Commerce, Awadh Bihari Singh College, Lalganj (Vaishali).

Dr. Naresh Kumar, Department of Political Science, B.R.A. Bihar University, Muzaffarpur

Kumar Rakesh Ranjan, Research Scholar, Department of Political Science Patna College, Patna.

Dr. Sayeed Sahnawaj C. Ajmeri, Department of Geography, Patna University, Patna.

Md. Irshad Ali, Research Scholar, Patna University, Patna.

Dr. Manjari Verma, Department of Political Science, L.S. College, (B R.A. Bihar University), Muzaffarpur.

Dr. Madhu Singh, Lecturer, in Political Science, R.B.B.M. College, Muzaffarpur.

Dr. Binda Kumari, H.O.D. Department of Political Science, Samastipur Mahila College, Samastipur.

Dr. Sita Sinha, Lecturer in Political Science, S.M.D. College, Punpun.

Dr. Krishnandan Singh, Department of Hindi, B.R.A. Bihar University, Muzaffarpur

Dr. Pramod Kumar Dubey, H.O.D. Department of Political Science,. S.M.D. College, Punpun.

Dr. Harishchandra Prasad Yadav, H.O.D., Department of Political Science, R.M.L.S. College, Muzaffarpur.

Dr. Mukul Roy, Lecturer, Department Sociology, B.N. College, P.U. Patna.

Dr. S.A. Hassan, Research Scholar, Patna University, Patna

Dr. Prem Singh, Lecturer, Deptt. of History, Sukhdev Mukhlal College, Hajipur.

Prof. Gita Sinha, Lecturer Deptt. of Home Science, B.P.S. College, Vaishali.

Dr. Shakil Asharaf, Lecturer, L.S.W., S.N.S.,R.K.S. College, Saharsa.

Dr. Manawwar Jalan, Principal, Women's Training College, (Patna University), Patna.

Rajni Rani, Deptt. of Hindi, B.R.A. Bihar University, Muzaffapur.

Ambuj Kumar, P.G.T., B N Collegiate Inter School, Patna.

Anju Sadhna, P.G.T., B N Collegiate Inter School, Patna.

Dr. Rakesh Ranjan, Department of Political Science, Patna College, (Patna University), Patna.

Dr. Amrendra Kumar Gond, Research Scholar, Department of Political Science, Patna University, Patna.

Shashank Kumar, Research Scholar, Department of Political Science, Patna University, Patna.

Bipin Chandra, Research Scholar, Department of History, Patna University.

Dr. Indira Sinha, Lecturer in Political Science, College of Commerce, (Magadh University, Bodh-Gaya), Patna.

Dr. Sudhir Kumar, U.G.C. NET Research Scholar, Department of Education, Patna University, Patna.

Dr. Kumar Amrendra Naraian, Lecturer in Economics., R.N. College, (B R A University) Hajipur.

Dr. Kamal Prasad Boddh, Principal, Nalanda Teacher's Training College, Nalanda.

Dr. Nutan Kumari, M.A. Home Science, M.U.

Dr. Mukesh Kumar Roy, Lecturer in Political Science, B.N. Collegiate Inter School, Patna.

Dr. Usha Chaudhari, Lecturer in Psychology, R.N. College, (B R A Bihar University), Hajipur.

Dr. Sudhir Kumar, Research Scholar, U.G.C. NET, Patna.

Dr. Syed Raza, PGT, M.S. K. + 2 School, Motihari.

Priti Kumari, Department of Economics, Baldev Inter College, Dinapu, Patna.

Kavita Kumari, Research Scholar, Deptt. of Sanskrit, Patna University, Patna.

Amit Vikram, Research Scholar, Patna.

Dr. Ram Prakash, Reader, Department of Political Science, L.S. College, (B.R.A.Bihar University), Muzaffarpur.

Dr. (Mrs.) Ratna, Research Associate, L.S. College, Muzaffarpur.

Dr. Prasannta, Educational Product Manager, Mac Milan Publishers India Ltd, Patna.

Dr. Shefali Roy, Senior, Lecturer in Politca; Science, Patna Women's College, (Patna University), Patna.

Dr. Sheo Kumar Ram, Lecturer in Political Science, R.P.S. College, Jaintpur (Muzaffarpur).

Sushri Bahalen Haro, Lecturer, Marwari College, Ranchi, Jharkhand.

Md. Irshad Ali, Research Scholar, UGC NET, Patna University, Patna.

Dr. Madhu Prabha Singh, Lecturer in Hindi, Y.N. College, (J P University) Dighwara, Chapra.

Shalendra Kumar Mandal, Lecturer, Department of Architecture, UGC, NET, Patna.

Dr. Rajendra Prasad Singh, D.M. College, (B R A Bihar University), Vaishali.

Dr. Minni, Thakur, H.O.D., Department of Political Science, R.N.A.R. College, (L N M University), Samastipur.

Santosh Kumar Ram, Department of Political Science, V.K.S. University, Ara (Bhojpur).

Ratnesh Ranjan, Deptt. of Politcal Science, Rajendra College, (J P University), Chapra.

Pallavi, Lecturer, Women's Training College, P.U., Patna.

Dr. Bimal Kumar, Research Scholar, T.M. Bhagalpur University, Bhagalpur.

Dr. Anil Thakur, Lecturer in Economics, Koshi College, Khagaria.

Ramayan Shastri, Research Scholar, Department of Political Science, T.M.Bhagalpur University, Bhagalpur.

Manish Kumar Pandey, Department of Political Science T.M.Bhagalpur University, Bhagalpur.

Dr. Vinod Shankar Jha, University Professor, Department of Political Science, L. S. College, Muzaffarpur.

Dr. Javed Ahmad Khan, Department of History, Jamuni Lal College, (B R A Bihar Univesity), Hajipur.

Dr. Mukhlal Roy, Lecturer in Political Science, K.S.S. College, Lakhisarai.

Avinash Kumar, Research Scholar, Department of History, Patna University, Patna.

Alveen Bakhla, Lecturer, Radha Govind, Inter College, Ramgarh, Jharkhand.

Dilip Kumar, Research Scholar, Department of History, Patna University, Patna.

Gajanfar Alam, Research Scholar, UGC NET, Department of Sociology, Patna University, Patna.

Amita Kumari, Lecturer, S.M. College, Hajipur.

Dr. Sanjay Kumari, Lecturer in Hindi, S.M. College, Patna.

Shakil Ahmad, Research Scholar, Department. of Sociology, P.U. Patna.

Dr. Asha Rani, Lecturer in Political Science, G.L. College, Bihta.

Hari Narayan Prasad Chaurasia, Advocate, Civil Court, Hajipur.

Abhay Kumar, Research Scholar, Department of Political Science, PatnaUniversity, Patna.

Ms. Navneet Khatri, Lecturer, N.C. College, Israna, Panipat Hariyana.

Dr. Ravindra Kumar Verma 'Ravi', University Professor in Hindi, B.R.A. Bihar University, Muzaffarpur.

Dr. Subhash Chandra Roy, Assistant Prof., Chankaya National Law University, Patna.

Dr. R. K. Verma, Lecturer, Deptt. of Pol. Science, R.N. College, Hajipur.

Dr. K.H. Siddiqui, Lecturer, Deptt. of Pol. Science, R.N. College, Hajipur.

Dr. Nawal Kishore Prasad Singh, H.O.D., Deptt. of Pol. Science, R.N. College, Hajipur.

Dr. Mona Tabassum, Lecturer in Psychology. R.N. College, Hajipur.

Dr. Suman Sinha, Lecturer in English, R.N. College, Hajipur.

Dr. Pawan Kumar Yadav, Lecturer in Pol. Science, R.N. College, Hajipur.

Dr. Manju Kumari, Department of Psychology., R.N. College, Hajipur

Dr. Kumar Rajani Kant Ranjan, Lecturer in Hindi, R.N. College, Hajipur.

Dr. Kavita Kumari Singh, Lecturer, Department of Hindi, R.N. College, Hajipur.

Santosh Kumar Singh, Research Scholar, Department of History, R.N. College, Hajipur.

Dr. L.N. Sharma, University Professor & Head (Retired), Department of Political Science, Patna University, Patna.

Dr. Sushma Yadav, Professor, Ambedkar Chair on Social Justice, Indian Institute of Public Administration, New Delhi.

Dr. Sanjeev Kumar Sharma, Editor, Indian Journal of Political Science, CCS University, Meerut (U.P.)

Prof. Vijay Kumar, University Professor, Department of Political Science, T.M.Bhagalpur University, Bhagalpur.

Dr. Baleshwar Prasad Singh, University Professor, Department of Political Science, Binova Bhave University, Hajaribagh (Jharkhand).

Dr. Upendra Mishra, University Professor, Department of Political Science, B/R.A. Bihar University, Muzaffarpur.

Dr. Sudhir Kumar Singh, Reader and Head, South Asian Studies Rajiv Gandhi Central University, Itanagar (Arunachal Pradesh).

Dr. Shefali Roy, Senior Lecturer, Department of Political Science, Patna Women's College (P.U.), Patna.

Part–1

Theorization of Women Political Leadership

1

Omni-Relevant But Dysfunctional Women Political Leadership (An Examination of the Phenomenon at the Apex Level)

L. N. Sharma

Feminism has brought gender considerations and new insights into political discourse. According to the feminist school of thought, political theorists and analysts have overlooked women. But according to the other school, it is not correct to say in the fast moving modem age that particular traits are masculine and particular traits are feminine. For example, for ages, competition, aggression and power, etc. were treated as masculine traits. But now a day, it is found that women are as competitive and prone to power-wielding or aggressive as their male counterparts. Mrs. Gandhi as the Prime Minister was said to be "the only man in the company of old women" in her cabinet. There is nothing that separates Sonia Gandhi, Mayawati, Vasundhara Raje, Sheila Dikshit, Renuka Chaudhary, Kanti Singh, Uma Bharati and Sushma Swaraj as less competitive, power-wielding or aggressive than Manmohan Singh, Pranab Mukherjee, Sharad Pawar, Arjun Singh, Digvijai Singh, L.K. Advani, Jyoti Basu, etc. Hence, the gender considerations are no longer entertainable.

It is a fact, however, that women have been poorly represented in traditional statecraft and high politics. In her celebrated work, *Bananas, Beaches and Bases,* Cynthia Enloe asks provocatively, 'where are the women?' thus drawing attention to the fact that politics subordinates the role of gender.[1] Peterson and Runyan persuade theorists to apply the lens of gender" to their theories.[2] However, the feminist theory itself suffers from several weaknesses. There is as yet no single comprehensive feminist theory. Feminism has many strands including liberal feminism, socialist feminism, radical feminism and even post-colonial feminism. Feminist scholars are themselves demanding a fundamental review of their theories and assumptions while they advocate the incorporation of the women's perspective into the traditional theories.

Indian parliament has not been able to ensure, despite some efforts being made in this direction for the last one decade, that 33% of its seats be reserved for women. But 50% of seats have been reserved for women in PRIs and the apprehension that women representatives would act in *purdah* behind their male counterparts or that their male counterparts would act on their behalf is being gradually eliminated. Recently, the Govt. of Bihar issued a circular that women representatives would not attend meetings along with their male counterparts. Such efforts would ultimately make women come on their own as political leaders in their own right and they will develop the mettle and acumen of political leadership as their sisters at the higher echelon at the state and national level have already done, though their number is comparatively small.

Having made gender—specific comments above, this writer would like to emphasise that many comments apply equally to men and women political leaders and one such comment is that when they occupy offices, both become omni-relevant. They play the most crucial role in politico-economic-administrative management and manipulate all the affairs that concern human existence. Their role becomes all pervasive and effects virtually all the spheres of political life from the Union down to the taluka or the village. They arrogate a bigger than their size image even while they function under the constraints imposed by the constitution which is imbued with the features of federation, secularism, rule of law, judicial review and periodical elections within a time frame.

A Case Study of Mrs. Gandhi's Leadership Style the Only Women Indian P.M. so far

Most of the political analysts characterize leadership style of Indira Gandhi as authoritarian and describe her methods as ruthless, deceptive and manipulative.[3] She is projected as a consummate practitioner of pragmatic politics (de-ideologied, amoral and uniformed by any compassion[4]) with no holds barred and possessing a superb sense of timing and political bargaining to match her single-minded pursuit of self-interest. She herself said, I am a tough politician". She had a strong conviction of self-righteousness. This acted as a delusion during the emergency when communication about others' perception of the rightness or wrongness of her actions did not reach her. However, when she learnt about what others did or felt, she made amends by calling for an election which indicated that she possessed the capacity of self-correction.

Mrs. Gandhi's assumption of leadership role in the initial years appears to have been inspired to overcome the inferiority complex that she was being undervalued and underestimated as Prime Minister (between 1966 and 1969). She wanted to be recognized and was "determined" to face challenges and problems with courage. She was stubborn enough to meet tests and transcend them. Therefore, she appeared imperial and domineering even while using power to serve social and national goals. In any case, she was a realist and when situation demanded, she did not shrink from being a confrontationist and user of unscrupulous means.

A set of commentators defend Mrs. Gandhi's role on the ground that it led to maintenance of order, socialist reconstruction and national cohesiveness and integrity by contributing to the liberation of Bangladesh. These goals would not have been realized without leadership initiative from a single centre of power.

Mrs. Gandhi's leadership strategies changed according to times. To begin with, she played a dormant role and adopted the style of a consensual leader. She consulted senior party leaders, gave the image of being pliable and appeared to be more concerned with maintaining continuity rather than change. She even appeared as indecisive and vacillating at times. She absorbed both external and internal pressure. But even at that time, she had the trait of disallowing others to read what was passing in her mind. She kept herself within a protected "shell" while talking to her colleagues and did not reveal her hand or mind on anything. That served the purpose of giving the impression to her senior colleagues that she was indecisive or vacillating. After the election of 1967 in which the congress did badly, she started asserting herself and showing her independence from the party bosses. She formed the cabinet in 1967 without party guidance and gave a fair representation to her personal allies like Dinesh Singh in it. She introduced charges in policy direction also. Though earlier, she was initiating growth-oriented economic policies and absorbing US pressure, she started orchestrating her support for populist policies, assumed image of a "progressive" leader and showed a tilt towards the *USSR. and the C.P.I.*

Mrs. Gandhi acted with such subtlety that her style worked as a mask so that her competitors or rivals were not able to guess what she was upto. She started building a personal power support structure gradually and tended to make her position dominating in the cabinet and in the bureaucracy. She started acting without consulting senior party colleagues between August 1968 and April 1969. By April 1969, she was in a confrontatimist mood but in her power gave, she chose ideological divergence on the issue of public sector US. Private sector as the external manifestation of the confrontation. The successful turning of a power game into an ideological confrontation marked Mrs. Gandhi's distinctive style.

S. Kaviraj aptly comments that Mrs. Gandhi did not set the terms of the game, she tried to win it within the terms set for her by others.[5] In the AICC session held in April 1969, the Deputy Prime Minister with the portfolio of Finance & Morarji Desai was taking the position that social control of banks had been started only three months previously, it ought to be given a fair chance. Mrs. Gandhi, along with her supporters, spoke in favour of public sector and nationalization of banks. The Congress President spoke against the public sector. The real battle was over the issue of nomination of candidate for the office of the President of India which Mrs. Gandhi wanted to be left to herself. She divested Desai of his portfolio of Finance and giving the battle ideological teeth thus started. Leaders of the Congress, combined in a grap called the syndicate, were not in a mood to give Mrs. Gandhi a free hand in the selection of candidate to this important office. Mrs. Gandhi did not propose any name in the meeting of the Parliamentary Board of the Congress Party which selected a name and Mrs. Gandhi not only kept mum but even signed the nomination paper of the Congress candidate. But one day after the passage of the bill on the bank nationalization, she and her supporters demanded that Congress MPs be left free to vote according to their conscience of Ram and two union ministers F.A. Ahmad, who sided Mrs. Gandhi vociferously spoke in favour of "free voting" and ultimately, the congress candidate was made to loose the election with the help of Mrs. Gandhi's group in the Congress party and the leftists, thus leading to the split of the Congress party. Though the Congress party was reduced to a minority group in the Lok Sabha, she managed to be in office with the help of the leftist support. Meanwhile, she set upon building an electoral base for herself among the masses. Apart from seeking support for some policies which were identified with her personal leadership, she adopted the strategy of seeking the support of S.C..s, S.T.s, minorities and OBCs for her leadership. They along with agricultural workers, students, youths and women were recruited as members of the new Congress Party. She reorganized the governmental departments in such a way that the major administrative, police and intelligence services came under her command.

The preparations at all the levels indicated pragmatic electoral strategy whereas she continued to adorn an ideological cloak. As a result she secured massive electorate mandate in the mid-term parliamentary poll of 1971. She pushed through some progressive measures and brought about the emergence of Bangladesh in 1971. She reached the pinnacle of glory and triumph in 71-72 but in 73-74, failures appeared in the areas of land reforms and reflected in price increase, unemployment, and corruption. The slogans of "committed bureaucracy" were reflections of institutional decay which was all the more reflected in the suppression of three senior most judges of the Supreme Court of India in the appointment of its Chief Justice. Mrs. Gandhi had broken all the institutions which could defend the system and in the wake of bad economic situation of 73-74, when the opposition groups launched movements in Gujarat and Bihar, and the Allahabad High Court delivered a judgment holding her guilty of 'corrupt practices" in election to her Lok Sabha seat on 12 June 1975, she declared emergency without consulting the cabinet - a desperate act of a desperate leader at bay. The emergency (25 June 1975 - early 1977) was an authoritarian interlude in the democratic history of independent India and its implementation by her son, Sanjay and his coterie gave the emergency a bad name particularly in north India. Mrs. Gandhi in fact became helpless and felt "imprisoned" and lost her treasured sense of self-righteousness. The mixture of populism and charisma that made her win bettles after battles abandoned her.

She still had the democratic instinct left for as some say that she relied on the IB report that she would win if elections' were held than) to announce elections in early 1977 in which she lost badly. Following her defeat, the Janata Party which came to rule made her face the Shah Commission for her various acts of omissions and commissions during the emergency. She also faced imprisonment in a parliamentary probe for suppressing facts in "Kissa Kursi Ke" case.

People, however, turned to Mrs. Gandhi again in 1980 because of bad performance of the Janata Party. She served four year term (1980-84) as Prime Minister before she was assassinated by a Sikh to avenge firing on the Golden Temple of Amritsar which she had to order to leer the temple from the terrorist siege. Once more, however Mrs. Gandhi showed that she could be tough to black marketers who feared her.

But some delay in policy making also characterized this phase. Political loyalty became more important as one of the norms for advancement to plum parts in the bureaucracy and a demoralized bureaucracy was not of help in the policy making process. Mrs. Gandhi's policy initiatives were characterized by ad-hocism. She tinkered with the planning Commission. She was being forced to liberalize economy in the name of fiscal refocus. She went in for a massive I.M.F. loan in addition to borrowing from the international market. She faced the crisis of credibility as she had moved away from her earlier policy of socialism. But she faced the biggest challenge on the front of law and order. Politically-motivated agitations by farmers in states like Maharashtra, Punjab, Karnataka and Tamil Nadu assumed serious dimensions. Punjab imbroglis, in particular, tried Mrs. Gandhi's patience out and she shed her "last drop of blood" for the cause of national integration.

Theorisation and Generalisation about Leadership Behaviour

The case of Mrs. Gandhi is not such that we can draw generalized conclusions about women leadership on the basis of the study of her leadership characteristics. Sheila Dikshit has made a hat trick as the Chief Minister of Delhi State recently. If she were to become Prime Minister tomorrow or if we make a case study of Sheila Dikshit, our conclusions of women leadership would be entirely different because of personality differences. We would, therefore, endorse the formula that L=P+S i.e. personality in interaction with situation constitutes the kernel of leadership. Unless we have visionary Realist Political Leader[6] (to use Koren's term) which we did not have after Gandhi, situation and personality in interaction would continue to constitute leadership style of men or women political leadership.

In any case, the political leadership, whether of male or female, is omni-relevant because of various causes. Its omni-relevance emanates from its positional centrality backed up by its power wielding and benefit dispensation capability.

Leadership is the object of a large amount and heterogeneous variety of societal, communal and individual expectations that keeps the leader at the centre stage except when election is around; and or she/he faces odds when his or her re-election is under serious challenge.[7] We generally have "transactional leadership".[8] Leaders grant gobs and receive votes instead or grant subsidies in lien of campaign contributions.

As we saw in the case of Mrs. Gandhi, leadership becomes omni-relevant through identification with big causes, goals and symbols. A large part of the Indian leadership claims to be the successor of the freedom struggle; a good part claims to be the participants of the J.P. and then of the Mandal movements, whereas the leaders of the old Madras and Bombay state claim to be the successors of the anti-Brahmin, anti-Hindi *Dalit* movements. Mrs. Gandhi was not a transformative[9] or an ideological leader but essentially a manipulative one who were the clock of false ideological consciousness (to use the term of Marx's 'The German Ideology, 1845) to hide her real intentions. We can also use Lasswellian formula to characterize Mrs. Gandhi's leadership. The formula is L=rdp i.e. a leader has the skill to rationalize and displace his or her personal motives by national goals.[10] Her personal motive was survival and glorification of her leadership but she hid this motive behind the veneer of ideology of public sector, nationalization and in the popular phraseology of 'garibi hatao'.

Mrs. Gandhi inherited 'charisma' from Nehru which he had inherited from Mahatma Gandhi so charisma has been routinized (to use Max Weber's phrase) in the Nehru clan even in the `successors of Mrs. Gandhi which include Sonia Gandhi and even Priyanka Gandhi. Maneka Gandhi could not be on good terms with her charismatic mother-in-law (Mrs. Gandhi), so she had to leave the Congress party. She went to the opposition where she was a minister for only some time and faded away from the political scene. Charisma could not be routinized in her case. Due to having the hesitate of queen of a princely state Mrs. Vasundhara Raje when she left as a socialite of Delhi to be the C.M. of Rajasthan, too, appeared to be a charismatic personality. But since the end of 2007, there appears to be a change in the lexicon of Indian politics. Good governance has made a space in it and anti-incumbency has lost its importance in electoral politics. That explains the defeat of Vasundhara Raje who annoyed the Gurjars by going back against the promise she had made of providing reservation in gobs for them and they resented that the Meenas had got a reservations at the first instance. Mrs. Sheila Dikst won as the Chief Minister for the third time because to the electorate she was deemed to be a performer and appeared to be doing her best under the existing circumstances.

Charisma has also been inherited by Mayawati from Kanshiram but she has added electoral pragmatism, like Mrs. Gandhi, to charisma. She has been arduously wooing the upper caste, particularly the Brahmins of U.P. and was able to gain Chief Ministership on the basis of astute electoral combination. If she gets more than 50 out of 80 seats from U.P. in Lok Sabha, she will be a contender for the Prime Ministership of the country with the support of the third or the fourth front.

Jayalalita also inherited charisma from Ram Chandran and for sometime, her stars appeared on the upswing. A characteristic of charisma is that the followers of such a leader think that he or she is doing or saying right things even when he goes wrong. Jayalalita, in that sense, has lost her charisma after the initial phase.

Dysfunctional of Women's Political Leadership

We have taken the position, in this paper, that most of the traits are common among male and female political leaders and generalization on the basis of a few women political leaders will not be correct. In this part of the paper, we tend to argue that like their male counterpart, women political leaders, too are prove to encourage crime, corruption, casteism, communalism, regionalism, linguism, etc. There is a demand for an inquiry into the alleged Rs. 22,000 crore corruption charges against Vasuandhara Raje, Former Chief Minister of Rajasthan and no less a person than the Ex-Vice-President of India is making this demand. Arrest her, send her to jail if found guilty, he says. It is also found that most re-elected, too were corrupt. As it this was not enough, there has been unprecedented 20% increase in crime in U.P. under Mayawati's regime between January 1 and October 15 as police records show[11] whereas 1,02,013 cases were registered during the mentioned period under Mulayam Singh's period in 2006, 1,21,030 cases have been reistered during the same period under Mayawati's regime in 2008.[12] Most of the cases relates to crimes against women and dalits who have been hit the hardest.[13] This is quite in contrast to what Mayawati had promised to the people. The alleged murder of an engineer by an M.L.A. of the B.S.P. has earned quite a bad name for the regime of Mayawati. Even a modest looking political leader like Sheila Dikshit spoke against the migrant Biharies and *UPwallahs* in Delhi. Uma Bharati raised slogans arousing passions for the demolition of Babri Masjid. We can give credit to Mrs. Gandhi who was able to bring down the number of persons killed each year to 68 between 1971 and 1978.[14] a bit of credit, though due to pragmatic considerations, is due also to Mayawati who brought balance to the imbalanced "Taraju" slogan of Kanshiram who was abusive against the upper castemen. So we can conclude that though the signs of functionalism are present among women political leaders as they are among male political leaders, there are also some signs of functionalism among women political leaders.

Notes

1. Cynthia Enloe, *Bananas, Beaches and Bases: Making Feminist Sense of International Politics*, Berkeley : University of California Press, 1990.
2. V. Spike Peterson and Anne Sisson Runyon, *Global Gender Issues* (2" d ed.), Oxford: Westview Press, 1999.
3. Much of the Materials of this Case Study is Based on L.N. Sharma, ICSSR-sponsored Research Project Report, Leadership Role of the Indian Prime Ministers: Styles, Authority and Effect, 1993, pp. 174-230 (in the Press).
4. Ashis Nandy, *At the Edge of Psychology: Essays in Politics and Culture*, Delhi: Oxford University Press, 1980, p. 114; and Stanley A. Kochanexk, "Mrs. Gandhi's Pyramid: The New Congress"

in Henry C. Hart (ed.) *Indira Gandhi's India,* Colorado: Westview Press, 1976, pp. 93-124.

5. S. Kaviraj, "Indira Gandhiand Indian Politics", *Economic and Political Weekly,* Sept. 20-27, 1986, p. 1697.

6. Michael Keran, "Moses as a Visionary Realist", International *Political Science Review* (1988), Vol. 9, No. 1, pp. 71-84.

7. This factor gains added significance in India because of follwership behaviour. In India, almost everybody thinks that he or she should knock the doors of politicians for getting his or her work (legal or illegal, personal, semi-public or public or for getting any kind of state patronage) done either by himself or herself as a pay-off if he or she had obliged the politician in the campaign or through intermedieries or contactman who are many in number.

8. James Macgregor Bums, *Leadership,* Delhi: Ambika Publications, 1978, pp. 141-400.

9. *Ibid.*

10. H.D. Lasswell, *Political Writings of Harold D. Lasswell,* Illinois: The Free Press, 1951.

11. Subhesh Mishra, "Apatriyashit Badhotri", *India Today,* November 19, 2008, p.20 (in Hindi).

12. *Ibid.*

13. *Ibid.*

14. B.L. Fadia, *Indian Government and Politics,* Agra: Schitya Bhawan Publications, 1997, p. 624.

2

Dimensions of Women Political Leadership

Sushma Yadav

> *"Perhaps no form of government, said Lord Bryce, "needs great leaders as much as democracy." For democracy is not self-executing. It takes leadership to bring democracy to life. Great democratic leaders are visionaries. They have an instinct for their nation's future, a course to steer, a port to seek. Through their capacity for persuasion, they win the consent of their people and call forth democracy's inner resources".*
> ***—Arthur Schlesinger Jr. "Pulitzer-prizewinning Historian"***

> *"In government, in business, and in the professions there may be a day when women will be looked upon as persons. We are, however, far from that day as yet".* ***—Eleanor Roosevelt, 1940***

> *"Whether there are innately female leadership styles... is not really the right question. It is more important to ask why there has been so little attention paid to women leaders over the years as well as why the styles of leading more often exhibited by women are particularly useful at this critical moment in history."* ***—Charlotte Bunch***

> *"In politics if you want anything said, ask a man. If you want anything done, ask a woman".*
> ***—Margaret Thatcher, British Politician***

> *"Leaders don't just appear out of thin air. They must be developed-nurtured in such a way that they acquire the qualities of leadership".* **—Warren Bennis**

Leadership is a topic with universal appeal. Much has been written about it. Despite this, leadership presents a major challenge to practitioners as well as researchers interested in understanding its nature. It is a highly complex, yet valued phenomenon. Leadership has been defined and conceptualized in myriad ways. The component common to nearly all classifications is that leadership is an influence process that assists groups of individuals toward goal attainment. It is defined as a "process whereby an individual influences a group of individuals to achieve a common goal".

A number of studies have also focused on leadership as a trait. The trait perspective suggests that certain people in our society have special inborn qualities that make them leaders. This view restricts leadership to only those who are believed to have special characteristics. In contrast, the process approach suggests that leadership is a process that can be learned and that it is available to everyone. Similarly, there are two common forms of leadership assigned and emergent. Assigned leadership is based on a formal title of position in an organization. Emergent leadership results from what one does and how one acquires support from followers. Leadership, as a process, applies to individuals in both assigned roles and emergent roles.

Then, there are certain concepts, which are integral to the process of leadership. Prominent among them is the concept of power, the potential to influence. There are two kinds of power: position and personal. Position power, which is much like assigned leadership, is the power an individual derives from having an office in a formal organizational system. It includes legitimate, reward, and coercive power. Personal power comes from followers and includes referent and expert power. It is given to leaders because followers believe leaders have something of value. Treating power as a shared resource is important because it de-emphasizes the idea that leaders are power wielders.

Leadership is usually associated with coercion but leadership and coercion are also not the same. Coercion involves the use of threats and punishment to induce change in followers for the sake of the leader. Coercion runs counter to leadership because it does not treat leadership as a process that includes followers, and it does not emphasize working with followers to achieve common goals.

Another related concept is management. In fact, leadership and management are different concepts that overlap. They are different in that management traditionally focuses on the activities of planning, organizing, staffing, and controlling, whereas leadership emphasizes the general influence process. Management is concerned with creating order and stability, whereas leadership is about adaptation and constructive change. It is also said that managers and leaders are different types of people, with managers being more reactive and less emotionally involved and leaders being more proactive and more emotionally involved. The overlap between leadership and management is centered on how they both involve influencing a group of individuals in goal attainment.

As more and more women begin occupying positions of leadership, questions as to whether they lead in a different manner from men and whether women or men are more effective as leaders have garnered greater attention. Writers are asserting that there are indeed gender differences in leadership styles and that in contemporary society women's leadership is more effective (Book, 2000; Helgesen, 1990, Rosener, 1995). However, academic researchers have a greater diversity in their views. Many argue that gender has little or no relationship to leadership style and effectiveness (Dobbins & Platz, 1986; Engen, Leeden, & Willemsen, 2001; Powell, 1990).

These views need serious consideration and deliberation, and, therefore, I again congratulate the organizers of this seminar who thought of the very contemporary and thought provoking subject for discourse in the land of the traditional and intellectual legacy.

Scholars started this discourse by asking, "Can women lead?" Can they be effective? Can they deliver? Can they cope?

Can they manage? Can they balance? This was done in the wake of the increasing presence of women in corporate and political leadership roles, including eBay's CEO Meg Whitman, Avon's CEO Andrea Jung, New York Senator Hillary Rodham Clinton, Secretary of State Condoleezza Rice, U.S. Army Lieutenant General Ann Dunwoody, and the founder of Teach for America, Wendy Kopp, German Chancellor Angela Merkel, Indian President Pratibha Patial, the exceptional Police Officer, Kiran Bedi, Kalpana Mor (CEO, J.P. Morgan), Radhika Roy (MD, NDTV), Neelam Dhawan (MD, HP India), Shobhna Bharatiya (Chairperson & Editorial Director HT Media), Anu Aga (Chairperson, Thermax Ltd), Kiran Mazumdar (Chairperson Biocan India Ltd.), Vinita Bali MD Britania Industries, Amrita Patel (Chairperson NDDB), Mother Teresa, Simone Tata (Lakme), Indu Jain (Chairman Times Group), Shehnaz Hussain, Indira Nooyi (Chirman Pepsi), Chanda Kochar (ICICI, CEO MD), Naina Lal Kidwai (HSBC Dy. CEO), Preetha Reddi (Apollo MD), Ravina Raj Kohli (Star News Ex-President), Vandena Shiva (Environmentalist) – the list seems to be endless.

The women have amply and very ably demonstrated that they can lead. In fact, they not only lead but they lead by example! The primary research questions now are, "What are the leadership style and effectiveness differences between women and men?" which is often subsumed under a large question: "Why women are starkly underrepresented in elite leadership roles?" So over the years the questions have changed.

Early research on leadership style differences between women and men compared either interpersonally oriented and task-oriented styles or democratic and autocratic styles. In a meta-analysis of 1990, it was found that contrary to stereotypic expectations, women were not found to lead in a more interpersonally oriented and less task-oriented manner than men in organizational studies. These differences were found only in settings where behavior was more regulated by social roles. The only robust gender difference found across settings was that women led in a more democratic, or participative, manner than men.

These studies also revealed that women were devalued and branded autocratic or directive when they led in a masculine manner, even when they occupied a typically masculine leadership role (e.g., athletic coaches or managers in manufacturing plants), and when the evaluators were men. This was a manifestation of the prejudice women experienced in leadership positions.

However, in the early 1980s, leadership researchers began studying a new style of leadership first articulated by J.M. Burns (1978) as transforming leadership, later modified and expanded into transformational leadership by B.M. Bass (1985; Chapter 9). Significant research has gone to illustrate that all four components of transformational leadership (idealized influence, inspirational motivation, intellectual stimulation, and individualized consideration) and the contingent reward component of transactional leadership are positively related to leadership effectiveness (Lowe, Kroeck, & Sivasubramaniam, 1996). A recent meta-analysis by Eagly, Johannesen- Schmidt, and van Engen (2003) has found that women's styles tend to be more transformational than men's, and they also tend to engage in more contingent reward behaviors than men, all of which are aspects of leadership that predict effectiveness.

Women and Leadership Effectiveness

In addition to leadership style, the relative effectiveness of male and female leaders has been assessed by a number of research studies (Jacobson & Effertz, 1974; Tsui & Gutek, 1984). It has been found that overall men and women are equally effective leaders, but there are gender differences. For instance, women were less effective than men in military positions, but they were some-what more effective than men in education, government, and social service organizations and substantially more effective than men in middle management positions, where communitarian interpersonal skills are highly valued. In addition, women were less effective than men when they supervised a higher proportion of male subordinates or when a greater proportion of male raters assessed the leaders' performance.

Thus, empirical research supports small differences in leadership style and effectiveness between men and women. It shows that the Women experience slight effectiveness disadvantages in masculine leader roles, whereas more feminine roles offer them some advantages. However, women exceed men in the use of democratic or participatory styles, and they are more likely to use transformational leadership behaviors and contingent reward, styles that are associated with contemporary notions of effective leadership (Fondas, 1977). But the glass ceiling exists.

The Glass Ceiling

The invisible barrier preventing women from ascending into elite leadership positions is commonly called *the glass ceiling* a term first introduced into the American vernacular by two Wall Street Journal reporters in 1986 ("Corporate Woman," 1986). Even in female-dominated occupations women face the glass ceiling, whereas men in general appear to ride a *"glass escalator"* to the top leadership positions (Maume, 1999; Williams, 1992, 1995).

The glass ceiling is a global phenomenon whereby women are disproportionately concentrated in lower-level and lower-authority leadership positions than men. Although the glass ceiling generally is conceived as a barrier against women, it can be generalized to encompass other non-dominant groups such as ethnic and racial minorities and other marginalized groups as well. There are a number of important motivations for removing this barrier into the upper echelons of leadership. First, doing so will fulfill the promise of equal opportunity by allowing everyone the possibility of taking on leadership roles. Furthermore, just as one is more likely to find a large fish in a lake than a pond, one is more likely to find the most talented human resources by increasing the pool of potential candidates. In addition to finding a large fish in a big lake, one is also more likely to find a great variety of fish. Promoting a richly diverse group of women into leadership roles will make societal institutions, businesses, and governments truly representative and more productive.

On the political front, women currently hold only 81 of the 535 seats in the U.S. Congress (15.1 %; 14% in the Senate and 15.4% in the House of Representatives), and women of color occupy just 20 seats (3.7%; Center for the American Woman and Politics, 2006). Indeed, as of March 2006, the world average of women's representation in national legislatures or parliament is 16.4%, with the United States ranked 68th and India out of 188 countries (Inter-Parliamentary Union, 2006). Moreover, women represent just 5.5% of military officers at the level of brigadier general and rear admiral or higher (U.S. Department of Defense, 2005).

In the Indian context, women represent 4.9% of the top earners and the top leaders in the corporate world. On the political front, women are representing 44 seats out of 543 (12%) in the 2004 Lok Sabha elections. Moreover, the representation of women in 2006 in the Rajya Sabha is only 24 out of 242 (10%) seats.

Although the predicament of women leaders has improved significantly in the last century, we still have a long way to go. Women currently occupy more than half of all management and professional positions (50.3%) in some countries, and they make up nearly half of the labor force (46.4%) the world over, but they are still underrepresented in the upper echelons of the world's corporations and political systems. Women represent only 5.2% of Fortune 500 top earners, they have a mere 7.9% of the highest titles in the Fortune 500, and they represent less than 2% of Fortune 500 CEOs (Catalyst, 2002). Women hold only 14.7% of Fortune 500 board seats (Catalyst, 2006).

Women's under representation in high-level leadership positions can be generally explained through three types of explanations. The first set of explanations highlights differences in women's and men's investments in human capital. The second category of explanations considers essential differences between women and men. The final type of explanation focuses on prejudice and discrimination against female leaders.

Human Capital Differences

One prominent set of explanations for the glass ceiling is that women have less human capital investment in education, training, and work experience than men. This supposed lack of human capital is said to result in a dearth of qualified women, called a "pipeline problem." However, a closer look at the numbers reveals that women are indeed in the pipeline but that the pipeline is leaking as it approaches the top. Women are obtaining undergraduate degrees at a far higher rate than men, earning 57.5% of the bachelor's degrees in the United States (National Center for Educational Statistics [NCES], 2003), and women are graduating at a rate nearly equal to that of men in most professional schools, earning 58.8% of all master's degrees and 46.3% of all doctorates (NCES, 2003). Although women earn 47.3% of all law degrees and make up 47.4% of associates, they make up only 17.1% of partners (National Association for Law Placement, 2005). Although women represent only about one third of those graduating with M.B.A.s from the top 20 business schools (C200 Business Leadership Index, 2005), their representation in the upper echelons of American business pales in comparison. Thus, there is clear evidence that the lack of women reaching the top is not due to the fact that enough time has not passed for natural career progression to occur (Heilman, 1997).

Although women occupy more than half of all management and professional positions, the researches prove that they have fewer developmental and progressional opportunities than men at work driven at least in part by the prejudice women experience in the domain of leadership. In addition to having fewer responsibilities in the same jobs as men, women are less likely to receive encouragement, be included in key networks/positions and receive formal job training than their male counterparts.

Moreover, women are disproportionately represented in business positions that are less visible, have less responsibility, and do not lead to top leadership positions. For example, women are clustered in the fields of accounting, education, nursing, hospitality, and what is called the velvet ghetto.

Interestingly, when women are promoted to leadership positions, they are more likely to be placed on a "glass cliff"; that is, they are more likely to be appointed to precarious leadership situations associated with greater risk and criticism.

In sum, there is very little evidence for the notions that women receive less education than men, that they quit their jobs more often than men, or that they opt out of the leadership track for the mommy motherhood track. There is enough evidence to support the notion that women have less work experience and more career interruptions than men, largely because women assume significantly more domestic responsibility. They also receive less formal training and have fewer developmental and progressional/promotional opportunities at work than men, both of which are related to prejudice against women leaders.

Gender Differences

Another set of arguments attempting to explain the leadership gap revolve around the notion that women are just different from men. One argument in this vein is that women's under representation in elite leadership positions is a result of differences in leadership style and effectiveness. As discussed earlier in this address, any substantial leadership style differences between women and men should not disadvantage women and can even offer them an advantage (Eagly & Carli, 2003; Powell, 1990; Vecchio, 2002). Because the glass ceiling makes it so difficult for women to attain elite leadership positions, the ones who do make it tend to be very competent.

Another oft-cited barrier to women's advancement is the presumed gender difference in commitment to employment/work/job and motivation to attaining leadership roles. However, research clearly and amply indicates that women show the same level of identification with and commitment to paid employment roles as men do, and both women and men view their roles as workers/employees to be secondary to their roles as parents and parterns. Empirical research does indicate that women are less likely to promote themselves for leadership positions than men. This research must be interpreted in light of the social costs, or backlash, women experience when they promote themselves or are competent in positions of authority and more aggressive and even at times less moral and less feminine.

Women face significant gender biases and social disincentives when they self-promote; for example, unlike men, self-promoting women are seen as less, socially attractive and less hirable. Thus, women who want to pursue leadership positions may choose not to do so because they have internalized these expectations or are simply aware of the social costs, perpetuating the glass ceiling.

One gender difference that comes out clearly from the empirical research and pertains to leadership is that women are less likely than men to ask for what they want. Reaching elite leadership positions is not done in a vacuum; people must negotiate with others to access the right positions, experiences, opportunities, resources, and assistance in both the professional and domestic spheres. However, women are less likely to negotiate than men. A recent research examining the initiation of negotiation clearly demonstrated how the conception of negotiation is gendered. Unfortunately, the negotiations needed to ascend the leadership hierarchy especially the political one, often are unstructured, ambiguous, and rife with gender triggers-exactly the type of situation that particularly disadvantages women. Moreover, women face greater social costs for initiating negotiation than men do, so their lower levels of negotiation may represent an adaptive response to social disincentives.

Thus, women are no less effective at leadership, committed to their jobs, or motivated for leadership roles than men. However, women are less likely to self-promote and negotiate than men, and although there are a few psychological differences between women and men, they may not be innate and are much more a result of socialization.

Prejudice

One prominent explanation for the glass ceiling is gender bias stemming from stereotyped expectations that women take care and men take charge. These biases can be seen in media coverage on the campaign trails. An American Research comparing the presidential campaign of Elizabeth Dole with the campaigns of George W. Bush, John McCain, and Steve Forbes found that Elizabeth Dole received significantly less media coverage on policy issues and more coverage on her personality and attire than her male counterparts (Aday & Devitt, 2000). India is no exception. Similarly, in a recent survey of women executives from Fortune 1000 companies, 33% of the respondents cited stereotyping and preconceptions of women's roles and abilities as a major contributor the glass ceiling (Catalyst, 2003).

Gender stereotypes are pervasive, well documented, and highly resistant to change. These stereotypes not only describe stereotypic beliefs about the attributes of women and men, they also tend to prescribe how men and women ought to be. Men are stereotyped with agentic characteristics such as confidence, assertiveness, independence, rationality, and decisiveness, whereas stereotypical attributes of women include communitarian characteristics such as concern for others, sensitivity, warmth, helpfulness, and nurturance.

In addition to conforming to the stereotype-based expectations, it is also expected that women should avoid behaviors that are incompatible with the stereo-type. The penalties for violating one's gender stereotypes are very interestingly illustrated in the classic. American Supreme Court case Price Waterhouse v. Ann Hopkins (1989). Price Waterhouse told Hopkins that she would not make a good partner because she was too masculine, going as far as advising her to go to a charm school, wear jewellery and makeup, and be less aggressive. In the end, the court ruled that Price Waterhouse was discriminating based on gender stereotypes.

In leadership roles, gender stereotypes are particularly damaging for women because agentic, as opposed to communitarian, tendencies often are indispensable. According to the role congruity theory, the agentic qualities thought necessary in the leadership role are incompatible with the predominantly communitarian qualities stereotypically associated with women, thus resulting in prejudice against female leaders (Eagly & Karau, 2002).

In the leadership roles, women are confronted with cross-pressures: As leaders they are expected to be masculine and tough, but as women they should not be "too manly". One can not but recollect here the references to Indira Gandhi as the only MAN in the Cabinet. The election of the current chancellor of Germany, Angela Merkel, brought these cross-pressures to the fore, with the press constantly focusing on both her toughness and her femininity. Indeed, in response to her perceived lack of femininity in conjunction with the media focus on her appearance, Chancellor Merkel had to drastically change her appearance by wearing bright colors and adopting a new hairstyle. These opposing expectations for women result in the perception that women are less qualified for elite leadership positions than men and harsh evaluations of effective women leaders for not being "female enough."

This prejudice helps explain the numerous findings indicating less favorable attitudes toward female than male leaders, greater difficulty for women to attain top leadership roles, and greater difficulty for women to be viewed as effective in these roles. These gender biases can be particularly detrimental in the decision-making processes for selecting elite leaders, given that the generally unstructured nature of those decisions allows biased decisions without accountability. Not only are the crucial decision makers influenced by the stereotypes that disadvantage women in the leadership role, but they may also succumb to homosocial reproduction, a tendency for a group to reproduce itself in its own image. People prefer similar others and report the most positive decisions about and evaluations of people who are most similar to them, biases that can clearly disadvantage women when male leaders are looking for replacements.

Thus, substantial empirical evidence reveals that gender stereotypes can significantly alter the perception and evaluation of female leaders and directly affect women in or aspiring to leadership roles.

Breaking the Glass Ceiling

Although the glass ceiling in political and business leadership clearly still exists, encouraging data suggest that we are on our way to cracking the glass. For example, since 1995 the number of Fortune 500 companies with no women directors has fallen nearly 50%, and those that have 25% or more women board directors increased nearly sixfold (Catalyst, 2006). Additionally, women have shown a marked increase in lower-level managerial and administrative positions that can funnel into higher leadership positions. On the political front, although there are only 14 women senators in America, 4 of them belong to three of the most populous states (California, Texas, and New York), and one of them, Hillary Rodham Clinton, was a serious contender for the 2008 U.S. presidential election. Furthermore, in a recent Gallup poll, 86% of Americans said they would vote for a qualified woman for president which they eventually did not, of course.

In India, though we have had a woman Prime Minister and still have a woman President, UPA Chairperson, state Governors, many Party Heads but the representation of women in parliament and state legislatures has hardly gone over 10% and even among them, their effectiveness as leaders in their own right without losing socially appropriate positions and roles remains largely an area of doubt or at least ambivalence and concern.

Women, who are aware of the limit of the glass ceiling looming ahead, at times circumvent these barriers by starting their own ventures. There is evidence to show that among privately owned businesses, those owned by women are the fastest growing; this includes the number of women-owned firms, the revenues generated by them, and the number of people employed by them. By leaving organizations, these entrepreneurial women do contribute to the glass ceiling; however, to the extent that they become some of the most successful entrepreneurs, they are beginning to change the face of business as we know it as well as the face of leadership.

PART II

Today, in the first decade of the new millennium, the Indian women find that while much has been achieved by way of constitutional rights and opportunities, they have still a long way to go to secure their due place in the leadership structure. That, the empowerment of women through equal opportunities is a basic requirement for national advancement is conceded both by policymakers and society. This itself is no mean achievement. However, while many have taken full advantage of the changed circumstances, a very large segment of womanhood, Indian as well as global still suffer discriminatory attitudes when it comes to the effective leadership positions and the power structures at the top.

Indian cultural evolution and national movement is singularly marked by the active role of a large number of women along with that of men. The relentless fight against social oppression and the social change ran parallel and sometimes got entwined with the nationalist movement.

Interestingly, Indian women did not have to go through a suffragette movement as in Britain and some other industrially advanced countries, but the barriers of social prejudice they had to overcome in all activities were formidable. The part played by the women pioneers/leaders constituted in itself an epic saga in the political and social history of this country. Many of them had to encounter stonewalling opposition at every level from the household, community, in area of functioning and the alien administration. This band of pioneer/leaders who evolved in the late 19th and early 20th century gave direction and purpose to the mass of the Indian women.

We have a number of women whose life stories have left their imprint on history and an inspiring legacy for subsequent generations to take their programmes further ahead. To name a few, Ramabai Ranade (1862-1924), Pandita Ramabai Saraswati (1858-1922), Savitribai Phule (1831-1897), Subhadra Kumari Chauhan (1904-1948), Lady Premleela Thackersey (1894-1977), Sarojini Naidu (1876-1949), Mahadevi Verma (1907-1987), Jyotirmoyee Devi (1894-1988), Kulsum Sayani (1900-1987), Rani Rajwade (1887-1984), Rukmini Devi

Arundale (1904-1986), Kasturba (1869-1944), Basanti Debi Chittaranjan Das (1880-1974), Nellie Sengupta (1886-1973), Anasuyaben Sarabhai (1885-1972), Asha Devi Aryanayakam (1901-1970), Prabhawati Devi (1906-1976), Maniben Patel (1903-1990), Rajkumari Amrit Kaur (1889-1964), Maniben Nanavati (1905-2000), Leela Roy (1900-1970), Vijaya Lakshmi Pandit (1900-1990), Sucheta Kripalani (1906-1974), Kamaladevi Chattopadhyaya (1903-1990), Mridula Sarabhai (1911-1974), Aruna Asaf Ali (1906-1996), Hansa Mehta (1987-1995), Durgabai Deshmukh (1909-1981), Indira Priyadarshini (1917-1984), Mary Clubwala Jadav (1908-1975), Lakshmi N. Menon (1899-1994), Nandini Satpathy, Rajkumari Amrit Kaur, Medha Patkar, Aruna Roy, Ila Bhatt besides of course, your own Rabari Devi, Mayavati, Jayalalitha, Sushma Swaraj, Sheila Dixit, Girija Vyas, Sonia Gandhi, Pratibha Patil and so on.

The richness of the movement was enhanced significantly by the contributions made by these women. In fact, the 20th Century, which was a continuous period of upheavals that shook time-worn beliefs, pulled down social barriers in the way of progress and aroused the conscience of society to the wrongs perpetrated through centuries, could well be called the century of the Indian women because of the ordeals they have gone through in the relentless struggle waged to secure their due place in society and which is still continuing. Thanks to them that today, women are in a position to speak up with conviction and courage, to lead and to demand their legitimate space in leadership positions.

These women in leadership came from all sections of the society; while some belonged to the fairly affluent and enlightened families, the contribution of those from middle class tradition-bound backgrounds is even more significant as they truly represented the wave of change which swept the masses; among them were literati, educationists and housewives turned crusaders. For instance, Ashadevi Aryanayakam was a leader in basic education and she developed it under Mahatma Gandhi and Dr. Zakir Hussain's leadership along with her husband Shri Aryanayakam.

When India won independence Kamaladevi Chattopadhyay's next priority was work for national reconstruction. Though she could have any office in the Government or outside for the asking, she chose to revive and rejuvenate the country's cultural heritage through promotion of arts and crafts. Similarly, Muthulakshmi Reddi gave organisation to women's work while Durgabai helped in codification of antiquated Hindu laws and set up institutions to usher in social change.

Subhadra Kumari Chauhan demonstrated through her writings what women could achieve through education and literary skills. Lady Premleela Thackersey's commitment to the underprivileged is testified by the educational and humanitarian institutions she had raised. Sarojini Naidu, was a brilliant orator, an outstanding poet, a person endowed with unusual charm and a sense of humour. Similarly Mahadevi Verma's poems inspired a large number of writers-men as much as women.

In the social sphere, dignity to womanhood and removal of their privations arising from early widowhood and absence of education were the main planks of the programme launched by activists like Ramabai, wife of Justice Ranade. Ramabai who herself did not have any formal schooling took up the cause of women's education as her life's mission. She left several institutions which remain monuments to a life of service. The achievements of these women crusaders/leaders have to be viewed in the circumstances of the times.

The social revolution, these women brought about was manifest in other developments as well. The first school for women in Pune signified such a revolution in 1848 when Savitribai Phule set it up. Savitri and her husband carried on one of the biggest campaigns against untouchability by totally identifying themselves with the deprived sections.

In political and administrative leadership there has been an array of world class women. The post-independence generation threw up the leadership of Indira Gandhi, who had influenced the course of contemporary history on a scale as few Prime Ministers ever could anywhere. Administrators and educationists like Lakshmi N. Menon and Lady Thackersey and social activists like Durgabai Deshmukh and Naoroji sisters are notable among the many makers of modern India. Ma Kasturba and Prabhavati Devi were embodiment of simplicity and compassion. The versatile Rajkumari Amrit Kaur and Sarojini Naidu, will remain a source of inspiration for all times to come. The present generation owes their relatively secure existence, status of equality and prospects of opportunity and leadership to them.

In the near east, we have the exemplary leadership of a courageous woman-Corazon Aquino. She fought dictatorship in Philippines, restored democracy and became president and after six years resigned to take up social projects and to look after her grandchildren. She survived seven coup attempts in six years tenure. The 'Time' magazine, which conducted leadership survey choosing 100 leaders of 20th century, has also conducted similar exercise for Asian leadership and the only one lady out of 20 leaders is CORAZON AQUINO. The salient features of her leadership are: She left her office voluntarily, a rare gesture, seldom shown by any head of state; She restored democratic institutions which her predecessor Marcos had destroyed, promulgated a constitution designed to be dictator proof, which still survives and She took number of unpopular decisions even by defying her core supporters, if they were in the interest of the nation.

A large number of books have been written on leadership, but *'Leading Minds' by Howard Gardner* is considered to be one of the best. The author has used stories and examples of world class leaders from different fields to focus, how leaders mind work, how they influence their subjects and how they lead. He has illustrated the life and works of around eleven leaders including Martin Luther King, Mahatma Gandhi, Eleanor Roosevelt, Pope John XXIII, etc. in this book to explain how leaders lead and remarkably the list includes two women leaders who are leaders in their own right namely, *Margaret Thatcher and Margaret Mead.*

The famous Management Counsellor and the author of "Thought Leaders: The Source Code of Exceptional Managers and Entrepreneurs" (2001), "Shrinivas Pandit has captured the life and thought process, of 22 exceptional leaders, managers and entrepreneurs after years of closely monitory over 2000 mangers/G.Ms/Vice Presidents etc and interviewing over 3500 people. They have high credibility, use vivid language with compelling evidence, and they connect emotionally". And most notably, he categorically declares that *"Gender is no bar to leadership. So in the course of this book 'he' applies to 'she' and vice-versa"*.

While women have made steady gains in participation in parliaments, business management, the media and the academic world, the pace is still too slow, even in wealthy nations, said the report prepared by UN Secretary-General Kofi Annan to mark International Women's Day. "Serious obstacles remain that hinder women's effective participation," said the report, which called for increased participation and greater say in the decision-making process. Recently, we had Angela Merkel (Germany's Chancellor), Ellen Johnson-Sirleaf, Liberia's President, Michelle Bachelet as Chile's president & Pratibha Patil as Indian President. But a handful of women leaders attending a meeting of the UN commission on the status of women said that these successes masked the many challenges they had overcome and the long and arduous preparations.

"Behind that progress, we can see that it takes time to get prepared, it takes time to have such awareness and openness in a society at the political level," said Rachel Mayanja, the special UN adviser on the advancement of women.

Even after winning a leadership post, women leaders face harsher judgment than their male counterparts when they make mistakes, simply because they are women. Among the obstacles facing women, Annan's report said, are their under-representation in such male-dominated fields as the military and foreign affairs and the persistence of stereotypical attitudes and behaviour toward women. Even though more women are being elected to parliaments every year, they soon discover 'the absence of gender-sensitive enabling environments' in the world's legislatures, it said.

Many of the impediments women face in the leadership domain stem from the incongruity between the female gender role and the leadership role. Women face a double standard in the leadership role: They must come across as extremely competent but also be seen as appropriately "female," a set of standards men are not held to. One way women can increase their perceived warmth and their influence is by combining communitarian qualities such as warmth and friendliness with agentic qualities such as exceptional competence and assertiveness. Because women engage in most transformational behaviors and contingent reward behaviors to a greater extent than men they probably will begin occupying and succeeding in a greater number of leadership positions in our society, helping to break down the think leader-think male stereotype. Moreover, the incongruity between the leadership role and the female gender role is gradually decreasing. Recent research indicates that women have become more assertive and valuing leadership and power more as job attributes, without losing their femininity. Besides the perception about the leadership role is also changing and it is being seen as less masculine and more androgynous (Schein, 2001).

Thus, despite the glass ceiling, women are showing a greater presence in top leadership positions. A confluence of factors contributes to leadership effectiveness and the rise of female leaders. Changes in societies, states and organizations are beginning to make it easier for women to reach top positions. The culture almost everywhere is changing; gendered work assumptions such as the male model of work, the notion of uninterrupted full-time careers, and the separation of work and family are being challenged. Also, flexible work schedules and diversity in top echelons are being preferred. These can augment women's career progression by involving them in career development programs and formal networks and offering capacity support. Women do need to take advantage, of the change to attain more positions beyond the velvet ghetto and gain high-visibility assignments that will put them on the leadership track.

The percentage of women in legislatures and decision making positions always remained low. Women do not share the power of decision-making and are not involved in policy making in Indian democracy in proportion to their numerical strength. Thus there is a gap between the formal idea of women's participation and their meaningful use of power. (Susheela Kaushik: 1993). The quest for greater political representation of women is, therefore, still relevant. (Asha Kapur Mehta *et al:* 2001).

Women in India constitute nearly half the population of the country, but they are poorly represented in the various governance and decision making bodies. The position depicted through the 14 general elections so far reflects a low representation of women in Parliament, State legislatures, in political parties and other decision-making bodies. Less than 8% of Parliamentary seats, less than 60% Cabinet positions, less than 4% of seats in High Courts and the Supreme Courts, have been occupied by women. Less than 3% of the administrators and managers are women. The average percentage of women's representation in the Parliament, Assemblies and Council of Ministers taken together has been around 10% (UNIFEM: 2000).

The percentage of representation of women in the Lok Sabha varies from 4.4 in 1952 to 8.1 in 1984, declining to 5.2 in 1989, rising to 7.9 in 1998 and 9.02 in 1999 and again declining to 8.1 in 2004. In Rajya Sabha, proportion of female members started with 7.3 per cent in 1952 and rose to 15.5 per cent in 1991, but again declined to 6 per cent in 1998 and rose to 10.3 per cent in 2005, again slightly declining to 9.9 per cent in 2006. On the whole the representation of women in Parliament (Lok Sabha and Rajya Sabha) and the State Assemblies remains low. Thus, despite the increase in electoral participation of women, their representation in the formal political structures has not changed much.

The Congress Party led by a woman had only 10% of women among the candidates. The BJP and the CPM had 7% of women among the candidates (Jayati Ghosh: 1999). The idea of 33% reservation for women in parliament was actively endorsed by most of the major political parties and this had raised expectation that many more women would be nominated to contest the elections. The election manifestoes and the public pronouncements of parties as well as the print and electronic media highlighted the idea of women's representation by reservation or by nomination of more women for elections signifying a more conscious political stand on women's representation.

In spite of the low political representation of women in Indian politics, it must be noted that some women leaders have an important place in Indian politics today. Jayalalithaa as leader of AIADMK, Mamata Bannerji as leader of Trinamul Congress and Mayawati as leader of Bahujan Samaj Party (BSP) are instance in point. Some of them head important and strong regional political parties which have been in alliance with major national political parties both outside and in national government. Even though the rise of some of these women leaders might be linked to their proximity to male leaders, they now had a position of leadership within the party in their own right who can influence the decisions of their own party as well as the course of national politics.

In addition, the example of Indira Gandhi who rose to be Prime Minister of India, and later of Sonia Gandhi, leader of the Congress Party, both of whom had the dynastic advantage underpinning their leadership and position of power and decision-making in the Congress Party and the government can hardly be ignored. But the positions of authority of these women leaders did not include any specific mandate to address only women issues. In this sense as leaders of political parties, they were as power driven as their male peers. Political leadership by women is not dramatically different from that of men. Women leaders are no better or worse than men. Nor have women leaders been typically anxious to give greater representation to other women within their own organizations or in the political process generally. Representation of women has not necessarily increased greatly under the leadership of women. In fact, interestingly the 73rd Constitutional amendment and the policy and implementation of 33% reservation for women in Panchayats, received strong support and impetus due to Rajiv Gandhi's interest and advocacy in the matter.

Thus, the Indian political system cannot be said to be non-receptive to the emergence and dominance of women leaders even though the political representation of women has not particularly registered a significant increase over the last 14 general elections. While on the one hand most women politicians have found it difficult to rise within male dominated party hierarchies, on the other hand some women have managed to become leaders when they have set up parties of their own. Once they have established themselves as leaders, there has been an unquestioning acceptance of their leadership and decisions by the party rank and file, even if it is largely male.

With changes in societal & organizational culture and the developmental opportunities for women within them; greater gender equity in domestic responsibilities; greater negotiation power of women, especially regarding the work-home balance; the effectiveness and predominance of women-owned businesses; and changes in the incongruity between women and leadership, we are likely to see more women in elite leadership roles in the present century and the years to come.

Deliberate approaches like 73rd & 74th Constitutional Amendments and decentralization, seek to create enabling conditions for women to take on leadership roles. Structural (institutional) factors/individual backgrounds/cognitive experiences and circumstances also influence women's leadership. While women with inherent personality traits naturally assume leadership roles, inexperienced can learn leadership skills. Strategies such as capacity building, training of women elected representatives to govern; mobilizing them to network with associations/collectives; mobilizing collectives to enhance their participation; and gender sensitisation can promote effective leadership of women and India is a living testimony to this.

I would like to end by agreeing that, "It is not merely that more justice must be received by women, but also that social justice can be achieved only through the active agency of women. The suppression of women from participation in social, political, and economic life hurts the people as a whole, not just women. The emancipation and empowerment of women is an integral part of social progress, not just a women's issue." Dreze and Sen (1999:178). And we must remember what Warren Bennis has said *"Leaders don't just appear out of thin air. They must be developed-nurtured in such a way that they acquire the qualities of leadership"*. Not only this, they must also be appreciated and applauded.

References

Aday, S. and Devitt, J. (2000), *Style Over Substance: Newspaper coverage of female candidates: Spotlight on Elizabeth Dole*. Retrieved April 12, 2006, from the White House Project Web site: *http://www.thewhitehouseproject.org/research/* Style-substance Dole _report. pdf.

Andrews, P. H. (1992), Sex and Gender Differences in Group Communication: Impact on the Facilitation Process. *Small Group Research*, 23(I), 74-94.

Aronson, E. (1995), *The Social Animal* (7th Ed.). New York: W. H. Freeman.

Babcock, L. and Laschever, S. (2003), *Women Don't Ask: Negotiation and the Gender Divide*. Princeton, NJ: Princeton University Press.

Bartol, K. M. and Butterfield, D. A. (1976), Sex Effects in Evaluating Leaders. *Journal of Applied Psychology*, 61, 446-454.

Bass, B. M. (1985), Leadership: Good, Better, Best. *Organizational Dynamics*, 13, 26-40.

Belkin, L. (2003, October 26), The Opt-out Revolution. *The New York Times*, p. 42.

Bell, E. and Nkomo, S. (2001), *Our Separate Ways: Black and White Women and the Struggle for Professional Identity*. Boston: Harvard Business School Press.

Bianchi, S. M., Milkie, M. A., Sayer, L. C. and Robinson, J. P. (2000), Is Anyone doing the Housework? Trends in the Gender Division of Household Labor. *Social Forces*, 79, 191-228.

Bielby, D. D. and Bielby, W. T. (1988), She Works Hard for the Money: Household Responsibilities and the Allocation of Work Effort. *American Journal of Sociology*, 93, 1031-1059.

Biernat, M., & Wortman, C. B. (199). Sharing of Home Responsibilities between Professionally Employed Women and their Husbands. *Journal of Personality and Social Psychology*, 60, 844-860.

Blank, R. and Slipp, S. (1994). *Voices of Diversity*. New York: AMACOM.

Book, E. W. (2000), *Why the Best Man for the Job is a Woman*. New York: HarperCollins.

Bowles, H. R., Babcock, L. and Lai, L. (2005, July). *It Depends who is Asking and who you Ask: Social Incentives for Sex Differences in the Propensity to Initiate Negotiation*. Cambridge, MA: Kennedy School of Government Faculty Research Working Paper Series, RWP05-045.

Bowles, H. R. and McGinn, K. L. (2005), Claiming Authority: Negotiating Challenges for Women Leaders. In D. M. Messick & R. M. Kramer (Eds.), *The Psychology of Leadership: New Perspectives and Research* (pp. 191-208). Mahwah, NJ: Lawrence Erlbaum.

Bowman, G., Worthy, N. and Greyser, S. (1965), Are Women Executives' People? *Harvard Business Review*, 43(4), 14-28, 164-178.

Browne, K. (2002), *Biology at Work: Rethinking Sexual Equality*. New Brunswick, NJ: Rutgers University Press.

Burgess, D. and Bergida, E. (1999), Who Women are, who Women should be: Descriptive and Prescriptive Gender Stereotyping in Sex Discrimination. *Psychology, Public Policy, & Law*, 5, 665-692.

Burns, J. M. (1978). *Leadership*. New York: Plenum.

Buss, D. M. and Kenrick, D. T. (1998), Evolutionary Social Psychology. In D. T. Gilbert, S. T. Fiske, & G. Lindzey (Eds.), *The Handbook of Social Psychology* (4th ed.) (Vol. 2, pp. 982-1026). Boston: McGraw-Hill.

C200 Business Leadership Index (2005), *Annual Report of Women's Clout in Business*. Retrieved April 12, 2006, from *http://www.c200.org/externall2005index2.pdf*

Carli, L. L. (2001), Gender and Social Influence. *Journal of Social Issues*, 57, 725-741.

Catalyst (1996), *Working with Business and the Professions to Effect Change for Women*. New York: Author.

Catalyst (2002), *Catalyst Census of Women Corporate Officers and Top Earners*. New York: Author.

Catalyst (2003), *Women in U.S. Corporate Leadership*. New York: Author.

Catalyst (2004), *The Bottom Line: Connecting Corporate Performance and Gender Diversity*. New York: Author.

Catalyst (2005), *Women "Take Care," Men "Take Charge": Stereotyping of U.S. Business Leaders Exposed*. New York: Author.

Catalyst (2006), 2005 *Catalyst Census of Women Board Directors of the Fortune 500*. New York: Author.

Census of India 2001. *online available at http://www.censusindia.net/*

Center for American Women and Politics (2006), *Women In elected Office 2006*. Retrieved April 12, 2006, from *http://www.cawp.rutgers.edu/Facts/Office holders/cawfps.html*

Chemers, M. M. (1997), *An Integrative Theory of Leadership*. Mahwah, NJ: Lawrence Erlbaum.

Chemers, M. M. and Murphy, S. E. (1995), Leadership and Diversity in Groups and Organizations. In M. M. Chemers, S. Oskamp, & M. A. Constanzo (Eds.), *Diversity in Organizations: New Perspectives for a Changing Workplace* (pp. 157-190). Thousand Oaks, CA: Sage.

Cooper, C. L. and Lewis, S. (1999), Gender and the Changing Nature of Work. In G. N. Powell (Ed.), *Handbook of Gender and Work* (pp. 37-46). Thousand Oaks, CA: Sage.

The Corporate Woman: A Special Report. (1986, March 24). *Wall Street Journal*, 32-page supplement.

Dasgupta, N. and Asgari, S. (2004). Seeing is Believing: Exposure to Counter Stereotypic Women Leaders and its Effect on Automatic Gender Stereotyping. *Journal of Experimental Social Psychology*, 40, 642-658.

Davies, P. G., Spencer, S. J. and Steele, C. M. (2005). Clearing the Air: Identity Safety Moderates the Effects of Stereotype Threat on Women's Leadership Aspirations. *Journal of Personality and Social Psychology*, 88, 276-287.

Deaux, K. and Kite, M. (1993), Gender stereotypes. In F. L. Denmark & M. Paludi (Eds.), *Psychology of women. A handbook of theory and issues* (pp. 107-139). Westport, CT: Greenwood.

Deshpande, Rajeshwari, (2004), How Gendered Was Women's Participation in Election 2004? *Economic & Political Weekly*, Vol. xxxix, No. 51, December 18, p. 5431-5436.

Dobbins, G. H., & Platz, S. J. (1986). Sex Differences in Leadership: How Real are They? *Academy of Management Review*, II, 118-127.

Dodge, K. A., Gilroy, F. D. and Fenzel, L. M. (1995), Requisite Management Characteristics Revisited: Two Decades Later. *Journal of Social Behavior and Personality*, 10, 253-264.

Eagly, A. H. and Carli, L. L. (2003), The Female Leadership Advantage: An Evaluation of the Evidence. *Leadership Quarterly*, 14, 807-834.

Eagly, A. H. and Carli, L. L. (2004). Women and Men as Leaders. In J. Antonakis, R. J. Sternberg, & A. T. Cianciolo (Eds.), *The Nature of Leadership* (pp. 279-301). Thousand Oaks, CA: Sage.

Eagly, A. H., Johannesen-Schmidt, M. c. and van Engen, M. (2003), Transformational, Transactional, and Laissez-faire Leadership Styles: A Meta-analysis Comparing Women and Men. *Psychological Bulletin*, 29, 569-591.

Eagly, A. H. and Johnson, B. T. (1990), Gender and Leadership Style: A Meta-analysis. *Psychological Bulletin*, 108(2), 233-256.

Eagly, A. H. and Karau, S. J. (1991), Gender and the Emergence of Leaders: A Meta-analysis. *Journal of Personality and Social Psychology*, 60, 685-710.

Eagly, A. H. and Karau, S. J. (2002), Role Congruity Theory of Prejudice Toward Female Leaders. *Psychological Review*, 109, 573-598.

Eagly, A. H., Karau, S. J. and Makhijani, M. G. (1995), Gender and the Effectiveness of Leaders: A Meta-analysis. *Psychological Bulletin*, 117, 125-145.

Eagly, A., Makhijani, M. and Klonsky, B. (1992). Gender and the Evaluation of Leaders: A Meta-analysis. *Psychological Bulletin*, 111, 3-22.

Ehrlich, E. (1989, March 20). The Mommy Track: Juggling Kids and Careers in Corporate America Takes a Controversial Turn. *Business Week*, pp. 126-134.

Election Commission of India. Online available at *www.eci.gov.in*.

Engen, M. L. van, Leeden, R. van der, & Willemsen, T. M. (2001), Gender, Context and Leadership Styles: A Field Study. *Journal of Occupational and Organizational Psychology*, 74, 581-598.

Ensher, E. A. and Murphy, S. E. (2005), *Power Mentoring: How Successful Mentors and Proteges get the Most out of their Relationships*. San Francisco, CA: Jossey-Bass.

Feingold, A. (1994), Gender Differences in Personality: A Meta-Analysis. *Psychological Bulletin*, 116, 429-456.

Fiske, S. (1998), Stereotyping, Prejudice, and Discrimination. In D. T. Gilbert, S. T. Fiske, & G. Lindzey (Eds.), *The Handbook of Social Psychology* (4th ed., Vol. 2, pp. 982-L026). Boston: McGraw-Hill.

Fiske, S., Bersoff, D. N., Borgida, E., Deaux, K. and Heilman, M. E. (1991), Social Science Research on Trial: Use of Sex Stereotyping Research in *Price Waterhouse v. Hopkins*. *American Psychologist*, 46(10), 1049-1060.

Fletcher, J. K. (2001), *Disappearing Acts: Gender, Power, and Relational Practice at Work*. Boston: MIT Press.

Fondas, N. (1997). Feminization Unveiled: Management Qualities in Contemporary Writings. *Academy of Management Review*, 22, 257-282.

Forsyth, D. R. (2006), Group Dynamics (4th ed.). Pacific Grove, CA: Brooks/Cole.

Franke, G. R., Crown, D. F. and Spake, D. F. (1997). Gender Differences in Ethical Perceptions of Business Practices: A Social Role Theory Perspective. *Journal of Applied Psychology*, 82, 920-934.

Gallup Poll (September 8-11, 2005), Poll Question Retrieved June 30, 2006, from Gallup Brain Academic database.

Geary, D. C. (1998), *Male, Female: The Evolution of Human Sex Differences*. Washington, DC: American Psychological Association.

Ghosh, Jayati (1999), Women in Indian Politics, *Frontline*, October 8, 1999.

Glick, P. and Fiske, S. T. (1999), Sexism and Other "Isms": Independence, Status, and the Ambivalent Content of Stereotypes. In W. B. Swann Jr. &. 1. H. Langlois (Eds.), *Sexism and Stereotypes in Modern Society: The Gender Science of Janet Taylor Spence* (pp. 193-221). Washington, DC: American Psychological Association.

Goldin, C. and Rouse, C. (2000), Orchestrating Impartiality: The Impact of "Blind" Auditions on Female Musicians. *American Economic Review*, 90(4), 715-741.

Greenwald, A. G., McGhee, D. E. and Schwartz, J. L. K. (1998), Measuring Individual Differences in Implicit Cognition: The Implicit Association test. *Journal of Personality and Social Psychology*, 74, 1464-1480.

Gurin, P. (1985), Women's Gender Consciousness. *Puhlic Opinion Quarterly*, 49, 143-163.

Hall, D. T. (1972). A Model of Coping with Role Conflict: The Role Behavior of College Educated Women. *Administrative Science Quarterly, 17(4)*, 471-486.

Hamilton, D. L., Stroessner, S. J. and Driscoll, D. M. (1994), Social Cognition and the Study of Stereotyping. In P. G. Devine, D. L. Hamilton, & T. M. Ostrom (Eds.), *Social Cognition: Impact on Social Psychology* (pp. 291-321). New York: Academic Press.

Heilman, M. E. (1997), Sex Discrimination and the Affirmative Action Remedy: The Role of Sex Stereotypes. *Journal of Business Ethics*, 16, 877-889.

Heilman, M. E. (2001), Description and Prescription: How Gender Stereotypes Prevent Women's Ascent up the Organizational Ladder. *Journal of Social Issues*, 57, 657-674.

Helgesen, S. (1990), *The Female Advantage: Women's Ways of Leadership*. New York: Doubleday.

Hennig, M. and Jardin, A. (1977), *The Managerial Woman*. Garden City, NY: Anchor.

Hewlett, S. A. (2002), *Creating a Life: Professional Women and the Quest for Children*. New York: Talk Miramax.

Hoyt, C. and Blascovich, J. (2006), *Leadership Efficacy and Women Leaders' Responses to Stereotype Activation*. Manuscript submitted for publication.

Human Development in South Asia (2000), The Gender Question, (2000), Oxford University Press.

Human Development Report (HRD) 2007/08, UNDP, Palgrave Macmillan, New York, p. 326-329.

Inter-Parliamentary Union (2006), *Women in national parliaments*. Retrieved June 30, 2006, from *http://www.ipu.org/wmn-e/classif.htm*

Jacobson, M. B. and Effertz, J. (1974), Sex Roles and Leadership Perceptions of the Leaders and the Led. *Organizational Behavior and Human Performance*, 12, 383-396.

Kanter, R. (1977), *Men and Women of the Corporation*. New York: Basic Books.

Kaufman, G. and Uhlenberg, P. (2000), The Influence of Parenthood on Work Effort of Married Men and Women. *Social Forces, 78(3)*, 931-947.

Kaushik Susheela (1993), *Women's Participation in Politics*, Vikas, New Delhi.

Kaushik, Susheela (1996), *Why Women in Legislatures?* Paper Presented at the Meet of Parliamentarians, New Delhi.

Kasturi, Leela., (1998), *Development, Patriarchy and Politics: Indian Women in the Political Process*, 1947-1992.

Keith, K. and McWilliams, A. (1999). The Returns to Mobility and Job Search by Gender: Additional Evidence from the NLSY. *Industrial & Labor Relations Review*, 52(3),460-477.

Knight, P. A. and Saal, F. E. (1984), Effects of Gender Dift'erences and Selection Agent Expertise on Leader Influence and Performance Evaluations. *Organizational Behavior and Human Performance*, 34, 225-243.

Knocking at the Male Bastion: Women in Politics, (1997) National Commission of Women, New Delhi.

Knoke, D. and Ishio, Y. (1998), The Gender Gap in Company Job Training. *Work and Occupations*, 25(2), 141-167.

Konrad, A. M., Ritchie, J. E. Jr., Lieb, P. and Corrigall, E. (2000), Sex Differences and Similarities in Job Attribute Preferences: A Meta-analysis. *Psychological Bulletin*, 126, 593-641.

Kray, L. J., Thompson, L. and Galinsky, A. (2001), Battle of the Sexes: Gender Stereotype Confirmation and Reactance in Negotiations. *Journal of Personality & Social Psychology*, 80, 942-958.

Kumari, A. and Kidwai, S. (1998) *Crossing the Sacred Line: Women's Search for Political Power*, Orient Longman, India.

Kunda, Z. and Spencer, S. J. (2003), When do Stereotypes Come to Mind and when do they Color Judgment? A Goal-based Theory of Stereotype Activation and Application. *Psychological Bulletin*, 129, 522-544.

Lowe, K. B., Kroeck, K. G. and Sivasubramaniam, N. (1996), Effectiveness Correlates of Transformational and Transactional Leadership: A Meta-analytic Review of the MLQ Literature. *Leadership Quarterly, 7,* 385-425.

Mahoney, R. (1996), *Kidding Ourselves: Breadwinning, Babies, and Bargaining Power.* New York: Basic Books.

Majumdar, Veena (1993), Women and the Political Process, *Durgabhai Deshmukh Memorial Lecture,* Council for Social Development, New Delhi.

Maume, D. J. Jr. (1999), Glass Ceilings and Glass Escalators. *Work & Occupations,* 26(4), 483.

Mohanty, Manoranjan Ed. (2004), *Class, Caste, Gender,* Sage Publication.

Morrison, A. and Von Glinow, M. A. (1990), Women and Minorities in Management. *American Psychologist,* 45, 200-208.

National Association for Law Placement, Women and Attorneys of Color in Law. (2005, February). *Women and attorneys of color at law firms.* Retrieved April 12, 2006, from *http://www.nalp.org/content/index.php?pid=143*

National Center for Educational Statistics (2003), *Digest of Education statistics, 2002 2003.* Retrieved April 12, 2006, frol11 *http://nces.ed.gov/programs/digest/ d04/lt3.asp#c3a_5*

Nieva, V. E. and Gutek, B. A. (1981), *Women and Work: A Psychological Perspective.* New York: Praeger.

Nussbaum, M. (2003), Gender and Governance: An Introduction, in *Essays on Gender and Governance,* Human Development Research Centre (UNDP), New Delhi.

Ohlott, P. I., Ruderman, M. N. and McCauley, C. D. (1994), Gender Differences in Managers' Developmental Job Experiences. *Academy of Management Journal,* 37, 46-67.

Powell, G. N. (1990), One more Time: Do Female and Male Managers Differ? *Academy of Management Executive,* 4, 68-75.

Powell, G. N. (1999), Reflections on the Glass Ceiling: Recent Trends and Future Prospects. In G. N. Powell (Ed.), *Handbook of Gender and Work* (pp. 325-345). Thousand Oaks, CA: Sage.

Powell, G. N. and Graves, L. M. (2003). *Women and Men in Management* (3rd ed.), Thousand Oaks, CA: Sage.

Ragins, B. R. and Cotton, J. L. (1999), Mentor Functions and Outcomes: A Comparison of Men and Women in Formal and Informal Mentoring Relationships. *Journal of Applied Psychology*, 84(4),529-550.

Ragins, B. R., Townsend, B. and Mattis, M. (1998), Gender Gap in the Executive Suite: CEOs and Female Executives Report on Breaking the Glass Ceiling. *Academy of Management Executive*, 12, 28-42.

Ranjana Kumari, (1994), *Women Parliamentarians*, Har Anand Publication, New Delhi.

Rosener, J. (1995), *America Competitive Secret: Utilizing Women as a Management Strategy*. New York: Oxford University Press.

Rudman, L. A. (1998), Self-promotion as a Risk Factor for Women: The Costs and Benefits of Counter-stereotypical Impression Management. *Journal of Personality and Social Psychology*, 74, 629-645.

Rudman, L. A. and Glick, P. (2001), Prescriptive Gender Stereotypes and Backlash Towatd Agentic Women. *Journal of Social Issues*, 57, 743-762.

Ryan, M. K. and Haslam, S. A. (2005), The Glass Cliff': Evidence that Women are Over-represented in Precarious Leadership Positions. *British Journal of Management*, 16, 81-90.

Schein, V. E. (2001). A Global Look at Psychological Barriers to Women's Progress in Management. *Journal of Social Issues*, 57, 675-688.

Sekaquaptewa, D. and Thompson, M. (2003), Solo Status, Stereotype Threat, and Performance Expectancies: Their Effects on Women's Performance. *Journal of Experimental Social Psychology*, 39, 68-74.

Sharma, Kumud (1998), *Power vs. Representation: Feminist Dilemmas, Ambivalent State and the Debate on Reservation for Women in India*, Occasional Paper No. 28, Centre for Women Development Studies (CWDS).

Small, D. A., Gelfand, M., Babcock, L. and Gettman, H. (2006), *Who Goes to the Bargaining Table? Understanding Gender Variation in the Initiation of Negotiation*. Manuscript submitted for publication.

Smith, A. and Stewart, A. J. (1983), Approaches to Studying Racism and Sexism in Black Women's Lives. *Journal of Social Issues*, 39, 1-15.

Stangor, C., Lynch, L., Duan, C. and Glass, B. (1992), Categorization of Individuals on the Basis of Multiple Social Features. *Journal of Personality and Social Psychology*, 62, 207-218.

Stoddard, T., Kliengklom, T. and Ben-Zeev, T. (2003, February), *Stereotype Threat, Assimilation, and Contrast Effects, and Subtlety of Priming, or: You say "bitch" like it's a bad thing*. Paper presented at the annual Society for Personality and Social Psychology conference, Los Angeles, California.

Subramanian, Malathi, (2002), 'Women in Indian Politics: Participation and Representation' in Lal, Malashri, & Paul Kumar, Sukrita, Eds., *Women Studies in India: Contours of Change*, Indian Institute of Advanced Studies, Shimla UNIFEM (2000) Progress of South Asian Women (2000). New Delhi.

Thoits, P. A. (1992), Identity Structures and Psychological Well-being: Gender and Marital Status Comparisons. *Social Psychology Quarterly*, 55, 236-256.

Tsui, A. S. and Gutek, B. A. (1984), A Role Set Analysis of Gender Differences in Performance, Affective Relationship, and Career Success of Industrial Middle Managers. *Academy of Management Journal*, 27, 619-635.

Twenge, J. M. (2001). Change in Women's Assertiveness in Response to Status and Roles: A Cross-temporal Meta-analysis, 1931-1993. *Journal of Personality and Social Psychology*, 18, 133-145.

UNDP (2003) *Gender and Governance*, (2003) Human Development Research Centre (UNDP), New Delhi.

U.S. Bureau of Labor Statistics. (2005). *Current Population Survey, Annual Averages: Household Data*. (Characteristics of the Employed, Table 9: Employed Persons by Occupation, Sex and Age). Retrieved April 12, 2006, from *http://www . bls.gov /cps/ cpsaat9 .pdf*

U.S. Department of Defense (2005), *Active Duty Military Personnel by Service by Rank/grade* (for September 30, 2005). Retrieved April 12, 2006, from *http:// webl.whs.osd.mil/mmid/military/ miltop.htm*

Varma, Sudhir, (1997) *Women's Struggle for Political Space*, Rawat Publications, Jaipur.

Vecchio, R. P. (2002). Leadership and gender advantage. *Leadership Quarterly*, J 3, 643-671.

Wadman, M. K. (1992, July 16), Mothers Who Take Extended Time off Find their Careers Pay a Heavy Price. *Wall Street Journal*, pp. B 1, B5.

Williams, C. L. (1992), The Glass Escalator: Hidden Advantages for Men in the "Female" Professions. *Social Problems*, 39, 253-267.

Williams, C. L. (1995), *Still a Man's World: Men who do "Women's Work."* Berkeley: University of California Press.

Wirth, L. (2001), *Breaking Through the Glass Ceiling: Women in Management*. Geneva, Switzerland: International Labour Office.

Wood, W. and Eagly, A. H. (2002), A Cross-cultural Analysis of the Behavior of Women and Men: Implications for the Origins of Sex Differences. *Psychological Bulletin*, 128, 699-727.

3

Theoretical Concerns of Women Political Leadership (A Reference to Democratic Consolidation, Social Capital, Voluntarism and Political Empowerment)

Ravindra Kumar Verma

Introduction

The phrase 'women in politics' has become the striking concern at global level as their share in politics has been marginal throughout globe. The feminists have been advocating strongly for assuring their proportionate share in power structure.[1] This concern is closely related to women political leadership phenomenon. As we know it cannot occur in vacuum, the societal norms, patriarchal dominance and socio-economic environment inhibiting them in politics are certain issues that need be addressed. In Indian case too, the phenomenon is intersected by various factors such as, women's position in society, their personal self (ability-inability), the patriarchal dominance, the nature of polity, working of democracy and the attitude of civil society. An array of studies can be found marking these factors as influencing the women political leadership in India. But there is lack of attempts to theorize the phenomenon in context of working of democracy and sensitization of women for political participation in a broader sense.[2] Indian social and cultural heterogeneity has shaped a peculiar character of emergence of political leadership and women's political participation. Thus there is need to theorize women political leadership in the garb of certain concepts namely democratic consolidation, political leadership, social capital and voluntarism. These concepts intersect interse, if the various dimensions of the phenomenon of women political leadership are to be understood properly. As such the present paper intends to examine the concepts and underline the relationship among them in context of women political leadership, particularly in Indian milieu. The paper has been attempted under influence of the following predominant assumptions/hypotheses:

i. Democratic consolidation demands women's share in power structure and governance proportionate to their population, if not at least one third.

ii. Women's proportionate share can only be assured if women are able to come up to acquire positions in politics through self assertion

iii. Self assertion can be facilitated through creation of social capital among the women actors by the voluntary action.

The present paper examines the above mentioned concepts with a view to conceptualize the phenomenon of women political leadership in its various dimensions. Let us start with an overview of the concepts concerned.

An Overview of Concepts

Democratic Consolidation

In present days state has to restructure the whole governance process in delivery of good and social justice to the people. On the other hand the state particularly in developing ones, has failed to eradicate maladies such as deprivation, subjugation and social injustice. In other words, the state only reinforces the existing inequalities in the society.[3] As such the politics becomes the destiny of the masses. Adi Ophir advocates that the purpose of politics should be to deliver 'good' to the masses and should not inflict sufferings in any form on them.[4] In this context, it has to be seen whether women are deprived of their rights, opportunities and due share, only then a democracy can be said to have consolidated. While we do not wish to belittle the importance of liberal democracy, two things are unmistakable: most citizens in any country expect more than a democratic political system (such as a fair share of economic resources), and there are degrees of democracy. There is a growing focus and awareness among social scientists on the latter fact. As Linz and *Stepan* have argued, "Within the category of consolidated democracies there is a continuum from low to high quality democracy; an urgent political and intellectual task is to think about how to improve the quality of most consolidated democracies".[5]

Consolidation of democracy or democratic consolidation, thus, has become cherished task to be accomplished by the democratic system. Democracy has been broadly defined not only as a political entity but also a way of life and socio-economic system which hardly be examined empirically. Robert Dahl has outlined eight pre-conditions of democracy of which four are normative and the rest operative. For proper democracy, he emphasized on equal political participation, liberties and healthy competition obviously among political actors, interests and groups. In other words, democracy has to be examined in context of consolidation in terms of its operative part not only in normative parts. The democratic politics confines to the basic elements like - competition (among political actors), people's political participation and provision of equal liberties to all.[6] Achieving this is consolidation of democracy. It is quite difficult to adjudge as to when democratic consolidation is complete. Thus objective indicators for consolidation of democracy should be underlined.

Many scholars have conceptualized democratic consolidation; important among those are Juan Linz, O'Donnell, Huntington, Mainwaring and a few others.

Juan Linz takes legitimacy of democratic process through which the power is acquired as objective criteria. He argues that no political group should challenge the way in which government is formed in a consolidated democracy. To him, the democratic process should provide healthy competition among political actors, greater participation of people in governance process and political justice to all sections of society. Allurements, violence, generation of hatred among social divisions and infliction of sufferings on the masses cannot be taken as legitimized.[7]

O' Donnell believes in establishment of a government elected in an open competitive context with exercise of universal franchise and guaranteed democratic rights and liberties to all sections of society.[8] It means deprivation of exercising political rights in any form and for any reason hinders the consolidation process. Similar views were expressed by Mainwaring and others. This school believes that conviction of political leaders and conscious people towards democratic methods of government formation which may last long are the essential components of consolidated democracy.

Huntington considers the transfer of power from one elected government to another as one of the most crucial tests a new democracy must pass in consolidation process. It can also be viewed as process whereby democratic institutions and practices become so ingrained in the political culture that not only political leaders but the masses come to see such institutions and practices as part of natural order of things.[9]

In nutshell, the discussion on consolidation of democracy boils down to certain basic aspects that may be reflected in consolidated from of democracy–those are legitimacy of practices, participation and liberties, acceptable modes of transfer of power and establishment of harmonious society. Thus in a consolidated democracy the following elements must be there- (i) democratic institutions are formed and developed to such a degree that they reconciliate diverse societal interests and demands, (ii) people and political leaders have conviction to adopt democratic methods in formation of government which may be endurable (iii) all the sections of the society be represented in formation of government. The whole thing indicates towards accommodation of deprived sections of society in an acceptable and durable mode of democratic practices and institutions. Women's (as a deprived section of a society) proper share in the formation of government is a pre-requisite to democratic consolidation.

Political Leadership

All pre-conditions of democratic consolidation and the three significant aspects of operative democracy veer around the political leadership. Who should be called political leader and what roles has a leader to play? People generally interchange the term 'leadership' with 'political leadership'. An array of discussions on this issue has come in light, but a few of such discussions in context of India can be seen.[10] Jean Blondel has provided a comprehensive analysis of political leadership but his examination has been based on experiences of western democracies.[11] As we know political leadership does not occur in vacuum and it rests and wields power from the community/ society. Scholarship on leadership has articulated the basic characteristics of leader that need not be discussed here.[12] It is confined to two basic dimensions - capacity dimension and role dimension.

The capacity dimension is related to leaders' capacity to provide guidance, direction and coordination (GDC) to the led community and role dimension is related to instill confidence, courage and obedience (CCO) among the led groups, community and nation. Political leadership is not exempted from these GDC and CCO dimensions. Here is a question- what makes a leader different from a 'political leader'? Those leaders who influence decision making process from a formal position with having legitimate power to influence the community or seek (aspire) a formal position on the basis of power he/she enjoys on the community. Again a question arises - are all formal position holders political leaders? Only formal position holder cannot be political leader. He / she must have capacity to influence the led community and wield power from both the community and the super structure (state). Even the head of state cannot said to be a political leader if his/her activities are limited to wholly symbolic functions. The monarch of U K and President of India cannot be said to be political leaders. However, formal position facilitates opportunities to hold real power. Political leader has the power in that it is exercised over a wide range of values and goals such as socio-economic progress, justice to deprived masses, communal harmony and responsive governance in view of the experiences of Indian polity in last six decades. R C Tucker[13] has clarified the areas of political leaders' roles such as diagnosis of the problems, prescription, of course, of action and mobilization of those who are made to ensure that the action does take place. Here 'those' is meant for members of the led community. The political leader in India has to diagnose the real problems faced by the society, prescribe action for the masses to influence the decision making process for the resolution of the problems and have to mobilize the masses in a way it does not inflict sufferings in any form. Gender discrimination in the political sphere is also one of the most significant issues in Indian polity. Women political leadership would have also to cope up with these shortcomings, if they really want to enjoy the political leadership.

Social Capital

Social capital has been in prolific use by the social scientists particularly in context of analyzing democracy, political participation or grading the quality of democracy. Putnam's works are worth referring.[14] The concept is not concerned with formal associations but refers to trust, networks and norms shared by a group of actors that enable them to act together more effectively to pursue shared objectives. It is a resource – a capital that consists of relations one has with other people. It is social since one cannot have it in isolation, contrary to human capital.[15] It does not refer to any social or political action rather a condition or situation in which a group of actors feel united or togetherness. For example, if a group of unprivileged people such as dalit and women live in the same place but do not trust each other and have not shared norms. It is much less likely to act together against the oppressor. On the other hand if they trust and share norms (social capital), they can act effectively against the oppressor. Thus this concept is useful in understanding the functioning of democratic institutions in the segmented societies like Bihar. The scholarship has examined the functioning of panchayats and the grassroots democracy in Indian states in context of social capital.[16] Empowerment is thus not merely a change of mind-set, but a visible demonstration of that change which the world around is forced to acknowledge, respond to, and accommodate as best it way. Armed with their growing collective strength, women begin to assert their right to control resources (including their own bodies) and participate equally in decisions at the family and community levels and levels of various political institutions.

Social capital facilitates coordinated action between individuals and hence a means of making collectively the problems less problematic. Social capital increases communication, since trust, works and shared norms becomes means precisely. Social capital has-been shown to increased democratic responsiveness as well economic performance. If it is not a part of social divisions and a collective fund, why we call it social capital? It is a resource - a capital–that consists of the relations one has with other people. It is 'social' since one cannot have it in isolation, contrary to human capital. The term social does not imply socially or politically praiseworthy actions or goals. A simple example may illustrate the idea. We can think about a group of underprivileged people- agricultural laborers, pavement dwellers or dalits. If these groups of people live in the same place but do not trust each other, do not know each other and do not have shared norms, it is much less likely to act together against a landlord, a threat of eviction or against oppressive behaviour by dominant castes. On the other hand, if the members of such a group trust each other and share norms -in other words, if they have social capital they can utilise this capital to act collectively. This social capital can be used for political action. But social capital is not synonymous with formal associations. Indeed, shared norms' can often be founded on shared identity. This point also brings us the fact that social capital is not a theory 'without agents'. Social capital can be created and it can be destroyed.

Rudolph has reviewed the concept and indicated towards certain challenges. Rudolph's[17] first challenge is whether the concepts of civil society and social capital cope "in the context of highly unequal societies in the grip of radical social change, the condition of many countries in the south." The theory of social capital speaks to the general issue of cooperation. As Elinor Ostrom writes, "The really big puzzle in the social sciences is the development of a consistent theory to explain why cooperation levels vary so much"[18] Thus social capital is a very useful concept, particularly when women self assertive political leadership is to be understood and encouraged on a large scale among the masses.

Voluntarism

The creation of social capital is not an evolutionary or spontaneous process; rather it will have to be created in a segmented society like India. The social capital can sensitize women for political participation and political roles and it is believed that voluntary action can make them aware and sensitize to participate in local governance process through various modes - such as voting enthusiastically, fighting elections and participating substantially in the meetings of the political institutions (panchayat bodies, urban local bodies, political parties and non governmental village development organizations). As we know political participation is itself a voluntary action, one can ask how one voluntary action can facilitate another voluntary action? It is very simple, a group of aware people can make the group of unaware people or section aware, enthused and sensitized for political roles.

What then voluntarism is? How can it facilitate creation of social capital and sensitization of women for self assertive roles in political sphere? All voluntary associations which are the expression of human impulse (will) have been the subject of study of, by and large, three disciplines - sociology, social psychology and public administration. Sociologist whose contribution is significant in this regard, studies the associations as part of the social system; social psychologists are concerned with voluntary associations in an environment of their individual members; and the students of public administration are concerned with their organizational processes.[19] Inequality among individuals is a perennial source of motivation for voluntary action in any society, whatever is the state of its development. Inequality may be in material, moral and intellectual terms. A F C Bourdillon[20] observes that there is always an element of betterment of compensating inequality, motivating individuals to volunteer their services.

At the operational level, the above components may not differ much from one another but each of them is moved by an impulse with dedication as the common motivation. G D H Cole believed that along with changing impulse, there emerged with the welfare state the impulse of mutual help with the social interiors paralleled to the altruism of philanthropists, to play a significant part in looking after themselves by creating associations of their own instead of receiving passively as individuals, the benefaction of the 'well to do'. Cole identified the problem of poverty as the running thread in all types of activities of associations.[21] Approaches that saw the communities primarily passive recipients of any policy reforms have been given way to those which seek to make more of the potential that more active community participation might offer for enhanced accountability and improve responsiveness in services. This has laid a greater emphasis on issues of governance and within that on the institutional dimensions community participation. In other words, simply involving people in the political bodies and institutions cannot vibrate the voluntary impulse but there should be vibrant and dynamic people's participation.

For women's political participation, the need is to make them aware and politically socialized for effective and sizeable roles. Thus, the establishment of the communication network to enrich and instill in them the courage and confidence to lead is essential. The volunteers have to act as an instrument and psychologically prepare them for taking to politics at grass roots level. Developing the leadership qualities is of serious concern. In the first place, they should be taught about the norms, the values and priorities of the political system preferably in the panchayat raj institutions (PRIs). The volunteers' nature, temperament and enthusiasm should be in consonance with the target groups of women for effective results.

Thus, it is imperative to examine the role of voluntarism in this area (WPL). It could not be imagined earlier as these did not exist then. The functioning of PRIs, in view of prevalent women deprivation, has been against the very spirit of the democracy and consolidation of democracy. Making women aware of their political rights, creating a vision for a good and dignified life as well as the nitty-gritty of elections are the potential areas for the voluntary agencies to devote their energies.

Women's Political Empowerment

The most conspicuous feature of the term empowerment is that it contains within it the word power. So, obviously empowerment is about power, and changing the balance of power. In every society, there are resources of various kinds. This is spiral not a cycle which leads to greater and greater changes, and more empowerment. Consciousness, problem identification, action for change and analysis of that action and its outcome lead to higher levels of consciousness and better planned and executed strategies. This empowerment spiral affects every person involve: the collective, and the environment, though not necessarily at the same pace or depth. By this definition, therefore, empowerment cannot be a top-down or one-way process. Thus, empowerment has three basic contents freedom enabling and control. Freedom refers to freedom from subjugation, deprivation and oppression, perpetuated through institutionalized methods. The women have been prey or victims of centuries old, deprivation, subjugation and oppression by patriarchal norms not only in India, but also in almost all societies. The women have been victim of all these kinds of shackles from centuries. Empowerment requires their freedom. Freedom alone cannot empower them rather they should be enabled to participate in social, economic, political and cultural spheres of life. Finally the patriarchal norms have so been designed that women are kept at bay from their control over the resources and the ideology. They should have control over available resources and social ideas and thoughts at par with that of men.[22]

Again the issue of political empowerment requires clarification. The term 'political' refers to the views of Catlin and Lasswell who posit that 'shaping and sharing the power is political'. In other words, any thing-action, idea, and incident that relates to 'power' can be termed as 'political'. Thus the political empowerment of women denotes their role in political sphere i.e. political participation, political behaviour and actions related to influencing the decision making process and participating in the process of governance. Political participation has been considered as any voluntary action employing legitimate methods to influence the choice of public policies, administration of public affairs or the choice of political leadership at any level local or national.[23] In other words, they would have to be incapacitated to face the social domain, enjoy the economic independence and roles in political spheres i.e. political participation and acquisition of political leadership, may it be of any level.

Women Political Leadership: Ground Realities

Women political leadership (WPL) can be examined in context of three major dimensions - emergence, nature and roles. Further all these dimensions are concerned with WPL at macro and micro levels. The emergence of WPL refers mainly to political recruitment at the grassroots level. The nature has concerns with socio-economic texture of WPL. Finally the roles of WPL should be examined in context of their substantial participation in the political bodies, public affairs and activities related to CCO among followers.

The situation of WPL at the macro level - state, national and international level - has been discouraging. If taken together, the parliaments of world have nearly 10 per cent of women legislators and very few countries have women as head of the state and government. According to a survey conducted by Inter Parliamentary Union (IPU) in 186 countries in 1995, the percentage of women representatives in the American Congress was merely 10.9, in the United Kingdom this percentage was 9.05. France known as the land of liberty, equality and fraternity, had women parliamentarians as less as 6.4%. The survey further reveals that in countries, such as Bhutan, Cameron, Djibuti, Papua New Guinea, Kuwait and UAE, the Legislatures are exclusively-a preserve of men. In fact, the Constitution of Kuwait and UAE provide for equality of all citizens but allow only men to become members of their Legislatures. The only exceptions are the Nordic countries of Sweden, Norway, Denmark, Finland and Netherlands where the women parliamentarians range between a healthy 30 to 40 percent of the total membership of the House. So far the situation in Commonwealth countries is concerned women's representation has been merely 14 per cent. The situation is more pitiable in parliaments of the regions like Asian, South East Asian and Pacific countries to the tune of 5.8%, 8.5% and 8.7% respectively.[24] As regards the situation in India, the share of women in Indian Parliament and state assemblies has been quite low since beginning of the parliamentary democracy in country. It never reached above ten per cent in any of the period of Parliament and Bihar Legislative Assembly. So is the case with their share in Council of Ministers both at Union and state governments. It is needless to discuss it in details.[25] The question is–why? The patriarchal dominance in almost all societies–developed or developing-is the single reason. Men in politics, despite having raised voice in their favour, never made efforts with the core of heart evident from the fact that the proposed Bill on women's reservation in legislative bodies has been hanging in balance for last 12 years. Besides, the women in macro level politics came from the affluent sections of the society and from those families who were in politics. So wives, daughters and sisters of the political elites and social elites acquire the membership of the apex legislative bodies in India. There are few women in Indian politics, even at present, who have come up by their own like Mamta Banerjee, Mayawati and a few may be counted. That is why the women parliamentarians and legislators continued in the legislatures for long periods. They did not facilitate common women taking up the political roles. Thus there is urgent need to sensitize women to play assertive roles in the political arena.

The WPL at micro levels was a distance thing in India till the passage of 73rd and 74th constitutional amendment in 1992. Since then women blasted into political leadership at grassroots level particularly in the PRIs and ULBs. The two historic constitutional amendments have paved way through reservation provisions for a sizeable number (33%) of women into the local self governance throughout India in one go. Bihar being late in implementing the new PRIs and ULBs in 2001 went one step forward in 2006 by reserving 50% of seats in these bodies. But a new era began of 'proxy leaders' among women. Most of the women representatives of these bodies became the puppet political leaders, operated by their male guardians. It was also marked that male guardians of such elected women representatives used to sit in the meetings of these bodies.[26] But with passage of time, women representatives of these bodies have started playing substantial and effective roles. It so happened because women representatives learnt to participate in the governance and exercise their political rights owing to experiments and awareness campaign by voluntary organizations. A large number of voluntary organizations (nearly 300) created awareness among weaker sections and women in Bihar for participation in panchayat bodies for years together (from 1995). A sizeable number of women volunteers of these organizations participated in election fray and got success to the tune of 70% (as claimed by the voluntary organizations).[27] Besides, the women of weaker sections have participated in the elections of PRIs very enthusiastically and these women have come up with assertion by resisting male bastion.[28] All these happen because the women volunteers have created social capital among them and faced the odds despite being resisted by their male counterparts.

Epilogue

The whole gamut of discussions on the concepts and the ground realities suggests that the aspects of emergence, sustenance and change in the phenomenon of women political leadership and process of political recruitment from among common woman must be conceptualized in a way it could be understood properly in Indian context. If India is a democratic polity, it must be consolidated and for consolidation of democracy the space for women would have to be created. Women's equal partnership in power structure, decision making process, and political participation in greater degree is the pre-requisite of consolidation of democracy. Women's self assertive attitude can make them come up to political arena which can be assured by creation of social capital. The voluntary efforts - organized or unorganized - can only sensitize women for political participation and resist the male bastion. Unless the women from the mass are sensitized, women political leadership cannot spring up and will be subject to patronization. The entire process will facilitate political recruitment and emergence of women political leadership from among the common women (bottom up). The present attempt of theoretical concerns of WPL can be presented through the following figure. The political scientists should make efforts to theorize women political leadership keeping in view the emergence, socio-economic texture and role taking in context of socio-economic and political ecology of countries like India.

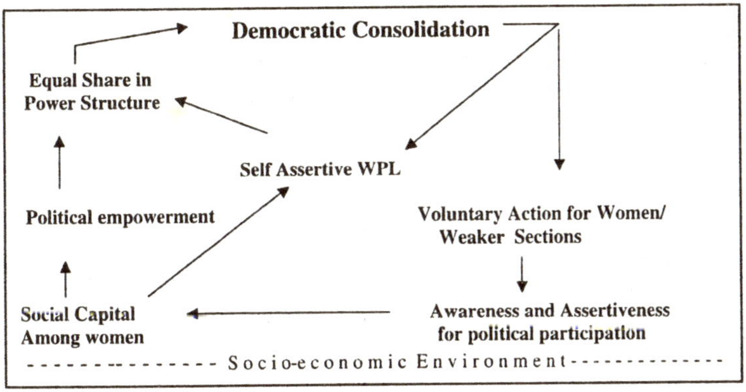

Figure: The Intersections and Relationships among Concepts

Notes

1. "Gender Sensitizing Commonwealth Parliaments" 1st Plenary Subject C, *The Parliamentarian,* Vol. LXXXIII, Issue one, 2002 p. 21
2. For Political Participation see (i) S. M. Lipset, *Political Man,* Doubleday Pub, New York 1960 (ii) S. Verba, "Democratic Participation", *Annuls of the American Academy of Political and Social Sciences,* September, 1967 (iii) L. W. Milbrath, *Political Participation,* Routledge McNally, Chicago, 1965 (iv) B. Ahmed, "Political Stratification of the Indian Electorate", *Economic and Political Weekly,* Annual Number, January 1971.
3. James Midgley, *Social Security, Inequality and the Third World,* John Wiley and Sons, Chicago, 1984.
4. See Upendra Baxi, Politics as Destiny, Foundation Lecture, A N Sinha Institute of social Studies, Patna 1993.
5. Juan Linz and Alfred Stepan, *Problems of Democratic Transition and Consolidation,* John Hopkins University Press, Baltimore, 1996.
6. Robert Dahl, *Polyarchy: Participation and Opposition,* Yale University Press, New Haven, 1971
7. (i) Juan Linz, "Transmission to Democracy", The Washington Quarterly, Vol. 13, No. 3, 1990 (ii) Larry Diamond, Juan Linz and S M Lipset (eds), Politics and Developing Countries: Comparing Experiences with Democracies, L Reinneer, Boulder, 1990.

8. S. Mainwaring, G O'Donnell and S Valenzuela (eds) Issues in Democratic Consolidation: The New South American Democracies in Comparative Perspectives, University Press of Notre dame, Notre dame, 1992
9. S. Huntington, *The Third Wave: Democratization in Late 20th Century,* University of Oklahoma Press, Norman, 1991.
10. (i) R K Verma, *Bases of Rural Political Leadership: A Study of Social Structure and People's Perception,* Amar Prakashan, Delhi, 1991 (ii) R K Verma, "Political Leadership: Issues in Concept and Approaches", *Journal of Social and Economic Studies,* Combined Volume, 1996 (iii) S. N. Mishra, *Emerging Pattern of Rural Leadership in India,* Associate Books, Patna, 1977.
11. Jean Blondel, *Political Leadership: Towards a General Analysis,* Sage Publication Incl, New Delhi, 1987
12. The detailed account on the issue is discussed in the author's paper. See R K Verma, *op cit* (1996).
13. R C Tucker as quoted in Jean Blondel, *op cit.*
14. Robert Putnam, *Making Democracy Work: Civic Traditions in Modern Italy,* Princeton University Press, Princeton, 1993.
15. H. Blomkvist and Ashok Swain, "Investigating Democracy and Social Capital in India", *Economic and Political Weekly,* February 24, 2001, pp. 639-43
16. For Various Studies on Social Capital in Context of Grassroots Level Politics see *Economic and Political Weekly,* 24 February, 2000.
17. Susanne Rudolph, "Civil Society and the Realm of Freedom" *Economic & Political Weekly,* May 13, 2000.
18. Elinor Ostrom, "A Behavioural Approach to the Rational Choice Theory of Collective Action" *American Political Science Review,* Vol. 92, 1998, pp. 1-22.
19. M. A. Mutalib (ed), *Voluntary Action in Education,* Sterling Enterprises, New Delhi, 1989.
20. A F C Broudillon (ed), *Voluntary Social Service: Their Place in Modern State,* Melthen, London, 1945.
21. As quoted in M A Mutalib, *op cit.*
22. Srilatha Batliwala; *Empowerment of Women in South Asia: Concepts and Practices.* (Second draft), Asian-South Pacific Bureau of Adult

Education and FAO's Freedom from Hunger Campaign- Action for Development, down loaded from Internet, June 1993.

23. (i) Myron Weiner, "Political Participation: Crisis of the Political Processes", in L. Binder et al (eds), *Crisis and Sequences in Political Development,* Princeton University Press, Princeton, 1971 (ii) S. Verba, "Democratic Participation", *Annuls of the American Academy of Political and Social Sciences,* September, 1967.

24. "Gender-Sensitizing Commonwealth Parliaments", *The Parliamentarian,* Vol. LXXXIII, Issue, 1, 2002.

25. Shobha Kumari Gupta, *Voluntarism, Social Capital and Women Political Empowerment,* MPS Publishers and Distributors, New Delhi, 2008.

26. (i) See "Proceedings of the Orientation/Training Camp for Newly Elected Panchayat Bodies", *Democracies,* Vol. XXI, Nos. 1&2 Jan-June, 2001 (ii) National Commission of Women, *Participation of Women in Panchayati Raj in India,* compiled by Shusheela Kaushik, NCW, New Delhi, 1998.

27. R K Verma and Singh, "Voluntarism and Panchayat Elections in Bihar 2001: A Study", *Indian Journal of Public Administration,* Oct-Dec., 2001.

28. R K Verma, *Panchayat Raj Elections in Bihar: A Study of the People, Parties and Electoral Process,* (mimeo), RN College, Hajipur, submitted to ICSSR, New Delhi, 2007.

4

Social Capital and Women's Political Leadership

Sonal Shree

According to Robert Putnam, a political scientist and professor at Harvard University , social capital consists of social networks and associated norms of reciprocity and it is made up of both instrumental (group involvement and social networks) and affective (norms of reciprocity and trust) components[1]. We need to understand the mechanisms by which it is created as well as its effects on other processes and institutions to recognize the role of social capital in political milieu for women. While the former provides insight into the particular sources of social capital, the latter provides it on the nature of political participation in modern democracies. Both can be examined for the degree to which they vary across various groups in modern societies. Putnam was clear in identifying that social capital provides both public and private returns although much emphasis has subsequently been placed on the public side. He was also clear in the distinction between bridging and bonding social capital. Bridging social capital brings people into contact with those who are different than oneself, while bonding leads to stronger ties with members of ones' own group. The former has positive benefits for democracy as it is likely to increase levels of trust and strengthen ties across groups. The latter introduces negative externalities in light of the increased tension between members and non-members of the group (that is, enhances feelings of us versus them).[2]

Social capital encompasses the fabric of social system and the credibility and 'norms of reciprocacity' associated with it. It has two facets, one that covers involvement with personal networks and the other, the professional and public one. For women, strong social networks can help advance their career through their ability to exploit the system of contacts. Here, Information technology comes to aid in modern times. Hillary Clinton made full use of it to build and encash on her supporters in the recently concluded presidential elections in the USA. Her profile can be found on the popular networking site, Facebook. It is important to understand whether, if at all, and how social capital is translated into political participation. That so many women continue to devote their energies and talents to various political and social organizations demands the attention of social scientists to better understand the public and private consequences of that participation.

Women in the Cosmos of Social Capital in India

Society is composed of both males and females and it would be against the laws of nature as well as against healthy political, social, economic, cultural and technological environment to let one group accumulate all the advantages of social capital at the cost of the other. Women's status is reciprocal to social capital comprising many dimensions of their lives like economics, politics, health, education. The existence of better women's status and high levels of social capital in juxtaposition is no coincidence. It indicates increased consciousness and awareness in the society towards empowerment of women. But so long as women do not have free hand in taking decisions based on their own might rather than others', political empowerment would remain a gimmick, a mockery of the cause of women empowerment.

Modern India has seen political parties taking up women's issues and appearing sympathetic towards them in order to capture the women's vote. At best, they are employing a populist strategy rather than being serious about espousing it on a priority basis. All political parties bury their 'ideological' differences in their unity against providing 33% reservation for women in the Parliament whenever a bill to that effect is introduced in the Parliament. Social capital is no guarantor of enhanced political status as long as changes are vague and sympathies remain mere claptraps. As a consequence, much of the women's movement has fragmented along ideological and political lines as women's organisations operate as progeny of the major political parties. This is not to say that there is no silver lining. We have some genuine elected women candidates who are contributing positively towards good causes and making their voices heard. Some female leaders have benefited from the changing political scene in terms of bargaining power within alliance formations with national parties. But one cannot say that the fragmentation and regionalisation of Indian politics has increased the support of women candidates by political parties. The changing political system has only worked to propel a few women into positions of power. Thus, the presence of women in top positions has made little apparent difference to the allotment of tickets to other women.

Social capital is about connectedness, co-operation and shared values that can occur across many different groups, rather than being about adherence to traditional family values as implied in the more communitarian elements of the literature[3]. Even though in a limited way with limited participation on the wider political platform, what women bring to political movements is a realization and attentiveness towards this as process. It arises out of the specific context of prior collective identification and common values and of forms of exclusion as well as inclusion and generally reflects a long term history of common identification and habitus. Because it becomes taken-for-granted, it is not necessarily reflected in the immediate degree of social interaction between the women, and is not easily analysed in a methodologically individualistic quantitative framework.

Role of Bihar in Expanding Social Capital for Women Leadership

A state as Bihar that had been scoring among the lowest across all human development indicators in terms of health, BPL families, literacy, per capita income, etc and was also known for its deeply ingrained caste and gender divisions took a giant leap and now has become the first Indian State to provide 50% reservation for women in Panchayats. Given this scenario, it is expected that the development agenda will positively improve with the advent of these newly elected women leaders. There are now a total number of 1, 35,805 members across all three tiers of the Panchayati Raj institutions of whom 73,204 are women.[4] This critical mass of women leaders of whom 4535 hold the posts of Presidents in Gram Panchayats, it is hoped, will definitely impact and change positively the path of Bihar's development.

An interesting case of woman leadership can be cited here in exception of the assumption that where levels of social capital are high, women have higher levels of political partaking and representation. Despite low level of social capital in the 1990s, Rabri Devi, wife of then Chief Minister Laloo Yadav, came to symbolize what one can call proxy leadership when she was instated as the leader of the state right out of her kitchen. Similar is the case at Panchayat levels, especially after the reservation policy enacted in the 73rd and 74th constitutional amendment reserving for women a third of all seats in the panchayat institutions, where most of the elected women leaders act simply as an agent on behalf of their male relations. It is hoped that with time, these women develop enough confidence in taking their own decisions without any outsider influence.

Gendered Power and Social Capital

The concept of social capital provides a basis for understanding the deployment of gendered power. This is true both of the way social capital is used to exclude and to outline separate areas, even in today's modern era, and of the way women have been sustaining themselves in the face of male segregation of all kinds, by building their own networks within the locality. Following are some examples:

(1) Women's networks serve to enable women in Africa to pool their resources and protect savings from their husbands.[5]

(2) At a basic level, too, Columbian women flower growers have been found more able to resist sexual violence and to find a negotiated solution with their partners where they can call upon social capital, developed in this case through outside employment.[6]

(3) In India, we have National Women's Rights Commission which looks after problems and complains of women and has an important say in matters pertaining to women on a national platform.

Women build networks in specific contexts, often in reaction to external threat and external power. Social capital- of whatever form - is built on specific concerns. Out of this bond develops cohesiveness amongst the members that is too strong to be curbed in the long run. As a consequence, it wouldn't be a surprise at all, if their issues start donning political colours. Male resistance and dominance is the primary cause behind women being relegated to the background in politics and almost every sphere. Underlying is the male fear of women dominating over them if the latter are armed with enlightened self awareness through political and economic power. It is thus more important for women to make their voices heard so as to establish themselves firmly in the house as well as country.

Social capital shows duality in its nature when women are involved- it is both inclusionary and exclusionary. In countries like Pakistan and Afghanistan, it is noteworthy that the Taliban is attacking and damaging the social capital and uprooting it with blasting of schools and declaring a ban on female education and appearance in public on their own. Can women show any political participation under such circumstances has now become a rhetorical question that supplies its own answer in silence. Women can show more attendance in the political arena only when their basic problems and issues as safety are addressed well. Consciousness raising groups in the early years of the women's movement also illustrate this double form of social capital: gaining strength from their new base excluding men, building links and understandings that have sustained individuals over the years, and taking what were hitherto personal, individual problems of domestic violence and sexual abuse, eventually, into the political arena.[7]

Conclusion

What women want is sense of their own identity. Several women's movements across the world form example of the exclusionary/inclusionary nature of social capital. Women are increasingly managing both their family as well as careers today so integrating work and family life requires a well-informed collaborative effort on the part of all the key actors that share interests and responsibilities for these issues. The need of the hour is a bit of sensitivity and co-operation. Families and family advocacy groups, government and communities all have roles to play in this balancing act as none of them can solve this problem acting alone. Social capital is an investment. It is an ever continuing process of bridging the gaps and linking the ends to incorporate and accommodate divergent interests. There are unlimited people competing for limited resources. We need to redefine social capital as part of a system of contending interests and values within a multidimensional space of difference, framed by large inequalities of power. Empowerment of women in all spheres is inter-related. Economic combined with political empowerment is required right away to instill confidence in the female population of the country if transformation has to be brought about in the larger social scene. It must be recognized that enriching social capital is obviously not a one-way process, and certainly not one in which conflicts of interest and values can be overcome overnight. Women leadership in politics will assume magnanimous proportions in quantity as well as quality if differences can be acknowledged and altered through the development and deployment of social capital. Numerous opportunities must be created for the younger female population of the country for entry into political platform right since the grass root level. Higher education centres like Delhi University and Jawaharlal Nehru University have good presence of female candidates at the time of contesting Students' Union elections which is a healthy sign. India is in a unique position to ensure political leadership for women considering its demographic dividend that boasts of having one of the youngest population in the world vis a vis aging economies like China's or the USA's. The path to a nation's progress demands intellectually aware, economically independent and physically sound youth, especially women, who can play a much larger role in the national and international context. Gender differences and inequalities must be things of past and if country has to grow and assure nurturing of more Indira Gandhis and Sarojini Naidus.

Notes and References

1. Robert Putnam (2001), "Social Capital: Measurement and Consequences," Isuma: *Canadian Journal of Policy Research*, 2, p. 41.
2. *Ibid*, p. 41.
3. *http://www.thp.org/where_we_work/south_asia/india/map/bihar*
4. Women and Social Capital, Edited by Jane Franklin With contributions from Irene Bruegel, Ruth Lister and Ginny Morrow. Families & Social Capital ESRC Research Group, London South Bank University, London ,April 2005, published by London South Bank University, p. 5.
5. *Ibid*, p. 9.
6. *Ibid*, p. 10.
7. *Ibid*, p. 10.

5

Gender Justice and Social Democracy

Subhash Chandra Roy

Introduction

An Infant born in any Society immediately becomes a member of various groups in a Cultural matrix. In India, as in most cultures, an infant is closest to its mother. At birth, all children are assigned a gender, which is based on the appearance of their genitals. Gender is then inculcated, at first by their mothers differentiating between children of different sexes through their behaviors towards them. Mothers respond differently towards their children on the basis of preconception about what biological sex differences are supposed to exist, and these differences include touching, Soothing and differential ideas about the autonomy of boy and girl children. Thus the direction of Personality, More specifically its feminity masculinity is set in the very early interactions between infant and its parents, More Particularly its mother. Thus, we can say that the mothering role of women differentially affects boys and girls universally.

When we look in to the socialization of girls, differential treatment can be seen right from the birth. Parents use double standards and differential codes of rearing a boy and a girl in terms of food, clothing. Social Contacts, Joys, games, responsibility of households, and development of personality of household. The girl is given food less nutritional value. In behaviour responses, she is taught to give in. In social behaviours, she is taught withdrawal. In terms of personality traits, Submissiveness is favoured. Hence, In comparison, preference is a accorded to the boy child over the girl child. This practice denies the girl child good health, education, recreation, economic opportunity and the right to choose her Partner violating her rights under the conventions on rights of the child as well as constitutional provisions, this gender discrimination leads to the extent of investment in her development.

The girl child is required to confine her space to the kitchen and backyard. She is forced to restrict her time, Space and mobility. The early socialization of girls emphasises on dutifulness, obedience, tolerance, sacrifice, timidity and conformity to 'feminine' qualities. She is never encouraged to be assertive what begins in infancy continues through the years.

At home, parents give priority to the satisfaction of the desires and interests of their sons than daughters. The adolescent girl is denied to involve in decision making in the family. She hardly takes decisions, which affects her life directly, by the time, she runs her own home. She realizes the discriminatory practices on her. But, she is so thoroughly imbibed such practices from her childhood, that she propagates the same. These practices militate against the interest of her own gender group. This situation reflects antidemocratic environment in the society. In fact, democracy does not signify political democracy only in which all the adult persons choose their representative to forma government for good governance, rather it has manifold concept , i.e. social democracy, religious democracy, economic democracy etc. Here, the term democracy signifies freedom, right to self determination, freedom from 'Pater familia system', equality, equal opportunity, freedom under Article 19 of the Indian constitution and the 'Right to life' under Article 21 of the constitution. Infact, the fundamental rights provides opportunity to man and woman to establish social democracy, by protecting girl child vis-a-vis women from discrimination. Hence, the paper seeks to explore the ways and means to establish gender justice in order to achieve social democracy which is an essence to achieve the goal of economic and social justice enshrined in the preamble of our constitution.

Impact of Education

Literacy and education are the indicators of social development. Improved literacy helps in the growth of awareness, eradication of unreasonable custom and social evils, proper understanding of human being and humanity, It is education which enlightens the concept of regards towards man and women each other, forming harmonious family life and society. But, according to 2001 census, the national average literacy rate is about 66% as against 18.33% in 1951. In isolation, it may look impressive, but the fact is dismal as per census 2001 itself with regards to female literacy, which is about 54.16% as against 75% males. Literacy, here, it can be observed that census data are exaggerated in terms of women literacy. National literally programme is also out of track which simply believe in training the women to write their 'names' and declare her as literate. The reason behind lies gender discriminations which continues all through women's life hampering democratic rights. Education is not only helpful in poverty eradication, rather it brings realisation of the importance of human life. Enlightened women develop their children who are asset to the nation. They are problem solver rather problem creator. In spite of right to Education under Article 21A in our constitution, girl children are deprived of such inherent need of life. Hence, the journey of exploitation and suffering starts from the hands of 'feudal males' which is ever lasting. Hence, they are deprived of the equal treatment from their childhood[2]. If they are provided education equally as male child, they will be not only good mothers rather good manager of the family leading to social democracy which is collective participation in social, political,economic and cultural life and decision making process[3]. It is the education which helps women to realise their human rights. Apart from the constitutional provisions, a large number of laws have been enacted to protect the human rights of woman. The women specific legislations are the immoral traffic (prevention) Act 1956, The dowry prohibition Act 1961, The Indecent Representation of women (Prevention) Act 1986, The commission of sati (Prevention) Act-1987, Domestic violence Act 2005. These legislations can be helpful to the women only if they are educated. The educated women can take benefit from the national policy for women 2001 and others relating to population, health, nutrition, agriculture industry, forest, water, housing, credit, science and technology, media etc. The participation in these area certainly, will bring social democracy.

Right to Life and Women

Gender discrimination is the violation of the very right to life of women and deprives them of the civil, political and economic liberty both within the family and the society. Women are not allowed equal access to the freedom of faith and religion, freedom of movement and residence. Right to equal opportunity either dejure or defacto is missing for them. Women suffer wage discrimination in spite of protection under labour legislation. They seldom get benefits under 'Maternity benefits Act' particularly in private organised as well as in unorganised sector. It tells upon their mental and family set up which hampers harmonious relations and participation in democratic process. Gender based violence, including wise battering, dowry, murders, incest, Marital rape, foeticide, infanticide, rape and sexual harassment, sexual slavery and exploitation are the examples of violations of 'Right to life' When ever there is upheaval the victim is girl child and women. They suffer injustice, superstition and cultural prejudices. More so, they are deprived from their reach. How can the women contribute in the evolution and development of Social democracy?

Political Rights and Woman

Mahatma Gandhi had announced at the second Round table conference that his aim was to establish a political society in

India in which there would be no distinction between people of high and low classes and in which women would enjoy the same rights as men and the teeming millions of India would be ensured dignity and Justice-social, Economic and political. With the Independence of country, We introduced ' Right to vote' and provided this right without any qualification - each adult person without any distinction of caste and creed, high & low, rich and poor, have right to vote. But the women's political rights are being enjoyed by the males counterpart and thus they are deprived from taking participation in the political activities right from Panchayti Raj institutions to Parliament. Therefore, now a day, a demand for 33 per cent reservation of seats in the parliament and state legislature is not enough. Actually, the condition of women either educated or uneducated is the same. Whether they belong to any religion or caste. Therefore, they can be categorised only in two parts educated and uneducated. Hence, 50 per cent reservation is essential for their upliftment not only for political empowerment rather for economic and social empowerment also, Here, 33 per cent reservation can be provided to the uneducated, dalit and adivasi women and 17 per cent reservation to the educated urban woman at least for ten years Manifesting the replacement of the politics of idea with a politics of presence, contain influential strands in feminist theory have stressed the importance of women's. presence in public /Political/ decision making bodies in 'critical mass'[4], while the 'notices of critical mass' subscribe to the view that the presence of women as a critical mass would some how set in motion a process that would engender politics, the difference between presence as 'critical action' has been emphasized by others, foregrounding the necessity of moving beyond numbers in to the realm of transformative actions.[5]

Gender Budgeting

Our society consists of almost fifty per cent of women population. It is quite obvious that with out progress of women, - society can not progress and the social democracy, socio-economic-politico justice can not be achieved. Therefore, there is a need of gender budget in all family as well as in Institutional planning too. Gender budgeting is a process in which allocation of resources as well as impact assessment is done right from childhood to old age-according to their Psycho-somatic needs and overall personality development. The planning for women needs micro level as well as external factors which affect the empowerment of women which leads the goal of social democracy.

The internal factors affecting the process of participation in democratic process are lack of proper schooling and lack of awareness about their role in family society and nation building, lack of leadership quality and exposure etc. It is noticed that women, representatives are not aware of their functions duties and responsibilities[6]. Lack of education or low level of education has become a major obstacle in the path of playing active role in the functioning of family and society.

The external factors which affect the process of participation and empowerment of women are - influence of family, caste, social outlook, partriarchy system etc. The male dominated society does not perceive women as capable or worthy of leadership. They say- "Females job is to cook and serve, governance is not their job." Patriarchal influences and traditional norms of our society hinder the path of women's empowerment which leads to social democracy.

Conclusion

Gender justice is a justice to the women folk from injustice. It is a mantra to protect their basic human rights so that they can participate actively in the family, society and nation. The active participation of women from courtyard enroute to farm, industry, offices, administration and finally parliament indicates the result of gender justice. We have no doubt, made some progress in the matter of women's education since 1947 and now many women are educated and they have entered in different professions as well as adventures. But, still the very essence of education is out of their reach. The measurement of women empowerment lies in their realization of their role from bearing-nurturing-developing the children to their stability in the social life–both male and female child. Secondly, her role is managerial in the family progress- economic as well as cultural. At the same time, it is women on whom responsibility lies for creating better citizen, i.e. 'human'–vaisnav, one who feels the pangs of other. This is the biggest role on the shoulder of women. And here needs gender justice to her. It is she who can fight all evils of society because many are either her own creation or supported by her willingly or unwillingly. Therefore, the schools and university should frame syllabus for women keeping in mind their psycho-somatic and sociological needs as extra and compulsory papers. At the same time, boys should also be compulsorily taught, as importance of women in all walks of life, in all courses throughout from school to higher education. In this way, the remnants of feudal culture, casteism, communalism and various abuses in the society can be eradicated. More so, women can confidently save themselves from various exploitation. Thus, the tryst of destiny, i.e, the harmonious and human society, i.e. social democracy can be achieved.

Notes

1. Dr. Rathi Devi (2006), Gender Discrimination in Socialization, *Legal News & Views,* April, p. 4.
2. Article 14, 15 & 16 of the Constitution.
3. Girija Vayas (2008), Remedy for Social Elevation, *Yojona,* October.
4. Anuparna Roy (2008), Empowerment Forchange, *Yojana,* October.
5. *Ibid.*
6. Desrathi Bhuyan (2008), Participation in Panchayati Raj, *Yojana,* October.

Part–2

Micro Level Women Political Leadership

6

महिला राजनीतिक नेतृत्व के आयाम

Archana Kumari

यह सर्वमान्य तथ्य है कि समाज में महिलाओं की स्थिति तब ही मजबूत होगी तथा उनकी प्रस्थिति (Status) में सुधार होगा, जब उनकी भागीदारी राजनीति में होगी तथा निर्णय प्रक्रिया में उनकी भूमिका होगी। इसी वैचारिक पृष्ठभूमि में राजनीतिक विधिक (वैधानिक) उपाय किये गये हैं यथा राजनीतिक संस्थाओं एवं नौकरियों में महिलाओं के लिए आरक्षण आदि। परन्तु अनुभव बताते हैं कि ये राजनीतिक-वैधानिक उपाय भी प्रभावी नहीं रहे हैं। वृहद् स्तरीय एवं सूक्ष्म स्तरीय महिला राजनीतिक नेतृत्व में कमजोरियाँ हैं। यह पाया गया कि इनमें छद्‌म नेतृत्व का विकास हुआ है। इस स्थिति में सुधार लाने की सख्त आवश्यकता है। जो भी राजनीतिक वैधानिक उपाय किए गए हैं उनकी प्रभावोत्पादकता को बढ़ाना है। नई पंचायती राज व्यवस्था में महिलाओं की सुनिश्चित भागीदारी का प्रावधन किया गया है। बिहार में तो महिलाओं के लिए 50% आरक्षण की व्यवस्था है जिसके चलते महिलाओं के लिए पर्याप्त अवसर उपलब्ध हुए हैं। परन्तु छद्‌म नेतृत्व परिघटना (Phenomenon) के कारण यह भी अप्रभावी प्रतीत होता है।

हाल में इस संदर्भ में जो भी अध्ययन प्रकाश में आये हैं उनमें इस बात पर बल दिया गया है कि महिलाओं को राजनीतिक एवं सामाजिक क्षेत्रों में स्वस्पफूर्त (self assertive) भागीदारी निभानी होगी। इसके लिए आवश्यकता है कि उनमें

राजनीतिक एवं सार्वजनिक विषयों के प्रति स्पंदन कराना होगा, तथा इन क्षेत्रों में भागीदारी के लिए जागृति एवं उत्साह विकसित करना होगा। हमारी राजनीतिक व्यवस्था में राजनीतिक दलों ने राजनीतिक प्रशिक्षण को महत्व एवं प्राथमिकता नहीं दी है। परन्तु खुशी की बात है कि कुछ स्वयंसेवी संस्थाओं ने इस दिशा में न केवल पहल की है अपितु वृहत स्तर पर कार्यक्रम भी चलाया है। इस संदर्भ में यह भी जानना आवश्यक है कि इन संस्थाओं के कार्य-कलापों का क्या प्रभाव पड़ा है।

हमारी सामाजिक व्यवस्था ऐसी है जिसमें संस्थागत तरीकों से महिलाओं को सार्वजनिक भूमिकाओं में आने से रोका जाता रहा है। खासकर अत्यन्त पिछड़े एवं दलित वर्ग की महिलाओं के बीच अनेक बाधाएं हैं। पुरुष-प्रधान समाज में उन्हें राजनीतिक नेतृत्व के लिए उत्प्रेरित करने एवं अपने अधिकारों के प्रति सजग रखने हेतु विशेष प्रयासों की आवश्यकता है। इस संदर्भ में सामाजिक परिप्रेक्ष्य में महिला नेतृत्व का परीक्षण आवश्यक प्रतीत होता है।

कतिपय महिलाएँ राजनीतिक भूमिका के लिए आगे आती हैं। परन्तु उनमें सामाजिक पूँजी (social capital) का अभाव पाया जाता है। फलस्वरूप उनके प्रयास प्रभावकारी नहीं हो पाते हैं एवं पुरुष वर्चस्व वाले परिस्थितियों पर उनका नियंत्रण नहीं हो पाता है। महिलाओं में राजनीतिक सशक्तीकरण के लिए विशेष उपायों को सुझाना आवश्यक प्रतीत होता है। खासकर कमजोर वर्ग की महिलाओं जिनमें व्यापक रूप से अशिक्षा एवं गरीबी व्याप्त है, में राजनीतिक जागरूकता एवं सामाजिक पूंजी के निर्माण की आवश्यकता है। सक्रिय महिलाओं के बीच परस्पर विश्वास, मेलजोल, विचार का आदान-प्रदान एवं उद्देश्य की समानता को ही हम सामाजिक पूंजी कहते हैं ।

उपरोक्त परिस्थितियों के आलोक में निम्नलिखित मुद्दों पर गहन विचार-विमर्श करने की आवश्यकता है।

1. महिला नेतृत्व का प्रादुर्भाव (उदय), उत्थान, एवं परिवर्तन
2. सूक्ष्म एवं वृहद् स्तरीय नेतृत्व की प्रकृति एवं भूमिकाएँ
3. राजनीतिक संस्थाओं एवं राजनीतिक दलीय संगठनों में उनकी भूमिका,
4. महिला नेतृत्व में सामाजिक पूंजी एवं अंतःक्रिया,
5. पुरुष नेतृत्व के साथ सम्बन्ध,
6. महिला नेतृत्व में स्वैच्छिक संस्थाओं की भूमिका,

उपरोक्त विवेचनों के आलोक में प्रस्तुत विषय के मूल तत्व निम्नलिखित

विषय खण्डों या (sub themes) विभाजित किये गये हैं ताकि महिला नेतृत्व के इन आयामों पर विषद् विवेचन किया जा सके ।

1. सैद्धांतिक विवेचन- इसमें अर्न्तनिहित मुख्य सैद्धान्तिक पक्षों एवं पदावली का स्पष्टीकरण आवश्यक है यथा राजनीतिक नेतृत्व, महिलाओं का राजनीतिक सशक्तिकरण, सामाजिक पूंजी और स्वैच्छिकवाद (voluntarism) महत्वपूर्ण हैं ।
2. वृहद् स्तरीय (राज्य, राष्ट्र एवं अंतर्राष्ट्रीय स्तर) महिला नेतृत्व (इसके तहत इन स्तरों पर विधयिकाओं एवं राजनीतिक दलों के संगठनों में उनकी भागीदारी, भागीदारी की प्रवृति एवं परिमाण पर विमर्श करना)
3. सूक्ष्म स्तरी (पंचायत राज संस्थाओं एवं नगरीय स्थानीय संस्थाओं में महिला राजनीतिक नेतृत्व का आकलन)
4. राजनीतिक-वैधनिक विधनों का अनुशीलन (खासकर महिलाओं हेतु आरक्षण प्रावधनों एवं प्रस्तावों का पुनर्परीक्षण एवं उनके कार्यान्वयन का अनुशीलन
5. सामाजिक पूँजी एवं महिला नेतृत्व- (इसके तहत महिला नेतृत्व के बीच सामाजिक पूंजी की स्थिति का आकलन करना ताकि उनकी प्रभावकारिता पर प्रकाश डाला जा सके।)
6. सामाजिक संरचना एवं महिला नेतृत्व (इसके तहत् महिला राजनीतिक नेतृत्व के समाजशास्त्रीय विवेचन किया जायेगा। महिला राजनीतिक नेतृत्व का विभिन्न सामाजिक स्तरों में वितरण एवं परिचालन का आकलन करना)
7. यह मान्यता है कि कर्त्ताओं (नेतृत्व) के बीच परस्पर विश्वास, नेटवर्क एवं उद्देय की एकरूपता होने से अभिवंचित वर्ग अपने अधिकारों के लिए प्रभावकारी ढंग से संघर्ष कर पाते हैं। इस अवधरणा को हम सामाजिक पूंजी के भी नाम से जानते हैं। भारतीय परिप्रेक्ष्य में भी यह पाया गया कि दलितों के बीच सामाजिक पूंजी होने के कारण उनकी राजनीतिक सहभागिता सामान्य की तुलना में अधिक रही है। बिहार के संदर्भ में एवं अन्य राज्यों के परिप्रेक्ष्य में सामाजिक पूंजी के स्थिति का आकलन आवश्यक प्रतीत होता है तभी हम महिला नेतृत्व पर प्रकाश डाल सकेंगे।

8. महिलाओं के बीच राजनीतिक जागरूकता एवं राजनीतिक भागीदारी को प्रशास्त करने में स्वैच्छिक संस्थाओं की भूमिका प्रकाश में आई है। कई तरह के कार्यक्रम इस उद्देय से चलाए गए जिसके अच्छे परिणाम भी आये हैं। यह जानना आवश्यक प्रतीत होता है इन स्वैच्छिक संस्थाओं की कार्य प्रणाली प्रभावोत्पादकता एवं व्यापकता की स्थिति क्या है? ताकि महिलाओं में राजनीतिक भर्ती की प्रक्रिया एवं स्वरूप का विवेचन किया जा सके।

इसके अतिरिक्त कुछ अन्य क्षेत्र भी हैं जहां की पृष्ठभूमि पर महिलाएं राजनीतिक क्षेत्र में प्रवेश कर सकती है। उदाहरणस्वरूप दबाव समूहों से, महिला संगठनों से, तकनीकी संस्थाओं से एवं अन्य कल्याणकारी संगठनों से महिलाएं राजनीतिक क्षेत्र में आ सकती है। इस दृष्टिकोण से भी महिला राजनीतिक नेतृत्व को देखना चाहिए ।

यह विषय आज की बदलती परिस्थितियों में महिलाओं की बढ़ती भूमिका एवं विश्वव्यापी महिला मुक्ति आन्दोलन के परिप्रेक्ष्य में अत्यन्त ही महत्वपूर्ण है। यह अकाट्य सत्य है कि जब तक महिलाएं राजनीतिक क्षेत्र तथा निर्णय-निर्माण प्रक्रिया में सार्थक भागीदारी नहीं निभाती तब तक समाज में उनकी स्थिति सबल नहीं होगी।

पाश्चात्य तथा भारतीय राजनीतिवेताओं सहित राष्ट्रीय महिला आयोग की भी यही धारणा है। इस उद्देश्य की पूर्ति हेतु कई राजनैतिक-वैधानिक प्रावधान भी किए गए हैं। किन्तु ये प्रावधान पिछले दो तीन दशकों में प्रभावी होते प्रतीत नहीं होते।

दूसरी ओर 73वें एवं 74वें संवैधानिक संशोधन के पश्चात् महिलाओं के लिए राजनीतिक भूमिका का मार्ग प्रशस्त कर दिया गया है। एकाएक राजनीतिक भूमिका में उनके प्रसार से कतिपय विडम्बनाएं भी प्रकाश में आ गई । जिसमें Proxy leadership उदासीन प्रतिभागिता एवं असमर्थता जैसे तत्व दृषटिगोचर होने लगे। इनके पीछे सामाजिक परम्पराएं, महिलाओं की अयोग्यताएं, तथा नारी सुलभ विलक्षणताओं के कारण महिला राजनीतिक नेतृत्व में विसंगतियां उत्पन्न हुई है।

पिछले दशक में स्वैच्छिक संस्थाओं ने इस ओर अपनी दृष्टि डाली है और अन्य कमजोर वर्गों की भांति महिलाओं के अन्दर राजनीतिक एवं सामाजिक भूमिका हेतु स्पंदन देने की दिशा में कार्य किया है। प्रतिवेदनों से आभास होता है कि इनका प्रभाव भी हुआ है। स्थानीय स्तर के महिला राजनीतिक नेतृत्व में social capital (सामाजिक पूंजी) का अभाव अभी भी पाया जा रहा है।

आज की यह मांग है कि जमीनी स्तर पर महिलाएं राजनीतिक एवं सार्वजनिक भूमिकाओं के लिए स्पंदित हो एवं स्वस्पफूर्त गतिविधियाँ करें। इसके लिए उनके बीच राजनीतिक एवं सामाजिक जागरूकता एवं राजनीतिक अधिकारों के प्रति उत्कृटता का प्रसार होना आवश्यक है। उनमें प्रभावोत्पादकता को बढ़ाने के लिए सामाजिक पूंजी का होना अति आवश्यक है।

इन बातों से भारतीय सामाजिक राजनीतिक परिवेश में महिला राजनीतिक नेतृत्व के कई पहलू एवं आयाम प्रकाश में आये हैं जैसे कि–

1. महिला राजनीतिक नेतृत्व का उद्भव एवं विकास एवं सामाजिक-सांस्कृतिक तत्वों का प्रभाव
2. महिला राजनीतिक नेतृत्व की प्रकृति-भूमिकाओं, तरीकों एवं प्रभावोत्पादकता के परिपेक्ष्य में
3. उनकी भूमिकाओं को प्रभावित करने वाले तत्व
4. पुरुष प्रधान सामाजिक संरचना एवं महिलाओं की राजनीतिक भूमिका विचार-विमर्श की इस पृष्ठभूमि में कुछ terms ऐसे हैं जिसको मैं उसी प्रकार प्रस्तुत कर रही हूँ जिस प्रकार मैंने स्वयं उसे समझा है।

अब हम राजनीतिक नेतृत्व को ही लें। यह नेतृत्व से सर्वथा भिन्न है और इसके प्रमुख घटकों में शक्ति, औचित्यपूर्ण घटनाएं, समुदाय का समर्थन तथा किसी पद को प्राप्त करना या प्राप्त करने का प्रयास करना। इस क्रम में उस नेता को समुदाय एवं निर्णय निर्माण प्रक्रिया दोनों को प्रभावित करना होता है।

दूसरे सशक्तिकरण वह प्रक्रिया है जिसमें महिलाएँ वंचनाओं एवं प्रताड़नाओं से मुक्त होती है, सार्वजनिक भूमिका की योग्यता आती है तथा संसाधनों एवं विचारों पर उनका नियंत्रण होता है और ये सारी स्थितियां नेतृत्व के लिए आवश्यक हैं। विगत दशक से नेतृत्व सुदृढ़ीकरण में सामाजिक पूंजी की भूमिका महत्वपूर्ण मानी जा रही है। इटली के Robert Putnam ने इसे प्रजातंत्र के कार्यकरण में प्रभावी माना है जिसके तहत् सार्वजनिक कर्त्ताओं के बीच विश्वास तथा अन्तःक्रिया स्थापित होता है और वे एक समान उद्देश्य के लिए क्रियाशील रहते हैं। इसके चलते दमनकारी संस्थाओं के विरुद्ध संघर्ष प्रभावकारी हो जाता है। सामाजिक पूंजी के निर्माण में स्वैच्छिक संगठनों की भूमिका भी सहायक होती है। इसके भी प्रमाण हमें देखने को मिले हैं।

स्वैच्छिकता (voluntarism) समाज सेवा के उद्देश्य से एक स्वस्फूर्त मानवीय इच्छा है जिसका शाश्वत श्रोत समाज में व्याप्त विषमता, अभिवंचना एवं असहाय स्थिति है जिनकी स्वैच्छिक प्रयासों द्वारा क्षतिपूर्ति की जा सकती है। यह चार तरीकों से प्रतिपादित होती है–

1. स्वनियमित गैर सरकारी संगठन (NGOs)
2. राज्य नियमित सहकारी संगठन,
3. कल्याणकारी संस्थाएं यथा चर्च, मिशनरीज आदि (philanthropic Institution)
4. असंगठित स्वैच्छिक प्रयास– जैसे राहत कार्य हेतु नवयुवक दल, श्रमिक विकास दल।

महिला राजनीतिक नेतृत्व का आकलन इन्हीं सैद्धान्तिक परिप्रेक्ष्य में किया जाना श्रेष्यकर हैं ।

अब हमें महिला राजनीतिक नेतृत्व के विभिन्न आयामों पर एक संक्षिप्त दृष्टि डालनी चाहिए। सर्वप्रथम महिला राजनीतिक नेतृत्व का उद्भव एवं विकास जो किसी भी प्रजातांत्रिक राजनीतिक व्यवस्था के लिए अत्यन्त महत्वपूर्ण है। राजनीतिक नेतृत्व का सामाजिक स्तर पर राजनीतिक भर्ती एवं राजनीतिक समाजीकरण की प्रक्रिया से गहरा सम्बन्ध है। अतः इसके उद्भव के परिप्रेक्ष्य को विभिन्न समाजशास्त्रियों ने अपने-अपने दृष्टिकोण से देखा है।

राजनीतिक नेतृत्व के उद्भव को चिन्हित करने के लिए समाज विज्ञानिकों ने कई उपागम प्रयास में लाये जिन्हें– नेता केन्द्रीत, परिस्थिति केन्द्रीत एवं नेता समर्थक सम्बन्ध केन्द्रीत श्रेणियों में रखा जाता है। प्रथम श्रेणी में Ordway Tead, Sanderson, Kreitlow तथा Hunter महत्वपूर्ण है। जिन्होंने नेतृत्व के व्यक्तिगत गुणों को महत्व दिया। अर्थात् नेतृत्व का उद्भव व्यक्ति के मनोवैज्ञानिक एवं अन्य व्यवहारिक गुणों के कारण होता है।

गॉर्डन एवं वेल्स की धारणा है कि समर्थकों एवं नेता के बीच सम्बन्धों के आध ाार पर भी पुराने नेतृत्व में परिवर्तन एवं नए नेतृत्व का उद्भव होता है।

भारतीय परिपेक्ष्य में एक चौथी श्रेणी भी प्रकाश में आई है जिसकी मान्यता है कि समुदाय की मंशा नेतृत्व के उद्भव में प्रेरक होती है और नेतृत्व का स्वरूप भी उसके अनुरूप ही होता है इसे समुदाय बोध का नाम दिया गया है। विगत् कुछ

वर्षों में सामाजिक पूंजी और स्वैच्छिक संस्थाओं की भूमिका ने भी महिला राजनीतिक नेतृत्व के उद्भव में उत्प्रेरक का कार्य किया है।

इन सिद्धान्तों की पृष्ठभूमि में हमारे परिवेश में महिला राजनीतिक नेतृत्व के उद्भव के स्वरूप को चिन्हित करना आवश्यक प्रतीत होता है। यह विवेचन किसी नये उपागम या नेतृत्व उद्भव के किसी नए सिद्धांत की ओर भी इंगित कर सकती है।

यह आरोप सदा लगते आया है कि राजनीतिक क्षेत्र में प्रवेश के बावजूद महिला प्रभावी भूमिका नहीं निभा पाती है। कभी छद्म नेत्री (proxy leader) के रूप में तो कभी अनुकरण (male directed) करने वाली नेत्री के रूप में और कभी दबाव पर सक्रिय (induced) होने वाली नेत्री के रूप में और इन सबके कई उदाहरण भी हमारे सामने हैं ।

पंचायत एवं नगरीय निकायों में Proxy leadership की बहुलता देखी गई है। निर्वाचित महिला प्रतिनिधि के बदले उसके अभिभावक ही कार्य करते हैं। वृहद् स्तर पर संभ्रात परिवार की महिलाएं अधिकतर सांकेतिक भूमिकाएं ही निभाती रही हैं। परन्तु राजनीतिक क्षेत्र में आने के बाद महिलाएं उत्तरोतर परिमार्जित हुई हैं एवं अपनी भूमिकाएं क्षमतापूर्ण निभायी हैं। अतः महिला राजनीतिक नेतृत्व का यह व्यवहारिक आयाम तीन दृष्टियों यथा Proxy leadership, Introduced leadership and self assentive leadership से देखना आवश्यक प्रतीत होता है। क्या Proxy leadership assertive में परिवर्तित हो सकता है? क्या भूमि सदा कारगर साबित होती है। इस पर विचार करना हमारा केन्द्रीय लक्ष्य है।

इन प्रश्नों को विधायिकाओं, राजनीतिक दल एवं दबाव समूहों, स्थानीय निकायों एवं स्वैच्छिक संस्थाओं में महिलाओं की भूमिका को भी चिन्हित करना हमारा लक्ष्य है।

हमें विदित है कि महिलाओं को सार्वजनिक एवं राजनीतिक भूमिका में प्रेरित करने के लिए कुछ राजनैतिक एवं वैधानिक उपाय प्रावधन भी किए गए हैं जिनमें स्थानीय स्वशासी संस्थाओं में महिलाओं के लिए आरक्षण, राज्य एवं राष्ट्रीय विधायिकों में महिलाओं के लिए आरक्षण का प्रस्ताव, महिलाओं के हितों एवं अधिकारों की रक्षा के लिए कानून आदि। इनका विवेचन एवं पुनरावलोकन महिला राजनीतिक नेतृत्व के उद्भव, उनकी भूमिकाओं की प्रवृति एवं उन्नयन पर प्रभाव का विवेचन आवश्यक है।

महिलाओं में सार्वजनिक एवं राजनीतिक भूमिकाओं को प्रोत्साहित करने, उन्हें जागृत करने एवं स्पन्दित करने में स्वैच्छिक संस्थाओं की भूमिका का परीक्षण करना इसलिए आवश्यक है कि महिला राजनीति नेतृत्व में हो रहे बदलावों को चिन्हित किया जा सके इस सन्दर्भ में स्वैच्छिक संस्थाओं का संगठनात्मक स्वरूप, कार्य प्रणाली एवं महिला राजनीतिक नेतृत्व व सशक्तिकरण पर प्रभाव का निरूपण करना भी हमारा अनिष्ट है।

उपरोक्त विवेचन एवं समीक्षात्मक चिंता को निम्नलिखित कुटों में दर्शाया जा सकता है।

विषय के अनुशीलन की आवश्यकता

1. विपरीत परिस्थितियां

- राजनीतिक एवं निर्णय निर्माण प्रक्रिया में निर्बल भागीदारी
- अप्रभावी राजनीतिक-वैधानिक प्रावधान
- स्थानीय स्वाासन में आरक्षण
- छद्म एवं असक्रिय महिला नेतृत्व

2. सम्भावनाएं

- स्वस्पफूर्त एवं राजनीतिक संवेदना
- स्पंदन एवं स्वस्पफूर्त भागीदारी
- राजनीतिक अधिकारों के प्रति उत्कृष्ठता
- सामाजिक पूंजी आवश्यक

महिला राजनीतिक नेतृत्व के आयाम

- उद्भव एवं विकास
- सामाजिक/सांस्कृतिक तत्वों का प्रभाव
- भूमिका की प्रकृति
- नेतृत्व के प्रकारों एवं प्रभावोत्पादकता का विवेचन
- वृहद् स्तरीय एवं सूक्ष्म स्तरीय नेतृत्व

- सामाजिक पूंजी का संदर्भ
- स्वैच्छिक संस्थाओं की भूमिका

संदर्भित अवधरणाएँ

- राजनीतिक नेतृत्व
- महिला सशक्तिकरण
- सामाजिक पूँजी
- स्वैच्छिकवाद एवं स्थानीय राजनीतिक नेतृत्व

राजनीतिक नेतृत्व

- नेतृत्व बनाम राजनीतिक नेतृत्व
- राजनीतिक नेतृतव के घटक
    1. शक्ति
    2. पद-धारण या प्राप्ति का प्रयास
    3. प्रभाव-निर्णय निर्माण प्रक्रिया एवं समुदाय पर
- समुदाय का समर्थन

महिला सशक्तिकरण

1. *महिला सशक्तिकरण के तीन अवयव*
    - मुक्ति-परम्परागत बेड़ियों एवं संस्थागत वंचनाओं से
    - योग्यता-सामाजिक, आर्थिक एवं राजनीतिक भूमिका
    - नियंत्रण-संसाधनों एवं विचारों पर
2. *सामाजिक, आर्थिक एवं राजनीतिक क्षेत्र में पुरुषों से समानता*
3. *राजनीतिक सशक्तिकरण*
    - समान राजनीतिक भागीदारी के अवसर
    - राजनीतिक एवं निर्णय निर्माण में तथ्यपरक भूमिका की संवेदना
    - पदधारण एवं पद प्राप्ति हेतु स्वस्पफूर्त प्रयास
    - समर्थकों के हितों का संरक्षण

सामाजिक पूंजी

- एक ऐसी स्थिति है जिसमें सक्रिय कर्त्ताओं के बीच होता है—
  1. परस्पर विश्वास
  2. परस्पर अंतःक्रिया
  3. उद्देश्यों की समानता

  (Robert Putnam, संदर्भ के लिए bibliography देखें)
- यह स्थिति अंतःसामाजिक घटकीय एवं अन्तर्घटकीय भी हो सकती है।
- इस स्थिति के लाभ—
  - राजनीतिक निर्णय निर्माण पर प्रभाव
  - विकास प्रक्रिया में सहायक
  - प्रजातांत्रिक प्रक्रिया में सजीवता

स्वैच्छिकता

- एक मानवीय क्रिया का स्वरूप
- समाजसेवा की मानवीय इच्छा
- इसका शाश्वत श्रोत समाज में व्याप्त
  - विषमताएँ
  - अभिवंचनाएं
  - लाचारी
- स्वैच्छिक प्रयासों से कमजोर वर्गों के बीच राजनीतिक जागरण

7

Women Administrative Leadership in Technical Institutions: A Case Study of S D Institute of Technology and Management, Israna

Rajesh Kumar & Anand Kumar

Introduction

The field of scientific study is not simply a crude form of learning scientific principles and applications, rather it involves a lot of human activities that need to be directed, guided and coordinated by some one who may be called leader. Power and influence are the two related terms which are generally confused with the physical force. But force is an abstract thing that is manifested only after application. Force as a factor that motors work, necessarily have connotation of physical force in the natural sciences, however, this force automatically refers to a capacity that is able to displace a body. In human activities power refers to a work i.e. in the shape of influencing the behaviour of others, especially the led. As such the leader exercises this capacity over the led (persons acting according to the guidance). The psychologists and sociologists have come to the conclusion that leadership is a phenomenon that grows with the individual capacities to guide the led community, direct the followers and coordinate action among them. Besides, a leader has to play roles to instill courage, confidence and obedience among the followers in order to exercise influence. The concept of leadership goes with this assumption that there will be no leading activity unless there is exercise of power and influence over the rest of the people. This can only happen when some body has some qualities in access to the rest of the people.

So far the political leadership is concerned, the political scientists have agreement that there is politics wherever power resides. Similarly in social and political areas too, the 'power' is considered as capacity to 'influence' others and in turn 'influence' refers to controlling others' behaviour. It has also been advocated that the major components of a political leader are-qualities to lead, power, formal position, influencing community (led community) and influencing the decision making process. Any body who has qualities of a leader, holds power, influences the community which he/she leads, acquires or aspires a formal position and influences the decision making bodies in context of the led is a political leader.

With this assumption in mind the author has taken venture to examine the women political leadership in context of the teaching, learning and imparting training among the students of an institution that impart training in technological and managerial fields. Thus the present paper intends to underline the characteristics of leadership exercising power over the led by the de-powered gender (women) in an educational institution imparting training in engineering and management. For this it discusses the case of S D Institute of Technology and Management, Israna (Panipat), Haryana state. It goes to articulate the profile of women leadership and followership, modes of actions taken by them in function of leading a group. As such the paper is divided in three parts-first part deals with the details of the case for the study (SDIT&M), second part, draws the profile of the leadership provided by the women teachers, and the modality of their functions and finally conclusions have been drawn in articulating the salient features of women leadership in a technical institution.

Profile of S D T M

Motto of the Institute: The Institution by Shanti Devi Charitable Trust strives to achieve academic excellence in the very formative years by developing a work culture where faculty and student work together to evolve teaching learning processes, which are most satisfying to the ignited minds of the students. The Institute thrives to create an academic environment, in which the students would feel pleasure in acquiring knowledge and cognitive skills to make them globally competitive technocrats. The Institute identifies key performance indicators, output indicators and outcome indicators, which would be monitored periodically on regular basis in a closed loop system. The Institute strives at developing low cost technology and transferring the same to the common man including the unorganized sector of the economy. The institute would also create healthy linkages for the upliftment of the community in its neighborhood to fulfill its social obligation with the active involvement of faculty and students so that the students develop themselves into responsible and accountable citizens. It offers under graduate, post graduate and doctoral programs in emerging areas of engineering and technology, computer application and management in a phased manner. As such the main motto is "To produce technically skilled and competent manpower of the highest quality capable of effectively meeting the global challenge to meet the growing technological needs of the country". Further, it has also the vision "To establish professional academic institutions for shaping careers of the ignited minds who could channel their energy and intellect for getting technological solutions for the sufferings of the common man and present a humane face of science and technology for mitigating the modern problems of the human race; and to create an environment which is free from physical and social ambiguities where an ordinary person could achieve one's aims and objectives of physical and spiritual attainments for the benefit of the society"

The Managers at Their Mission: The Institute is named after a woman who devoted her life to the service of the community. The managers of Institute have established similar institutions in the service of the society, like stablishing institutions like N.C. College of Engineering, Israna (Panipat), N.C. Institute of Computer Sciences, Israna (Panipat), Sudha Devi Dental College & Research, Faridabad, Gurgaon Institute of Tech & Management, Tauru Road, Gurgaon. They are committed to provide the high quality of faculty in our Engineering Institute. This will result into providing excellent technical education. The College is committed to recruit excellent faculty and provide various promotional and career advancement schemes. Director of Institute writes, "Information Technology, Electronics and Telecommunications has become the key potential area for Haryana in the last few years. This supported by the first information Technology Policy, 2002 w.e.f. May 1, 2000 has helped transforming Haryana into an IT driven economy. We at SDITM are committed to provide high quality technical education, training and develop skills of the students to improve the quality of their life, capabilities, thinking process, etc to achieve the same. The College is unswerving to recruit excellent faculty and provide various promotional and career advancement schemes A well chalked out quality policy is to be implemented as per the norms of the ISO so that quality education is imparted to students by using Total Quality Management tools and procedures. The able advisory committee of the college and the members of the board will guide us in completion of our mission." Further the Chairman observes, "Our colleges has always stood for professionalism & quality education. As the spirit (Late Lala Nemi Chand Ji and that of Late Shanti Devi Ji) behind this college, were persons with a vision to educate the people of Haryana, our commitment to the country & stress on ethical values become part & parcel of our mission. Our new college will maintain quality as per the standards of ISO Standards. All-round development of our students will be given utmost priority and preference so that they can put their share of efforts in increasing the country's knowledge and spiritual wealth."

The entire discussion about the profile of the S D Institute depicts that the mission, commitment and vision of the leaders of the organization make its faculty members committed to the cause who lead the students to acquire perfection in their lives. So is the case with women faculty members who take the leadership roles for the mission.

Profile of the Women Leaders

There altogether eleven women faculty members in the Institute who have been given some assignment for providing leadership to the students. Some of them have been assigned with special tasks. The women of the S D Institute of Technology and Management were given special tasks like leading National Service Scheme, Admission after conducting tests at various stages, Sports and conducting tests for merit scholarships. A look at the Table 1 will give the picture.

Table 1
Profile of the Women Faculty with Leadership Roles

Age (yrs)	*Post*	*Qualification*	*Family background*	*Speciall assignment*
23	Lect	M Sc	GS+HW	
24	Lect	M Sc	G S + H W	
23	Lect	B Tech IT	RGS+HW	
25	Lect	MBA	B+HW	
26	Lect	MSc, MPhil B Ed	B+HW	NSS, Admn
25	Lect	MSc, MPhil, B Ed	B+HW	Sports
24	Lect	B Tech, CSE	GS+HW	
22	Lect	B Tech CSE, GATE	GS+GS	
26	Lect	M Tech, ECE	B+GS	Scholarship
24	Lab Tech	BSc, MBA	GS+HW	
31	Asst Prof	M Tech CSE, MSc	B+HW	

Note: GS-Government Service, HW- Housewife, B- Business, RGS- retired government servant.
First before plus (+) mark is profession of the father and the second after plus (+) mark is professional status of mother.

The names of the women faculty members are- Ms. Sonal Jain, Ms. Rajni Bhoker, Ms. Monika Dahiya, Prerna Gupta, Ms. Vinod Kumari, Mrs. Sumita Dahiya, Ritu Sharma, Sulekh

Sharma, Pooja Rani, Mrs. Ruby Pandey and Mrs. Priti Singla. All of them are of relatively younger age group. If we categorize these women faculty members age wise, they can be kept in two categories matured young (from 25 years to 30 years) and quite young (from 22 years to 24 years). Out of eleven there were five women faculty members in the category of 'matured young' of whom three were given special assignment and one lecturer and one Assistant Professor were kept free. Rest six women who fell in the category of 'young women' were made to assist the elder women and keep the students disciplined. Out of the total faculty members all these women have been functional and identical in performance with their male counter parts.

Since all of them are faculty members, they are highly qualified for their respective assignments. However, the women of matured young category are found more qualified than others. Out of these five two have the M Phil degrees, one has the MBA degree and one has the M Tech and M Sc degrees.

Performance of Leadership Roles

It is to be noted that MBA degree holder might have the extra quality of leadership. But no special leadership training was possessed by them. Despite they delivered their best in instilling confidence, courage and maintaining obedience among the students. They guided, directed and coordinated among the students in order to achieve the goals of the particular programme.

So family background is concerned, none of the women of the Institute are found to have family with leadership specific background. Five of the eleven women faculty members have the family background of parents under GS+HW category that means that father in the government service and mother remains the house wife. Five of them belong to the families in which father is a businessman and mother is a house wife. Rest one of them belongs to both parents in the category of government service.

It is interesting to note that all the three women faculty members having special assignments belong to the father having business as profession and two of the mothers housewife and one in government service. The brothers and sisters of almost all the women faculty members were in higher education except three of the brothers and sisters were in job.

The performance of all the women faculty members having the special assignment has been of very high order. The NSS (National Service Scheme) student volunteers are well disciplined and perform better than students of other institutions in the NSS meets. The NSS volunteers always obey their women Programme Officer and the women teachers have instilled in them the value of national and public service. The students of the Institute perform well in sports meet and bring shields almost from every tournament.

The tests conducted for admission and scholarship are also of very high order and none of the students or the guardians have ever complained of inefficiency or dishonesty in the selection process.

The conduction of examination has always been found fair and predictable. The supporting staffs under these teachers are found working properly and to the full capacity. These women do not even require any kind of help from the male counterparts.

Conclusions

The whole gamut of discussions suggests that factors like age, experience and family background have less impact over the leadership roles and exercise of power rather; energy, capacity to deliver and commitment to achieve the given objectives are more likely to have impact on the leadership roles among the leading women. This is evident from the fact that all the women in the studied Institute ranged between the age of 22 to 26 years and guided, directed and coordinated the led students to almost the perfection and instilled in them the confidence to do something, courage to accept the challenges and obedience to the level of desired needs. The span of control was found even wider that what it has been considered in the books of management. Besides, the family backgrounds of such women leaders in the studied institution were not found conducive to the leadership training as is evident from the fact that more than 80 per cent of the mothers of the studied women leaders were housewives and nearly 40 per cent of their fathers had business as occupation. The rest of the mothers (20%) were either in teaching job or in government job whereas rest of their fathers (60%) were in government job or retired from government service. Such family background is not conducive to leadership training. Whatever the factors that led the women to deliver the roles of a leader were the commitments to the goal, mutual trust, networking and shared objectives. So my paper finds it that family and social background or the experience do not make leaders rather personal qualities, working environment and power, position and support of the led community are the influencing factor of leadership emergence among the women.

References

Biernat, M. and Wortman, C. B. (1991) "Sharing of Home Responsibilities Between Professionally Employed Women and their Husbands", *Journal of Personality and Social Psychology,* 60.

Book, E. W. (2000), *Why the Best Man for the Job is a Woman,* New Delhi, Harper Collins

Browne, K. (2002), *Biology of Work: Rethinking Sexual Equality,* New Brunswick, Rutgers University Press, NJ.

Burns, James Macgregor (1978), *Leadership,* Delhi Ambica Publication.

Eagly, A., Makhijani, M. and Klonsky, B. (1992), "Gender and the Evaluation of Leaders: A Meta-analysis," *Psychological Bulletin,* 111, 3-22.

Forsyth, D. R. (2006), *Group Dynamics* (4th ed.), Pacific Grove, CA: Brokks/Cole.

Jha U. S. & P. L. Pujari (1996), *Indian Women Today : Tradition, Modernity and Challenge,* Kaniohka Publishers, New Delhi.

Mishra, Jugal Kishore (2006), "Empowerment of Women in India", *The Indian Journal of Political Science,* Vol. LXVII, No. 4, Oct.-Dec..

Powell, G. N. and Graves, L. M. (2003), *Women and Men in Management* (3rd ed.), Thousand Oaks, CA: Sage.

Sharma, Priyanka (2008), Women Empowerment and Working Women, Book Enclave, Jaipur, p. 132.

Verma, R. K. (1996), "Political Leadership: Issues in Concept and Approches", *Journal of Social and Economic Studies,* Combined Issue.

Verma, R. K. (1991), *Rural Political Leadrship: A Study of Social Structure and People's Perception,* Amar Prakashan, Delhi.

8

Emerging Pattern of Women's Political Leadership at Grass roots Level in India

U. P. Mishra

The 73rd Constitutional Amendment Act (1992) introduced a three=tier system of local governance ranging from the village to the district level. Through this, reservations of seats for women raised from 33% to 50% were introduced at the panchayat level.[1] This was the first step towards ensuring women's leadership at the grass-roots level. The legislation has the potential to enable women to transform the state structure. This proved crucial in enhancing the confidence of women in rural India. After taking the reins of villages as Mukhias and Sarpanches, hundreds of untutored women in rural India have led a silent revolution, which has brought a paradigm shift in rural development.

The advent of Panchayati Raj marked a new chapter in the political history of India as it sought to recast Indian polity in a new mould where the historically disadvantaged groups would take control of their own destiny. The panchayats have been projected as an answer to the ubiquitous social order and a harbinger of social justice and social equity. The dream of the father of nation to make every village a "little republic" or "Power to people in the rural India" may be fulfilled by the sincere implementation of the provisions of this historic act by the people in power in states and at the centre and India may be made a prosperous and democratic country.

The primary objective of the 73rd Amendment to the constitution is to decentralise the decision-making process and encourage the villages to identify and implement the plans. This is a departure from the so-called "top-down approach" where all decisions are taken by the central and state governments. The system has been developed on the concept of delegating the responsibility to the village panchayats and its allied bodies. This is to ensure that the elected representatives of the villages can take the right decisions pertaining to developments.

Women after being marginalized for a long period are being brought to the forefront through their involvement in the decision-making process. Through their reservation leadership of women was given statutory status. This status is a channel to address the issue of women empowerment and to wipe away inequality prevailing in the society. The 73rd Amendment Act provides for one-third reservation for women in all the three-tiers of the Panchayat Raj system and is a step forward towards removing inequality, invisibility and powerlessness of women. The amendment is a landmark in the history of women's empowerment and a revolutionary step in women's participation in decision-making and political process in the country at least at the grass-roots level. With this amendment women's representation in panchayati raj institutions increased in many states from almost 2-3 per cent to at least 30 or 32 per cent. Before 1985 whereas only 2 women in each of the states of Gujarat, Madhya Pradesh, Punjab, Rajasthan and West Bengal participated in panchayati raj institutions, their representation in 1995 increased to 33.3 per cent, 38 per cent, 30.2 per cent, 32.4 per cent and 35.4 per cent respectively. As regards U. P. there was no representation of women before 1985 in panchayati raj institutions but after 1995 they occupied 29.6 per cent representation in them.[2]

Table 1
Women's Participation in PRI Before 1985 and after 1995

States	*Overall percentage in GPS 1985*	*Overall percentage in GPS after 1995*
Gujarat	Only 2 women	33.3%
Haryana	Only 2 women	33%
Karnataka	Only 1-2 women	37.0%
Madhya Pradesh	2 women	38%
Kerala	1 woman	38.2%
Punjab	2 women	30.2%
Rajasthan	2 women	32.4%
West Bengal	2 women	35.4%
Uttar Pradesh	0 woman	29.6%

Source: Panchayati Raj Development Report, 1995, Institution of Social Sciences, New Delhi.

The above figures show increased trend of representation of women in grass-roots democratic institutions. These figures also show the trend of women assuming leadership in the decision-making. This trend is also an indication of the changes in the socio-economic life of women. There are changes also in the value-orientations of people and in leadership.

Several significant facts have emerged from the nation-wide study on elected women representatives in panchayati raj institutions done by AC Nielson ORG-MARG for the Union Ministry of Panchayati Raj. The study shows that becoming a Pradhan or a ward member augments respect within the family as well as in the community at large besides increasing their self-esteem, confidence and decision-making ability.[3] Some of the important findings of the survey are worth mentioning here.

Socio-economic Profile

Elected female representatives were found to be generally younger than their male counterparts. Educationally, women were far behind men. Women representatives prior association with any form of politics was low, and for most women the act of contesting the first election signaled their entry into active politics. Husbands (30%) and other family members (12%) were reported as playing an important role in motivating women representatives to contest elections for the first time.

Reservation

Reservation emerged as an important motivator (43%) for contesting the first election as much as its withdrawal was an important reason for not contesting the election among former women representatives (39%). Ex-women representatives, who faced defeat in their attempts to continue their careers, accepted that there was less social interaction and/or no proper campaigning (52%) on their part. The problem of unacceptability/ conflict across different social categories was another important reason mentioned by two-fifths of them.

Training

Training was not available to a large proportion of newly elected representatives (43%). The chief reason was simple : 'training not being held (61%), followed by 'not called for training' (22%). Three-fifths felt. the need for training on the 'Rules & Regulations of Panchayats' (91%).

Quality of Participation

A significantly large proportion of female pradhans (86%) reported that they were executing the important role of being a local panchayati raj functionary. Interaction with the police, local bureaucracy and officials in the line departments was slightly lower in case of female representatives. The high performers among elected women representatives were from Kerala, followed by Karnataka, Tripura, Maharashtra, Sikkim and West Bengal. On the other hand, the, performance score was on the lower side in Orissa, Arunachal Pradesh, Bihar, Gujarat and Madhya Pradesh.

Impact of Participation

The positive impact of entering politics and working as a panchayati raj functionary is evident from the fact that a sizeable proportion of women representatives perceive enhancement in their self-esteem (79%), confidence (81%) and decision-making ability (74%). Becoming a pradhan or ward member augments respect within the family (67%) as well as in the community at large (82%). They also perceive an increased voice in decisions related to economic matters and other issues in their families (66.71%). While no gender discrimination in the panchayat is reported by 60 per cent elected women representatives, acceptability in panchayat meetings and enabling them to raise issues freely was mentioned by 94 per cent.

The performance of women representatives who belonged to a younger age category (21-35 years) was better than those who were above 35, suggesting that younger women should be encouraged to join politics. A large proportion of women who received training have performed better. The data show that 43 per cent elected women did not receive any training in their current political term. Hence training should not only be made mandatory for all elected representatives, but it should also be organized regularly. In order to increase the effective participation of women, they should be given more honoraria, as the findings show that the representatives who devoted more of their time in doing panchayat work register better performance. Reservation becomes more meaningful when women can sustain their political activity through re-election. The data shows that 85 per cent women representatives were first timers, and only 15 per cent could get re-elected because the seat from where they were elected was dereserved in the next round. Hence, the rotation of seats may be discontinued for the women-headed panchayats and wards. The data show that the duration (in years) of political involvement is directly proportionate to the performance of women representatives. Therefore, the effort should be made to maintain not only the representation of women in politics in terms of their percentage, but also their ability to remain in politics.

Be it health, water, cleanliness or alcohol consumption, villages in rural Maharashtra are witnessing a silent movement in the last few years. Women, who never even thought of opening their mouths in front their men, are now talking about iodized salt, safe delivery, clean drinking water, exclusive breast-feeding, sanitation and even safer sex to avoid HIV infection. Water management, Wastewater disposal, toilets, solid waste disposal, house and environment sanitation, personal hygiene, health education and communication, unconventional energy sources, family welfare activities, community participation and innovative programmes have become focal points on the agenda of woman Sarpanches.[4] Of the 27,876 gram panchayats in the state, 8,351 panchayats are defection free thanks to the initiative taken by rural women leadership. Out of these, 2367 panchayats have been awarded the Nirmal Gram Award while 6164 panchayats are awaiting the formal approval for the award from the central government.[5] Popular participation of women Sarpanches have brought tremendous change in rural Maharashtra by involving large population in decision-making process and actual implementation.[6]

However, women leadership has still to cross many stumbling blocks in establishing themselves as leaders in comparison to males. In rural areas culture and traditions are observed more rigidly. Family as well as caste play an important role in directing the course of life of individual. To cope with the inhibiting factors women need to be more articulative in coordinating social and economic roles for creating space for themselves in political fields. Reservation is just a means towards equality and not an end in itself. To make it successful both men and women must strive to ensure that the end is achieved.[7] Considering the long history of suppression of women under patriarchy, women seem to be on the path to empowerment although at slower pace. The fact that women have come forward to fight elections, come out of homes to attend panchayat meetings and sit with men of different castes and age groups is itself a step on the road to empowerment.[8]

The ideal of strong, truly representative and responsive Panchayati Raj Institutions is still a distant dream. But a silent revolution has already begun to take governance beyond governments. With the new stakeholders–women, SCs and STs-coming to power, the governance is now more horizontal and accountable.[9] Women leaders are adding small little jewel to their crown of success every now and then. Our administrative system can be made participatory, transparent, responsive and accountable only by strengthening women leadership at least at grass-roots level. Let us hope this dawn would lead to a brighter day for women leadership in India.

Notes and References

1. In Bihar Nitish Kumar government has given 50% reservation to women in Panchayati Raj Institutions.
2. R. C. Agrawal, "Women and Panchayati Raj Institution", No. 3, p. 69.
3. Panchayati Raj Update, Institute of Social Sciences, New Delhi, May, 2008, p. 8.
4. 'Women can do it', Radheshyam Jadhav, Panchayati Raj Upadate, Institution of Social Sciences, New Delhi, October, 2008, p. 6.
5. *Ibid.*
6. *Ibid.*
7. *Kurukshetra*, New Delhi, November, 2005, p. 18 quoted by S. Waseem. Ahmad, Nilofer & Gazala Parveen in 'Women's Political Participation and Changing Pattern of Leadership in Rural Areas of U. P., *Indian Journal of Political Science,* Vol. LXIX, No. 3, July-September, 2008, P. 670.
8. B. S. Baviskar and George Mathew (eds), Inclusion and Exclusion in Local Governance: Field Studies From Rural India,' Delhi; Sage Publications, 2009, pp. XIV+ 453.
9. *Ibid.*

Readings

Ashwini Chliatre, Political Articulation and Accountability in Decentralisation Theory and Experience from India, Conservation & Society 6 (1).

G. Palanithurai (2005), "Dynamics of New Panchayati Raj System in India", Vol. IV, Concept Publishing Company, New Delhi.

Gopi Nath Ghosh (2008), Trasparency and Accountability, *Yojna,* August.

George Mathew (2008), A New Deal for Panchayats, Panchayat Raj Update, April.

Institute of Social Sciences: NREGA and Panchayats.

Mani Shankar Aiyar (2008), State of Panchayats: The Journey Thus Far, INCLUSION March.

Mihir Shah (2008), The Real Radicalism of NREGA, *The Hindu*, 22 May.

Ministry of Panchayati Raj, State of Panchayats, 2007-08 (Three Volumes), New Delhi.

M. R. Biju (2008), Women's Political Empowerment: Imperatives and Impediments, *South Asian Journal of Socio-Political Studies*. Jan-June.

Nilika Mehrotra, S. M. Patnaik (2008), Culture versus Coercion; Other side of Nirmal Gram Yojna, *Economic and Political Weekly*, October 25.

9

73rd Amendment of Indian Constitution and Women's Empowerment

Mrs. Ratna & Ram Prakash

The development process assume men and women to be abstractly equal; both making rational choice. In fact, Indian women have contributed significantly since the beginning of the civilization. The moral values and dedications towards the humanity from the old age till the present era Sita, Anushiya, Ahilya, Laxmibai, Mirabai, Razia Sultan, Sarojini Naidu, Indira Gandhi, Sonia Gandhi, Kalpana Chawla, Kiran Bedi, Medha Patkar amongst many others are remarkable. The history repeats lots of revolutions through the dedicated efforts of great women in India and one has to be proud of it. However the social values dramatically decreased for various reasons.

After independence in India, it was felt that women, as a class, are oppressed and subdued by the hegemony of social patriarchy. Gender discrimination is stubbornly cultural and this enquality is very sharp within the rural households. Women have been viewed as a deprived section of the society requiring welfare measures. Women are saddled with multiple burden. Hence, they need political empowerment. The government of India consequently passed a piece of progressive legislation in 1993 to enable the presence of a 'critical mass' of women in the decentralized decision making process.

The constitution of India was adopted in 1950. It had envisaged in article 40 that "the state shall take steps to organize village Panchayats and endow them with such powers and authority as may be necessary to enable them to function as units of government". This provision of the constitution was primarily advisory. In the following four decades, some sporadic and indifferent steps were taken by some of the state governments to organize Panchayats, but they were invariably denied any meaningful powers and authority and worst of all, the elections were seldom held at the interval of five years. Another deplorable state of affairs was that women's entery into formal structures of government was quite low at grass root level.

In post independence decades, the government of India did take various initiative to improve the status of women in India. The government initiative towards women empowerment can be characterized as "women in development", "Gender and development' and finally "rights based development". The constitution 73rd Amendment Act as an enabling measure can be characterized as the facilitator of 'rights based approach' to women's empowerment the expectation was that this would redress some of the deprivations which face Asian women in general and Indian women in particular.

Efforts towards women's empowerment by reservation in local self governing institutions was first of all experimented in the southern state of Karnataka. The law included a clause that 25 per cent of the seats in local councils would be reserved for women. The constitution 73rd Amendment Act was originally initiated by the Late Rajiv Gandhi as 64th Amendment but got defeated in the Parliament. It was passed after the death of Rajiv Gandhi during the tenure of Narsimha Rao. This Act was a landmark in the history of the local government or Panchayati Raj system. The most important feature of the Act from the women's perspective is the reservation of at least one-third of total seats for women both at the functionaries and membership level.

The relevant lines regarding women's participation in local self governing institutions in the 73rd amendment Act can be illustrated as follows, "In all the Panchayats, seats shall be reserved for scheduled castes and scheduled. Tribes in proportion to their population and one-third of the total number of seats will be reserved for women. One-third of the officer of chairpersons of Panchayats at all levels shall also be reserved for women".

The Millennium Development Goals (2000) expressed serious concern about suppression of women from participation in social, political and economic life of the society. These goals include the eradication of extreme hunger and poverty, universal primary education, gender equality, empowerment for women, reduction of child mortality, improvement of maternal health, combating HIV/AIDS, malaria and other diseases as well as ensuring environmental sustainability and developing a global partnership for development. All these goals assume additional significance once it is realized that women suffer a lot of deprivation due to lack of achieving the above goals. As for example it is well known that majority of the poor in the world are found among women, the percentage of illiteracy among the women in higher than those of men, access to primary health care is always denied to large percentage of women and so on and so forth. Realizing the above picture various governments all over the world have been taking various measures to improve the conditions of women. Indian government is no exception. The local government institutions have been given a new lease of life to plan and execute the local development planning in which not less than one-third seats have been reserved for women. It is contention that being in the panchayats the women themselves have been involved in the task of local development. This in turn will fulfil the Millennium Development Goals (MDG) in a big way and Indian women would assume the role of leadership in Asia in spite of being the beginners in the political process.

The impact of 73rd constitutional amendment on Indian women is tremendous and far reaching. Various studies in this field has revealed that this legislation intending the reservation of seats in the local council has provided a critical mass of women with an opportunity to empower themselves by being partners in decision making process.

The first and foremost impact of the above act has been the widened and strengthened base of participatory democracy. Because of reservation a large number of women has been elected particularly from the lower socio-economic strata. Further at least 90 per cent of the ward members are from low socio-economic background and those of higher categories are from the high caste or class. The elections for the panchayat offices are held in time. About three million elected representatives have been elected to these political institutions of which about one million are women as mentioned in the Act.

The most significant result of the legislation has been inclusion of five million women to active politics till now. It is interesting to speculate that this number would enlarge much more in the coming years and women leadership at the level of grass root politics would become more firm and strong. The arithmetic of the five million women can be explained in the following manner. First of all in each tenure one million women get elected. Secondly for each seat, two, three or four women on an average contested the elections and thus participated in the election process. Thus, all together five to six million women participated in the political process.

Yet another impact of the PRIs is the reduction of poverty ratio from 38 per cent to 26 per cent and a slight increase in the rate of urbanization by 2 per cent between 1991 and 2001. (Economic Survey 2002). At least a major part of these results can be explained by the implementation of schemes meant for poverty alleviation through panchayats. It is interesting to note that within a span of two years, between 1999 to 2001, about 35793 million rupees were allocated, out of which 72 per cent was utilized. About 2.4 million swarozgaries (self earners) were assisted out of which 44 per cent are women. (Govt. of India, Annual Report, 2001-02). The government, however, has a policy to allocate at least 30 per cent of the total amount of money available for any scheme for women.

The impact of panchayat on women's life has been tremendous and varied. In fact the entery to the panchayats has been described by some as a beginning of a silent revolution. These panchayati raj institution have influenced social political and economic lives of the village women in more that one ways.

About 80-90 per cent women attend the panchayat meetings regularly. Given their sheer numbers, one might conclude that democracy has become more participatory than before, at least at the grassroots level. This argument is strengthened by the fact that the socio-economic background of these women showed that majority of them come from the lower income group, particularly in the case of membership at the village panchayat level. As for example about 85 per cent of the elected women representatives (EWRs) who came to the above programme were from village panchayats and most of them belonged either to SC, ST or other backward castes–all three castes are at the bottom of the caste hierarchy. So far they have been excluded from the decision making process.

The surveys and studies revealed that so far as the effective participation of these women is concerned, if they get outside support in terms of NGO intervention, women's groups, or any other social or political movement, the women become relatively more vocal. Their knowledge about the functioning of the panchayats increase.

Related to the theme of women's political empowerment, the issue of 'proxy women' has cropped up. It is alleged that since many of the women are first timers and are illiterate, they depend on their men folk without understanding the implications.

Several issues are involved and interlinked with the phenomenon of 'proxy women'. First of all, the husbands or other male relatives shield them from the panchayat secretary and B.D.O. if they try to harass the women. In fact, some of the state governments namely U.P. and Rajasthan have passed a rule that women elected representative should be accompanied by their male relatives. This is because in some cases the secretaries of the panchayats and male colleagues tried to implicate inexperienced women by asking them to sign blank cheques. Some of the women chiefs went to jails because of these acts and were implicated on false charges.

Because of reservations, the power relation between husband and wife has changed. The husband gets a chance to come to the public sphere because of the wife and in the process, the character of patriarchy gets altered. As a result, in many low income families, the husband-wife relationship has not soured. On the other hand, the husband supports the wife and also helps her in her domestic work.

Even other members of the family including the mother-in-law and sister-in-law help her to complete domestic responsibilities and obligations.

The practice of 'proxy women' is not true with women leaders who are recruited from the white collar background. Since they are educated and know about the working of the official system, they will not remain silent in the panchayat meetings.

Women not only take up issues relating to basic needs, such as drinking water, availability of doctors and teachers in the villages which are dear to them, but also general developmental activities, for example, augmenting the income of the panchayats and generating irrigation facilities for the paddy field. The schemes of widow welfare and old age pensions are better targeted. The women of the neighbourhood act as the 'watch dog' in compelling the elected women to deliver at least some goods. Women of the villages can easily approach the women elected members for justice and favour.

The net conclusion can be drawn that the standard of the political institutions at the grassroots level has not been lowered as a result of women's reservations. The development process has been engendered to some extent.

Involvement of three million women in grass roots politics by itself has created an expansion of public space as well as that of private space for the women. In the public space they have been allowed to attend the panchayat meetings along with other colleagues. In addition women get opportunity to network and facilitate conditions for creating the social capital. These conditions get reinforced with another set of forces which also involve a large number of women through various rural programmes. In the private sphere, their working relations change. The area of cooperation increases at the family level also. Sometimes it has been seen that the husbands of elected women representatives take them on bike or motor bike to the panchayat office if it is far away from their own villages.

The results of the census of India, 2001 shows that the female life expectancy at birth has exceeded that of males marginally. It indicates that women's self perception has changed and they look after their health and nutritional status. Similarly the female literacy rate has jumped from being 39 per cent to 53 per cent within a span of ten to fifteen years.

It would not be out of place to mention here some of the constraints which prohibit this legislation in contributing towards women's empowerment. Firstly women as a class are not a homogenous category. They represent different interest group depending on their class and caste Secondly, predominant trend of Indian Culture is still very patriarchial and the women are looked down upon. The women representatives are not taken seriously by their male colleagues and the bureaucrats and they have scant information about the functioning of panchayats. Thirdly, in many places the women are not immune to systemic corruption. Again, violence against women has also increased.

At the end it can be concluded that in India, a bold step has been taken up in the form of giving more power to the panchayats to tone up the development of rural areas in which not less than one-third seats have been reserved for the women in all three tiers. The impact of panchayats in the lives of women has been quite significant because it affects women's lives socially, politically and economically since they got enough space to negotiate at the private and public space. It has led to social mobilization and created conditions for social capital. It has provided a space for Asian women to emerge as a formidable force to fight for social justice and human rights.

10

Scheduled Caste Women Leadership in Jehanabad District

Kr. Amrendra Narain

The 73rd and 74th Amendments (1993) of the Indian Constitution is the landmark which ensures equal access and increased participation in political power structure for women at the grassroots level.

Based on these amendments, almost all the status have enacted new Panchayati Raj Acts. So it is high time to examine the problems and prospects involved in this attempt to establishing gender justice and the changes brought about in the political affairs by the one-third participation of women in PRI and in the society at large.

In Bihar, there are 1,37,239 elected members of three tier Panchayati Raj Institutions in which women occupy 44,824 seats in different capacities. (according to 2001 Panchayat Election).

In Bihar, there are 37 districts in which 8438 village Panchayats, 529 Panchayat Samitis and 37 Zila Parishad exist. The total member of ward members stands for 1, 16,028 and the member of seat reserved for women is 40472. With first election, under the new arrangements held in 2001, a large number of women (at least 33% of the total strength) got

Position of 2001 Panchayat Election in Bihar

	Seats	*Elected Mukhia*	*Elected Members ward*	*Reserved seats for Women*
Members of village Panchayat	8438	8438	116028	40472
Panchayat Samiti	529	11611	-	3954
Zila Parishad	37	1162		398

Source: Society for participatory Research in Asia: 2000-2001.

opportunity to participate in local bodies during 2001-2006 and half of the strength in 2006 panchayat elections. Never before such a large number of women were made to play roles in the political arena of the state. This indicates a revolutionary change which brings a sense of political aptitude specially among women. This is nothing but a political inducement of women in the grass root level democracy and administration of development programmes to get the desired objectives of rural development.

Leadership is itself a better level of knowledge and thinking which denotes 'to invest with power'. It further instills the ability to influence the behaviour of others with or without hindarance. It also includes guidance and power to control the existing capacities. It or empower women with the ability to generate and control resources, develop physical and psychological capacity to challenge the prevailing gender norms and ensure changes. It is most appealing and noticeable attitude of the women which enamour social, economic and political relations between the individuals in the distribution of resources and control over it. The novel lauriate Prof. Amartya Sen is of opinion that "women are less likely to secure favorable outcomes for themselves in household decision making process. They feel that their long term securities lies in subordinating their well being to that of male authority figures."

Though the women are engaged in a wide variety of occupations in the organized and unorganized sector like-in services, weaving, sowing, transplanting, cattle breeding, working in the handlooms, producing handicrafts, low paid wage earners and unpaid family worker, they are least interested in leadership. Traditionally women have less public roles in the main stream of the society. From dawn to dusk; they are primarily engaged in household work. They do not come out from the corridor of their house either because of their tradition or social and economic barriers. They are highly marginalized and oppressed. All their attempts to come out of their predicaments are nipped in the bud. It can be reproduced in the words of noted writer Arundhati Ray who said, as such the actual situation will be 'soul of India dies in the villages'.

The present paper highlights the role of women in village Panchayats in Bihar: This is a case study of SC women leadership of Jehanabad district.

Jehanabad district is primarily an agricultural district with a population of 15,11,406 (according to 2001 sensus) out of which 2,78,215 belong to scheduled caste communities. The 80 per cent of the total population are wholly or partially engaged in cultivation. It consists of six C.D. Blocks and a sub-division with its head quarter at Jehanabad town. The socio-economic and political condition of rural women are very negligible. Socially women of the district is oppressed and politically they are dwarf. Meager income also puts hindrance on the path of their development Jehanabad is full of evidences which show the discrimination done by the feudal lords or big farmers in the political atmosphere of the district. They have initiated the political scenario of the district. It was 1967 Assembly Election for Makhdumpur Assembly, Constituency where a scheduled caste socialist leader Lohari Ram was contesting. Though the seat was reserved for the scheduled caste, the upper caste so called bhumihar (the assembly is also partly dominated by bhumihar) tortured him many times and made upsurd statement of snatched him flag and slonganed against him. (though he was got elected with the support of SC and OBC votes).

The 73rd Amendments of the Indian Constitution has given berth to the participation of women in elections. But the ground reality tells something awkward. The women of the district are far away four on equal status of men. Politically women are not interested in active politics and they are hesitate/ inclined to participate in political deliberations either because of poverty, ignorance, illiteracy, or their family burden and other socio economic conditions. They do not at par with male counterpart. Male members always put barrier on their leg and the women do not get rid of those chains. Social obligation and traditional control of women folk by their family members and their commitment to household work also put obstacles in permitting the women representatives to perform their function effectively.

Women leaders particularly scheduled caste women leaders or panchayat representatives, fell in the grip of political stalwart due to lack of political consciousness and powerful organization. Though such type of stories area lot, I would like to give an example. This is a story of one Kranti Devi of village Amain an adjacent village of Jehanabad town. She belongs to scheduled caste (chamar) community. She is a little bit literate, takes part in village panchayat election. Being a ward member of the panchayat, she has never been allowed to keep her Views in the general body meeting by the Mukhia of the Panchayat, several times she has been rebuked and molested.

Women leaders of the scheduled caste community are also tortured beaten and neglected by her sons and husband. Some other relatives are also against her decision. Sometimes the situation becomes so grave that her conjugal life becomes pitiful and full of horror, Naina Devi alias Naina Manjhi of village Koiria chatar under Makhdumpur P.s. contested for ward member in the 2006 panchayat election for Jagpura Panchayat. Though she could not be elected, she has been beater up by her son and husband. She was thrown out of her house, now living separately and struggling for life. Her husband Naresh Manjhi married another woman.

Some scheduled caste women leaders are intelligent and best crarater also. In the year 1990 Assembly election, I.P.F. (Now CIP-ML) leader Kunti Devi contested for Makhdumpur Assembly seat. She belongs to (chamar community) scheduled caste community. She is no more but even today she is known for her talent and advocacy. She had challenged the muscleman of the area though she was defeated by congress leader Prof. Ramjatan Sinha.

Elected female members of ward, mukhia, panchayat samiti and Zila Parishad are deprived of their power and responsibilities, generally her husband and her like person take part (in her place) in the proceedings of the meeting and take decisions either for and against keeping in view of their interest. Those women representation put signature either on the blank paper or on then proposal designed by their husbands. This is a clear violation rights of the women representatives. Take an example of a woman Mukhia of Makarpur village Panchayat. Abhinta Devi was elected Mukhia of the Panchayat in the year 2006. She never attended the general meeting if it is necessary, it is presided by her husband.

Women political leaders in general and scheduled caste women leaders generally hesitate to utter their views on matters related to common conflict. As they are mostly literature, they do not go through in detail of the situation and it becomes a bone of contention. This is a story of village Patiyama Tola Lohia nagar under Sakurabad P.S. A fateful night of 9th September 2008, a group of anti-social elements attacked the Dalit village and raped a scheduled caste (Musher) woman, Tileshwar Manjhi the husband of the deceased woman (who is also a Panch of village 'kachhari') protested against the occurrence but he was beatch up mercilessly. His son and a little grandson were also beaten up. Later on the statwart groupd snatched ornaments, cloths and utensils, caught then on fire and fled away. In the F.I.R. several years of the another village were named. But this is not the ground reality. The next day, the heavy weights of the upper caste approached Tileshwar Manjhi and forced him to lodge F.I.R. against the Yadavas who were innocent and unknown to the matter. Few days ago the women (Panch) had given her judgment which was against purview of the upper caste landholder. Earlier two bighas of government land were distributed to the mushars which was captured by the bhumihar community.

It is ironic that when the entire nation is celeberating the dawn of the Republic, the scheduled caste workers and leaders of the district are being subjected to caste oppression and discrimination.

11

पंचायत स्तरीय राजनीतिक सहभागिता तथा महिला नेतृत्व : सबौर प्रखण्ड भागलपुर के संदर्भ में अध्ययन

अजय कुमार, देवकान्त एवं शरत् चन्द्र

महिला सशक्तिकरण का अभिप्राय महिलाओं को पुरूषों के बराबर राजनीतिक, सामाजिक, आर्थिक, क्षेत्रें में उनके परिवार, समाज एवं राष्ट्र की सांस्कृतिक पृष्ठभूमि में निर्णय लेने की आजादी से है। महिलाओं में इस प्रकार की क्षमता का विकास तभी हो सकता है। जब वे अपने जीवन का निर्वाह इच्छानुसार कर पाने में समर्थ हो, उसके अन्दर आत्मविश्वास और स्वाभिमान की भावना पैदा हो। यह सही है कि किसी भी प्रकार के सशक्तिकरण को गति प्रदान करने के लिए राजनीतिक सशक्तिकरण आवश्यक शर्त्त है जिसका अर्थ है एक न्यायपूर्ण तथा सम-समाज की स्थापना। लिंगगत समानता को सुशासन की कुंजी कहा जाता है। महिला सशक्तिकरण में पंचायती राज का विशेष महत्व है, क्योंकि इसके द्वारा ही सामाजिक स्तर पर परिवर्त्तन संभव है। राजनीतिक सशक्तिकरण के द्वारा ही समाज में सशक्तिकरण लाने का प्रयास किया जा रहा है। भारत में महिला सशक्तिकरण के प्राचीन काल से अबतक अनेक प्रयास एवं आन्दोलन हुए हैं। ऐसे तीन दौर आये जब महिलाओं की अस्मिता को बड़े पैमाने पर मान्यता दी गयी तथा उन्हें अपने बारे में निर्णय की आजादी मिली। पहला दौर था बौद्ध धर्म के अविर्भाव का, दूसरा दौर भक्तिकाल को माना जाता है, और तीसरा दौर स्वतंत्रता संघर्ष को, जिसमें लाखों महिलाओं को घर से बाहर आने और सार्वजनिक जीवन में शामिल होने का अवसर मिला।

महिला सशक्तिकरण की दृष्टि से 20 अप्रैल 1993 की क्रांति का दायरा बहुत ही व्यापक है। इसी वर्ष पंचायतों को संवैधानिक मान्यता दी गयी। स्त्री की स्वतंत्रता के पूर्ववर्त्ती प्रयास माहौल में परिवर्त्तन और व्यक्तिगत निर्णयों तक सीमित थे। सामाजिक ढाँचे में कोई ऐसा परिवर्त्तन नहीं किया गया, जिससे स्त्रियों की हैसियत में संरचनात्मक सुधार हो। राजनीतिक तंत्र में परिवर्त्तन का माध्यम बनी पंचायती राज की नई व्यवस्था जिसमें पंचायतों को संवैधानिक मान्यता दी गई, उनका कार्य क्षेत्र परिभाषित किया गया, उनके संसाधनों के स्त्रोत निश्चित जातियों तथा अनुसूचित जन जातियों के लिए आरक्षित पदों पर भी इन वर्गों की तिहाई महिलाओं को आरक्षण दिया गया। इस तरह पंचायत क्रांति को समाज के सभी वर्गों तक ले जाने की कोशिश हुई। पंचायतों में महिलाओं की भागीदारी से उनकी स्थिति में व्यापक परिवर्तन आया है। पंचायतों के द्वारा महिलाओं को प्राप्त राजनीतिक सशक्तिकरण की ही देन है कि विगत वर्षों में राजनीति में महिलाओं की भागीदारी बढ़ी है। राजनीतिक प्रक्रिया और राजनीतिक संस्थाओं में महिलाओं की भागीदारी से शासन की गुणवत्ता में सुधार आया है। आर्थिक तथा जीविका से जुड़े मुद्दों, सामाजिक एवं सांस्कृतिक मूल्यों में भी कई स्तरों पर महत्वपूर्ण प्रभाव पड़ा है ।

पंचायतों के माध्यम से समाज की जड़ता, धार्मिक अंधविश्वासों, रूढ़ियों, कुशासन एवं भ्रष्टाचार के उन्मूलन में महिलाओं ने प्रतिकूल वातावरण में भी अच्छा काम किया है। पंचायतों में महिलाओं की भागीदारी से ग्रामीण विकास एवं महिलाओं के विकास जैसे चिन्तन का विकास हुआ है और एक नई चेतना का सूत्र्पात हुआ है। महिलाओं के सम्पूर्ण एवं वास्तविक सशक्तिकरण के लिए आवश्यक है पंचायतों का सशक्तिकरण। देश के लिए सामाजिक और आर्थिक विकास की सुनियोजित प्रक्रिया में पंचायती राज व्यवस्था का विशेष महत्व है। उसके तीन पक्ष हैं–

1. स्थानीय– स्वायत्त शासन।
2. विकास।
3. सामाजिक और राजनीतिक चेतना।

पंचायती राज नेतृत्व परम्परागत समाज को आधुनिकता से जोड़ता है, भ्रष्टाचार और प्रशासनिक ढील वैसी समस्याओं से पंचायती राज के माध्यम से बहुत हद तक निपटा जा सकता है। राजनीतिक संदर्भ में नारी सशक्तिकरण का ज्ञान इस

आधार पर होता है कि सत्ता के स्वरूप निर्धारण और उसमें सहभागिता के मामले में कितनी स्वतंत्रता और समानता उन्हें प्राप्त है तथा उनके योगदान को कितना महत्व दिया जाता है। राजनीतिक शक्ति संरचना और निर्णय प्रक्रिया से जुड़े कार्यकलापों में सशक्त और सुनिश्चित भागीदारी ही महिलाओं को राजनीतिक रूप से सबल कर सकती है। आज सम्पूर्ण विश्व की महिलाएँ समाज में शक्ति के असमान और एकपक्षीय वितरण को चुनौती देने हेतु निरंतर प्रयास कर रही है। असमानता पर आधारित लैंगिक संबंधों में परिवर्तन के लिए आवश्यक हैं कि वर्तमान वैश्विक सामाजिक आर्थिक व्यवस्था में सत्ता और शक्ति के मुक्त केन्द्र विन्दुओं जैसे– राज्य, बाजार व नागरिक समाज का नेतृत्व करने के लिए महिलाएँ आगे आएँ, स्वयं को प्रभावित कर सकने वाली योजनाओं और नीतियों को अपने अनुरूप निर्मित करवाने के लिए सत्ता के गलियारों में पैठ बनानी होगी और ऐसी शक्ति अर्जित करनी होगी कि वे स्वयं के संदर्भ में लिये जानेवाले निर्णयों को प्रभावित कर सकें। महिलाओं की उन्नति और विकास के लिए आवश्यक है कि जीवन के प्रत्येक क्षेत्र, विशेषकर राजनीति में उनका सशक्तिकरण हो, उनकी सहभागिता का स्तर उच्च हो। ऐसा होने पर ही लैंगिक आधार पर समतामूलक समाज की स्थापना संभव है। नारी राजनीतिक सशक्तिकरण के लिए तीन आधारभूत सिद्धांत है–

1. स्त्री-पुरुष के बीच समानता।
2. स्वयं की क्षमताओं के पूर्ण विकास के लिए महिलाओं को अधिकार।
3. स्वयं के प्रतिनिधित्व और स्वयं के संदर्भ में निर्णय लेने के अधिकार।

भारत को स्वतंत्र हुए छः दशक बीत चुके हैं। इस अवधि में स्त्रियों की सामाजिक स्थिति में भी सुधार हुआ है। विगत वर्षों में महिला सशक्तिकरण की अवधारणा का प्रयोग हो रहा है जो नारियों को शक्ति, क्षमता तथा योग्यता प्रदान करता है ताकि वह अपने जीवन स्तर का सुधार कर अपने जीवन की दशा को स्वयं निर्धारित कर सके। दूसरे शब्दों में यह वह प्रक्रिया है जो महिलाओं को सत्ता की कार्यशैली समझने की न केवल समझ दे वरन् सत्ता के स्त्रेतों पर नियंत्रण कर सकने की क्षमता भी प्रदान करें। स्वतंत्र भारत में महिलाएँ जीवन के अनेक क्षेत्रें में महत्त्वपूर्ण भूमिकाओं का निर्वाह कर रही है। किन्तु उनकी राजनीतिक भूमिका को बहुत अधिक निर्णायक नहीं माना जा सकता। किसी भी सभ्य समाज की स्थिति उस समाज में स्त्रियों की दशा देखकर ज्ञात की जा सकती है। किसी भी

समाज के विकास मापक को महिलाओं और बच्चें की स्थिति निर्धारित करती है। बच्चे जहाँ देश के भविष्य है; वहीं स्त्री उसकी प्रथम शिक्षिका, पोषिका और दिगदर्शिका है। तमाम प्रयासों के बावजूद महिलाओं की स्थिति दयनीय है। संवैधानिक प्रावधानों के अंतर्गत महिलाओं के लिए कई प्रकार के कार्यक्रम चलाए जा रहे है। पंचायतीराज विधेयक पारित हो जाने के पश्चात उनकी राजनीतिक सहभागिता बढ़ी है, महिलाओं का पंचायत स्तर से लेकर राष्ट्रीय स्तर तक नेतृत्व बढ़ा है ।

उद्धेश्य

प्रस्तुत शोध प्रपत्र महिला सशक्तिकरण के संदर्भ में उनकी राजनीतिक सहभागिता एवं नेतृत्व क्षमता को पंचायत स्तर पर आकलित एवं रेखांकित करने का लघु प्रयास है। पंचायती राज विधेयक में महिलाओं की भागीदारी के स्पष्ट प्रावधान हैं। महिलाओं की स्थिति की बेहतरी के लिए उन्हें पर्याप्त शिक्षा की सुविधा प्रदान की जा रही है। पंचायत स्तर पर राजनीतिक सहभागिता से नारी सशक्तिकरण साकार हो सकता है।

अध्ययन क्षेत्र– बिहार राज्य के भागलपुर जिले में सबौर प्रखण्ड नगर का निकटवर्ती प्रखण्ड है, जहाँ नगरीय प्रभाव को स्पष्टतः देखा जा सकता है। इस प्रखण्ड के प्रतीक अध्ययन के माध्यम से महिलाओं की पंचायत स्तर पर राजनीतिक सहभागिता का अध्ययन किया गया है तथा सशक्त महिला नेतृत्व के मार्ग की बाधाओं का आकलन करते हुए समस्याओं के निराकरण हेतु सुझाव प्रस्तुत किया गया है ।

भागलपुर जिले का सबौर एक प्रगतिशील प्रखण्ड सह-अंचल है। इसके अंतर्गत कुल 14 पंचायत आते हैं जो 106 वर्ग कि.मी. में फैला हुआ है। इसकी कुल जनसंख्या 2001 की जनगणना के अनुसार 109551 है। बिहार पंचायत अधिनियम, 2006 के अनुसार महिलाओं को 50 प्रतिशत आरक्षण दिया गया है। अध्ययन क्षेत्र में 2006 के पंचायत चुनाव में मुखिया पद के लिए अनु. जाति पुरुष और महिला के लिए एक-एक पद आरक्षित है। पिछड़ा वर्ग में एक पुरुष और एक महिला के स्थान आरक्षित है। 9 पंचायतों को अनारक्षित कोटी में रखा गया है। पंचायत समिति पद के लिए एक अनु. महिला और एक अनु. जाति के पुरुष के लिए स्थान आरक्षित किया गया है। पिछड़ा वर्ग में एक महिला और एक पुरुष के लिए पद आरक्षित है। 5 पंचायतों में अना. महिला के लिए स्थान आवंटित है।

सरपंच पद के लिए अनु. महिला के लिए एक और पुरुष के लिए एक पंचायत आरक्षित किये गये है। पिछड़ा वर्ग में पुरुष और महिला को क्रमशः एक-एक पंचायत आरक्षित किये गये है। अनारक्षित महिला के लिए चार पंचायत आरक्षित किये गये हैं ।

स्पष्टतः महिलाओं के लिए 50 प्रतिशत पद आरक्षित कर नारी सशक्तिकरण को मजबूत बनाने का साहसिक कदम उठाया गया है। महिलाओं को राजनीतिक क्षेत्र में भागीदारी के लिए संविधान में संशोधन किये गये है तथा पंचायतों में महिला नेतृत्व को गति देने के लिए आरक्षण दिया गया है ताकि अब महिलाएँ भी पंचायतों के काम में पुरुषों के साथ कंधा से कंधा मिलाकर कार्य कर सकें।

ग्रामीण क्षेत्र में महिलाओं की भागीदारी निश्चित रूप से सराहनीय है। सबौर प्रखण्ड के 14 पंचायतों में मुखिया के लिए 5 पद आरक्षित है जिसमें 2 पद महिलाएँ संभाल रही है। पंचायत समिति पद के लिए 5 पद आरक्षित है जिसमें 3 पद महिलाएँ कार्यरत है। सरपंच पद के लिए 6 पद आरक्षित है तथा कुल 4 पद महिलाएँ सत्ता संभाल रही है। इस तरह इन तीनों पदों में यानि 42 सीटों के विरुद्ध 22 सीटें महिलाएँ चुनाव जीत कर आयी हैं। तालिका 1 महिलाओं की भागीदारी को स्पष्ट करता है।

सबौर प्रखण्ड : पंचायतों में महिला प्रतिनिधित्व 2006

पंचायत	पद मुखिया	पंचायत समिति	सरपंच
बरारी	अना.	अना. महिला	अना.
फतेहपुर	पि. महिला	पि. वर्ग महिला	पि. वर्ग महिला
रजन्दीपुर	अना.	अना.	अना.
सबौर	अना. महिला	अनु. जाति (पु.)	अना. महिला
लोदीपुर	पिछड़ी जाति	अनारक्षित	पि. वर्ग
सरधो	अनु. जाति (पु.)	पिछड़ा वर्ग	अनु. जाति
खानकित्ता	अना.	अना.	अना.
फरका	महिला	अना. महिला	अना. महिला
चंधेरी	अना. महिला	अना. महिला	अना. महिला
ममलखा	अनाद्र महिला	अनाद्र महिला	अना. महिला
शंकरपुर	अना.	पिडछी जाति	अना.
लैलख	अना.	अनारक्षित	अना. महिला
बैजलपुर	अना. महिला	अना. महिला	अनु. जाति महिला
परघड़ी	अनु. जाति महिला	अनु. जाति महिला	अनु. जाति महिला

स्त्रोत– व्यक्तिगत सर्वेक्षण पर आधारित

इस प्रकार महिलओं का पंचायत स्तर पर अपेक्षित प्रतिनिधित्व हुआ है और उन्हें सक्षम नेतृत्व करने का सुअवसर प्राप्त हुआ है। जहाँ तक उनके दायित्वों का प्रश्न है तो इस दिशा में महिलाओं से अपेक्षा हैं कि वे सरकार की योजनाओं के क्रियान्वयन तथा पंचायत स्तर पर सफल नेतृत्व के लिए आगे आए। उनके ऊपर लोकतांत्रिक ढंग से काम करने का दायित्व है। महिलाएँ शिक्षा, बाल विकास, जनसंख्या नियंत्रण, स्वास्थ्य तथा अन्य सामाजिक कार्यों में रुचि लेकर इन दायित्वों को पूरा कर सकती हैं।

महिला प्रतिनिधियों की नेतृत्व संबंधी समस्याएँ

जागरूकता की कमी

गाँव का विकास तभी संभव है जब पंचायत के प्रतिनिधियों, पदाधिकारियों को इससे सबंधित सही जानकारी हो। साथ ही वे अपने जिम्मेदारी के साथ काम करने को तत्पर रहें।

संबंधों से जुड़ा होना— पुरुष प्रधान समाज वर्चस्व को बनाए रखने के लिए संबंधों का उपयोग कर रहा है। महिला सरपंच की खुद की कोई राय नहीं है। सबौर प्रखण्ड में सरपंच पति, सरपंच पुत्र जैसे सम्बन्ध स्वतंत्र नेतृत्व में बाधा उत्पन्न करते हैं।

भ्रष्टचार

पहले से व्याप्त नौकरशाही के भ्रष्टाचार के कारण भी महिलाएँ काम करने में असमर्थ हैं। कोई भी संचिका बिना हिस्सा दिए आगे नहीं बढ़ती, जिससे ग्रामीण विकास में अड़चने आती है।

चरित्र हनन

गाँव की रूढ़िवादी नीतियों के कारण भी प्रतिनिधि कार्य करने में असमर्थ है। महिलाएँ घर से बाहर निकलकर ग्रामीण विकास का कार्य करती हैं तो समाज उनके चरित्र पर उंगली उठाकर उन्हें हतोत्साहित करता है।

अविश्वास प्रस्ताव

पंचायत या गाँव का पुरूष वर्ग यह नहीं चाहता कि महिला प्रधान हो । बिना किसी कारण अविश्वास प्रस्ताव लाकर उन्हें हटा देना चाहते हैं ताकि पुरुष उपप्रधान प्रधान बन जाय। उन्हें भ्रष्टाचार के मामलों में फंसाया जाता है।

अधिकार के प्रति अनभिज्ञता

अधिकार प्राप्ति के बाद भी महिलाएँ उन्हें उपयोग करना नहीं जानती, क्योंकि पंचायती राज की कार्य प्रणाली से वे अनजान होती है।

अशिक्षा

अशिक्षा महिला सहभागिता एवं नेतृत्व के मार्ग में बाधक तत्व है। पंचायती राज की सफलता के लिए महिलाओं का शिक्षित होना आवश्यक है। सबौर प्रखण्ड में पंचायती स्तर पर महिलाओं की भागीदारी तो हुई है, किन्तु उनका सफल नेतृत्व न हो पा रहा है। जिसके लिए उपयुक्त कारक उत्तरदायी हैं।

समाधान

- पंचायती राज की सफलता के लिए जागरूकता एक महत्वपूर्ण शर्त्त है। महिलाओं को उनके अधिकार, शक्तियाँ और कर्त्तव्य के बारे में प्रशिक्षण देना अनिवार्य है। महिला जन प्रतिनिधियों के लिए ग्रामीण स्तर पर प्रशिक्षण केन्द्र लगाकर उन्हें विकास के बारे में समझाना चाहिए। साथ ही साथ कम्प्यूटर के द्वारा भी प्रशिक्षण दिया जा सकता है।
- चूँकि पंचायत प्रतिनिधि पढ़ने-लिखने की सामान्य अवस्था पार कर चुके होते हैं। इसलिए उने स्तर का प्रशिक्षण हो, साथ में स्थानीय महिला प्रशिक्षिका जरूर हो।
- पंचायत प्रतिनिधि अधिकतर काम करनेवाले है। अतः प्रशिक्षण के दौरान इस बात का ख्यालरखना होगा कि उनके जीविकोपार्जन में किसी तरह का व्यवधान न आए।
- बाल बिवाह पर रोक हो जिससे बालिकाओं को पूर्ण व्यक्तित्व विकास का अवसर मिल सकें।
- हाई-स्कूल से उपर की बालिकाओं को व्यावसायिक शिक्षा दी जाय।
- निर्धनता निवारण कार्यक्रमों में महिलाओं की भागीदारी बढ़ाई जाए।
- महिला विकास कोष से अधिक ऋण दिया जाय।
- राष्ट्रीय महिला कोष का प्रचार-प्रसार किया जाय।

- ऐसे परिवारों की पहचान की जाय जिसकी मुखिया महिलाएँ हो तथा जिनके पास रोजगार, आवास और स्वच्छ जल के स्त्रोत नहीं हैं, उन्हें यह सभी सुविधाएँ उपलब्ध करायी जाय।
- ग्राम सभा में अधिक से अधिक महिलाओं की भागीदारी बढ़ाई जानी चाहिए।
- महिला पंचायत प्रतिनिधि बड़ी संख्या में अशिक्षित है जो उनके लक्ष्य तक पहुँचने में मुख्य बाधा है। अतः महिला साक्षरता पर विशेष ध्यान देने की जरूरत है ।
- महिलाओं को लघु एवं कुटीर उद्योगों में लगाया जाना चाहिए, जिससे उत्पादन में वृद्धि के साथ-साथ रोजगार एवं आय में वृद्धि की जा सकें।
- महिलाओं को संगठित होकर पुरुष प्रधान मानसिक व्यवस्था को बदलना होगा। यह तभी संभव है जब महिला प्रतिनिधि संगठन बनाया जाय।
- महिला को समझौतावादी नीति-छोड़कर स्वयं की राय को महत्व देना होगा।

निष्कर्ष

सरकार ने पंचायतों में आरक्षण के आधार पर महिलाओं की भागीदारी कागजों पर सुनिश्चित कर दी हैं तथा महिला सरपंचों, पंचों एवं अन्य प्रतिनिधियों को पुरुष प्रधान राजनैतिक व्यवस्था में अपनी भूमिका निभाने के लिए खड़ा कर दिया, मगर इस भूमिका की सफलतापूर्वक अदायगी के लिए महत्वपूर्ण आधार प्रदान नहीं किया गया। आकड़ों का विश्लेषण ही अगर महिलाओं की सक्षम एवं सफल भागीदारी की ओर इशारा करता है तो आज देश में कुल 7,16,234 महिला पंचायत प्रतिनिधि है। पुरूष वर्ग, महिला सशक्तिकरण की प्रक्रिया के विरूद्ध अपनी सम्पूर्ण शक्ति का प्रयोग कर रहा है।

वास्तविकता तो यह है कि जब तक निर्णय प्रक्रिया में सम्पूर्ण मानव आबादी के इस आधे भाग की आवाज नहीं सूनी जायेगी तो हमारी निर्वाचित संस्थाओं व कार्यपालिका की निष्पक्षता पर प्रश्न चिन्ह लगा रहेगा । इसलिए सबौर जैसे पिछड़े एवं सभावनाशील प्रखण्ड में वास्तविक रूप में महिलाओं को सशक्त करने के लिए जरूरी है कि महिलाओं को सम्मान, सहयोग और सुरक्षित वातावरण उपलब्ध कराने की ।

संदर्भ

पाण्डेय जितेन्द्र कुमार (अगस्त 2006 कुरूक्षेत्र), महिला सशक्तिकरण में पंचायती राज की भूमिका, पृ. स. 30, 31।

शोध यात्रा : शोध एवं शिक्षण परिषद् ग्वालियर (म. प्र.)।

शोध वीथिका : पंचायती राज एवं ग्रामीण विकास शासन, महाराजा स्वशासी महाविद्यालय छतरपुर (म. प्र.)।

आज की नारी : 22 बी. प्रोफेसर्स कॉलोनी भोपाल (म. प्र.)।

पंचायती राज : इंस्टीच्यूट ऑफ सोशल साइंसेज।

आपकी चिट्ठी आपके नाम : 40, इंस्टीच्यूशनल एरिया, साउथ ऑफ आई.आई. टी., नई दिल्ली।

पाठक इन्दु (मार्च 2007 कुरूक्षेत्र), राजनीतिक सहभागिता एवं महिला सशक्तिकरण; कुमाय विश्वविद्यालय, नैनीताल, पृ. सं. 26-30।

12

भारत में पंचायती राज संस्थाओं में महिलाओं के नेतृत्व का विकास : सशक्तिकरण का एक प्रयास

नरेश कुमार

इस तथ्य से हम सभी सहमत हैं कि किसी भी स्वस्थ्य एवं विकसित समाज के निर्माण में स्त्री एवं पुरुष दोनों की सहभागिता आवश्यक है। वैसे भी मानव समाज के समुचित और सर्वांगीण विकास में महिलाओं का योगदान कभी भी कम नहीं रहा। भारत में आजादी के आन्दोलन के साथ-साथ विशेष तौर से महिलाओं को समान रूप से शैक्षणिक, आर्थिक, सामाजिक, राजनीतिक अवसर उपलब्ध कराने के लिये आवाजें उठती रही तथा इस दिशा में की गई पहल के काफी सार्थक परिणाम भी दृष्टिगोचर हुए।

सभी क्षेत्रों में प्रगति सुनिश्चित करने के लिये लिंग की समानता और महिलाओं को अधिकार प्रदान करने के सिद्धांत को विश्व भर में एक पहलू के रूप में स्वीकार किया गया है। भारत में भी कानूनी तौर पर स्त्री पुरुषों को समान अधिकार प्राप्त है। सामाजिक क्षेत्र की घटनाओं के सन्दर्भ में स्त्री पुरुष समानता पर जोर देने का अर्थ है– सामाजिक आर्थिक परिवर्तन के एजेन्ट के रूप में महिलाओं को अधिकार प्रदान करना। औरतें और बच्चे जो देश की कुल जनसंख्या का 67.7 प्रतिशत है, आज विकास के सन्दर्भ में सबसे महत्वपूर्ण लक्ष्य वर्ग है। इस बात की ओर तत्काल ध्यान देना आवश्यक है कि देश की विकास में मजबूत और प्रभावी शक्ति बनाने के लिए महिलाओं को सामाजिक और आर्थिक दृष्टि से

अधिकार सम्पन्न करना जरूरी है। वर्तमान कानूनों और महिलाओं का समुचित अधिकार एवं उनकी सामाजिक हैसियत सुधारने की सरकारी योजनाओं की समीक्षा के लिये महिलाओं और बच्चों पर एक कार्यदल का गठन किया गया है।

नौवीं योजना (1997-2002) में खासतौर पर कहा गया है कि महिला संघटक योजनाओं की पहचान की जाये जिसके लिये कम से कम 30 प्रतिशत विधियाँ महिलाओं के विकास योजनाओं में लगाई जाये। महिला कल्याण के लिये कुछ विशिष्ट योजनायें हैं। जिनके लिये बजट में कुछ धन मुहैया कराया जाता है। जिनमें महिला समृद्धि योजना, बालिका समृद्धि योजना, वर्किंग वुमेन्स होस्टल स्वशक्ति परियोजनाएँ इत्यादि।

स्वतंत्रता प्राप्ति के पश्चात् सरकार द्वारा महिलाओं की स्थिति बेहतर बनाने के लिए अनेक योजनायें बनायी गई। तभी आज देश में सामाजिक आर्थिक एवं राजनीतिक क्षेत्रों में महिलाओं ने भी अपनी पहुंच बनाई है। लेकिन साथ ही यह भी सच है कि आर्थिक सामाजिक क्षेत्रों के साथ राजनीतिक अंगों में जिस अनुपात में उन्हें अपनी उपस्थिति दर्ज करानी चाहिये थी, उतनी आज भी संभव नहीं हो पायी है। राजनीतिक क्षेत्र में मुख्यमंत्री, प्रधानमंत्री एवं राष्ट्रपति जैसे– नेतृत्व के शिखर पदों पर महिलायें पहुंचने में सफलता जरूर हासिल कर ली है। लेकिन अनुपातिक दृष्टि से आज भी नेतृत्व पदों पर उनकी संख्या नगण्य ही हैं। इण्टर पार्लियामेन्ट्री यूनियन द्वारा जारी सूची के अनुसार भारत में लोकसभा के 543 सदस्यों में महिलाओं की संख्या 45 दर्शाया गया है जो मात्र 8.3 प्रतिशत है जबकि राज्यसभा के 242 सदस्यों में महिलाओं की संख्या मात्र 28 दर्शाया गया है जो मात्र 11.6 प्रतिशत है। (इण्टर पार्लियामेन्ट्री यूनियन राजनीति में महिलाएँ)-(1995-2005) संयुक्त राष्ट्र के अवधरणा को क्रियान्वित करने के लिए सार्वजनिक जीवन के प्रत्येक स्तर पर लैंगिक समानता और महिलाओं का सशक्तिकरण महत्वपूर्ण निर्यय प्रक्रिया के प्रत्येक स्तर पर उनका प्रतिनिधित्व न केवल कम है वरन् अदृश्य है और उनकी आवाज अनसुनी रह जाती है। आवश्यकता यह है कि प्रत्येक स्तर पर न केवल उनकी सहभागिता को बढ़ाया जाये बल्कि निर्णय प्रक्रिया को वे प्रभावित भी कर सके।

भारत में सामाजिक एवं राजनीतिक क्षेत्र में महिलाओं के नेतृत्व के विकास में पंचायती राज की भूमिका कापफी महत्वपूर्ण है। भारत के प्राचीन इतिहास की पृष्ठभूमि के अवलोकन से भी स्पष्ट होता है कि पंचायत एवं पंचायती राज की परम्परा भारतीय संस्कृति के रूप में विद्यमान रही है जो कि मनु के महान ग्रंथ

मनुस्मृति तथा कौटिल्य के अर्थशास्त्र से लेकर मुगल काल तक अनवरत देखी जा सकती है। ब्रिटिश काल में केन्द्रीय सरकार की प्रमुखता के कारण पंचायत राज व्यवस्था हाशिये पर चली गयी थी जिन्हें लॉर्ड रिपन ने पुनर्जीवित किया।

स्वतंत्रता के उपरान्त भारतीय संविधन में स्वतंत्रता समानता एवं न्याय को अत्यधिक महत्व देते हुए लोकतांत्रिक जन सहभागिता को बढ़ावा दिया गया। जिससे महिला एवं पुरुषों में किसी भी आधार पर भेदभाव नहीं किया गया। सहभागिता के आधर पर यह समानता सैद्धान्तिक ही रही। व्यवसायिक रूप में इसे तभी प्राप्त किया जा सकता था जबकि महिलाओं को राजनीतिक संस्थाओं में सहभागिता को बढ़ाया जाता। इस कदम की शुरूआत भारतीय राजनीतिक व्यवस्था के प्रथम स्तर पंचायत में महिलाओं की बराबरी की भागीदारी सुनिश्चित करने के साथ हुई। इसके लिये 2 अक्टूबर 1952 में सामुदायिक विकास योजनाएँ चलाई गई परन्तु जन जागृति एवं उत्साह के अभाव में यह कार्यक्रम जन जीवन की परिधि से बाहर ही रहे। इस जनसहयोग को बढ़ाने एवं प्रशासन में सीधी भागीदारी के लिये 2 अक्टूबर 1957 में बलवन्त राव मेहता समिति गठित की गई। त्रिस्तरीय पंचायत की रूपरेखा तैयार कर लोकतंत्र के निचले स्तर पर अधिक सहभागिता के रूप में नया अध्याय शुरू किया गया। इसे आगे बढ़ाने के लिये 1977 में अशोक मेहता समिति, 1985 में जी.वी. राव समिति, 1986 लक्ष्मीमल सिंधिया समिति तथा 1988 में पी. के. थुगन समिति ने योगदान दिया परन्तु पंचायती राज एवं उसमें महिलाओं की भागीदारी सुनिश्चित करने का ठोस प्रयास 73वें संविधन संशोधन अधिनियम 1992 द्वारा किया गया। इसी अधिनियम के द्वारा पंचायतों को मान्यता दी गई। स्त्री की स्वतंत्रता के पूर्ववर्ती प्रयास माहौल में परिवर्तन और व्यक्तिगत निर्णयों तक सीमित थे। सामाजिक ढांचे में ऐसा कोई परिवर्तन नहीं किया गया। जिससे महिलाओं की हैसियत में संरचनात्मक सुधार है। नतीजा यह हुआ कि माहौल बदलते ही पुनर्मूषिको भवः की स्थिति आ जाती थी। इसके विपरीत 73वें संशोधन के द्वारा जो ऐतिहासिक प्रयोग किया गया (1) वह राजनीतिक तंत्र में परिवर्तन पर आधरित है तथा (2) महिलाओं के लिये संस्थागत प्रतिनिधित्व का प्रावधन करता है।

राजनीतिक ढंग में परिवर्तन का माध्यम बनी पंचायती राज की नई व्यवस्था जिसमें पंचायतों को संवैधनिक मान्यता दी गई, कार्य क्षेत्र परिभाषित किया गया तथा उनके संसाधनों के स्रोत निर्धारित किये गये। इन्हें भारतीय राज्य का तीसरा संस्तर कहा जाता है, ये संस्थायें नागरिक समाज एवं सरकार के बीच कड़ी का

कार्य करती है। यही सुनिश्चित हुआ है कि तीनों स्तरों की पंचायतों की एक तिहाई सीटों और पदों पर महिलाएं होगी। यह आरक्षण यदि मात्र महिलाओं को दिया गया होता तो ज्यादातर सवर्ण एवं सम्पन्न परिवारों की महिलायें ही दिखाई देती। इसीलिये सामान्य वर्ग से ही नहीं, अनुसूचित जातियों एवं अनु.जनजातियों के लिये आरक्षित पदों पर भी इन वर्गो की एक तिहाई महिलाओं को आरक्षण प्रदान किया गया।

पंचायती राज के माध्यम से महिला सशक्तिकरण को मानव अधिकार के परिप्रेक्ष्य में भी देखा जा सकता है। इस सम्बन्ध में बीजिंग में विश्व स्तर पर सम्पन्न हुए महिलाओं पर विशाल चतुर्थ सम्मेलन (4-15 सितम्बर 1995) में जारी किया गया बीजिंग घोषणा के कुछ बिन्दुओं पर भी ध्यान देना होगा। उक्त सम्मेलन का नारा था कि दुनिया को महिलाओं की दृष्टि से देखो (Look at world through women's eyes)। बीजिंग घोषणा के बिन्दु 14 में यह वर्णित है कि महिलाओं के अधिकार मानव अधिकार है। महिलाओं की नीति निर्धारण प्रक्रिया में भागीदारी के सम्बन्ध में बीजिंग घोषणा के बिन्दु 13 में यह स्पष्ट उल्लेखित है कि महिलाओं को समाज के सभी अंगों में समानता के आधार पर पूर्ण भागीदारी तथा सत्ता तक पहुँच भी सम्मिलित है। समानता विकास और शांति को आगे बढ़ाने के लिये मूल मंत्र है भारत में पंचायती राज संस्थाओं में महिलाओं की भागीदारी। महिलाओं के सम्बन्ध में बीजिंग घोषणा के उपयुक्त बिन्दुओं को मूर्त रूप प्रदान करना है तो भारत में पंचायती राज के स्तर पर महिलाओं का व्यापक भागीदारी को सही ढंग से प्रस्तुत करना होगा।

महिला सशक्तिकरण की दृष्टि से यह महत्वपूर्ण है कि भारत में 73वें संशोधन के द्वारा जो पंचायती राज व्यवस्था अपनायी गई है जिसके अन्तर्गत महिलाओं के लिये त्रिस्तरीय पंचायतों के हर स्तर पर एक तिहाई स्थान आरक्षित करने का प्रावधन किया गया है। इसके आलोक में बिहार पंचायत राज अधिनियम 2006 के द्वारा बिहार में पंचायती राज संस्थाओं में सभी स्तरों पर 50 प्रतिशत सीट आरक्षित कर दिया गया है। बिहार की इस नई प्रणाली के तर्ज पर हिमाचल प्रदेश, राजस्थान और उत्तराखंड की राज्य सरकारों ने भी जनवरी-मार्च 2008 में पंचायती राज संस्थाओं में आरक्षण को 33 प्रतिशत से बढ़ाकर 50 प्रतिशत करने की घोषणा की है। उत्तराखंड राज्य विधन सभा ने इस सम्बन्ध में 13 मार्च 2008 को उत्तराखंड पंचायत कानून (संशोधन) विधेयक को पारित कर दिया है।

महिलाओं को समान अधिकार प्रदान करने हेतु बिहार पंचायत राज अधिनियम 2006 में यह प्रावधान है कि आरक्षित स्थानों में से भी आधा स्थान महिलाओं के लिये आरक्षित होगा। अतः सामान्य के अलावा अनु. जाति एवं अनु. जनजाति तथा पिछड़े वर्ग के लिये आरक्षित स्थानों में से आधा स्थान महिलाओं के लिये आरक्षित है।

पंचायती राज मंत्रालय 27 मई 2004 से अस्तित्व में आया है। इसे पंचायती राज के माध्यम से ग्रामीण गरीबी उन्मूलन और समृद्धि के लिये नीतियां तथा कार्यक्रम बनाने का कार्य सौंपा गया है। इस मंत्रालय का गठन मूलतः 73वें संविधान संशोधन अधिनियम 1992 (सीएए) द्वारा जोड़े गये संविधान के खण्ड 9 के कार्यान्वयन की निगरानी करने के लिए कहा गया है। पंचायतों की संख्या की वर्तमान स्थिति (1 अप्रैल 2005) इस प्रकार है ग्राम पंचायत 2,34,676, मध्यवर्ती पंचायत 6097, जिला पंचायत इसकी कुल पंचायत संस्थायें 241310 है। इन संस्था में महिलाओं की संख्या और उनका प्रतिशत इस प्रकार है– जिला पंचायत में 41 प्रतिशत, मध्यवर्ती पंचायत में 43 प्रतिशत, ग्राम पंचायत में 40 प्रतिशत इन पंचायतों के माध्यम से महिलाओं के सशक्तिकरण का कार्य किया जा रहा है। पंचायतों में महिलाओं की भागीदारी उनके लिये आरक्षित 33 प्रतिशत की न्यूनतम सीमा से अधिक है। देश में पंचायतों में 22 लाख निर्वाचित प्रतिनिधियों में लगभग 9 लाख महिलायें हैं। तीन स्तरों वाली पंचायत प्रणाली में 59000 से अधिक महिला अध्यक्ष हैं।

73वें संशोधन के पश्चात् पंचायती राज संस्थाओं के जहां कुछ राज्यों में 50 प्रतिशत स्थान आरक्षित कर एवं अन्य राज्यों में 33 प्रतिशत स्थान आरक्षित कर महिलाओं को नेतृत्व पदों पर आसीन किया गया है जिसके फलस्वरूप पिछले 12 वर्षों के भीतर पंचायती राज संस्थाओं के माध्यम से महिलाओं ने नेतृत्व पदों पर महत्वपूर्ण स्थान प्राप्त की है। कई राज्यों में पंचायतों के सभी स्तरों पर महिलाओं की उपस्थिति 33 प्रतिशत से अधिक है। जैसे कर्नाटक में 43 प्रतिशत, केरल में 39 प्रतिशत, बंगाल में 37 प्रतिशत, जबकि बिहार में 50 प्रतिशत से अधिक है। पंचायतों के माध्यम से समाज की जड़ता, धार्मिक अंधविश्वासों में, रूढ़ियों, कुशासन एवं भ्रष्टाचार के उन्मूलन में प्रतिकूल वातावरण में भी महिलाओं ने अच्छा काम किया है। पंचायतों में महिलाओं की समुचित भागीदारी से ग्रामीण विकास एंव महिला विकास जैसे चिन्तन का विकास हुआ है तथा एक नई चेतना का सूत्रपात हुआ है। पंचायतों में महिलाओं के एक-तिहाई आरक्षण के प्रावधान

लागू होने की वजह से संसद एवं राज्यों की विधानसभाओं में भी महिलाओं को आरक्षण देने का दबाव बढ़ता जा रहा है, बहुत संभव है कि आनेवाले दिनों में यह बदलाव देखने को मिले जो महिला सशक्तिकरण की दिशा में एक बेहतर प्रयास है।

निःसंदेह, पंचायती राज संस्थाओं की निर्णय प्रक्रिया में नेतृत्व पदों पर महिलाओं की 33 प्रतिशत से अधिक भागीदारी सामाजिक क्रान्ति की दिशा में एक प्रगतिशील कदम है, महिला सशक्तिकरण की दिशा में एक बेहतर प्रयास है परन्तु इस बात को भी सुनिश्चित करना होगा कि ग्राम स्तर पर विकास और लोकतांत्रिक क्रियाकलाप से गांव की आम महिलायें भी जुड़ सके। वर्तमान ग्रामीण परिदृश्य इस बात को दर्शाता है कि अभी भी महिलायें समाज के हाशिये पर है अभी भी वह जागरूक नहीं हो पायी है कि अपने कर्तव्यों को भली-भांति निर्वहन कर सके। सामंतवादी दृष्टिकोण पुरुष प्रधन ग्राम्य जीवन पर्दा प्रथा तथा पंचायत के प्रति उदासीन भावना जैसे सामाजिक परिवेश में महिला आरक्षण से जुड़ी हुई महिला सशक्तिकरण को चुनी हुई महिला सदस्यों और अध्ययनों के साथ गांव की आम महिलाओं तक ले जाना सहज कार्य नहीं है।

इसके साथ ही सामाजिक एवं राजनीतिक आयाम के अतिरिक्त महिलाओं के आर्थिक सशक्तिकरण हेतु पंचायती राज संस्थाओं में नेतृत्व पदों पर आसीन प्रतिनिधियों को गरीबी रेखा से नीचे जीवन-यापन कर रही ग्रामीण महिलाओं को रोजगार उपलब्ध कराना होगा। इस दिशा में राष्ट्रीय ग्रामीण रोजगार गारन्टी योजना के तहत महिलाओं को भी काम मिले इसका सम्बन्ध करना होगा। महिलाओं के आर्थिक उत्थान हेतु स्वयं सहायता समूहों का गठन अपरिहार्य है। पंचायती राज संस्थाओं में 33 प्रतिशत आरक्षण राजनीतिक सशक्तिकरण का द्योतक है, इस राजनीतिक सशक्तिकरण के माध्यम से सामाजिक और आर्थिक सशक्तिकरण की दिशा में आगे बढ़ना होगा।

इस सन्दर्भ में यह भी ध्यान देने की बात है कि केन्द्र के पंचायती राज मंत्रालय ने एक संस्था द्वारा पंचायती राज संस्थाओं के महिला प्रतिनिधियों पर शोधकार्य कराया था जिसकी रिपोर्ट से यह तथ्य उभरकर आया कि पंचायती राज संस्थाओं में महिलाओं हेतु निर्वाचन क्षेत्रों का चक्रानुक्रम के आधार पर आरक्षण एक अवधि (5 वर्ष) के लिये होता है और उन क्षेत्रों का आरक्षण समाप्त कर सामान्य क्षेत्र बना देने पर उन सामान्य क्षेत्रों से 15 प्रतिशत से भी कम महिलायें चुनाव जीत पाती है। अतः किसी पंचायत के महिलाओं हेतु आरक्षित स्थान को दो

अवधि (कुछ दस वर्ष) तक आरक्षित करना महिला सशक्तिकरण की दृष्टि से सही माना जा सकता है। उत्तराखण्ड राज्य द्वारा की गई इस तरह की व्यवस्था भारत के अन्य राज्यों के लिये अनुकरणीय है। भारत सरकार के पंचायती राज मंत्री मणिशंकर अय्यर का मानना है कि महिलाओं हेतु आरक्षित एक ही निर्वाचन क्षेत्र को दो अवधि तक आरक्षण देना महिला सशक्तिकरण की दिशा में सही कदम होगा उन्होंने इस पर विचार करने का सुझाव दिया है।

इस प्रकार इक्कीसवीं सदी के भारत में सामाजिक बदलाव का एक ऐसा चित्र उभर कर आया है जब पंचायती राज संस्थाओं में निर्वाचित प्रतिनिधि के रूप में महिलाओं के नेतृत्व का विकास हुआ है जिसका प्रभाव आनेवाले दिनों में संसद में भारतीय संसद एवं राज्यों के विधान सभाओं में महिलाओं के लिये 33 प्रतिशत आरक्षण विधेयक पर भी पड़ेगा। इस सम्बन्ध में लम्बित विधेयक को हम अधिक दिनों तक लम्बित नहीं रख सकते। इस प्रकार पंचायती राज संस्थाओं में महिला नेतृत्व का विकास महिला सशक्तिकरण की दिशा में एक सार्थक प्रयास माना जा सकता है।

संदर्भ सूची

इण्टर पार्लियामेन्ट्री यूनियन : राजनीति में महिलायें (1995-2005)।

अन्नान कॉफी (2006), विमैन इन डिसिजन मेकिंग *www.un.ovg/events.*

महाजन सुमित्रा (2001), महिला सशक्तिकरण-दर्शन लक्ष्य और उपलब्धियाँ, *योजना,* अगस्त।

पाण्डेय जितेन्द्र कुमार (2006), महिला सशक्तिकरण में पंचायत राज की भूमिका *कुरूक्षेत्र,* अगस्त।

दत्त विजय शंकर (2009) महिला सशक्तिकरण की क्रांतिकारी पहल, (*प्रतियोगिता दर्पण,* मार्च, 2009/1420)

निशिथ राकेश शर्मा (2006), पंचायती राज संस्थाओं में महिलाओं की बढ़ती भूमिका, *कुरूक्षेत्र,* अगस्त।

13

बिहार की पंचायती राज व्यवस्था में दलित महिलाओं की सहभागिता

विपिन चन्द्रा

राष्ट्रपति महात्मा गांधी के शब्दों में,

"मैं ऐसे भारत के लिए काम करूँगा, जिसमें सबसे निर्धन व्यक्ति भी इसे अपना देश समझे और इसके निर्माण में उसकी प्रभावी भूमिका हो, एक ऐसा भारत जिसमें लोगों का कोई उच्च-निम्न वर्ग न हो। जिसमें सभी समुदाय पूरे सद्भाव के साथ रहते हों, इस प्रकार के भारत में छूआछूत नामक कोढ़ के लिए कोई जगह नहीं होगी। स्त्रियों को पुरुषों के बराबर अधिकार होंगे। मेरे सपनों का भारत यही है।"

महात्मा गांधी के मुखारविंद से निकले यह शब्द स्वतंत्रता पूर्व भारत के तस्वीर को रेखांकित करते हैं। गांधी जी के सपनों को मूर्त रूप देने के लिए तथा तत्कालीन परिस्थितियों के अनुकूल संविधान निर्माताओं द्वारा भारतीय संविधान की प्रस्तावना में घोषित किया गया कि इसका लक्ष्य न्याय प्राप्ति व समस्त नागरिकों को स्तर और अवसर की समानता प्रदान करना है। देश की आधी आबादी को विशेष अवसर प्रदान करके ही समस्त नागरिकों के स्तर को सुदृढ़ किया जा सकता है।

हमारा भारतीय समाज विशेषकर हिन्दू समाज आज भी पुरातन स्मृतियों के प्रावधन के अनुसार चल रहा है। यद्यपि आधुनिक युग के आगमन से खासकर

अंग्रेजी राज की स्थापना के पश्चात् भारतीय दण्ड संहिता (आई.पी.सी.) तथा दण्ड प्रक्रिया संहिता (सी.आर.पी.सी.) द्वारा भारतीयों को व्यवस्थित करने का प्रयास किया गया, पर सामाजिक आचार-विचार पुरानी स्मृतियों के आधार पर ही संचालित होते रहे। वर्ण-व्यवस्था के कारण हिन्दू समाज हजार-हजार जातियों में विखण्डित होकर एक-दूसरे से शत्रुवत व्यवहार करने लगा। डॉ॰ अम्बेडकर के अनुसार, ''हिन्दू समाज जाति-व्यवस्था के कारण न केवल पृथक्करण या विभाजन का शिकार हो गया बल्कि सभी जातियाँ यहाँ तक कि उपजातियाँ भी एक-दूसरे से युद्धरत की स्थिति में रहने लगी।'' फलतः समाज में कुछ वर्ग कुटिल बुद्धि के कारण साधन-सम्पन्न होकर सुख भोगने लगा तथा बहुसंख्यक भाग गरीबी तथा अभाव की स्थिति में दम तोड़ने की स्थिति में पहुँच गया। समाज की इसी स्थिति ने स्वतंत्रता प्राप्ति के पश्चात् इन दबे-कुचले वर्गों के लिए आरक्षण की व्यवस्था करने के लिए हमारे संविधान निर्माताओं को बाध्य किया और संविधान की धारा-46 के द्वारा प्रावधान किया गया है, ''सरकार समाज के कमजोर वर्गों, खासकर अनुसूचित एवं जनजाति वर्ग के लिए शैक्षणिक एवं आर्थिक हित को विशेष ध्यान देकर विकसित करेगी तथा हर प्रकार के शोषण एवं सामाजिक अन्याय से बचायेगी।''

इन्हीं सारी बातों पर ध्यान देते हुए 1992 में संविधान के 73वें संशोधन द्वारा यह प्रावधान किया गया कि लोकसभा तथा विधानसभाओं में अनुसूचित जाति एवं जनजाति को प्रदत्त आरक्षण की तरह पंचायतों में भी अनुसूचित जाति, पिछड़ा वर्ग तथा महिलाओं के लिए आरक्षण किया जाए ताकि इन कमजोर वर्ग के लोगों को भी विकास का अवसर प्राप्त हो सके। इसके आलोक में बिहार पंचायत राज अधिनियम 1993 की धारा -13(1), 13(2) तथा 13(3) द्वारा पंचायत स्तर के पदों पर धारा-36(1), 36(3) द्वारा पंचायत समिति के पदों पर और धारा-63(1), 63(2) तथा 63(3) के द्वारा जिला परिषद् के पदों पर आरक्षण की व्यवस्था की गई। आरक्षित पदों का निर्धारण इन जातियों की जनसंख्या के प्रतिशत के अनुसार किया गया तथा महिलाओं के लिए निर्धारित पद के एक-तिहाई पर आरक्षित किये गये। बिहार पंचायत राज अधिनियम 2006 द्वारा पंचायत राज संस्थाओं में महिलाओं के लिए आधी सीटें आरक्षित की गई तथा इसमें 16 प्रतिशत दलित महिलाओं के लिए आरक्षण की व्यवस्था की गई। इसी आरक्षण प्रावधान के अन्तर्गत अनुसूचित जाति, जनजाति एवं अत्यंत पिछड़े वर्ग के लिए उनकी जनसंख्या के अनुपात में आरक्षण प्रदान किया गया है।

इस आरक्षण के कारण समाज के विशेषकर सुविधाभोगी वर्गों में असंतोष की भावना भी प्रस्फुटित होती रहती है, पर जो सदियों से शोषित एवं दबे-कुचले रहे हैं, उन्हें अवसर देने के लिए भारतीय संविधन के प्रति सम्मान प्रकट करते हुए इसे स्वीकार करना है तभी समाज आगे बढ़ सकेगा और बिहार अन्य राज्यों की तुलना में विकसित तथा समृद्ध हो सकेगा अन्यथा ये आपस में लड़ते रहेंगे और विकास के मार्ग में पिछड़ जायेंगे।

दलित महिला आरक्षण की उपलब्धियाँ

पंचायती राज व्यवस्था में दलित महिलाओं के लिए किए गए आरक्षण से उनकी स्थिति में सुधार हुआ है, यह भी सच है कि उन्होंने अपनी शक्ति को पहचाना है। पंचायत में दलित महिला प्रतिनिधि के आ जाने से उनमें राजनैतिक चेतना का प्रसार हुआ है। अब इनमें चुनाव में सक्रिय भागीदारी के लिए लालसा पैदा होने लगी है। गांव की पढ़ी-लिखी महिलाओं के साथ-साथ अनपढ़ महिलाएं एवं दलित तथा पिछड़े वर्ग की महिलायें भी पंचायत को अपने राजनीतिक भविष्य का प्रथम पायदान मानने लगी है।

गांव के बुजुर्ग लोगों का कहना है कि बिहार सरकार ने महिलाओं को पंचायत चुनाव में 50 प्रतिशत का आरक्षण देकर देश के नेताओं को यह दिखा दिया है कि केवल ऊंची-ऊंची बातें करने से महिलाओं के मुकद्दर को नहीं बदला जा सकता। अगर महिलाओं का उत्थान चाहते हैं तो उन्हें अधिकार सौंपे जाए तथा निर्णय कि प्रक्रिया में भागीदार बनाया जाए। संचार क्रांति के कारण देश के अन्य हिस्सों में घटने वाली घटनाओं का व्यापक असर बिहार में भी होता है और यहां की महिलाओं में भी पंचायतों में पचास फीसदी पदों पर काबिज होने से उनका आत्मसम्मान बढ़ा है।

पंचायत में महिला आरक्षण के व्यवस्था के कारण आज राज्य की आधी आबादी को सत्ता के निचले स्तर पर सहभागिता प्राप्त हो गई है। वे भी आज प्रखण्ड तथा जिला मुख्यालयों में जाकर पदाधिकारियों से समाज में घटित होनेवाली घटनाओं के बारे में जानकारी ले रही हैं तथा किसी महिला पर हुए अत्याचार के संबंध में आवश्यक कार्रवाई करने हेतु दबाव बना रही है।

दलित महिला पंचायत प्रतिनिधियों को परिवेश का ज्ञान, प्रशासनिक कार्यों में भागीदारी तथा अन्य संस्थाओं से संपर्क निरंतर बढ़ रही है। उन्होंने खुलकर बोलना शुरू कर दिया है। इससे पर्दा-प्रथा में कुछ उदारता आई है और अब

महिला प्रतिनिधियों की पहचान किसी पुरुष के पत्नी, पुत्री या पुत्रवधू के रूप में कम होती जा रही है। उल्टे पुरुष की पहचान किसी महिला प्रतिनिधि के पति, पुत्र या श्वसुर के रूप में हो रहा है। इस प्रकार पंचायतों में महिला आरक्षण की व्यवस्था की खासकर दलित महिलाओं के सामाजिक प्रतिष्ठा में बढ़ोतरी हुई है।

पुरुष प्रधान सामाजिक मानसिकता के तमाम दबावों के बावजूद महिलाओं ने अपने विवेक से निर्णय करने की शुरुआत कर दी है। अब वे भी पहले की तरह रबर स्टाम्प की भूमिका में नहीं है। महिला प्रतिनिधि भी अब अपने बुद्धि विवेक से नीतियां तय करना शुरू कर दी है। स्वभाविक रूप से उनके निर्णय करने की क्षमता में वृद्धि हुई है। विदित हो कि अलवर जिले के लिम्मो गांव की सरपंच कोयल देवी ने अपने पति और ससुर को अधिसूचना जारी की कि वे बताएं कि पंचायत की जमीन हड़पने की वजह से उनके विरुद्ध कार्यवाही क्यों न की जाएं। भले ही यह घटना बिहार राज्य की बाहर की है परन्तु इस घटना का प्रभाव बिहार के महिलाओं पर भी पड़ा है।

दलित महिला प्रतिनिधित्व के कारण सार्वजनिक विषयों तथा निर्णयों पर विचार-विमर्श का दायरा रसोईघर तक पहुंच गया है। जबकि पहले ये चौपालों तक ही सीमित था। सार्वजनिक मामलों में पुरुष वर्ग एवं सामान्य महिलाओं के साथ-साथ दलित महिलाएं भी नीति निर्धारण में महत्वपूर्ण भूमिका निभा रही है। फलस्वरूप कार्य-प्रणाली में स्पष्टवादिता तथा खुलापन पहले की तुलना में अधिक है। इससे भ्रटाचार के अवसर भी कम हो रहे हैं।

महिला आरक्षण की विफलताएँ

महिला आरक्षण की विफलताएँ के तौर पर अधिकांशतः वे कारण और समस्याएँ हैं जिनसे दलित महिला पंचायत प्रतिनिधियों को अपने अधिकार एवं कर्त्तव्य के निर्वहन में सामना करना पड़ता है तथा जिससे महिलाएं अपने कर्तव्य को संविधान सम्मत तरीके से निर्वहन करने में पूरी तरह से सफल नहीं हो पाई है।

गांव का विकास तभी संभव है जब पंचायत के प्रतिनिधियों, पदाधिकारियों को इसके संबंध में उठाये जाने वाले कदमों की जानकारी हो। वे इनकी बारीकियों से परिचित हो तथा उनके अंदर जिम्मेदारी के साथ काम करने की तत्परता दिखें। महिला आरक्षण के लागू हो जाने से निःसंदेह पंचायतों में उनका प्रतिनिधित्व बढ़ा है लेकिन जागरूकता की कमी के कारण वे उन उद्देश्यों को प्राप्त करने में सफल नहीं हो पा रही है जो उनसे उपेक्षा की गई है।

दलित महिलाओं का अशिक्षित होना उनके कार्य में सबसे बड़ी बाधा है। शासन तंत्र के अथक प्रयास के बावजूद भी महिला साक्षरता दर 39 प्रतिशत (सन् 2001) है। इसका मुख्य कारण हैं कि महिला साक्षरता के लिए जनजागरण की कमी है। अशिक्षित एवं अल्पशिक्षित होने के कारण महिलाएं अपने अधिकार एवं कर्तव्य बोध से सही तरीके से परिचित नहीं हो पाई है तथा वे सही तरीके से अपने कर्तव्य का निर्वहन नहीं कर पा रही है।

दलित महिला प्रतिनिधियों का गरीबी रेखा से नीचे रहना भी एक समस्या है। आरक्षण के माध्यम से पंचायतों में निर्वाचित महिला प्रतिनिधि गरीबी के कारण अपने दायित्व के निर्वहन में पूरे मन से समय नहीं दे पाती है तथा बिहार के कई जिलों में महिला के लिए आरक्षित पदों का खाली रह जाने के लिए गरीबी भी एक उत्तरदायी कारक है। गरीबी, महिलाओं के लिए पंचायत प्रतिनिधि बनने की तुलना में बड़ी जिम्मेवारी अपने परिवार का पेट पालना है।

दलित वर्ग की महिला प्रतिनिधियों की गांव में कोई सुनना नहीं चाहता। गांव में उच्च वर्ग के लोगों का ही प्रभाव रहता है। सरकारी अधिकारी भी उनके यहाँ न आकर गांव के अमीर व्यक्तियों के यहां जाते हैं। कभी-कभी निम्न जाति के होने के कारण महिलाओं को उच्च जाति के दबंगों का कोपभाजन बनना पड़ता है। जहाँ-तहाँ स्वतंत्रता दिवस, गणतंत्र दिवस तथा सार्वजनिक समारोहों के अवसर पर झण्डोत्तोलन करते या भाषण देते वक्त महिला प्रतिनिधियों को जलील किया जाता है। वास्तव में यह आरक्षण की विफलता न होकर पुरुष प्रधान समाज की सामंती सोच का परिणाम है।

गांव के रूढ़िवादी नीतियों के कारण भी प्रतिनिधि कार्य करने में असमर्थ हैं, महिलाएं घर से बाहर निकलकर ग्रामीण विकास का कार्य करती है तो समाज उनके चरित्र पर उंगली उठाकर, हतोत्साहित करता है। महिला प्रतिनिधियों को पुरुष प्रतिनिधियों के बीच में बैठकर कार्य करना पड़ता है तथा पंचायत राज से जुड़े सरकारी अधिकारियों से भी उनका बराबर मिलना-बैठना होता है जिसके कारण पुरुष प्रधान समाज उनके पवित्रता पर शक करने लगते हैं, जिसके कारण भी महिलाएं अपने कर्तव्य को सही तरीके से नहीं निभा पाती है।

बिहार के ग्रामीण अंचलों में आज भी महिलाएं घूंघट के अन्दर रहती है। पर्दा-प्रथा के चलन के कारण महिलाएं स्वतंत्रतापूर्वक अपने कर्त्तव्य के निर्वहन में कठिनाई महसूस करती है।

महिला आरक्षण के उपलब्धियों एवं विफलताओं के संबंध में अध्ययन करने के पश्चात् यह मालूम होता है कि आरक्षण व्यवस्था के लागू होने से निश्चित ही महिलाओं की सत्ता में सहभागिता सुनिश्चित हुई है। उनमें राजनीतिक जागृति का संचार हुआ है। वे स्वतंत्र पहचान बनाने के लिए जद्दोजहद कर रही है। आरक्षण की व्यवस्था की महिलाओं का सामाजिक उत्थान निश्चित रूप से हुआ है। लेकिन पुरुष प्रधान समाज की पुरातन पंथी, सोच, महिलाओं में अशिक्षा तथा जागृति के अभाव के कारण उनका उतना सामाजिक उत्थान नहीं हो सका है जितना कि महिला आरक्षण की अवधरणा में उनसे उपेक्षा की गई है।

महिला आरक्षण की सफलता के लिए सुझाव

महिला आरक्षण की सफलता के लिए प्रशिक्षण एक महत्वपूर्ण शर्त है। महिलाओं को उनके अधिकार, शक्तियाँ तथा कर्त्तव्यों से अवगत कराने के लिए उनको प्रशिक्षित करना अनिवार्य है। महिला प्रतिनिधियों के लिए ग्रामीण स्तर पर प्रशिक्षण केन्द्र लगाकर इन्हें विकास के विभिन्न पहलुओं से परिचित कराया जाना चाहिए। उन्हें उनकी क्षेत्रीय भाषा में ही प्रशिक्षण दिया जाना चाहिए। जिससे महिलाएँ आसानी से बातों को समझ सकें। प्रशिक्षण छोटे-छोटे ग्रुप में देना चाहिए, जिससे प्रत्येक महिला प्रतिनिधि पर प्रशिक्षण उचित समय दे सके। फिल्मों तथा कम्प्यूटर के द्वारा भी प्रशिक्षण दिया जा सकता है। चूंकि पंचायत प्रतिनिधि पढ़ने-लिखने की सामान्य अवस्था पार कर चुके होते हैं, अतः उनके स्तर पर ही शिक्षण-प्रशिक्षण देना चाहिए। इसके लिए स्थानीय महिला प्रशिक्षिका आवश्यक है। पंचायत प्रतिनिधि अधिकतर काम करने वाले हैं। अतः प्रशिक्षण देते समय इस बात पर ध्यान रखना होगा कि इस प्रशिक्षण से उनके जीविकोपार्जन में किसी प्रकार का व्यवधन नहीं हो।

बहरहाल पंचायती राज तथा महिला आरक्षण पर चाहे कोई कितनी भी उंगली उठाये या उसका नकारात्मक पक्ष खोजें लेकिन बिहार में महिला पंचायत प्रतिनिधियों की कामयाबी बताती है कि बदलाव की बयार मंद ही सही, लेकिन बहने लगी है। पंचायती राज व्यवस्था ने महिलाओं को स्वतंत्र पहचान बनाने तथा अपना सामाजिक उत्थान करने का एक सबल मंच प्रदान किया है।

संदर्भ सूची

एम. के. गांधी (1948), हरिजन।

73वां संविधान संशोधन अधिनियम, 1992

पी.सी. अरोड़ा, पंचायत राज विधन एवं नियमावली, पाहूजा लॉ हाउस, पटना।

बिहार पंचायत राज अधिनियम, 2006।

कुरूक्षेत्र, मार्च 2008

योजना, जनवरी 2009

बहार समग्र, (नैनो), सुरेन्द्र राउत

PART–3

Macro Level Women Political Leadership

14

Social Texture and Women's Political Leadership in India

Baleshwar Prasad Singh & Sarita Singh

Lord Budha's observation in reply to a question by the Prime Minister of Ajatshtru about Lichhivi Republic long ago that 'so long as the people of Lichhivi would keep on taking decisions after the due deliberations in Assembly .... and keep on honouring the women in, they would not be conquered"[1] hold truth for all times and all societies. India's own past is a testimony of his observation. It has not been mere a chance that the deterioration of India's great civilization has coincided with the deterioration in the condition and status of women and as our great epics Ramayana and Mahabharat testify any blow to women's honour brings in its wake vast destruction and turmoil in political and social life.

Democracy is one of the most coveted inventions humankind has made so far. It provides freedom to decide the way of life human being want for themselves. It gives an opportunity for exercising the creativity they are endowed with. Human society has been struggling to achieve the goal of democracy. Women and men are two important components of society. A good balanced between both the genders can help in making a developed society. According to 2001 census, the population of women in India is around 48% of the total population of the country.

The concept of political democracy implies that power is in some sense accountable to those affected by its exercise. But political democracy has no meaning in the absence of social democracy, especially when society is caste-ridden and there is a market difference between high and low, rich and poor. Social democracy implies provision of equal opportunities to all sections of society irrespective of caste, colour, creed, sex or religion. In this sense, social democracy or equal opportunities for all, is a pre-requisite to true democracy.

India, the largest democracy in the world, has historically little background of democracy. In fact, India strayed into democracy as a result of a long association with the British as a part of the British Raj. India has yet to adopt democracy as a way of life. But something can become a way of life only after a long and gradual process involving generations. Nevertheless, despite the numerous trials and tribulations, India has proved to be a shining example of democracy.

Despite tremendous advancement of human civilization, even in twenty first century, there is not a single country in the world where women have achieved equality with men. The historical, traditional and cultural portrait of women has been made under the veil of social norms and systems, which has always put women into the dockyard of society. A look into the thoughts in the ancient texts and also by ancient scholars reveals the poor status of women in our society. As far as the ownership of her offspring is concerned, it is found that the dominance of the male is considered to be normal. In Manu as well as Kautilya, long discussions can be found as to whom the fruit belongs to the owner of the "field" (women) or to the owner of the "seed" (men) (Devi 1999).

Women have been denied their political rights in reality though the constitution and the electoral laws have given them the right of adult suffrage and right to elected. Due to their position economically, socially and politically, women do not enjoy the political rights. There number in the parliament and state legislature is much less as compared to their population. They represent even less than 10% in the legislature.

Democracy cannot be realized if marginalized sections, which include women, remain outside the political system of power. Political participation does not mean only the right to vote but includes the ability to influence policies and decision making.

In the world as a whole women are under represented in all wings of the government-Legislative, executive and judiciary. In the political arena women have made the least headway in contemporary world and politics appears to be last made stronghold. Although the recent years have witnessed an increase in female other, changes in voters participation have been accompanied by changes in similar magnitude in the number of women occupying decision making positions. Notwithstanding the fact that females make up approximately 50 per cent of the world's population, rather throughout the world, their representation in public life is remarking small.

In India, women's representation in parliament and in the state Assemblies has never gone beyond nine per cent and ten per cent respectively. 'Political empowerment does not imply just a right to vote. The cardinal goal of democracy "of the people, by the people and for the people." Therefore can not be optimally accomplished, if the fifty per cent of population remains out of political empowerment. This can be observed from the following Table 1, Table 2 and Table 3.

Table 1
Representative of Women in Lok Sabha

Election Year	*Total Seats*	*Set own by Women*	*Percentage of Women*
1952	499	22	4.40
1957	500	27	5.40
1962	503	34	6.70
1967	523	31	5.91
1971	521	22	4.20
1977	544	19	3.40

Contd...

Election Year	*Total Seats*	*Set own by Women*	*Percentage of Women*
1980	544	28	5.20
1984	544	44	8.10
1989	517	27	5.30
1991	544	39	7.16
1996	543	39	7.18
1999	543	52	9.20

Table 2
Women Members Elected for Bihar Vidhan Sabha from 1952-2001

Year	*Total Seat*	*Women*
1952	330	13
1957	319	34
1962	319	25
1967	319	10
1969	319	04
1972	319	13
1977	325	13
1980	325	14
1985	325	15
1990	325	13
1995	325	12
2001	243	16

Tickets allotted by various political parties to women aspirants in Feb. 2006, Bihar Assembly Elections—

Party	*Total Candidate*	*Women*	*Percentage %*
R.J.D.	215	12	5.58
Cong.	083	06	7.22
I.J.P.	169	17	10.05
J.D. (U)	138	12	8.69
B.J.P.	105	08	7.61
C.P.I.	016	00	00
C.P.M.	013	01	7.69
C.P.I. (M.L.)	109	09	8.25
B.S.P.	243	20	8.23
S.P.	155	11	7.09
Total	1264	96	7.59

Unfair Stats

- India ranks 134th among 183 countries with just 8.3% women members in the Lok Sabha.
- Even Pakistan does better than us with 21.3% women Parliamentarians.

How Others Fare

Rwanda	48.8%
Sweden	45.3%
Norway	38.2%
Finland	37.5%
Denmark	36.9%

Table 3
Percentage of Female Vote in Lok Sabha Elections

	Voting Percentage		
Year	*Male*	*Female*	*Difference in male and female voting percentage*
1952	53.0	37.1	-15.9
1957	56.0	39.6	-16.4
1962	62.1	46.6	-15.5
1967	66.7	55.5	-11.2
1971	69.7	49.15	-20.55
1977	65.62	54.91	-10.71
1980	57.69	51.29	-6.40
1984	63.61	68.17	+4.56
1989	66.13	57.32	-8.81
1991	61.58	51.36	-10.22
1996	62.06	53.41	-8.65
1998	NA	NA	NA
1999	NA	NA	NA

Table 4
Total Number of Male and Female Contestants in Lok Sabha Elections

Year	*Total No. of Seats*	*Male Candidate*	*Female Candidate*
1952	489	1823	51
1957	494	1473	45
1962	494	1915	70
1967	520	2302	67

Contd...

Year	*Total No. of Seats*	*Male Candidate*	*Female Candidate*
1971	520	2698	86
1977	542	2369	70
1980	542	4478	142
1984	542	5406	164
1989	529	5962	198
1991	521	8374	325
1996	543	13353	599
1998	543	–	425
1999	543	–	–

Table 5
Percentage of Women MPs

Year	*In Lok Sabha*	*In Rajya Sabha*
1952	4.4	7.3
1957	5.4	7.5
1962	6.8	7.6
1967	5.9	8.3
1971	4.2	7.0
1977	3.4	10.2
1980	7.9	9.8
1984	8.1	11.4
1989	5.3	9.7
1991	7.2	15.5
1996	7.2	9.0
1998	7.9	–
1999	8.6	–

Table 6
Percentage of Women MLAs in Some State Assemblies

State	*1952*	*1993-97*
Andhra Pradesh	2.9	2.7
Assam	0.5	4.8
Bihar	3.6	3.4
Goa	–	10
Gujarat	–	1.1
Haryana	–	4.4
Himachal Pradesh	–	4.4
Jammu & Kashmir	–	2.3
Karnataka	2.0	3.1
Kerala	0	9.3
Madhya Pradesh	2.1	3.8

Contd...

State	*1952*	*1993-97*
Maharashtra	1.9	3.8
Orissa	9.6	5.4
Punjab	2.2	6.0
Rajasthan	0	4.5
Sikkim	-	3.1
Tamil Nadu	0.3	3.8
Uttar Pradesh	1.2	4.0
West Bengal	0.8	6.8
Delhi	4.2	4.3

If we examine women's representation in different country of the world, we find in USA it is 11.07 per cent, Japan it is 4.04 per cent, Belgium and Argentina there is reservation for women 15 to 20 per cent. In Morocco, 10 per cent of Parliamentary seats are reserved for a women. In France, a 1999 constitutional amendment requires political parties to include 50 per cent of women candidates on party lists. Obviously, while quite a few other countries are string to induct women into their political system, in India women have to wait a bit longer.

The secondary status of women in society is one of the causes of less participation in Politics women are not considered physically and mentally strong enough to undertake outdoor activities and, therefore, they remain confined mostly indoors which results in depriving them of virtually every opportunities to carve out an independent status in life. This leads to their perpetual and complete economic dependence because they can not partake in any such activities and can not avail themselves of the various opportunities.

Another reason for non-performer in politics is that women are not true right from birth to decide their own future. They are so inextricably bound to the social system that there is hardly any freedom for them to act. Their dress, their food, their movement, their dress, their food, their movement, their desires, their behaviours and even how much they are to be cared for are so much bound by customs and regulations that they have to follow them like a machine with very little scope for flexibility or change. Traditionally, our society has been patriarchal in character; hence patriarchal norms, values, principles and systems determine the social and political status of women.

In Mizoram Assembly elections 2008, only two women candidate were elected despite the fact that the female voters are more in numbers than male. In Kashmir Assembly election, 2008 only three female candidates were elected out of 67 seats.

In the central and state legislature, there has been a demand for reservation of one third of seats for the women. A seeking reservation for women in the Parliament is sought to be passed. The bill seeks reservation of 33% in the Parliament and State Legislature. It will improve the human resources base of the nation, as 50% of the total resource in unproductive in our country. Indian Parliament has only 8.8% women as its representatives.

It is clear that the 73rd constitutional amendment has played major role in the empowerment of women as a whole and Dalit women in particular. In a state like U.P. and Bihar, especially in the rural area, where caste and class inequalities are wide-spread, Dalit women have not only contested but won seats that were not reserved for them. There were a number of cased in which a woman who was elected in the previous election on a reserved seat, won this election in an unreserved constituency. Besides this, working as a Pradhan or in any other position, gave her much exposure and experience that she herself became the leader instead of being one's wife. It is not only the candidate that gets exposure but other women too come out for campaigning, which also represents a new trend in rural U.P. and Bihar. This change leads the society from a hierarchical society to a democratic society, as the rural elites are losing their grip over the power structure of the villages[2].

The structural features of political life also tend to exclude women from positions of power. In spite of having a woman Prime Minister, a few women Chief Ministers or Governors or some other women holding political and important offices, the level of representation of women in decision making has been very low. The women, who started as a small minority in the domain of politics in India at the time of Independence, have not become a large minority even after 47 years. An early study by Usha Mehta in 1973 brought out the fact succinctly that "although the representation of women in Parliament, in the Assemblies and the Union and State cabinets in India is larger than it is in many other countries of the world , it is not proportionate to their number in the total population and does not even approximate to the figure that political parties consider to be fair allocation". Usha Mehta also asserts on the basis of public opinion survey that women show less interest in information on political issues and are conservative in their opinions. The 'token women' who are perceptible here and there do not represent the real situation of women in Indian democracy. Interestingly, the numerical strength women had in Indian Parliament at the time of Independence has ever since remained static. They continue to be a negligible minority.

A cumulative analysis of Lok Sabha and Rajya Sabha women members shows that in the Lok Sabha the highest number of women was 43 in the 8th Lok Sabha, and the lowest figure was in the 6th Lok Sabha when only 19 members could be elected. The highest proportion of women was 8%, in the 8th Lok Sabha (1984). In the Rajya Sabha, in absolute terms the highest number of women (29) was in 1980 and the lowest (14) was in 1970 not only women in the Indian parliament are few, but their participation is also not encouraging. Anju Dubey's study brings out some startling facts in this regard. Dubey overves:

> *Majority of women are there as either their husbands/fathers/ mothers were in politics or the family has a history of politics. Not many women from the grassroots level are coming up to the national legislature. It is, therefore, pertinent to question if they are the 'true' representatives of people's interest? Moreover, in cases where both husband and wife are in politics, there are two consequences – a positive one is that the woman has more exposure and support, but the negative one is – if they belong to the same political party then there is not merely comparison between the two but women are also discriminated against regarding positions of power. Further, even if she is capable, the credit goes to the husband.*

After 73rd and 74th Amendment Act were enacted, women have been conferred one third reservation in the local bodies elections. Even after this, their position has not improved much. They are being used by their male relatives as a rubber stamp.

The vast gap between theory and reality with regard to women's actual role in democratic functioning in modern India makes it clear that women's empowerment is a precondition for the success of democracy in India. A cursory look at the women's movement for empowerment in India would show that it could be divided into four phases. The first phase was indeed not one of the women's movement by women, but by the social reformers who were, by and large, men. They were moved by the most pitiable conditions of women in society and felt that Indian society could not develop unless the conditions of the women improved. The crusaders in the dominant Hindu society were Raja Ram Mohan Roy, Swami Dayanand Saraswati, Ishwar Chandra Vidya Sagar, etc. These social reformers fought against the system of sati (women's cremation with her dead husband) *purdah* (diel) and child marriage. The reformers supported widow remarriage and education of women. The movement launched by these social reformers had a limited goal. Their main aim was the reform of Hindu society and women's issues were tackled from that point of view. Basically, none of the social reformers challenged the male domination of the patriarchal system. Rather, it could be said that the movement launched by them was to make the patriarchal system a bit humane. Nevertheless, the social reform movement has created some social awareness amongst women.

Some very specific notions which are prevalent in the dominant ideological framework to the intellectuals, social reformers and politicians have to be examined here. One such notion is that women in India, in contrast to the women of advanced countries, have achieved political and democratic rights without much struggle. "The Indian Constitution guarantees political equality through the institution of adult franchise and Article 15 which prohibits discrimination inter-alia on grounds of sex. It should be kept in mind that this recognition of political equality of women was a radical departure not only from the socio-cultural norms prevailing in traditional Indian but also in the context of the political evolution of even most advanced countries at the date." It is also said that in spite of India being a backward country, a large number of women had participated in the national movement, especially after Gandhi's entry. Besides, it is also emphasized that the social reform movement, which contributed to the emancipation of women, was a launched in India primarily by male social reformers.

Women still lag for behind men in top political and decision-making roles, a waste of talent given that their access to education and healthcare is nearly equal, the World Economic Forum said on the Wednesday.

In its 2008 Global Gender Gap report, the think tank ranked Norway, Finland and Sweden as the countries with the greatest equality between the sexes, while Saudi Arabia, Chad and Yemen were the least equal.

Averaging 130 national scores, the report found that girls and women have reached near-parity with their male peers in educational attainment, health and survival, in both rich and poor countries. But economically, in terms of workforce participation and earning opportunities, and politically, in terms of empowerment, the gap between the sexes remains large.

"The world's women are nearly as educated and as healthy as men, but are nowhere to be found in terms of decision-making," said Saadia Zahidi of the WEF, a Swiss-based think tank.

"Given that women have almost closed the gap with men on health and education, it is a waste of their talents if they are not catching up in economics and politics", she said. The report uses UN and other data to weight how evenly each country shares it resources and opportunities between men and women. The Nordic countries of Norway, Finland, Sweden and Iceland once again took the first four places, with Norway the highest-ranking. China climbed 17 places from the previous year but still ranked just 57th.

Outside the Nordic region, which traditionally scores well on measures of gender parity, New Zealand placed fifth, in part because of its female political empowerment including the tenure of Helen Clark as Prime Minister. The Philippines, whose president is a women, followed in sixth place, and Ireland, the Netherlands, and Latvia placed eighth, ninth and tenth respectively. The US ranked 27th , ahead of its neighbour Canada for the first time since the gender gap report was launched three years ago. Trinidad, Argentina and Cuba were rated highest among Latin American and Caribbean countries, and Lesotho was the top-rated African state in gender parity. Muslim countries had some of the worst ratings with Yemen at the bottom of the list.

Women's participation in decision-making is not only a demand of democracy or simple justice, but also a necessary pre-requisite of fighting out gender-based oppression and discrimination as also for their interests to be taken into account. Increasingly, the democratic system that assures equal citizenship and rights to women, its institutions and processes are providing themselves to be in no position to guarantee or implement these assurances. Hence, it is imperative to get into these institutions and processes, gain entry into the functioning of state and share the control over the apparatus of state. This along would lead to preserve and promote equality and justice, monitor and reverse the existing situation if these values are absent and bring about necessary policy changes and social structuring so as to usher in a humane and equitable social order. Women in decision making position in government and legislative bodies would contribute to redefining political priorities, placing new items on the political agenda that reflect and address women's gender-specific concerns, values and experiences.

It has been the long sustained gender-bias which has obstructed their entry into the politics. Sir William Blackstone's observation in this 'Commentaries on the Laws of England' that "no vote can be given by lunatics, idiots, minors, aliens, females, persons convicted or perjury, subordination of perjury, bribery, ... or by those tainted of felony or outlawed in a criminal suit simply reveals the impact of gender-bias from which even intellectuals cannot keep away. Even in twentieth century, a

British member of Parliament has the nerve to argue, "A women in the House of Common is a contradiction in terms". Al Bukharian Islamic text ordained that "A nation will never attain success whose control has been entrusted to a woman". So women had to fight hard for getting their claim transformed into legal political right. No phase of the feminist movement has been responsible for so much enthusiasm as the women's struggle for their enfranchisement. It was only after the First World War that this right was recognized for them. Even then, when the United Nations Charter was signed in 1945, the right was recognized only in 30 countries. There were still many states where the distinction between two sexes in this respect existed.

Thus, woman is trapped into the web of gender bias. In ancient civilization women were worshiped as mother goddesses and personification of the principle of the creation of life, of birth of nature after the death of winter and of the hope of resurrection of men himself. In ancient Egypt, Celtic Britain and Japan for example, Queens and empresses ruled their kingdoms and empires.

In Indian concept of Ardhanarishwar very well depicts this view. The 'Nirakar Bhahma' (the Almighty without a tangible farm) when willing to create the universe, assumes a tangible farm, the half of which is male - the 'Nar', while the other half is the female the "Nari". Together these two components make a complete body. Unfortunately this balance has always been lacking in human society. In India, there are numerous examples in great Hindu spics like Mahabharat and Ramayan which indicate the position of woman in general and of wife of particular as a piece of property[3].

Notes

1. Balraj Madhok, 'Hindu Raj', Vaicharik Vikalpa Prakashan, New Delhi, 1983, pp. 136-37.
2. P. K. Trivedi, From Hierarchy to Democracy: Rural Transformation and Political Empowerment of Dalit Women, *Vikash Vani Journal, A Quarterly Review,* Vol. 1, Issue 3, July-September 2007, pp. 12-13.
3. Valmiki Ramayan, IV 35, VI 101-15

15

The Myth of Gender Equity
Why are Women Missing from Politics

Narayan S. Kotvi

In his famous book, 'women in the past, present & future', August Bebel opine that oppression has been the lot of women from the beginning of the time. In spite of all changes in form this oppression has remained the same. In the explanatory note the Editors of the book Subrata Mukerjee and Sushila Ramaswamy says: "Women rather than slaves were the first human beings that tasted subordination and domination. The subservience of women from primitive times and the consequent differentiation made between men and women is rooted in the unique sexual functions women performed as child bearers. In course of time women's responsibilities got confined to bearing and rearing children, and managing their homes. As a result, the women were educated primarily to perform these tasks there by stunting their development and growth. This was used as a reason to exclude them from political participation and duties of citizenship and thus were reduced to a status of second rate beings. Women were denied property and inheritance rights, making them economically dependent on men. Socially, politically and economically women were made to expect an inferior and secondary status which was justified and defended with the help of scriptures, customs and traditions."

It is only at rare intervals during the long course of history that women became alive to the consciousness of servitude. Her position was lower even to the slaves. They further says,

"Servitude which lasts for hundreds of generations ends by becoming a habit. Inheritance and education teach (her) to regard it as a natural state. Consequently, women accepts her subordinate position so entirely as a matter of course, that it costs no little trouble to convince her of its degeneration and rouse in her the aspiration to become a member of society enjoying the same rights as man and in every respect his peer".

The basis of all oppression is undoubtedly economic dependence on the oppressor. This has been the condition of women in the past and it continues to be so to this day.

The question of gender equity, as we know it today, is a recent phenomenon which gained prominence especially during the last decades of the 20th century. Of course, now it is being critically analysed by a large number of women themselves. At first glance, it does seem as if women have made a quantum leap in terms of access to greater employment, better health facilities and improved standard of living. But on a closer look, we find that this has been confined mainly to the urban educated middle and upper middle class women. By and large, majority of women particularly in smaller towns and villages, lag far behind their male counterparts as they still carry the burden of patriarchal social structure and cultural ethos.The political and constitutional arrangements, all over the world tend to assume that masculine majority in offices and in politics can and does champion the cause of women. In other words, in a male dominated society, whatever men perceive as important assumes women's tacit approval and agreement. It has been so ever since mankind came into being, barring of course a minor difference here and there. It is also because women continue to be regarded as weakling both mentally and physically. In the words of Tennyson, "Woman is the lesser man." Unfortunately everything in our social and political set-up has conspired to give credence to this statement.

In the United States of America, which otherwise claims to be the most advanced democracy of the world, there is a saying that in every great national emergency there is always a man ready to meet the challenge and meet the same nobly and with understanding. There is no mention of women's contribution in the progress of the nation. It was because of this chauvinistic approach that women did not get right to vote, let alone contest for the legislative bodies in America, till full suffrage was introduced in 1920. It was also this mindset that the democrats were reluctant to nominate Hillary Clinton for the Presidency. Thus, male chauvinism has always underestimated the contribution and potential of women.

Roles Ascribed by the Society

Though as individuals, women have been participating essentially in all spheres of human activities, yet as a group, they have been and are being identified with particular roles ascribed by Society. These roles are commonly presented as naturally linked to child bearing and infant care. Even in societies where women have been given broader responsibilities and power, men have normally dominated formal political life. With the emergence of classes, religions and States, male chauvinism has been strengthened. However, despite this discrimination, neglect and suppression for ages, it goes to women's credit that whenever they have been called upon by circumstances to enter in to the so-called man's domain, by sheer dint of hard work and courage they have always left a distinct mark.

Women's Emancipation

Emancipation of women depends on three aspects- education, social and economic status and political empowerment. Education and social & economic status acts as locomotive for social change. However, it is not something that happens on its own rather, it has to be made to happen. The State should not only give priority to women's education and try to uplift their economic and social status but also encourage social reforms movement to rid society of dogmas.

Political empowerment on the other is key to gender equity. Perhaps it is with this realisation that it is being increasingly debated today at various fora all over the world. It has evoked enough heat and, in a peculiar sense, has shaken the man's citadel. Even though women have now earned the right to vote in almost every country, yet their struggle for exercising political power in proportion to their number appears to have just begun. There are far too men in politics and that, according to Harold Wilson, is its problem. The role of women in politics is still nominal.

There are two aspects to male domination. First, politics perpetuates the traditional patriarchal father-son relationship in the form of patronage and clientship, which excludes women from material benefits. Second, it is a fraternal perspective from which politics is seen as a form of male solidarity. As a result, women remain subject to a political culture that is essentially patriarchal. This has definitely proved to be a stumbling block in the path of women's emancipation. It should be understood that women, and women alone, can comprehend issues concerning their welfare. To ensure this, they must be represented in Legislatures and decision-making bodies in large number. Their emancipation is not possible as long as men continue to take decisions on their behalf.

Representation in Legislatures

The figures brought out by the Inter Parliamentary Union (IPU) in its Survey of 186 countries in 1995 are startling even to the most optimist. According to the survey, the percentage of women representatives in the American Congress was merely 10.9, in the United Kingdom this percentage was 9.05. France known as the land of liberty, equality and fraternity, had even less women parliamentarians at 6.4 per cent. The survey further reveals that in countries, such as Bhutan, Cameron, Djibuti, Papua New Guinea, Kuwait and UAE, the Legislatures are exclusively-a preserve of men. In fact, the Constitution of Kuwait and UAE provide for equality of all citizens but allow only men to become members of their Legislatures. The only exceptions are the Nordic countries of Sweden, Norway, Denmark, Finland and Netherlands where the women parliamentarians range between a healthy 30 to 40 per cent of the total membership of the House.

To make further mockery of the participatory character of women in Legislatures, of the few women who attained the higher political offices, a large majority of them consists of the wives and daughters of the deceased heroes of the masses. It is very rare that women have achieved the highest offices on their own. Be it Indira Gandhi, Benazir Bhutto, Sheikh Hasina or Bandarnaike, none rose to positions of power on their own. They were pushed there because of the charisma of their fathers or husbands who happened to be the national heroes. There are only a few women such as Margaret Thatcher, Golda Meir, Sarojini Naidu, and for that matter, even Mamta Benerjee who rose from the ranks and created their own political space.

Why has this been so? It has to do with social set up, the male ego, their approach towards women and the male psychology of being superior that is explicit in the American saying as cited above. The political parties, being dominated by men who have a vested interest, also perpetuate this by fielding women candidates who do not have their own political bases or have no tangible work to their credit. This explains why women politicians in recent times have made no significant impression nor have any of them initiated significant legislations upholding women's rights or improving their social and economic status. The UN Commission on Status of Women in 1990 observed:

> "Despite the fact that most countries use democratic methods of choosing political leaders and making policy choices and that women make up half the electorate, relatively few women reach the highest level of political participation and even fewer become public decision-makers. Women are largely absent from most forums where policy decisions affecting women's daily lives are being made".

The Commission, therefore, recommended that "a critical 30 per cent participation threshold be regarded as the minimum for decision-making positions at the national level." Taking cue from this, Sweden was the first country to establish reservation for women in 1992. Thereafter, Costa Rica promulgated a law of equality for women. Argentina, Cuba and Venezuela have since established quota laws to ensure increased female representation in Legislatures.

Similarly, The ANC in South Africa offered quota for women from its first democratic election onwards. In Argentina the quota resulted in increased women representatives from four per cent in 1991 to more then 16 per cent in 1993, and women's participation has risen to 28 per cent in Brazil, Mexico, Taiwan and Chile. In Japan reservations have been used to ensure appointment of more women to ministerial positions.

Reservation policy for women in formal political institutions, however, must not be viewed as a panacea for all social evils. It is nothing more and nothing less than an 'enabling condition' one that any State claiming to support equal justice to all has inevitably to create. How this is to be transformed in to an instrument for long term and broad-based empowerment of women depends largely on the effectiveness of grassroot movements working for oppressed and marginalised women in enabling them to seize and use such space. Women's empowerment is essentially a political task. It can not, therefore, be achieved until and unless a critical mass of women have access to formal political power by entering political institutions on a large scale.

The critics feel that reservation may divert women from the mainstream of politics and power; and push them into segregation whereby they will fight only women contestants. The elected women also run the risk of being looked upon as inferior representatives as they come to the House of people not because they are efficient and talented, but because they are women. However, this should apply equally to other weaker sections of society as well. Also, in the absence of political parties not volunteering to provide enough tickets to women there is hardly any other alternative to their empowerment.

Position in India

We Indians never tire of praising our past, especially our glorious vedic period. As legend has it, along with Rishis there were Rishi Kanyas to chant the holly words. It is said there was no discrimination based on gender, and both men and women were treated as children of God; the creator of the mantras of the Rigveda was Risika, a women sage, known as Surya Savitri. Unfortunately, after the end of this golden age the status of women in our society nose-dived.

What we were, is indeed important but what we are is even more important. The so-called protectors or exponents of our cultural heritage often forget, or avoid this aspect for obvious reasons. The issue, therefore, needs to be debated in its proper perspective.

The fact remains that women in our society are treated or even maltreated as second-rate citizens. How this prejudice started, or when it started is of little or no consequence. If, we are inheritors of the glorious past, as we are often told, we must prove it by making our present even more so. To do so, first we must accept that our society is riddled with social evils; especially discrimination against women. The discrimination against women begins from the womb itself, when female foetus is killed. The birth of a boy is celebrated while the birth of a girl is not. Ironically, discrimination against a girl child in respect of education, nutrition and domestic work begins at the hands of the mother who herself has under gone all this. Child marriage, forced marriage, dowry, resistance to widow re-marriage and *sati* system besides a host of other customary inhibitions, add up to make the girl child feel socially insecure and psychologically let down. Coming down to us as they do, as part of our cultural heritage for ages, we unfortunately try either to hide or to provide legitimacy to these social evils.

After independence, the task before us has been to rectify this imbalance by creating situation for meaningful and actual participation of women in the political and economic decision making-process. Ram Manohar Lohia once remarked that "caste is class in India" and if unity in Indian society is to be real, the women's question should be understood realistically within this fractured social, economic, cultural and political structure of our country. Unity in diversity is to be brought about by co-option and inclusion and not by imposition and exclusion. This is as true of women's representation in the political domain as it is in the case of other marginalised and oppressed groups in contemporary Indian society.

Striving for this goal the Constitution of India provides for among after things, equal opportunities in the matter of education, employment and other fundamental areas. There has been a progressive legislative measure relating to abortion, marriage, divorce, right to have children, right to property, maintenance, and family courts for speedy settlement of disputes and so on. The laws in relation to dowry, rape and violence against women have been made more stringent. All these measures should have emerged as enabling factors in the development of women but the laws did not achieve the desired result. Why? Because besides legislation, a radical change in outlook and perception of women's role along with appropriate support system is also important. All this have been very slow to come by. Consequently, even after more than a century of social reforms, the change, though discernible, is far from being indicative of parity between men and women. Even today "the cultural police" in our country spend their energies in demonstrating against films based on the plight of widows and night or pub culture (the protest against filming of a movie water and the recent incident in Mangalore where women were beaten up in a Pub are the instances of intolerance towards women's endeavour to equal rightst) rather than making use of their capabilities for rehabilitation and improvement in the lot of such hapless women. What more proof is needed to describe our ill-defined priorities and the sick state of mind.

Never the less, the Government on its part has taken a number of steps to set right the wrong done to the girl child. By one such step a 'Committee on the State of Women' was appointed in 1971.The report of the Committee entitled

'Towards Equality' was published in December 1974. Subsequently a separate department of 'Women and Child Development' was created. A 'National Perspective Plan for Women,' the 'Rashtriya Mahila Kosh' and a 'National Commission for Women' (NCW) were also established.

The Committee in its report concluded that even though women's number is large, yet their impact on politics has been marginal. As remedial measure the Committee proposed that each political party set a quota for women candidates. In the meantime as a transitional measure, it was decided that seats would be blocked for women in municipal councils and panchayats.

Subsequently, all the major parties in their respective election manifestos, decided to set aside 30 per cent nominations for women but they failed to keep their promise. It was because of this ambivalent behaviour of political parities and their leadership that 73rd and 74th amendments to the Constitution reserving 33 per cent seats for women at grass root level were passed by the Parliament in 1992. This has resulted in thousands of women being elected to positions of leadership and decision-making at village, block and district level. It was expected that this would overcome the centuries-old inhibition among women and encourage them to gradually shoulder greater responsibilities in Legislative Assemblies and in Parliament.

Unfortunately, the overall attitude to women's participation in politics has not yet changed. There have been reports, and correct ones, that men are enjoying power in rural and urban local bodies by getting their wives and daughters elected to seats of power. In most cases, it is actually the men who rules the roost and not the women who have been elected. In Haryana, U.P. and Rajasthan, it has been noticed that the elected women presidents of panchayats are not allowed to take independent decisions by their fathers and husbands, as the case may. The proposed Women Reservation Bill, reserving 33 per cent seats in Parliament and State Legislatures which has since been introduced many times in Parliament should be seen against this background. The aforesaid mental block that is coming in the way of the passage of this Bill. Besides Sharad Yadavs and Mulayam Singh Yadavs who have been openly opposing the Bill there are scores of other members across all the parties who play every dubious card to scuttle its passage even while supporting it publicly.

The approach of all the three Govts.- Narshima Rao, Vajpayee and Man mohan Singh on this issue been simply escapist. During the election campaign all parities pledges support for the Bill but their hypocrisy is soon revealed first, during distribution of tickets and then by their contradictory stands insides and out side the House. While distributing tickets for the 13th Lok Sabha, Congress Party nominated 51 out of 400 seats to women contestants. This was by far the maximum number, followed by 29 out of 319 by Bhartiya Janata Party, and four each by CPI (M) and CPI out of 73 and 54 seats contested respectively .The total number of woman contestants has shown a decling trend since 1991. It was only in 1996 Lok Sabha election that number of women constestants rose to 599 .But for this exception ,the trend has been one of steady decline that is 324 in 1991, 274 in 1998 and 247 in the 1999 elections. The situation has been similar in the fourteenth Lok Sabha. Out of 543 elected members only 46 are woman(Indian National Congress 13 of 147, Bhartiya Janta Party 10 of 136 ,CPI(M) 5 of 43, SP 3 of 38). In State Assemblies also the position is not any better either.

In short, all parties have so far failed to live up to women's expectations .When Sonia Gandhi assumed the office of Congress President ,she began on a positive note by promising to implement 33 per cent reservation for women in the party organisation but under pressure from within the party she failed to deliver. Because of the existing permutations and combinations in all the parties, the all-important question still remains whether the 'Women Reservation Bill' will be passed during this Lok Sabha at all. Doubts arise because the main persons opposed to the Bill not only constitute an important section of the United Progressive Alliance (UPA) but are also important members of the Man mohan Singh Government. Whatever be the shortcomings in the Bill, the best immediate course would be to let it be passed, keeping the option open to remove the flaws by an amendment at a later stage.

A Deeper Malaise

Be that as it may, women's empowerment remain a fundamental issue as it is linked to the broader question of the status of women in society. Besides reservation in Parliament/ State Assemblies, the real issue worrying women today is the growing decline in the male female ratio in certain States of the Country. The marriage and succession laws of both Hindus and Muslims, provides little space for their individuality. The inequality that stems from lack of educational opportunities and economic dependence is also a major concern. To achieve the desired status in society women will have to win their own battle. First of all, they will have to strive to change the male chauvinistic mindset nurtured over the ages.

As for electoral politics there are people who question the decision making and competitive capabilities of women during elections. The fact, however, is that these arguments are used as a ploy by political parties and by men controlling them to keep women away from politics. The 'winnabilty' criterion falls to pieces if, we look into figures since 1957 (data for which is available). The percentage of winning woman candidates in all these elections have been higher as compared to men as shown in the table below.

Percentage of Winning (Men and Women Candidates Separately) during Lok Sabha Elections from 1957 to 1998

Election year	*Percentage of winning men*	*Percentage of winning women*
1957	31.70	60.00
1962	24.00	50.00
1967	21.03	44.08
1971	18.05	24.04
1977	22.01	27.01
1980	11.05	19.07
1984	09.02	25.06
1989	08.05	13.06
1991	05.09	12.00
1996	03.08	06.01
1998	10.02	15.07

Today, the need to bring in more women members into the Legislatures is felt more strongly as on the whole women are found to be less corrupt and responsible .They are natural managers and can manage society and the government as well as they manage the families. Because women manages the families well, they need not be confined to it, rather for this very reason, they should be inducted into politics so that society and governance are managed better. Even otherwise, why leave politics to being the hunting ground for men alone, leaving fifty per cent of the populace out of it. The question which is more pertinent is, why should men go on taking decisions on issues relating to women's problems?

A beginning has to be made at some stage. The year 2001 was declared women's empowerment year. It was expected that all parties would come together in both the Houses of Parliament and pass the 85th Constitutional Amendment Bill. Unfortunately, it could not happen due to lack of consensus and even today its fate continues to hang in the balance. But seeking of consensus on this issue should not be the end in itself nor should lack of consensus be used as an alibi to postpone or dump it. The latter seems to be the strategy of all the Central Governments ever since this Bill was introduced in 1996. If, the government would have been really sincere, it should have put the Bill to vote, if need be a joint session of Parliament could have been called as was done by the NDA Govt. in the case of the 'Prevention of Terrorism Act (POTA). If a joint session can be called to pass POTA why not for the 'Women's Reservation Bill'. Among all the parties the left parties' stand on this issue has been most consistent. The Congress and the BJP have also publicly declared their support to the Bill but pressures from with in these parties have put a question on their sincerely. These together constitute enough numbers in Parliament to pass the Bill of they are sincere to this cause.

Yet, the all-important question is whether the political elite of this country really wants to pass such legislation. Do they really have the political will to do so? Let us hope that despite bickering on the issue within the ruling parties and in the

Opposition ranks better sense would prevail and the Bill will finally be passed during the on going session which is last session of the Manmohan Singh Govt., otherwise, gender equity will remain a myth, a subject to be discussed in seminars and coffee houses only.

References

Explanatory note provided by the Editors (Subrata Mukerjee and Sushila Ramaswamy) to the first chapter of the book 'Women in the Past, Present and Future' written by August Bebel in 1879. A book which is considered as the most-authoritative text with in the tradition of socialist feminism. Deep and Deep Publication's, New Delhi.

Ibid.

16

Women Political Leadership in Bihar (A Study of Inhibiting Factors and Prospects)

P. K. Yadav

Introduction

The poor participation of women in political process is a problem not only of India but it is so every where. A study made by United Nations Development Fund for the year 2000 to achieve greater participation while the so called developed countries lag for behind. U.S.A. has only 12% share of women in the Congress. In India women's position in the family and society and her participation in public affairs has been traditionally low. The reservation for women in political reservation in the political process can not change the status of women in the family and society[1].

The committee on status of women appointed in 1971 which submitted its report in 1974, opined that participation of women in the political process is almost negligible and because of inequality in their status and political power they have acquired the features of minority groups. The intentions of a male dominated society may be better gauged from the fate of the 81st Constitution Amendment Bill which was introduced in the Parliament in 1996. Barring few, most of the political parties are not sincere in providing 1/3rd reservation of seats to women in Parliament and State Legislatures. It is clear from the positions they give them in their organizations and the tickets they give to women candidates for elections to the Parliament Constitution Amendment has no impact on the political participation of women has increased enormously. The efforts of the State governments in this direction are commendable. Though the elections for grass roots institutions in 1995 and 2000 have resulted in the greater political participation of the women in the Pradesh yet the dependence of women on men in the decision making process continues. It may require social and family efforts particularly from male members.[2i] Despite constitutional and statutory provisions in favour of women's political participation, there is enough evidence to prove that they have been found less participative in politics. Those few who have been into politics, are largely either patronized or proxy leaders. In Bihar, their share in power structure has been far behind their male counter part.[3] Thus it is also pertinent to examine the factors inhibiting them (women) in taking roles in the politics in Bihar milieu.

The Historical Factors

The pitiable plight of women in our society needs no introduction. However, a precise illustration of their position in the political system of Bihar needs to be underlined. The women have been placed at the weakest point in our social arrangement and in family structure. They have been victim of perpetual violence and oppression in family and in society which inhibit them to take part in public affairs. The situation is more deplorable in terms of exercising franchise, contesting elections to legislatures, being members of Council of Ministers and party organizations etc. even though their share in electorate is in proportion to their share in the total population. Further more, those few who get an opportunity to represent their constituencies take little interest in legislative business perhaps driven as they are by patriarchal notions of our society.[4]

Historically speaking women in India have been deprived, at least politically. Let us look in modern times. Hindu women rarely, if ever, encountered a British or western woman besides the missionaries. Nevertheless, while discussing the Hindu women's movement or their education, one may presume that it must have been influenced by the presence of British women in India. The Hindu and British women, however, continued to live in isolated worlds and interaction between them was limited and exceptional. The stereotype portrait that they had of each other gave no impetus to imitate, identify or seek mutual communication. The British woman lived in the company of women from her own country and was preoccupied by the social entertainment provided by the clubs. Their knowledge of Indian women was based on the writings of missionaries and journalists who portrayed them as backward, oppressed and religious. The Indians regarded the British women as bold and aggressive with a peculiar standard of morality and propriety. They derogatorily referred to them as *mems* a term also used by them to put down the anglicized Hindu woman.

Hindu and British women occasionally came together for charitable or philanthropic work. Wives of important government officials and Viceroys interested themselves in the welfare of Indian women and children. Women from elite and progressive families or women heads of state were similarly involved. Lady Reading and the Begum of Bhopal met occasionally to discuss the political problems of the Begum as well as their mutual concern and interest in the welfare of women and children.[5] The practice of *purdah* observed by high caste/class Hindus, the rules of caste and lack of a common language were effective barriers to any significant communication between the two groups of women. Formal social events, at which a few Hindu women were hesitatingly present, did not lead to any understanding of each other's life styles, attitudes or values, Interaction was inhibited, artificial and meaningless.

With passage of time, elite Hindus, under the influence of the West, had recognized the need to modify traditional mores concerning women. The life of a Hindu woman would conform to the standards of humanitarianism and rationality, women would be educated and oppressive customs would be prescribed. Interestingly enough, although the elite accepted and recommended this change, they had as yet not formulated their image of the new woman, since in this case, more than in any other situation, they desired to retain the essential spirit of Hindu culture. The Hindu woman, despite, her education and liberation was expected to identify and reflect the virtues of womanhood as portrayed in literature and mythology, and fulfil her prime responsibility as a wife and mother. The inherent contradiction of education threatening the traditional pattern of relationships between dominant males and females was not recognized.

The upper caste/class Hindu were suspicious of the missionaries and of their efforts to educate women. They feared that the schools were being used by them for evangelization. Elite families were, therefore, faced with a dilemma if they desired education for their women they had necessarily to expose them to the efforts of the missionaries either in their schools or the zenana missionaries and Christian governesses. Reform organisations such as the Brahmo Samaj and the Arya Samaj opened schools for girls to stem the tide of conversion and to meet the need of women's education. In schools such as the Arya Kanya Pathshala established in 1890 by the Arya Samaj, Hindu girls could be educated without being exposed to the threat of conversion and westernization.[6]

The political actors (males) were with the women of India, and the enthusiastic acceptance of their new roles, can be explained within the framework of nationalist politics. Indian politicians were no doubt concerned with women's welfare; nevertheless their attitude towards the women's movement had political implications. The political controversy between Indian nationalists and the British Government centred not only on the right of Indians to govern their country, but raised the issue of their ability to do so. British bureaucrats expressed doubts about the capacity of Indians, once they were possessed of political power of creating and administering a modern, independent sovereign state. In addition they were sceptical about the commitment of Indian leaders to introduce social, economic and political change. The political debate emphasized the goals that Indians should necessarily follow if they were to emerge as an industrialized state. Indian leaders were confident that they could change India socially, economically and politically once the British were removed from the centre of power.

Gandhi took the lead in early 20th century who emphasized not merely political reform but included social regeneration and change as an integral parts of his policy. The oppressed situation of Hindu women was regarded by the British as an example of the backwardness of all Indians. The congress party was therefore committed to inclusion of women in almost every aspect of their programme. The equal participation of women in public affairs was expected to demonstrate the progressiveness and moral superiority of all Indians. The politically conscious Indians were anxious to overcome the image of a backward and colonized race whose inadequacy had provided the opportunity for a foreign government to administer their country. Nationalist politicians were seeking to assert to the British Government and their Indian and Western audience the dignity and self-respect of all Indians. There is no evidence that reflects any doubt or controversy among the leaders and political parties about the new and active role of women outside the home. There must have been some apprehension and concern over its impact on the family or on the women themselves, but due to a consciousness of the oppression against women in the past, as also for political reasons, a discreet silence was maintained. The autobiographies and biographies of male leaders generally commend and support liberalization of oppressive conventions and restrictive customs. Small and Whatever, it may be, the anti-colonial struggle attracted women from various castes and communities. The issues involved in the discussion of women's presence and role in politics such as the desire to counteract criticisms of Hindu social organizations or the question of role definition were problems associated with Hindu conventions and traditions. A handful of British women such as Mira Behn, Annie Besant and Margaret Cousins were involved in the various issues of this period. The exceptional case like that Annie Besant's participation in the nationalist movement did indicate to Indian society that political roles were available to women.[7] The problems encountered by British women in Indian society or their acceptance in the roles of politicians, reformers or religious devotees was from a set of values different than that applied to Indian women. British women in India did not provide a role model for The category of immensely isolated women were the Muslim. Muslim women's involvement in the movement is slightly different from that of the British women. Hindu and Muslim women had shared a common experience of subordination and oppression. British women also did not enjoy an egalitarian status in their society, although the difference between them is in the nature and extent of sub-ordination. The Indian National Congress was dominated by Hindu politicians and further Gandhi's leadership and propaganda had strong religious (Hindu) overtones. Wives of Muslim politicians did participate in a limited way in politics. For example, the wife and mother of Muhammad Ali gave up their life of seclusion and joined politics after his arrest. A direct attempt to mobilize Muslims to join public life was made by the Muslim League in the 1940s. A large number of Muslim women participated in the movement for the formation of Pakistan. Such activities of women politicians does not suggest that they were questioning or challenging Hindu social organizations or the position of women within it, Rather, women politicians expressed their commitment to Hindi ideals of womanhood and accepted the prevailing division of roles and functions by sex.

Social Factors

Backward and dalit categories of women in the state are the worst sufferers, particularly in political arena. These categories of women cannot cope up with affluent women who have better economic and educational background. Human Rights Watch (H.R.W.) report rightly observes, "dalit women face the triple burden of caste, class and gender ..... Sexual abuse and other forms of violence against women is used by landlords and the police of inflict 'lessons' and crush dissent with in community"[8]. The dalit women can hardly be found in Bihar politics but for a few exceptions like Bhagwati Devi. The dalit women have to be encouraged to take part in politics at least at the grass roots level. They are engaged on a continuous basis to earn their livings in most cases as agricultural labour, it is rather difficult, if not impossible, to draw their time and energy towards political participation.

Simple political participation cannot be said to be sufficient opportunity to exercise political rights at par with the male counterparts who acquire dominance in decision making process. If we take gender biases are always dominant round the globe. It is a global phenomena that there are very few women in powerful and influential public position. Even in western world, politically sensitive, women are supposed to be have not been adequately participative. Stacey and Price have rightly observed, "Acceptance as persons in their own right in the western world has not brought to women an equal share of the power or even with considerable share. In politics the situation of women is worse in numerical terms in Britain now, despite there being a woman prime minister.[9] Not only this the communist thought do also not place women as class-proletariat, petty burgoise etc. The central point of which is equality among social classes. Socialist societies, communes, reformists and revolutionary societies have remained male dominated. In advanced capitalist societies, the older forms of women's power have been so far eroded and their private domain so utterly invaded by husband, father and state advisers, that women have no choice left to them but to seize an equal share of political power.[10] Social, economic and psychological situations of women in India has placed women at the bottom of political power hierarchy. They have been branded as weaker race, tender, mother housewife, and they have weak public domain, political awareness, activities and are placed at weaker points in social arrangements. Some perceive them as 'neither ruler nor ruled, they are simply invisible in the world of public affairs'. Scholarship has found that women enjoy lesser power with little discussion on the issue.[11] Siddiqui finds that the laws and legislations, made in favour of women in India, do also not properly empower them to come forward to acquire power positions.[12]

The few women politicians, who have been closer to power structure, are either patronized by male politicians or are proxy leaders. It will not be out of place to mention that the rise in women voters turnout is more often than not caused by votes polled by malpractices during polls. They hardly are placed at the decision making bodies of the political parties in the States.

A study of National Commission for Women in India finds that most of the women said they were affected by the problems in shape of malpractices during the elections evident from the fact that a sizeable number of respondents in Harayana came out with much dissatisfaction by way obstacles and problems that the women faced during the polls. Quite a few (30 per cent) said they had no problems[13]. There were, of course, a few families, which did not allow or were not happy with the women entering politics. In Haryana a Joint family broke up, in Dehradun two cousins contested against each other, and the families broke up. One Haryana woman said clearly that she was not allowed to campaign. In Garhwal region, 22 women had not received any co-operation from the family, the main reason being, the husband who was away in service, had no interest in politics. Many women also had to face derisive comments, particularly from males that the women were illiterate, old, incapable and poor, and that they were not financially sound and cannot extend loans.[14]

Most significant to note that the social factors heavily came out as obstacle in their political role taking. Many mentioned the patriarchal view of men and even women, which considered that women were not capable and not fit for politics. Some women candidates also found illiteracy to be a handicap. Inability to read and write, or because they were economically not well off. Quite a few women also found social environment to be unfriendly and the *purdah* system disabling them. Domestic work, childcare duties, lack of mobility partly due to social reasons etc. have also been the main handicaps in electioneering. This was also found in case of Bihar. Many elected women found themselves unable to take roles in the panchayat bodies due to domestic work and childrearing related functions.[15]

Besides most of the women contestants faced a variety of problems. Most of them faced opposition from political parties (Possibly those to which they were not affiliated). Many women from various parts of India mentioned that the opposition of political parties who even held out threats and perpetuated violence in one case in Garhwal, the opposition party distributed liquor in her home and spread malicious rumours about her. There was also opposition to women contesting from general seats. This was particularly true at the higher levels of Zila Panchayats where the elections were fought on party tickets and the parties had much stake. Many women also found it difficult to campaign because of lack of mobility, transport and social taboos. Campaigning in late evenings and nights was difficult. In Tamil Nadu, instances of teasing, financial constraints, non-availability of support services and lack of transport were reported. Further, a respondent reported that she was forced to withdraw her candidature, because she was not a native of the constituency as she had been living there only after marriage. She was a Muslim and had married a Hindu. Her family was threatened of dire consequences if she did not withdraw. Women in her area refused to co-operate though she had been living there for nearly a decade. But the Mahalir Mandram of the area, which helped her to win, supported her. On the contrary, many women all over India said that the family members were helpful, that they gave them moral and even financial support and campaigned for them. In some case, of course, men alone campaigned.[16]

Physical harassment, battering, assaulting, dowry killings, depriving of property rights, economic independence, male dominance in marriages divorce, immoral trafficking, eveteasing, repes, and so on are some prevalent modes of oppression and discrimination against women. These forms of violences generate fear among them.[17] Threat of use of force make women to do or not to do a thing which they would have not done or done respectively in a normal situation. Crime against women is no doubt a universal phenomenon but the situation in India is very alarming. The government of free India incorporated several provisions in the constitution, enacted laws, made five-year plans for women empowerment but they have not met with any tangible result. No effort can soothe the frustration of women unless they come forward to shape their destiny from the grass root level. In rural areas of India the position of women is in dire straits. It is the irony of the fate that the soul of India reside in villages and their position is at lowest ebb. Village development hinges critically on improvement of living conditions of men, women and children in them.[18] The primary crime against women begins in the womb itself. "Man asserted that inferiority of women was willed on heaven and advantageous on Earth". The hundred million "missing women" of India as Amartya Sen has termed them go missing as daughters and sisters not widows or wives. They are all the victims of that original discrimination a girl child faces at the fetal, natal of postnatal stage, which decides whether she is 'empowered' to live at all. Gender-based inequality in social, economic and political life is worldwide.

Million of girls and women suffer from violence and their consequences are caused by their sex and their unequal status in society. Violence against women is a serious violation of women's human rights. Yet little attention has been paid to the serious health consequences of abuse and the health needs of abused women and girls. Women who have experienced physical, sexual or psychological violence suffer a range of health problems, often in silence. They have poorer physical and mental health, suffer more injuries and use more medical resources than non-abused women. The most common forms of violence against women are physical, sexual and emotional abused by a women's husband or intimate partner. Preliminary results from a World Health.

The empowerment process is one where women find a 'time and space' of their own, and begin to re-examine their lives critically and collectively. This enable women to look at old problems in new ways, analyse their environment and situation, recognize their strengths, after their self image, access new kinds of information and knowledge, acquire new skills, and initiate action aimed at gaining greater control over resources of various kinds. This is spiral not a cycle which leads to greater and greater changes, and more empowerment. Consciousness, problem identification, action for change and analysis of that action and its outcome lead to higher levels of consciousness and better planned and executed

Bihar is a state of simple societies under the domination of men. It is an agrarian society operative within a semi feudal framework of social relations. Therefore social life in Bihar is characterized by growing violence, disorder leading to political turmoil. Literacy rate is very low. Exploitation breeds dissatisfaction among women and they keep themselves aloof of public life. Taking into account the socio-economic background of women in Bihar we can assess their status in politics.

Let us conclude with the words of Mrs. Krishna Bose, a Member of Parliament who said, "Women are distributed all over the country. They fear that they may be deflected from the main stream of politics and power and pushed into segregated corner where women will fight women in election. And the elected women run the risk of being looked upon as an inferior representative. As if she has come to house of the people not because she is efficient and talented but just because she is a women. No self respecting women can agree to such a situation."[19]

But the situation has now changed. There are bigger scopes created for women in politics. The need is to make them self assertive and enabled with inner strength. There is a paucity of strong women personalities in politics from central to local level. There is also lack of representation of women issues in most elected bodies. Women need to participate more actively in the political process. One may wish that empowerment had come about through the natural evolution of society as a whole and society should transform, as change is desirable. Society should change through the effects of education and family welfare measures rather than by legislation from the top. But since every thing cannot be left to time reservation of seats for women in legislature can be taken as a positive step.

Notes

1. O. C. Sud , "Empowerment of Women", *Vidhanmala*, Volume 8 Nos. 1 & 2, January-December 2001, pp. 87-90.
2. *Ibid*
3. (i) R K Verma and G K Yadav, "Women in Bihar Politics", *Economic and Political Weekly*, 13 February 1996 (ii) Henna Tabassum, Women in Politics, Bharati Pustak Sadan, Patna, 2008
4. Prabhawati, *Mahila Vidhayak: Bihar Vidhan Sabha Mein Unki Bhumika,* Bharat Pustak Sadan, Patna, 1996.
5. David Laushey, The Bengal Terrorists and their Conversion to Marxism: Aspects of Regional Nationalism in India, University of Virginia, Ph.D. Dissertation, 1969, Unpublished, p. 235.
6. Kenneth Jones, Arya Dharm : Hindu Consciousness in 19th Century Punjab (Berkeley: University of California Press, 1976), pp. 103-108 and 215-18.
7. Kalpana Dutt, Reminiscences, Transcript of Interview with Kamladas Gupta.
8. Human Rights Watch, Broken People of India: Caste Violence Against Untouchables, H R W, New York, 1999.
9. M.N. Srinivas, Social Change in Modern India (Bombay: Orient Longman's, 1972), pp. 46-89.
10. See Vijay Agnew, Elite Women in Indian Politics, Vikas Publications, New Delhi, 1984.
11. This is not necessarily limited to that generation or time. Evidence of similar situations can be found throughout the 19th and 20th century.
12. (i) Fatima E. Siddiqui, Political Women: Country Experiences in Identity and Gender Debate, Kanishka Pub; New Delhi, 1999 (ii) also see Prakash Tandon, Punjabi Century (Berkeley: University of California Press 1968); Nirad Chaudhuri, Autobiography of an Unknown Indian (Bombay: Jaico Publishing House, 1951).

13. National Commission for Women, Women in Panchayat Raj, NCW, New Delhi, 2004.
14. *Ibid.*
15. Prabhawati, *op. cit,* pp. 54-55.
16. National Commission for Women, *op. cit.*
17. M.N. Srinivas, Social Change in Modern India (Bombay: Orient Longman's, 1972), pp. 46-89.
18. Niroj Sinha (ed), Women and Violence, Vikas Publishing, New Delhi, 1989.
19. Kalpana Dutt, Private interview, 28 September 1973; Kalpana Dutta, Reminiscences: Chittagong Armoury Raiders (Bombay: People's Publishing House, 1945); Transcript of interview with Kalyani Bhattacharjee and Kamladas Gupta.

17

Women's Share in Power Structure (A Study in Context of Political Justice)

Henna Tabassum

Proportionate share in the decision making process is a vital component of political justice to a particular section of society. Simple political rights at par with their male counterpart sections which acquires dominance in decision making process will not suffice. If we take political justice in consideration at the highest level of political arena, the gender biases are always dominant round the globe. It is a global phenomenon that there are very few women in powerful and influential public positions. Even in western world where women are supposed to be more exposed to public affairs, lack power in public domain. Stacy and Price have rightly observed, "Acceptance as persons in their own right in the western world has not brought to women an equal share of the power or even with considerable share. In politics, despite there being a woman prime minister, the situation of women is worse in numerical terms in Britain now ..."[1] (p. 173-74). Not only this communist taught do also not place women as class-proletariat, petty burgoise etc-the central point of which is equality among social classes. The women leadership has a very faint potentiality in our world. If women wish to make changes in the society, they live in; they must seek and achieve power positions. It is essential that woman should enter the political arena since the societies are all male dominated. State socialist societies, communes, reformists and revolutionary societies have remained male dominated. In advanced capitalist societies, the older forms of women's power have been so far eroded and their private domain so utterly invaded by husband father and ssate advisers, that women have no choice left to them but to seize and equal share of political power.[2]

The typical Indian society has a peculiar placement of women in the social setting as well as in family settings that inhibit women to acquire political formal positions and even roles in public domain. Social, economic and psychological situations of women in India have placed women at the bottom of political arena. The male dominant Indian society inhibits women avail political justice particularly in power sharing. They have been branded as weaker race , tender, mother housewife and they have weak public domain , political awareness, activities and are placed at weaker points in social arrangements. Some perceive them as neither ruler nor ruled, they are simply invisible in the world of public affairs. Scholarship has found that women enjoy lesser power with little discussion on the issue.[3] Siddiqui finds that the laws and legislations, made in favour of women in India, do also not properly empower them to come forward to acquire power positions.[4]

Violence against woman has been the major factor that inhibits women to come into political arena. Women in Indian society are subject to various kinds of violence, oppression and discrimination. Physical harassment, battering, assaulting, dowry killings, depriving of property rights, economic independence, male dominance in marriages divorce, immoral trafficking, eve teasing, rapes and so on are some prevalent modes of oppression and discrimination against women. These forms of violence generate fear among them.[5] Enormous Indian women face severe harassment due to unfulfilled dowry demands and many are victims of homicide, pre-malnutrition and poor medical facilities. All these foster a deep and inescapable sense of dependency in women who left with no alternative but to continue to live with and depend on abusive partners for want of any other choice. Threats of use of force make women to do or not to do a thing which they would have not done respectively in a normal situation.[6]

Despite all these, women have roles to play in the decision making process of our polity. It has been seen that level of women's political participation has been increasing day after day, may it be far below the men. There is general agreement that women have very less share in power structure particularly in India.

Now the question is-what do we mean by power structure? Every nation has a national government with authority over the entire nation and a series of local governments each of which has authority over a particular sub-national geographical area known variously as state, province, country, shire, department commune etc. All the levels have governments manned by politicians and bureaucrats. Thus these governments are run really by certain set of persons placed in the structure of the government the oldest and most persons placed in the structure of the government the oldest and most persistent typology of governmental forms rests on the key variable i.e. location of power. The Greek philosophers have typified the government on the basis of location of power.[7] In the democratic systems, many political scientists conceive of democracy as a form government, decisions are ultimately controlled by all the adult members of society. But another school of political scientists believe that government decisions do not emanate from the commands of any sovereign, not ever the people or the popular majority rather emanate by the political elites. C.W. Wrights Mills angued that behind the façade of popular elections in representation public policy a small identifiable ' power elite' make the decisions.[8] Here we come to a conclusions that it is the council of Ministers which really take the decisions, if taken the case of Indian political system or other such systems.

But it cannot be safely said that only the council of Ministers constitute the power structure of a democratic political system. It is argued that the decisions are taken by negotiations and compromise among the social groups concerned and each group has something closely approaching a veto over any proposed policy. These social groups and their interests are articulated in federal systems.[9] Thus the members of legislatures can be taken to be part and parcel of the power structure is the council of Ministers and a broader power structure is the legislature. Thus the issue of political justice to women has been examined here by discussing their share in ministry and legislature. In this context, their roles and share in ministry has been discussed here.

The Council of Ministers

According to government of India Act 1935, four seats were reserved for women in federal assembly of which one was reserved for Muslim women. However, in Bihar executive body, there is no evidence to prove that women were included in Executive Council of Bihar before independence according to congress manifesto10 of 192, 15 per cent of seats were to be spared for women in Bihar but it could not be complied with.[11]

After independence, the women's share in Union Executive has been very meagre if we look it in proportion to population. But in Comparison to their share in legislature, it can be found that their share has been greater. The following Table 1 shows the actual position.

Table 1
Women in Union Council of Ministers

Lok Sabha period	*Size of Ministry*	*No. of all kinds of women Ministers*	*Percentage of women Ministers*
1st L.S.	35	3	8.57
2nd L.S.	41	4	9.75
3rd L.S.	54	6	11.11
4th L.S.	55	5	9.90
5th L.S.	55	4	7.27
6th L.S.	45	2	4.44
7th L.S.	54	5	7.72
8th L.S.	40	4	10.0
9th L.S.	40	2	5.0
10th L.S.	60	8	13.44
15th L S	78	8*	11.2

Source: A. P. Kohli, Council of Ministers, Gitangali Pub. New Delhi,1983 and Manorma year book

* for these figures see The Times of India, 29-5-09

The above table shows that instead of increasing the number of woman ministers it, has gone down with the passage of time and change of Ministers has declared. However, at present the number of women ministers has increased in percentage terms.

Since we are more concerned with Bihar, let us have an idea of women Union Ministers from Bihar.

The following Tables 2 reveals the pictures.

Table 2
Women From Bihar in Union Ministry

Lok Shabha Period	*Size of Ministry*	*Women Ministers*	*Percentage*
1st L.S.	35	–	–
2nd L.S.	41	1	2.43
3rd L.S.	54	1	1.85
4th L.S.	55	1	1.81
5th L.S.	55	00	0.00
6th L.S.	45	00	0.00
7th L.S.	54	2	3.70
8th L.S.	40	1	2.50
9th L.S.	40	1	2.50
10th L.S.	60	1	1.67
15th L S	78	1	1.23

Source: India: A Reference Annual and The Times of India, Patna 29-5-09.

The figures of above table show that Bihar has had poor share in union ministry. The aspect of coin tells different story. All the time, the women minister from Bihar were not of the cabinet rank, they were either minister of state or deputy minister. This shows that, in the real decision making process, women have been kept away. At present, only women minister in union ministry, it can be found that similar women cabinet minister were placed each time except during third Lok Sabha while there were three cabinet rank women ministers.

The Bihar Council of Ministers have had given very little share to women during the initial decades of independent India. The following Table 3 will justify it.

Table 3
Women in Bihar Ministry (upto 1970)

Year	*Size of Ministry*	*No. of women*	*Percentage*
1952	13	0	0.0
1957	21	2 (Deputy)	9.52
1962	21	2 (part. Secy.)	9.52
1967	21	1 (Deputy)	4.76
1969	32	1 (Cabinet)	3.01

Source: Bihar Vidhan Sabha Library Documents.

It is markable fact that there were altogether six women ministers in Bihar of which one was in the rank of cabinet, there in rank of state minister and two in the rank of parliamentary secretary. It did not improve in post 1970 period in number terms but every time women minister of which one was in the rank of cabinet, three in rank of state minister and two in the rank of parliamentary secretary. It did not improve in post 1970 period in number terms but every time one women minister was one cabinet women minister out of 32 sized ministry. There was one each in cabinet and state rank woman minister during 1972 to 1975 out of 33 ministers. During 1975-77 there was only one women minister of cabinet rank.

It is also a notable fact that the women ministers were not changeably picked up in the council of ministers, rather similar woman was made minister every time. The following table shows the picture.

Table 4
Women Ministers who Sustained Share

Name of woman Minister	*Years*
Jyotirmay Devi	1957,1962
Rajeshware Saroj Das	1957, 1962
Manorama Pandey	1962,1972-73,1973-75
Sumitra Devi	1962,1963,1967,1977,1988
Ram Dulari Sinha	1971,1972,1973,1975
Uma Pandey	1980-83
Prabhawati Gupta	1580-83
Shusheela Karketta	1985-88,1988-89,1989-90

Besides these women minister, there were some more women ministers who could not repeat their terms. Those were Shushila Sahaya, Lalita Rajlakshami, Kaushalya Devi, Gayatri Devi and Jyoti. However, it is clear that after 1977 new faces entered into the power structure of Bihar who remained in the power seat till 1990. after the general electrons of 1990 no party could get the clear majority. As a result the Janata Dal with support of left parties, jharkhand Mukti Morcha and Bhartiya Janata Party initially the government was formed with formed with only nine ministers inclusive of one women cabinet minister named Sudha Srivastawa who was parliamentary secretary in 1977. Even after expansion of the cabinet of Bihar to 1991 the number of women ministers could not go up considerably. A new trend could be marked that the women included in ministry were drawn from non-dominant social groups.[12]

There is need to examine the trend of political parties in providing share to the women in the council of Ministers. The facts reveal that the congress party provided greater share to women in comparison to other political parties. The following Table 5 shows that women ministers were greater whenever congress was in power and Janta Dal, Rashtriya Janta Dal, Samata Dal and NDA and remained renamed in power. The Table 5 shows the situation upto 1990.

Table 5
Women Ministers and Political Parties (1952 to 1983)

Year	*Congress*	*SSP/BKD*	*J.P.*
1952	0	NIP	NIP
1957	2	NIP	NIP
1962	0	NIP	NIP
1967	1	NIP	NIP
1972	6	1	NIP
1977	NIP	NIP	6*
1980	2	NIP	NIP
1985	6	NIP	NIP

* includes five parliamentary secretaries

Notes: NIP stands for Not in Power

The situation after 1990 changed which is reflected in the following:

Table 6
Women Minister and Political Parties (1990-2000)

Year	*Congress*	*J.D./NDA*	*RJD*
1990	NIP	1	NE
1995	NIP	NIP	3
1997	NIP	NIP	1+2=3
2000 (3rd to 10 march)	NIP	0	NIP
2000 (11 March onwards)	1	NIP	2

It is to be noted here that in July 1997 Mrs. Rabri Devi became Chief Minister of RJD government and again on 11th march, 2000. it can also be marked that Mrs. Rabi Devi is said to be a proxy leader and the real power is enjoyed by her husband Laloo Prasad Yaday. A list of women ministers is enclosed with this chapter.

It is difficult to mark the role of women ministers in the proceedings of cabinet meetings.

Notes and References

1. Margaret Stacey and Marion Price, Women Power and Politics, Travistock Pub., London, 1982.
2. *Ibid*, p. 189
3. Fatima E. Siddiqui, Political Women: Vountry Experiences in Identity and Gender Debate, Kanishka Pub.; New Delhi, 1999.
4. *Ibid.*
5. Niroj Sinha (ed), Women and Violence, Vikas Publishing, New Delhi, 1989.
6. *Ibid.*
7. See Austin Ranney, Governing: A Brief Introduction to Political Science, 2nd ed; Dryden Press, Illinois, 1975.
8. C. Wright mills, The Power Elite, Oxford University Press, New York, 1956.
9. Austin Ranney, *op. cit.*, pp. 208-231

10. AICC, *Economic Review*, Vol. 8, No. 1-4.

11. Sarojini Sharan, "The Role of Women in Bihar General Elections 1967". *Journal of Public Administration*, Institute of Pub. Admn... 1968 (P.U.)

12. Prabhawati, *Mahila Vidhayak: Vidhan Sabha Meion Unki Bhumika*. Bharati Pustak Sadan, Patna 1997.

PART–4

Women Political Empowerment

18

Women and Political Empowerment

Manjari Verma

People's participation in political activities is the essence of democracy. Attendance at public meeting, taking part in agitational activities, attendance at study circles of political parties, voting in elections, membership of a political party, participation in election campaign, party activism etc. are some of the important indicators of political participation[1] wherein the world over, women are struggling to challenge the uneven distribution of power and authority today. It is being commented in both print and electronic media that the time has come to recognize that the hand that rocks the cradle is the power that rules the world. Pandit Nehru had clearly visualized that a country can develop only when women have a full chance to play their part in public life: "when women move forward, the family moves, the village moves and the nation moves"- are the words delivered by him about empowerment of women for the development of the country. Viewed thus, women should have every right to be recognized as co-citizens of the country and secure a gender- equal space in the horizon of politics.

Recognising the growing importance of political empowerment for women, the United Nations adopted

Convention on the political Rights of Women in 1952. Since 1975, four international conferences on women have been held under its auspices[2]. But the global awareness concerning the issue came to the forefront during the Fourth World Conference on Women in Beijing in 1995 when women's equal access and full participation in decision making was emphasized in the platform for Action as being one of the critical areas of concern. It unequivocally declared:

> "...women's equal participation in political life plays a pivotal role in the general process of advancement of women. Women's equal participation in decision making is not only a demand for simple justice or democracy but can also be seen as a necessary condition for women's interests to be taken into account."[3] Accordingly, various recommendations were issued to all national and international governmental agencies for enhancing women's participation in political arena and decision making. It also affirmed that women should have at least a 30 % share of decision making positions.[4]

Obviously, the issue of political empowerment of women has attracted the global attention. But many scholars in developing countries dismiss the idea until their socio-economic status is improved and more pressing need for health, nutrition and education are fulfilled. But Dr. Niroj Sinha has supported the Human Rights argument that as 50% of the population, it was unjust that women are underrepresented in Parliament[5]. Historically, instances of women's active political participation during national freedom struggle and J.P.Movement particularly in Bihar bears testimony to the fact that women had successfully proved their potential strength and courage to meet the potential strength and courage to meet the challenges of time. During that period, women came out of their houses to move freely in society and attained political status resulting in the automatic lifting of many social restrictions earlier places on them.

After independence, the government of India has been successful at the macro level in initiating a number of legislations, programmes, policies and planning procedures for the last six decades. However, it was only with the setting up of the committee on the status of women in India in 1971 that the demand for greater women representation in political institutions was systematically taken up for consideration. Earlier, the focus had been only on improving the socio-economic status of women. The committee recommended reservation of seats for women in municipalities and urged political parties to adopt a definite policy regarding percentage of women candidates[6]. In 1990, the National Policy for the Empowerment of Women, 2001, has assured that "women's equality in power sharing and active participation in decision making including decision making in political process at all levels will be ensured for the achievement of the goals of empowerment. All measures will be taken to guarantee women equal access to and full participation in decision making bodies at every level, including the legislative, executive, judicial, corporate, statutory bodies as also the advisory commissions, committees, Boards, Trusts etc. Affirmative action such as reservations/quotas including in higher legislative bodies will be considered whenever necessary on a time bound basis. Women friendly personnel policies will also be drawn up to encourage women to participate effectively in the development process."[7]

Experiences in the past decades have shown that despite general acceptance of the need for a gender balance in the political process, the actual political participation of women at the higher levels of decision making has not changed significantly in terms of inclusion of marginalized sections within governance process. In fact, very few women have been successful in subverting the boundaries of gender and in operating in a very aggressive male dominated sphere. The Lok Sabha elections in May 2004 elected just over 8% female candidates to the Lok Sabha with proportions of contesting and elected women candidates varying considerably among political parties as shown in the table given below.[8]

Partywise Women's Electoral Performance

	Female Contestants			*Male Contestants*				
	Contested	*Won*	*Women candidates elected (%)*	*Contested*	*Won*	*Men candidates elected (%)*	*Proportion of women in the fray (%)*	*Presence of women in Lok Sabha (%)*
Bharatiya Janta Party (BJP)	30	10	33.3	334	128	38.3	8.2	7.2
Bahujan Samaj Party (BSP)	20	1	5.0	415	18	4.3	4.6	5.3
Communist Party of India (CPI)	2	0	0.0	32	10	31.3	5.9	0.0
Communist Party of India (Marxist) (CPI) (M)	8	5	62.5	61	38	62.3	11.6	11.6
Indian National Congress (INC)	45	12	26.7	372	133	35.8	10.8	8.3
Nationalist Congress Party (NCP)	5	2	40.0	27	7	25.9	15.6	22.2
Total for national parties	110	30	27.3	1241	334	26.9	8.1	8.2

Source: Election Commission of India, *www.eci.gov.in*

In 1973, the passing of 73rd and 74th Amendments to the Constitution of India in 1973 has served as a breakthrough towards increasing political empowerment of women which provided for reservations of seats in the local bodies of Panchayats and Municipalities for women, laying a strong foundation for their participation in decision making at the local levels. Female political participation and leadership in the local panchayats does have political implications for the future became evident from women outnumbering men in 2006 in Bihar when the government granted 50 per cent reservation for women in Panchayats and local bodies, thus ensuring fair share to the fair sex. Undoubtedly, this decision brought about a crucial change in the patriarchial mindset of the people of rural Bihar according to a report published in the Hindustan Times, dated 7th of March, 2006 given below:

> *"It seems male domination of society is going to be a thing of the past as a large number of men all over the district are reported to have taken over the responsibilities of the household kitchen where till yesterday, they thought it unmanly even to be seen."*[9]

On 15 Dec,2008, in Jaipur at a State level consultation on women's representation in local politics, Geeta Sharma presented a ground reality by informing that 83% of the elected women were from the non-political families, 29% illiterate and majority were elected for the first time. Very encouraging indeed. But due to many underlying hurdles like male dominance from background in decision making, failure to understand technical aspects of budget, etc. the participants underlined the need to build relationship between informal networks and civil society organizations for women's advancement in politics.[10]

Thus, it is evident that mere provisions for women cannot bring about miraculous changes overnight. Of course, factors like apathetic attitude of political parties and other vested interests, women's lack of access to skill and training, illiteracy, information isolation, cultural and traditional barriers, stereotypical gender roles etc. are there to restrict their entry into political arena. But the million dollar question still remains how to achieve political empowerment for women? Personally,

I feel that this crucial goal can be achieved to a great extent by using technological devices. Getting Information technology to women, particularly in rural areas, will be a difficult and huge undertaking but as other alternatives are few and more expensive, the know how and training in computer literacy is becoming an indispensable tool for organizing and mobilizing women from local to international levels. If our women can make use of cellular phones to know the welfare of their near and dear ones and can use electronic voting machines during elections, they can also benefit themselves from emerging new technologies in many ways. For example, the Self Employed Women's Association in our country organizes electronic discussions through Panchayati Raj in which village women often pose questions that are answered promptly by a panel of experts. Through translation modules, responses go to the women in their vernacular language. Recently, Microsoft on 3 February 2009 announced several initiatives aimed at enabling Indian users to compute using several Indian languages (The Hindu, Feb. 4, 2009, p. 18) with a view to overcome language barrier. The company has also made available for free download 45 virtual keyboards for use in 12 Indian languages[11]. Thus promotion and training in IT can enhance political empowerment of women in the following ways:

- To end women's isolation and give them a voice
- As a tool for networking women for social and political advocacy
- To strengthen women's participation in the political process
- To improve the performance of elected women officials
- .To improve women's access to government and its services
- For education
- For the dissemination of indigenous knowledge

IT is a dynamic tool to improve governance and strengthen democracy. It is particularly powerful for giving a voice to women who so frequently in developing countries have been isolated, invisible, and without a voice. Information technology can contribute to the political empowerment of women as tools for networking to perform social and political advocacy, to strengthen women's participation in the political process, to improve the performance of elected women officials, to improve women's access to government and its services, to educate, and to disseminate indigenous knowledge. IT is particularly useful in increasing the transparency of accountability of government—an application from which women can particularly profit. IT increases the number of ways in which women can participate directly in politics and civic life. As Vikas Nath says:

The new models of governance open up avenues for direct participation of women which so far has been limited to representative forms of participation in which women were insufficiently represented. These models would lead to a more interactive and proactive form of communicating with officials in the local governance spheres in a process which will lead to greater transparency and accountability of their actions. The notion of distance and time would become meaningless as the technologies have the capability of working at all times and from all geographical locations. It also means that women in rural areas for whom time is a scarce commodity and for whom it is absolutely impossible to commute to public offices—the new technologies would enable them to leapfrog to an altogether different platform where they can voice their opinions and communicate to the concerned person without additional burden on their time or commuting large distances.[12]

It is encouraging to note that attempts are being made by various government and non governmental agencies to bring about modern technological devices within the reach of the poor and the illiterate women of our country. With two women stalwarts, Mrs. Pratibha Patil and Mrs. Sonia Gandhi sitting at the top of nation's politics, let us hope that our women will march forward towards 21st century with IT equipped education and training-a must for their political empowerment.

Notes and References

1. Sethi, Renu (1988), "Determinants of Women's Active Political Participation,"the *Indian Journal of Political Science,* Madras, Vol. 49, No. 4, Oct.-Dec., p. 565.
2. Pam Rajput (2001), Women's Political Participation in India: An Agenda for Empowerment, in Promilla Kapoor "Empowering the Indian Women" by, Publication Division, Government of India, New Delhi, p. 226.
3. *Ibid.*
4. *Ibid,* p. 227.
5. Sinha, Niroj (1989), Women as Marginals in Politics, article published in Pramila Dandvate (ed.), 'Widows, Abandoned and Destitute Women in India,' Radian Publishers, New Delhi, p. 68.
6. Sharma, Priyanka (2008), Women's Empowerment and Working Women, Book Enclave, Jaipur, p. 132.
7. Shalini, Women Empowerment, Novelty & Co., Patna, p. 197.
8. Election Commission of India, *www.eci.gov.in*
9. *Hindustan Times* (Patna edition), 7th March, 2006, p. 5.
10. *The Hindu,* Dec. 17, 2008, p. 3.
11. *The Hindu,* Feb. 4, 2009, p. 18
12. Vikas Nath, "Digital Governance: Building and Sustaining Democratic and Accountable Governance Structures using ITs," p. 9. *http://www.cddc.vt.edu/digitalgov/gov-menu.html.*

19

Political Empowerment of Women in the New Millennium

Saloni Prasad

Gender and political empowerment have been a major issue in the 21st century, and it is necessary for both the civil societies and governments to set an agenda for these in the new millennium. The absence of democratic context has contributed to slow progress in empowering women, particularly in South Asia, mainly due to gender subordination and ideologies of male dominance. Even in India, democracy is more than 50 years old, yet the ideals of democracy are far from destination specially for women in India. Women play a marginal role in politics. Their political participation is almost invisible, However, importance of women's political participation is being increasingly realized in all the corners of the world and to think of a democratic government without their participation is unthirkable. To empower them socially, economically, educationally and politically should be of utmost importance.

Prema Cariappa, Chairperson of the Central Social Welfare Board, while inaugurating the one-day national conference on "Empowerment of Women in Parliament and Local Self-Government Institutions: Role, Status, Participation and Decision-making" organized under the aegis of the Tirupati based NGO, Academy of Grassroots Studies and Research of India, said Ahat political empowerment of women alone would ensure participation of women in decision making and changing India's future. She pointed out that with every panchayat raj elections, ten lakh women were being inducted into the democratic process I of the country. She also added that it is necessary that women should be a part, of the decision process of the nation and that political empowerment is essential for gender justice and equitable society.

One finds that women elected representatives are unable to exercise their leadership because they are unable to articulate the priorities of the their constituency and influence the decision making. Their naivety is exploited by men both within household and institutions of governance. In the absence of support group, they are unable to articulate strongly their concern. Women leaders need to articulate the needs and priorities related to rights, entitlements and basic service provision of their constituency, participate in social planning and policy development and act upon them. They need skills, knowledge and information to articulate their concerns and influence the decision making as per their concerns.

With a view towards strengthening women's leadership in governance, studies on women leadership towards gender' mainstreaming in governance and an exploratory study on gender violence in local governance in UP and Bihar have revealed that there has been discrimination against women in these institutions. They have often faced serious problems in performing their duties, mainly because they are undereducated and inexperienced and are ignorant of administrative proceedings. Indifference and non-cooperation of the male counterparts constrain their ability to perform better. So, what is now needed is that social perceptions about women leadership needs to be changed through gender sensitization. In order to participate efficiently, they need to be backed by strength and support from the constituency. Strengthening of women leaders can help in addressing gender priorities.

In the new millennium, with women participating more and more in politics, myriad of innovative political education programmes have been developed. Information dissemination, capacity building, awareness raising, translation of skills into practice – all aim to increase women's understanding of social, economic and political forces and enable them to gain control over such forces. The scope of education for political empowerment today includes a wide gamut of arenas of human resource development such as education, poverty, alleviation, gender equality, environmental sustainability, reduction of HIS'/AIDS etc. The women leaders need to understand the new issues and trends so that they can take up programmes that are action-oriented, practical and relevant to the needs of the women leaders directly. Education for political empowerment would enable the women leaders to articulate their needs and priorities clearly as well as negotiate the unequal structures of power from a position of strength. Empowerment can be seen as providing the capabilities. Multifarious learning needs of potential women leaders needs to be assessed as a basis for developing their political empowerment as well as self- development. Life- histories, challenges, motivation and milestones of selected women-leaders should be tracked down for the upcoming women leaders in order to boost their participation in politics.

So, political empowerment of women in the new millennium has only two goals:

1. take measures to ensure women's access to and full participation in power structures and decision making.
2. increase women's capacity to participate in decision making and leadership.

In order to achieve these goals, the governments have to establish:

(i) the goal of gender balance.
(ii) create a critical mass of women leaders in strategic positions.
(iii) let women hold 50% of marginal and decision making posts.
(iv) political parties should integrate women in elective and non-elective positions.

(v) protect and promote women's equal rights.

(vi) support women public leaders through an active vibrant women's movement to provide technical support., information and solidarity.

(vii) ensure economic empowerment of women.

(viii) conceptualize a framework of women's leadership such as the responsible use of power, challenge corruption and promote a culture of peace and non-violence.

> Political empowerment of women can only be complete when women empower themselves as well as 'be empowered'. This relates both to individual and collective empowerment. Indicators of true empowerment show that increasingly women are breaking the traditional boundaries and stereo-types-for instance taking up ministerial positions in previously male-dominated sectors such as defence, finance and finance affairs. Condolezza Rice and Hillary Clinton are befitting examples. Indeed, it would be a true delight to reverse the positions and appoint men to positions previously viewed as women's domain such as women's affairs, children and community services. A fresh impetus is required with a modern approach, in order to politically empower women. An Equal Opportunity Commission needs to be created. Post the 4th World Conference on Women in Beijing, Hong Kong has been the only Asian country to create an E.O.C. While Gandhi's dream of gender equality has been adopted successfully by the West and implemented elsewhere, it remains a distant dream in India. Only together, on an independent platform, can we change this and bring Gandhi's vision of equality to India's women.

India has a rich history of exemplary political leaders who happen to be women- from the might of Rani Ahalya Bai, Rani Laxmi Bai to the continual influence of Indira Gandhi - all attest the strength and wisdom women have brought into the political domain. Although India has been inching towards the increased political empowerment of women, there is still 'a long way to go. Today women only account for a dismal 3%

of the current administration and 8% of India's political representatives. The formation, in the early 1990's of the National Commission for women has been an important step forward. However, it's main role is to "wipe the tears of women", whereas we also need an E.O.C. counterpart to "strive to bring smiles on women's faces".

Various alternative strategies to increase women's political representation are being suggested every day, widely debated, but are mired in discussions and difficulties. Potentially, a third house for women's representation can be set up. Another suggestion has been the expansion of the Rajya Sabha by 100 seats set apart for women acamedicians, professions, journalists and NGO's.

What we need is to mobilize our efforts together to build a neutral lobby group. Only then can our respective voices find the visibility necessary for change. Together on a single and neutral platform', we can concentrate our efforts to raise our vibrant voices for 'Vaishvik Bhagnivad' i.e. global sisterhood.

The planned neglect of women is a major concern for Modern India. Today, the female literacy rate, stands at 54%. The percentage of women in different sections is 'as follows: 8% in the Parliament, 3% in the ministerial posts, executive bodies of political parties 9%, High' Court judges 3% and 7% in civil services. The demand qf medJ4 fpr q sRpor women is dwarfing the achievements of the average woman who is making tremendous contribution in nation building which is almost going unnoticed. The 20'h century cry 'women demand half the sky' has created a base for the lobbyists to work for one-third representation in the legislative bodies, jobs, awards etc. There is however a growing need by women to have their own space in Indian society.

There must be a networking forum which can" be called '100 Women's Forum'- which can have women representatives from various sectors like govt. departments , political leaders, business icons, social activists , academicians and women from media, art and culture. They all can work together as a think tank to influence the policy makers for providing more space to women in India. They can interact and arrive at a consensus on key issues like leadership, insights into best management practices and become role models for young generation of women in the country.

Thus, women's political empowerment is definitely a quintessential cornerstone concept in social change theory, much discussed, often elusive and sometimes abused. Yet in the context of development in the new millennium, women's leadership and agency in social change have' been levers for women's empowerment within communities. Women have indeed garnered through their collective strength, a new' The tight rope walk that requires gender equality ideals to be sought and pursued all the time and with the greatest passion even while the fight against poverty, oppressive social structures or repressive state policies is on.

References

Mehra Rekha, Women Empowerment and Economic Development: Director of economic analysis at the International Centre for Research on Women in Washington DC.

Batliwala, S., The Meaning of Women's Empowerment 1994. (Harward Series on Population and International Health).

Political Empowerment of Women: High Level Inter-governmental Meeting to Review Regional Implementation of the Beijing Platform for Action, 26-29 Oct. 1999.

Margaret Schuler and Shakuntala Kardigaman, Legal Literacy, a Tool for Women Empowerment: Edited by New York, United Nation Development Fund for Women, 1992.

20

Theory and Practice of Women's Political Empowerment (An Analysis in Context of Voluntarism and Social Capital)

Shobha Kumari Gupta & Anjana Kumari

Introduction

Centuries old subjugation, deprivation and oppression against women perpetuated with institutionalized methods by the male-dominant society, particularly in Indian milieu, have inhibited women to take up roles in social domain. This is high time to free them from these traditional shackles and enable them to take activities and put the resources and ideology under their control.[1] So far our society is concerned, there are classes among the women, say Scheduled Castes, Scheduled Tribes, Backward Castes, rural, poor, slum dwellers and uneducated are among those categories of women who are more vulnerable than other categories. They interface two pronged deprivations–from family and society–as a result, they remain in fetters at large till life. There are following predominant assumptions that prompt us to attempt this paper as a curtain raiser:

1. The Indian socio-economic and cultural environment is inadequately conducive to improve their situation,
2. The political institutions and actors (political parties) have largely ignored the women lot, particularly the

weaker categories of women in terms of giving them adequate opportunities and political education,

3. Their psyche and unique physical texture have also inhibited them to come up despite the feminist movements.

As such the present paper intends to examine the key words–voluntarism, social capital and women's political empowerment in their theoretical and practical contexts. Of course the analysis is based on special reference to Bihar polity. Thus paper has been organised in two parts - the theoretical tenets involving women political empowerment, social capital and voluntarism and practical issues in the same context.

Conceptual Considerations

Voluntarism: The voluntarism (actions taken by the voluntary associations) has been the subject of study of, by and large, three disciplines–sociology, social psychology and public administration. Sociologists whose contribution is significant in this regard, studies the associations as part of the social system; social psychologists are concerned with voluntary associations in an environment of their individual members; and the students of public administration are concerned with their organizational processes.[2] There is lack of comprehensive research efforts so far to explore the motivating sources of voluntarism, which is required in case of political motivation among the deprived classes. Inequality among individuals is a perennial source of motivation for voluntary action in any society, whatever is the state of its development. Inequality may be in material, moral and intellectual terms. A F C Bourdillon[3] observes that it has always an element of betterment of compensating inequality and motivating individuals to volunteer their services. Social services are designed to help compensate for the inequality and to uplift the under privileged. There are five sources of voluntarism - religion, government, business, philanthropy and mutual aid. The Missionary zeal of the religious organizations, the commitment of government organization to the public interest, the enterprising urge in business, the altruism of philanthropist and motive of self-help among fellowmen, all are reflected in voluntarism. At the operational level, the above components may not differ much from one another but each of them is moved by an impulse with dedication as the common motivation. On the other hand, its character changes in conformity, both with changing views of the problem of the state action and with the growth of spirit and substance of democracy. In deed, as long as there are rich and poor, privileged and deprived and subjugated and dominant exist, the social service will continue in some degree. Voluntarism has always been present in the society but with it has been mingled, from time to time, motives and impulses which have changed greatly from age to age, whether attributing the sufferings of the poor people to religious or secular roots.

India has had a long tradition of voluntary services for the upliftment of the underprivileged groups like women, children and others in social welfare field. In recent years there has been a major shift in attitude to community involvement. Approaches that saw the communities' primarily passive recipients of any policy reforms have been given way to those which seek to make more of the potential that more active community participation might offer for enhanced accountability and improve responsiveness in services. The voluntary organizations can also be means of empowerment of those with least power, by acting for, on behalf and under the control of them. They can do this as a campaigning organization exercising more political leverage on behalf of the needy or by transferring state resources into the control of least powerful. This ideological alliance left and right on behalf of devolution of power has created immense pressure for expansion of the roles of the voluntary and non-governmental organizations. The development funds are channeled through such organizations. Thus their role becomes significant. Here another dimension is added, that is 'political' perspective of the voluntarism, which sounds unique but not impossible.[4]

Political Empowerment: The term 'empowerment' denotes that there is a class de-powered in the society, which needs sensitization and empowerment. Thus, empowerment has three basic contents control, freedom and enabling. Freedom refers to freedom from subjugation, deprivation and oppression, perpetuated through institutionalized methods. The women have been prey or victims of these for the centuries. Maladies perpetuated by patriarchal norms not only in India, but also in almost all societies need to be eliminated if women are to be really empowered. Empowerment requires their freedom. Freedom alone cannot empower them rather they should be enabled to participate in social, economic, political and cultural spheres of life. The women have been victim of all these kinds of shackles from centuries. In other words, they would have to be incapacitated to face the social domain, enjoy the economic independence and roles in political spheres i.e. political participation, may it be of any degree.[5] Power itself can be simply defined as control over resources and ideology. The resources over which control can be exercised fall into five broad categories: Physical resources like land, water, forests, Human resources like people, their bodies, their labour and skills; Intellectual resources like knowledge, information, ideas; Financial resources like money, access to money, and the Self that unique combination of intelligence, creativity; self esteem and confidence. Similarly control of ideology means the ability to determine beliefs, values, attitudes, virtually, control over ways of thinking and perceiving situations. Those who have power are those who control material and knowledge resources and the ideology, which governs both private and public life, and are thus in a position to make decisions, which benefit themselves from independence and participation in public affairs without fear and patronage.

This control confers on decision-making power, which is used to increase access to and control over resources. If we accept this definition, then it is clear, women in general, and poor women in particular, are relatively powerless because they do not have control over resources, and hence little or no decision-making power. Yet the decisions made by others affect their lives every day. Often, even the limited resources at their disposal such as a little land, a nearby forest, their own bodies labour and skills are not always within their control. They have always attempted, from their gendered position as mothers, wives and workers, to not only influence their immediate environment; but also expand their spare. But the prevailing patriarchal ideology, which promotes the values of submission, sacrifice, obedience and silent suffering, often subverts even these attempts to assert them or demand some share of resources.

Thus, the process of gaining control over the self, over ideology and the resources which determine power-may be termed empowerment. The term empowerment is rooted in the theories of Paul Freire[6], who put forward the notion of 'conscientization' as a process by which the poor could challenge the structures of power and take control to their lives. Freire's analysis, however totally ignored gender as a determinant of power. Thus, by expanding Freirian analysis and giving gender an integral place, feminists put forward the concept of women's empowerment.[7]

The term 'political' refers to 'shaping and sharing the power is political'. In other words, any thing–action, idea, and incident that relates to 'power' can be termed as 'political'. Thus the political empowerment of women denotes their role in political sphere i.e. political participation, political behaviour and actions related to influencing the decision making process and participating in the process of governance. Political participation has been considered as a voluntary action employing legitimate methods to influence the choice of public policies, administration of public affairs or the choice of political leaders at any level local or national. Voting, the most common, is one of those actions that are considered as political participation. S M Lipset, Sidney Verba and many others have defined political participation as participatory engagement of aggregate individuals either in formal or informal modes, of course to influence the decision-making processes.[8] Milbrath, Ahmed and several others have categorized the level of political participation right from expression of political will to hold a public or political office.[9]

Social Capital: The term has been in prolific use by the social scientists particularly in context of analyzing democracy, political participation or grading the quality of democracy. Putnam's works are worth referring.[10] The concept is not concerned with formal associations but refers to trust, networks and norms shared by a group of actors that enable them to act together more effectively to pursue shared objectives. It is a resource - a capital that consists of relations one has with other people. It is social since one cannot have it in isolation, contrary to human capital.[11] It does not refer to any social or political action rather a condition or situation in which a group of actors feel united or togetherness. For example, if a group of unprivileged people such as dalits lives in same place but do not trust each other and have not shared norms. It is much less likely to act together against the oppressor. On the other hand if they trust and share norms (social capital), they can act effectively against the oppressor. Thus this concept is useful in understanding the functioning of democratic institutions in the segmented societies like India in general and Bihar in particular.

Women's Political Participation

A sizeable of the women contestants and PRI members were found to be dependent on their male family members who either provided immense support to their leadership roles or alone performed on their behalf in almost all spheres of grassroots politics. The issue of women's affiliation with political parties throws light on the fact that women leaders were largely dependent on their male family members. The affiliation of women to political parties was not based on any ideology but on merely socio-political contacts of their mentors or some one who were known to them. Besides, most of the women contestants in the PRI elections had no prior experience of political activities. A sizeable of them did not even participate in campaign for their own elections as their male family members took up the responsibility. In short, despite their ensured entry in the grassroots level power structure, they are found less vibrant to utilize the opportunities created by politico-legal arrangements (reservation provisions) for acquiring share in power structure at the micro-levels.

The situation in Bihar has been found a bit better in comparison to the national findings. It was found after Panchayat elections (2001) that women could win 37 per cent of positions as against 33 per cent reservation. The post of panchayat headship (mukhiya) saw trivial share for women (0.9%); however, their share at the upper layers of PRIs (Panchayat Samiti and Zila Parishad) was higher in that comparison (ranging between 10 and 20 per cent). Their higher share at the two upper layers of the PRIs does also not match with their male counterparts. It is interesting to note that Bihar Panchayati Raj Act 2006 has made a drastic provision of reservation in favour of women (50% per cent of all categories for women). This has assured certain entry of women into the power structure at lower levels in proportion to their population. But the trend of proxy leadership among women does also prevail in the state of Bihar. The illustration in various studies depict that their family members pitted the women candidates, as the seats were reserved for women. A sizeable of the women PRI leaders admitted that they had neither awareness nor interest in the 'power-play'. Their male family counterparts on their behalf, do all. However, in those areas where voluntary agencies were active, the women were able to win from even unreserved seats. It has also been found interesting that most of the women candidates in those areas (falling under the operation of the voluntary organizations) were from the voluntary activists and nearly 70 per cent of them were elected from their respective seats.[12] In short, it is evident from the present study that though the substantial share to women in power structure at the grassroots level is not visible, yet the voluntary agencies have made them assertive to the endeavours for acquiring the their due share. It will take some time to mature, as we know that Rome was not built in a day.

The Voluntary Agencies At Work[13]

The core voluntary organization working in the field of preparing people, particularly the deprived sections of the society, for the Panchayat election in Bihar has been 'Centre for Communication Resources Development' (CENCORED) popularly known as 'Sansarg' in Hindi. It had promoted a large number of grassroots level voluntary development organizations. Established in 1989, the jurisdiction of 'Sansarg' is limited to the territory of Bihar. Its main objective is to support voluntary development organizations (VDOs), which promote people-centered development through participation and partnership with special focus on women and people from the deprived sections of society. It also aims at providing training, communication network and conducting research and evaluation studies to support and promote the working of VDOs at village level.

'Sansarg' took up the Panchayati Raj related programmes and activities in the State of Bihar, just after the passage of 73rd Constitutional Amendment Act 1992, in order to promote and strengthen the grassroots level democratic institutions. This voluntary organizations has conducted over 100 programmes in which around 5000 participants from over 350 VDOs took part, out of which as many' as 2736 were female. The 'Sansarg' has taken upon itself the task of educating the poor, illiterate, ignorant, deprived people for participating in the democratic process at grass roots level from which they distance themselves because of the fear of oppression.

It launched the programme way back in 1995 and covered activities such as (i) people-centered communication based learning programme, (ii) coaxing people to learn (iii) instilling courage and confidence in them to share and exercise their rights, (iv) intonating the available instruments, and (v) impact assessment. In performing these activities, 'Sansarg' chalked out a systemic line of action and entrusted hundreds of local voluntary development organizations. The 'Sansarg' brought all the like-minded NGOs on a common platform, which is known as 'Panchayati Raj Chunavpurva Jagrukta Abhiyan Samiti' in Bihar. The focus was on building people's critical consciousness, ideas, values and attitudes and making people behave rationally. Promoting maximum participation of the masses during Panchayat elections, maximize the participation of the woman as voters as well as candidates, and (iii) to minimize violence during the polling process etc. are among the broad objectives of this Samiti.

The Samiti has developed a system of two way 'communication net work' by establishing information centers at district, block, panchayat and gram Sabha level which are equipped with trained volunteers to impart training to the people and effectively liaison with government functionaries. These centres were entrusted to the VDOs working in the area. They imparted training by organizing rallies, cultural shows, plays, meetings, door-to-door canvassing, wall writings as well as using audio visual modes. These were planned to function in three periodic frame i.e. pre-election, during election and post-election scenario. Besides making people conscious of their participation in political process, these intended to support the measures for the conduct of peaceful and free and fair election. As such, after taking up the programme, 'Sansarg' first of all held meetings with networking VDOs' arranged for the training or grassroots resource person at all levels and reviewed its on going programmes. Having these centres, programmes and objectives, Sansarg focused especially on women and dalit sections of society as target groups. For this purpose *'Kishori Panchayats, Paramshakti Mahila Samiti'* at *Gramsabha* level were formed. The Kishori Panchayats, literally means Panchayats of young girls, were formed of adolescent girls of the village who would be incubated into future women leadership. These girls are trained with an objective to educate elder women in their families and community about the Panchayat system and elections. To quote 'Sansarg', "the Kishori Panchayat is a setting, designed and developed to have access beyond the barricaded segments of the community without breaking the barricades. If the information centre as an instrument provided the backward-linkages, backward in the sense of age groups, in the sense of deprived sections, in the sense of gender discrimination and in the sense of income groups, in the years to come when these adolescent girls blossom into womanhood, they become the active participative/responsive women of the society". These girls are also made to participate in other communication modes such as street plays, cultural programmes etc. It is interesting to note that there is no formal organizational structure for these Kishori Panchayats. 'Paramashakti Programme' (an abbreviation for 'Panchayati Raj Mahila Sashaktikaran Programme') is meant for women empowerment as the name itself suggests. It aims at ensuring participation of women, children and deprived sections of the society, in becoming active citizens, participating fully in the democratic process for their socio-economic growth and development, for achieving gender equity and for living copingly with the geo-naturic conditions'. In order to achieve these objectives workshops of concerned officials, ex-office bearers of Panchayats, and social activists of the area, and folk media are organized. Women volunteers in each Panchayat are selected in large number and they are imparted training from time to time. Three most active of them in each case are selected for leadership training for furtherance of the programme.

Social Capital and Women's Political Empowerment

The political empowerment here refers to the level of political participation in shape of voters' turnout, contesting the elections and working as the election workers at the grassroots level. We have taken the contesting panchayat elections as the major indicator. The study conducted by NCW[14] across the country in the selected states like Hariyana, Orissa, Tamil Nadu, Uttranchal, Chhatishgarh, Madhaya Pradesh, Rajasthan, Uttar Pradesh throws ample of light on the level of political participation by women at the grassroots democracy and the issues related to the components of social capital. It finds that women lacked the social capital at large; therefore, they could win only from those constituencies or wards, which were reserved for them (women). Most of the contesting women candidates interviewed (97 per cent) were from the reserved constituencies. This is, however, not surprising, as politics had not been too friendly to women all these years. Out of these, some came from the special reservation for women under SC, ST and OBC categories. A few had also come through constituencies reserved for SC and ST in general. Out of the total of 600, 17 women had contested from such constituencies. However, there were regional variations evident from the fact that in Tamil Nadu 7 women had come by contesting in the general open constituencies. In this state the women have shown a good sign that most of these women had contested the elections, rather than elected by consensus. The latter method, while possibly earning the agreement and good will among the villagers for the women, would have failed to utilize the occasion of elections to raise issues, educate the people and bring out the best in the candidates. Haryana, Orissa and Tamil Nadu, however, had a large number (20 to 30 per cent) of elected candidates through consensus while the other states did not have any. Consensus do not necessarily reflects the prevalence of social capital, however, it seems that in these states the women found some meeting grounds of understanding viz. having trust on each other and sharing the objectives, norms and modes of action.

The issue of taking up roles in the political arena and the influencing factors are very significant in our case. The study finds that while most of the women were put up by the villagers or by family members, the political parties have done so in a few cases for them. There were quite a few who were confident enough to say that they stood on their own and that it was their decision. The family members, particularly the husbands, brother-in-laws and father-in-laws, put up most of the women for political purposes. This applies to Bihar too. For many women it may be more of an order to stand than a process of consultation. In many cases, the men in the family might have put them up in order to keep the 'cushion hot' for them to contest when the constituencies are de-reserved. Nearly 57 in Tamil Nadu had close relatives in politics and this acted as incentive. There are however, other reasons for women entering politics. Many (61) in Tamil Nadu found an opportunity to serve the society, particularly on women's problems. It is also pertinent to examine the factors inhibiting them (women) in taking roles in the politics at the grassroots level. The study finds that most of the women said they were affected by the problems in shape of malpractices during the elections evident from the fact that a sizeable number of respondents in Harayana came out with much dissatisfaction by way obstacles and problems that the women faced during the polls. Quite a few (30 per cent) said they had no problems.

Most significant is to note that the social factors heavily came out as obstacle in their political role taking. Many mentioned the patriarchal view of men and even women, which considered that women were not capable and not fit for politics. Some women candidates also found illiteracy to be a handicap. They also came under scrutiny because of their inability to read and write, or because they were economically not well off. Quite a few women also found social environment to be unfriendly and the *purdah* system disabling them. Domestic work, childcare duties, lack of mobility partly due to social reasons etc. have also been the main handicaps in electioneering. This was also found in case of Bihar. Many elected women found themselves unable to take roles in the panchayat bodies due to domestic work and childrearing related functions.

There were, of course, a few families, which did not allow or were not happy with the women entering politics. In Haryana a Joint family broke up, in Dehradun two cousins contested against each other, and the families broke up. One Haryana woman said clearly that she was not allowed to campaign. In Garhwal region, 22 women had not received any co-operation from the family, the main reason being, the husband who was away in service, had no interest in politics. Many women also had to face derisive comments, particularly from males that the women were illiterate, old, incapable and poor, and that they were not financially sound and cannot extend loans.

Besides most of the women contestants faced a variety of problems. Most of them faced opposition from political parties (Possibly those to which they were not affiliated).Many women from various parts of India mentioned that the opposition of political parties who even held out threats and perpetuated violence in one case in Garhwal, the opposition party distributed liquor in her home and spread malicious rumors about her. There was also opposition to women contesting from general seats. This was particularly true at the higher levels of Zila Panchayats where the elections were fought on party tickets and the parties had much stake.

Many women also found it difficult to campaign because of lack of mobility, transport and social taboos. Campaigning in late evenings and nights was difficult. In Tamil Nadu, instances of teasing, financial constraints, non-availability of support services and lack of transport were reported. Further, a respondent reported that she was forced to withdraw her candidature, because she was not a native of the constituency as she had been living there only after marriage. She was a Muslim and had married a Hindu. Her family was threatened of dire consequences if she did not withdraw. Women in her area refused to co-operate though she had been living there for nearly a decade. But the Mahalir Mandram of the area, which helped her to win, supported her.

On the contrary, many women all over India said that the family members were helpful, that they gave them moral and even financial support and campaigned for them. In some case, of course, men alone campaigned. Villages and family members seemed to have given the women maximum support in the elections. The women from Chhattisgarh had, however, no problem in campaigning. All of them participated fully in their own campaign, and 15 of them managed single handedly. There were, also many instances of women receiving much help and encouragement from the family. In one case, the husband left his post of a panchyat, so that the wife can contest. There were also instances (69 cases) in Tamil Nadu where the husbands met the campaign expenses.

In context of social capital, it is pertinent to mark the issues taken up by women in the campaign. Many women from Haryana did not raise or campaign around any specific issue. However, drinking water, construction of roads/culverts, provision of electricity and other community needs and infrastructure issues, seemed to dominate even the campaigning by and for women candidates. Obviously the domination of males in organizing the campaign for women, led to not many women's issues being raised in Haryana, Orissa and Tamil Nadu. However, some of the prevalent schemes for poverty alleviation, widows pension, old age pension etc. camp up-more for speedier implementation.

By way of conclusion we may find that the reason of whatever the success they got in the panchayat elections were to some extent influenced by social capital evolved among them. Many of the elected women claimed that villagers supported them as a whole, consisting of both males and females. This support, in turn, they attributed above all to their own personal work, popularity and influence. The women of Haryana and Tamil Nadu emerged, thereby, self confident, with a high self-image. Not many attributed this to family political connections or to political parties. In short we can say that there is still scope uniting them for political empowerment.

The political scenario in Bihar had been very discouraging because political participation cannot be separated from social progress and economic independence. Very few women get elected. Those, who get elected, mostly hail from political or dominant family background. Indian democracy hope to elect mature and independent women who are not 'ready made' leaders by virtue of being daughters or wives of powerful, influential men. Rabri Devi. Former C.M. of Bihar is wife of more famous Laloo Pd. Yadav, Mrs. Veena Shahi the minister for co-operative daughter in law of seasoned politician Mr. L. P. Shahi, Rama Devi, widow of Brij Bihari Prasad the then minister for energy, and the list is much more longer. It is said that male politicians vacated 'ladies' seat for their wives and sisters. So they actually retained power in their own hands.

Though there was 33% reservation for women seats till 2001 panchayat elections but surprisingly approximately 37% of women won elections. Now the Bihar Panchayat Raj Act 2006 makes provisions of 50 per cent seats reserved for women in all categories. This is indeed a very healthy trend. Even women voters turned up in large numbers during Panchayat

Polls. At some booths, like Danapur, Naubatpur, Bhojpur, Bakhatiyarpur, they even out numbered their male counterparts. Interestingly such an awakening was not witnessed in Bihar assembly or parliamentary elections. Experts say that it is due to the fact that good number of seats for the membership of local bodies has been reserved for women. Election Commission report shows that tribal women won more seats than tribal men both in Purnea and Katihar in Gram Panchayat election. The numbers are 43 males and 56 females, 84 Males and 87 Females respectively in both the districts. 7 Males and 9 Females, 7 Males and 12 Females at Panchayat Samiti election respectively the studied districts 2 Males and 6 Females in Purnea and 2 Males and 6 Females in Katihar at Mukhiya level. It is interesting to note that these districts were under the programmes of the SANSARG the voluntary agency worked intensively in Bihar. Such a change is a welcome move towards women empowerment. It will be evident from the discussions below.

Another novel experiment was done in Panchayat Raj by allowing adolescent girls (Kishoris) just out of teens to participate in Panchayati Raj system of administration in the rural area with surprising results. Two girls Guriya and Sangita of the "Kishori Sabbha" in Karnapur Bochahan in Muzaffarpur district were assigned the task of going to every house where a woman lived to a varying degree of purdah to talk to them to come out to cast their vote in Panchayati Raj elections. Similar incidents happened in other districts too. A study on the innovations, awareness generation on the Panchati Raj was under taken by Centre for Communication Resources Development (CENCORED) during 1993 found that "kishori Sabha" not only helped to create awareness about electoral process. Voter's rights and duties but also empowered them to deal with adverse situation and articulate their problems in forum comprising their own peers. Hence they were more enthusiastic. There is a wind of change in our villages and people are more aware of their rights.

No doubt criminals and local powerful persons got their wives and relatives pitted into the electoral fray by virtue of force and dominance, but on the contrary, at Kaura village (Bhojpur) women voters outnumbered men. Huge turnout of women kept booth grabbers away and they have come to vote because they knew that powerful intervention of women would strengthen democracy. It is important here to note that women of Bihar in pre-independence days came out with fathomless patriotic spirit to fight against the British rule. The whole environment was emotionally charged with the clarion call of Mahatama Gandhi. Ganga Devi, Prabhavati Devi, lady Imam rani of Tekari Saraswati Devi and many others literate or illiterate jumped into the freedom movement. Roy and Kumar write, "But the sitatiion drastically changed in post independent era. The crux of the problem is that women always remained as a recipient of charge. Never as an agent of change and at any time if she will so she faces stiff resistance by the society as a whole." This was reflected during Panchayat elections that Mrs. Munni Devi a contestant from Nawalpur Champaran in her struggle for freedom from domestic bondage counts upon her husband. Ajit Kumar for campaigning as Ajit's recognition in the area in Munni's passport to polls raised a slogan '*Rabri Ke Pecchey Laloo jee Munni Ke peechey Ajit.*'[15] Whatever the changes are brought in case of political empowerment of women at grassroots level, it has been motored by the voluntary agencies.

Epilogue

To cap it all, the whole gamut of discussion suggests that the voluntarism may play a very effective role in creation of social capital towards political empowerment of women. The programmes of 'Sansarg' in Bihar sound systematic and fruit bearing. When the government and the political parties are hypocritical in their approach towards empowering women, voluntarism may work wonder. It may make women politically more socialized, participative and assertive. It is clear that the new panchayatraj system has given rise to involvement of more women into political arena. But still there is need to enable them economically, educationally and socially so that they substantially participate in local level governance.

Notes

1. Srilatha Batliwala; *Empowerment of Women in South Asia: Concepts and Practices.* (Second draft), Asian-South Pacific Bureau of Adult Education and FAO's Freedom from Hunger Campaign-Action for Development, down loaded from Internet, June 1993.
2. R. K. Verma and M. Singh, "Voluntarism and Panchayat Elections in Bihar: A Study", *Indian Journal of Public Administration,* Oct-Dec. 2001.
3. A.F.C, Bourdillion; (ed.), Voluntary Social Service: Their Place in Modern State, Metheu, London, 1945. McGlosky, H.; "Political Participation", in David Shills (ed.) *International Encyclopaedia of Social Sciences,* Vol. 12, 1968.
4. R. K. Verma and M. Singh, *op. cit.*, IJPA, Oct-Dec. 2001.
5. Srilatha Batliwala, *op. cit.*
6. *Ibid.*
7. (i) S.M. Lipset; *Political Man: The Social Bases of Politics,* Doubleday & Co., New York, 1960.

   (ii) S. Verba, "Democratic Participation", *Annuls of the American Academy of Political and Social Sciences,* September, 1967 (iii) Huntington, S.P. and Nelson, J. M.; *No easy Choice,* Cambridge, Harvard University Press, 1976.
8. (i) L.W. Milbrath; *Political Participation,* Rand Mckenley, Chicago, 1965. (ii) B. Adhmed, "Political Stratification of the Indian Electorate", *Economic and Political Weekly,* Annual Number, January 1971.
9. Robert Putnam, *Making Democracy Work: Civic Traditions in Modern Italy,* Princeton University Pdress, Princeton, 1993.
10. H. Blomkvist and Ashok Swain, "Investigating Democracy and Social Capital in India", *Economic and Political Weekly,* February 24, 2001, pp. 639-43.
11. State Election Commission, *Grassroots Democracy Incarnate,* SEC, Patna, nd.
12. The entire section is based on *Sansurg,* Panchayat Raj Programme and Activities of CENCORED; Five Years of Growth and Development, CENCORED Office, Patna, 2000.
13. National Commission for Women, Participation of Women in Panchayati Raj in India, compiled by Shusheela Kaushik, NCW, New Delhi, 1998.
14. As reported by *Times of India* dated 18.4.2001

21

Women Empowerment Through Self Help Groups (A Study in Context of Bihar)

Sandhaya Rani

Introduction

It has always been argued that economic empowerment is the key to women empowerment. If we talk of women political empowerment, their economic independence as well as well being is essential. As the larger chunk of poor women reside in rural areas in India in general and Bihar in particular, it is quite difficult to imagine the political empowerment of women. In the backdrop of this assumption the present paper intends to examine the women political empowerment in context of economic weakness of rural women which is being strengthened through self help groups (SHGs) very fast. As such the paper first examines the concept of women political empowerment and the linkages between grassroots level economic activities and governance and political participation. Finally it goes to assess the role of SHGs in political empowerment of women in Bihar milieu.

Conceptual Considerations

The most conspicuous feature of the term empowerment is that it contains within it the word power. So, obviously empowerment is about power, and changing the balance of power. In every society, there are resources of various kinds. This is spiral not a cycle which leads to greater and greater changes, and more empowerment. Consciousness, problem identification, action for change and analysis of that action and its outcome lead to higher levels of consciousness and better planned and executed strategies.[1] This empowerment spiral affects every person involve: the collective, and the environment, though not necessarily at the same pace or depth. By this definition, therefore, empowerment cannot be a top-down or one-way process.

Now the issue boils down to the concept of 'Empowerment of Women' that denotes that there is a class de-powered in the society, which needs sensitization and empowerment. Thus, empowerment has three basic contents control, freedom and enabling. Freedom refers to freedom from subjugation, deprivation and oppression, perpetuated through institutionalized methods. The women have been prey or victims of centuries old, deprivation, subjugation and oppression by patriarchal norms not only in India, but also in almost all societies. Empowerment requires their freedom. Freedom alone cannot empower them rather they should be enabled to participate in social, economic, political and cultural spheres of life. The women have been victim of all these kinds of shackles from centuries. In other words, they would have to be incapacitated to face the social domain, enjoy the economic independence and roles in political spheres i.e. political participation, may it be of any degree.[2]

Again the issue of political empowerment requires clarification. The term 'political' refers to the views of Catlin and Lasswell who posit that 'shaping and sharing the power is political'. In other words, any thing–action, idea, and incident that relates to 'power' can be termed as 'political'. Thus the political empowerment of women denotes their role in political sphere i.e. political participation, political behaviour and actions related to influencing the decision making process and participating in the process of governance and development. Political participation has been considered as any voluntary action employing legitimate methods to influence the choice of public policies, administration of public affairs or the choice of political leaders at any level local or national. Voting, the most common, is one of those actions that are considered as political participation[3]. S M Lipset, Sidney Verba[4] and many others have defined political participation as participatory engagement of aggregate individuals either in formal or informal modes, of course to influence the decision-making processes. Milbrath, Ahmedand[5] several others have categorized the level of political participation right from expression of political will to hold a public or political office. Here we are concerned with manifest action like women's activities in public affairs, voting, motivating, fighting for electoral positions and holding a public office. Simple expression of political will is not included in our analysis.

The people's participation, though came into academic sphere through political participation, has now been specifically a part of people's participation in the development process in all its four stages - formulation of development plans (planning process right at the grassroots level through decentralized development planning), implementation and of the development plans and monitoring, evaluation of the ongoing development work and finally sharing the benefit of the development work equally.[6] Now a question is raised - whose participation? It is obvious that the participation is required of those who are not in the helm of decision making process. Those are the common masses, the poor, the deprived sections such as women. If we talk of political empowerment of women, their participation in the development process is a must.

Relationship Between Economic Empowerment and Good Governance

Good governance has increasingly been recognized as a crucial prerequisite for development effectiveness and the growth that it fosters. It is critical for ensuring a positive investment climate, and it has a two-way relationship with empowerment—that is, good governance promotes empowerment, and empowerment further enhances good governance. The components of good governance range very widely; some of its aspects have close relationship with empowerment. Kaufmann, Kraay, and Zoido-Lobatón (1999) found a large, significant, and causal relationship between the rule of law and the income of nations (and also between rule of law, higher literacy, and reduced infant mortality). In its equity (or inequity) aspects, the rule of law also affects empowerment: if poor people can obtain impartial justice, their freedom is enhanced. By the same token, empowerment can improve the quality of the judicial and enforcement system, especially by increasing the availability and dissemination of information about the working of the system.[7]

One specific aspect of empowerment—enhanced women's rights and participation—deserves special mention in this context. Empowerment of women is associated with cleaner business and government, and better governance. Specifically, the greater their involvement in public life, the lower the level of corruption, even in countries with the same income, civil liberties, education, and legal institutions. At the micro level, studies have shown that women in business are less likely than men to pay bribes to government officials, either because they have higher ethical standards or because they are more averse.

Here again, aspects of empowerment, including provision of information to citizens and government commitment to transparency and accountability with respect to public spending, can play a critical role. When stakeholders, including civil society, the private sector, and intended beneficiaries (including poor people), can monitor public expenditure outcomes, performance can be enhanced. Public spending on education in Uganda provides a case in point. When Uganda, instituted public monitoring of funds with Bank support that went to primary schools, then the share of non wage allocations the percentage of actual reaching rose from 22 per cent in 1995 to about 80–90 per cent in 2000.[8] Here is an example of how key aspects of empowerment and government performance (and development effectiveness) go hand in hand: spending on improvements in education service delivery is critical for empowerment, while empowerment, in the form of citizen monitoring, is helping to ensure that public spending on education is actually reaching its intended beneficiaries—and thereby enhancing the effectiveness of public action and growth prospects.

There is a large cross-disciplinary literature and substantial development experience on the links between empowerment, growth, and poverty reduction[9] Income poverty has fallen most rapidly in economies that have grown dynamically, and poverty has remained high or has increased in countries with poor growth records. But experience also shows that growth alone is not enough to ensure substantial and sustainable poverty reduction. Country data indicate that similar growth rates can lead to very different poverty reduction outcomes.

For a given rate of growth, poverty will fall faster in countries where the distribution of income becomes more equal, as in Uganda, than in countries where it becomes less equal, as in Bangladesh.[10] And even where income distribution does not become more unequal with growth, country differences in initial inequality produce different poverty reduction outcomes for a given rate of growth. Hence, if poverty reduction is taken as a measure of development effectiveness, then the development effectiveness of growth efforts varies with levels of inequality.

A critical aspect of the empowerment agenda is to reduce inequality by broadening human capabilities (through, for example, universal basic education and health care, together with adequate arrangements for social protection12) and improving the distribution of tangible assets (such as land or access to capital). Such an approach brings with it the potential to enhance the poverty-reducing development effectiveness of growth- inducing policies and investments. The converse also applies. When inequality is high, poor people lack capabilities and assets (ranging from literacy to collateral for credit) and thus have difficulty in taking advantage of economic opportunity. This limits a society's potential for growth in general and pro-poor growth in particular, and consequently the effectiveness of development efforts.13

Gender discrimination, whether legal or customary, is a particularly important aspect of inequality. By curtailing the economic contribution of half the population, it limits overall prospects for growth and higher living standards—a situation perpetuated into future generations by inadequate investment in female education. Empowerment also implies more participatory, bottom-up approaches to working toward development objectives. There is now substantial agreement that such approaches, giving poor people more freedom to make economic decisions, enhance development effectiveness at the local level in terms of design, implementation, and outcomes.

Impact of SHGs on Women's Political Empowerment

The reports of Women Development Corporation suggest that there has been sea of change in Bihar owing to SHGs. It writes, "There are several indicators to suggest that Bihar is now embracing change at a faster pace than ever before. The state has seen a significant improvement in its law and order situation, educational institutions and health delivery systems. Its government—which completes three years of existence in November—has professed a commitment to "good governance".[11] Besides the women's political participation was also found greater among the dalit categories of women in rural Bihar. A study[12] suggests that Scheduled Caste women were found more enthusiastic in casting their votes in the panchayat elections of 2001 and 2006.

WDC, Bihar has started the process of women empowerment through a World Bank-IFAD support project-Swa Shakti, in which WDC, Bihar has showed the innovative ideas to unit rural women non-deterministic approach and need based facilitation. For WDC, SHG is the mean of a women owned community based organization, where women analyze critically their own situation & drive strategy to overcome difficulties, providing mutual support & serving the social change, take loan for economic development and sustaining a framework for raising awareness on literacy, information dissemination, health, etc.

The following Table 1 shows the projects undertaken by the WDC for facilitating SHGs and empowerment of women.

Table 1
Statement Showing WDC Projects with Financial Support Institutions

Name of Projects	*FundSupport*	*SHG*	*Project Duration* *Start*	*End*
Swa-ShaktiProject	World Bank/IFAD	400	1999	2005
SwawlambanPhase I	AdditionalCentral Assistance GOI	1000	2004	2007
SwawlambanPhase II	AdditionalCentral Assistance GOI	1000	2005	2008
Swayamsiddha	GOI	6300	2004	2006
Deep	SpecialComponent Plan GOI	1885	2004	2008

Source: Women Development Corporation, Final Report, 2008.

As we talked earlier that enabling the women is one of the basic components of women's empowerment but more important is their control over resources and ideas.The functioning of SHGs in Bihar has shown the enhancement of their abilities and control over resources. It will be evident from the fact that Behaviour Change Communication (BCC) programme created a cadre of more than 1500 Community Resource Persons capacitated to facilitate community on Health, Hygiene, Sanitation and Education. Mass level sensitization on 5 key behavioural issues i.e. Breastfeeding, Routine Immunization, Hand Washing, Girl Education and HIV/AIDS were created through these SHGs. A large number of demand generations on construction of toilets was created. Hand holding support need sensitized towards basic service delivery system of health, sanitation and education clusters. The Swawlamban Project is sign of achievement of self reliance. The government of Bihar has taken up the initiative for the empowerment of women living in the state. WDC takes this developmental intervention of the government along with CSOs into P-P-P mode and set five liner objective of women empowerment goal namely SHGs for greater access and control over resources, sensitizing institutional capacity support agencies and linkages between SHGs and lending institutions.

The achievements of the SHGs movement can be placed here for better understanding of the women's empowerment in the different areas. The report says, "IN 2006-07, WDC - UNICEF partnership contributed to establishing an evidence-based model for integrated communication activities around key behaviors through a widespread base of over approx. 10,000 active and vibrant women's Self Help Groups (SHGs) in 19 districts of the state. In phase 1 (2006), the project interventions focused on building the capacity of SHGs on key behaviors, IPC and social mobilization in integrated district 'Vaishali' .The BCC programme experience provided important lessons on enhancing the impact of behaviour change systematically, repeatedly and at a large scale. Consequently, in phase 2 (July-Dec '07) the project was scaled up to cover 19 WDC operational district where trained cluster coordinators and SHG members engaged in intensive IPC and community dialogue to reinforce behavior and social change."[13]

Women Development Corporation claims that 'its impact can also be read on the women's political participation at the grassroots level evident from the fact that panchayat elections held in 2006 saw women emerge as winners in over 58 per cent of the seats', as against the fifty per cent reservation of seats for women as per Bihar Panchayat Raj Act 2006. It can be inferred that such changes take place in a state like Bihar, which is not just one of India's least developed states, but one of the poorest regions in the world, it is significant. Change such as this needs to be recognized, analyzed, replicated, improved upon and sustained.

Notes

1. Srilatha Batliwala; *Empowerment of Women in South Asia: Concepts and Practices.* (Second draft), Asian-South Pacific Bureau of Adult Education and FAO's Freedom from Hunger Campaign- Action for Development, down loaded from Internet, June 1993.
2. See R. K. Verma and M. Singh, "Voluntarism and Panchayat Elections in Bihar 2001: A Study", *Indian Journal o f Public Administration*, Oct-Dec, 2001.

3. (i) Bidyut Mohanty (ed), Women and Political Empowerment, Institute of Social Sciences, New Delhi, 1996, pp 13-15 (ii) Shobha Kumari Gupta, *Voluntarism, Social Capital and Women's Political Empowerment of Women at Grassroots Level,* M P S Publishers, New Delhi, 2008.
4. (i) S. M. Lipset, *Political Man,* Doubleday Pub, New York 1960 (ii) S. Verba, "Democratic Participation", *Annuls of the American Academy of Political and Social Sciences,* September, 1967.
5. (i) L. W. Milbrath, *Political Participation,* Routledge McNally, Chicago, 1965 (ii) B. Adhmed, "Political Stratification of the Indian Electorate", *Economic and Political Weekly,* Annual Number, January 1971.
6. See S. N. Mishra, Development Through Participation, IX Course, Indian Institute of Public Administration, New Delhi, 1991.
7. As quoted in Government of Bihar, *Introduction Women Development Corporation,* WDC, Patna, 2008.
8. *Ibid.*
9. See especially World Development Report, 2000/2001(and Stern's *A Strategy for Development*)
10. GOB, WDC, *op cit.*
11. As in reference no 7 above.
12. Ravindra Kumar Verma, *Panchayat Raj Elections in Bihar: A Study of the People, Parties and Electoral Process,* Mimeographed report submitted to Indian Council of Social Research, March, 2007.
13. W D C, Final WDC_Report_Doc, available on WDC website, visited in March, 2009.

22

Women Empowerment

Ms Navneet

Introduction

Women's empowerment is not a Northern concept. Women all over the world, including countries in the South, have been challenging and changing gender inequalities since the beginnings of history. These struggles have also been supported by many men who have been outraged at injustices against women and the consequences for society. It would be yet another instance of imperialism to say all these women and men did not have minds of their own. Most men view themselves as being the superior life form in society. They justify this belief by saying that they are stronger and more capable; thus, making them more qualify for the more important roles in society. They place themselves on pedestals and force women to believe in their own inferiority to men and their incapability to excel educationally, politically, economically, and domestically. But the truth is that women will eventually advance in all these areas and come to realize that they do not need men to survive.

John Steinbeck, in his short story "The Chrysanthemums" depicts the trials of a woman attempting to gain power in a man's world. Elisa Allen tries to define the boundaries of her role as a woman in such a closed society. While her environment is portrayed as a tool for social repression, it is through nature in her garden where Elisa gains and shows off her power. As the story progresses, Elisa has trouble extending this power outside of the fence that surrounds her garden. Elisa learns but does not readily accept, that she possesses a feminine power weak for the time, not the masculine one she had tried so hard to achieve through its imitation.

Through the years, women have challenged the traditional female roles and have gradually climbed up the social ladder [5]. The word empowerment, although it gained widespread usage in the context of the US Civil Rights and Women's Movements is an extension of earlier concepts of equality, justice and freedom, which were expressed, in many anti-imperialist and political struggles. These are also enshrined in international agreements and also underlie the precepts of many religious traditions, including Islam.

International Women's Rights Agreements

Women's rights are well established by international agreements, notably the international Convention on Eradication of Discrimination Against Women (CEDAW), which explicitly include women within the definition of 'human' and hence in all International Human Rights Conventions. CEDAW has been ratified by most governments and underpins official gender policies of all major development agencies.

Women's rights in Islam

It is often argued, by some women as well as men, that these International Rights agreements are somehow 'unislamic'. This justification of inequality in terms of religious precepts, 'culture' or tradition is by no means confined to Islam. Powerful interests in most religions and cultures have referred to 'tradition' to justify maintaining gender and other inequality. Islam grants many rights to women, which are currently ignored. To argue that Muslim women should not be granted their human rights is to wrongly argue that under Islam women are less than equal. This is totally against the most fundamental teachings of Islam.

Dominance of the 'financial sustainability paradigm' as donors have required micro-finance institutions to rapidly become financially sustainable, definitions of empowerment have become diluted to mean insignificant increases in individual income and 'self-confidence'. The current concern with poverty targeting conflates women's empowerment with household well-being. This is despite the overwhelming evidence of both women's own demands for gender equality and the need to overcome constraints to achieving them [1].

Empowerment refers to increasing the spiritual, political, social or economic strength of individuals and communities. It often involves the empowered developing confidence in their own capacities.Empowerment is probably the totality of the following or similar capabilities:

- Having decision-making power of their own
- Having access to information and resources for taking proper decision
- Having a range of options from which you can make choices (not just yes/no, either/or.)
- Ability to exercise assertiveness in collective decision making
- Having positive thinking on the ability to make change
- Ability to learn skills for improving one's personal or group power.
- Ability to change others' perceptions by democratic means.
- Involving in the growth process and changes that is never ending and self-initiated
- Increasing one's positive self-image and overcoming stigma

Marginalization."Marginalized" refers to the overt or covert trends within societies whereby those perceived as lacking desirable traits or deviating from the group norms tend to be excluded by wider society and ostracized as undesirables.

Charitable organizations lead from outside of the community; for example, can disempower the community by entrenching a dependence on charity or welfare. A nonprofit organization can target strategies that cause structural changes, reducing the need for ongoing dependence. Red Cross, for example, can focus on improving the health of indigenous people, but does not have authority in its charter to install water-delivery and purification systems, even though the lack of such a system profoundly, directly and negatively impacts health. A nonprofit composed of the indigenous people, however, could insure their own organization does have such authority and could set their own agendas, make their own plans, seek the needed resources, do as much of the work as they can, and take responsibility - and credit - for the success of their projects [2].

Of the 1.3 billion people who live in absolute poverty around the globe, 70 per cent are women. For these women, poverty doesn't just mean scarcity and want. It means rights denied, opportunities curtailed and voices silenced. Consider the following:

- Women work two-thirds of the world's working hours, according to the United Nations Millennium Campaign to halve world poverty by the year 2015. The overwhelming majority of the labor that sustains life-growing food, cooking, raising children, caring for the elderly, maintaining a house, hauling water – is done by women, and universally this work is accorded low status and no pay. The ceaseless cycle of labor rarely shows up in economic analyses of a society's production and value.
- Women earn only 10 per cent of the world's income. Where women work for money, they may be limited to a set of jobs deemed suitable for women – invariably low-pay, low-status positions.
- Women own less than 1 per cent of the world's property. Where laws or customs prevent women from owning land or other productive assets,

from getting loans or credit, or from having the right to inheritance or to own their home, they have no assets to leverage for economic stability and cannot invest in their own or their children's futures.

- Women make up two-thirds of the estimated 876 million adults worldwide who cannot read or write; and girls make up 60 per cent of the 77 million children not attending primary school. Education is among the most important drivers of human development: women who are educated have fewer children than those who are denied schooling (some studies correlate each additional year of education with a 10 per cent drop in fertility). They delay their first pregnancies; have healthier children (each additional year of schooling a woman has is associated with a 5 to 10 per cent decline in child deaths, according to the United Nations Population Fund) A rights-based approach:
- Insists that poverty is neither natural nor inevitable, but has roots in political and economic decisions;
- Helps us identify the structural and societal causes of poverty and marginalization;
- Aims to address relations between those who wield power and those who do not;
- Provides a means of strengthening people's capacities to claim and exercise their rights; and Clarifies authorities' duties to those they serve. Before we adopted this approach, CARE's practical attempts to empower women often missed this simple starting point:

Until men as equally human accept women, attempts to help women change their lives will necessarily always result in achievements that are limited in scope and longevity. Women alone cannot empower themselves, nor should we expect them to bear that burden. Men too–especially in their status as power holders in the family, community and formal government–must act. Most recently, CARE has developed what we call the unifying framework to bring together the salient aspects of our poverty eradication approaches. This framework is designed to help us the thousands of CARE staffers around the globe and the people we serve - consistently look beyond the immediate and most evident causes of poverty to three categories of cause that shape the lives of the poor. These are causes related to: basic material or human conditions; influence and social positions; and the structure of laws, norms and institutions that constitute the enabling environment in which an individual lives. Our use of the framework as an analytical tool consistently underscores that women's disempowerment is a universal factor in extreme poverty; in turn, a focus on women's empowerment offers a pathway out of extreme poverty and toward dignity and security - for women, their families and whole communities [3].

Achievements and Role of Department of Women and Child Development

The provisions of the Constitution of India granting equality to women in various spheres creates the legal framework within which the Department of Women & Child Development functions for women's development. Women as a mother hood of the nation should be strong, aware and alert; that is main motto of the Department and mother with child is the future of the nation. formulating strategies and initiating processes to bring women into the mainstream. Women constitute half of the country's population (accounting for 407.1 million in absolute numbers as per the 1991 census), and it is abundantly clear that there can be no development unless their needs and interests are fully taken into account. to protect and safeguard the rights of women. to give the much needed impetus to the holistic development of women and children. For advancement of women and children All these efforts are directed to ensure that women are empowered both economically and socially and thus become equal partners in national development along with men.

Conclusion

In present paper we have focus on the issue of women empowerment and how we can achieve it. Male dominated cultural traditions discourage female education, restrict their legal rights and participation in decision-making, and permit women little control over their lives. The keystone plan is gender equality, equity and empowerment of women. The division of responsibilities is such that sometimes the man cooks and the woman looks after the rest of the house. The National Commission for Women set up in 1992 covers issues relating to safeguarding women's rights and promotion of their empowerment. A mother of a girl child born on or after 15th August, 1997 in a family below the poverty line in rural and urban areas is given a grant [4].

Tulsidas' verse from Ramayana 'Dhol, janwar, shudra, pashu, nari ye sub nindan ke adhikari' highlights the discrimination and deep-rooted gender bias which still exists in all sectors on the basis of caste, community, religious affiliation and class. The Constitution of India grants equality to women in various fields of life. Yet a large number of women are either ill equipped or not in a position to propel themselves out of their traditionally unsatisfactory socio-economic conditions. They are poor, uneducated and insufficiently trained. They are often absorbed in the struggle to sustain the family physically and emotionally and as a rule are discouraged from taking interest in affairs outside home. Oppression and atrocities on women are still rampant. Patriarchy continues to be embedded in the social system in many parts of India, denying a majority of women the choice to decide on how they live.

References

http://www.genfinance.info/1Empowerment.htm

http://www.selfgrowth.com/articles/Articles_Women_Empowerment.html

http://www.care.org/newsroom/publications/whitepapers/woman_and_empowerment

http://www.megaessays.com/viewpaper/29102.html

[7] http://www.123helpme.com/preview.asp?id=64201

23

Psychodynamics of Women Political Leadership Some Reflections

Mona Tabassum

The present paper intends to examine the psychological factors influencing women political leadership in Indian society. In this context it deals with concept of political leadership, roles of political leader, social power structure and psychological factors in order to examine the women political leadership.

About Leadership

Leadership is basically the execution of a particular kind of role with an organized group or society and this role is defined essentially in the terms of power or the ability to influence others. Like any roles, leadership involves not only the overt display of certain kind of action in the group but also certain patterns of interpersonal perception and certain expectation about the behavior of a leader. Leadership is not necessary an 'all –or – nothing' phenomenon is a group of dynamics. In some groups, leadership functions maybe concentrated almost completely in one individual. In other groups, leadership maybe shared by a number of individuals. The conception of leadership as a role involving power relationship provide the base for defining 'leadership as a frequency with which an individual in a group maybe identified as one who influences or directs the behavior of others within the group'. During the 19th century the idea of 'born leaders' was widely accepted. It was assumed that man of genius emerged from time to time within a society and that these men were destined to exert profound influence upon their society. Galton an important figure in the field of psychological measurement was a strong proponent of the notion that individuals processing outstanding talents or ability tended to emerge as leaders who shaped crucial changes in the social organization in which they participated. In 20th century the alternative position came into popularity. George Simmel (1902) a social scientist and Pigons (1935) reconsidered leadership as a product of situational condition within a group or society. From this point of view, the leader is not conceived as endowed inherently with powers or ability to influence others but his followers grant him their powers as his role evolves within the structural organization of the group. With the development of socio-metric technique for measuring inter personal relationship, it was accepted by the social psychologists like Helen Hall Jenings (1943) that is necessary to know the interpersonal qualities of a leader.

Social Power

In the late 1940's a group of investigators who were influenced and trained by Kurt Levin at the University of Iowa, conducted first major experimentation, exploration of social power and found that behavioral contingent and the 'dynamics of power' is the manifestation of the behavioral influence of one person on another within organized groups. These studies distinguished attributed 'power' as a set of preceptors and expectation held by members of the group about each other, and thus defined leadership and the power function in terms of role perception and role expectation.

Bases of Social Power: French and Raven (1958) have distinguished five particularly important and common different kinds of social power - (i) Reward Power–Having this power a person is able to control the consequences of another's behavior by manipulating the reward or punishment,

(ii) Coercive Power - This power occurs when one can deliver punishment to another who fails to comply, (iii) Represent Power - It occurs when one person has power over another's. The latter allows him to be identified with him. A person allows himself to be influenced by another he wishes to gain approval (i) or acceptance to gain similarity to others, (iv) Export Power- It occurs when a person power over others because they regard him as possessing knowledge or ability that are potentially useful to him, (v) Legitimate Power- It is a complex form of power relationship. When one person perceives another as externally empowered by virtue of his formal position.

Roles of Leadership

Leadership is not a phenomenon of leaders but it is a social phenomenon (R. K. Verma, 1991). To understand the phenomenon of political leadership we have to understand the roles played by the political leaders at various levels. To understand the phenomenon of political leadership we have to understand the roles played by the political leaders at various level which are going simultaneously political, social and economic change without sufficient incubators in democratic experience.

By examining the leadership theories, R K Verma has posited that leadership signifies role of providing guidance, direction and co-ordination to a group, organization, community, nation etc. Leadership also refers to the capacity to inspire confidence in the rightness of one's purpose; courage is their collected execution and sense of obedience in the threat of resistance. As such leaders possess capacity and exert roles clubbed as GDC and CCO (R K Verma: 1996). Sanderson, Kreitlow, Aiton, Torrence and many others have articulate a variety of qualities which can be classified into three broad divisions - Physical , Psychological and Development .

Political Leadership: There is a general agreement upon the term 'political '. Anything or act that relates to decision making in public affairs or power of the -super structure- is 'political'. This should be considered for the leadership also. Power is the capacity to influence others behavior and is the capacity to influence others behavior and is exercised through a formal position either legitimate or legal , having contents of state power. This indicates that power and office makes a 'leader ' a political leader. The basic components political leadership are the power, formal position (acquired or aspired) and supported of and acceptance by the community. This component s is in addition to the roles and personal qualities a leader as essential in perfecting GDC and CCO. The political leadership influences the community for support building and decision making process for rendering benefits to the community. As such political leadership influences both the community and the decision making process (*Ibid*).

Another dimension is related to the perception of the community the leaders lead. Politics by leadership is a universal trend but the nature of emergence of political leadership lies at the root of democratic experiment, development prospect and direction of change. These factors lead us to a question - who becomes a leader and how he comes to terms with society with which he interacts but has to improve upon through his leadership roles? This question is closely related to tensions and values of a particular community. Here the roles will be decided by the 'samudaiboth'. Again leadership is a function of acceptance by community, this the community perception (samudaiboth) well determine the kinds of person acceptable as leaders and will reflect the reasons of acceptance and/or rejection. The aspect is rural power structure, which suggests the aspects of political leaders and the community of people. Almost all the studies ignore the latter in general and the perception of latter is particular. The Samudaiboth approach is essential to be applied particularly in developing societies. The major postulates of the approach are (i) it is the community that leaders wield power from, (ii) the characteristics of the leadership depends on the perception of the community, (iii) the micro level leaders are the community for the macro level leaders, and (iv) the degree and naure of political socialization is the determinant of the peoples perception.

Women Political Leadership (The Gender issue that be)

For the leader in the old sense of boss (the commander) used traits superficially thought of as masculine, while the leader as influencer (the teacher) uses traits many of which are often thought of as feminine. Of course an admixture of these traits is necessary in effective leader, man or woman. But the women as leader usually have an intuitive sympathy for the approach, which is persuasive, rather than for that, which is strong arm. Woman has capabilities but their choices and preference are socially conditioned. Amity Sen , Nobel Laureate , views that social pressures 'mentally conditions' women to give up opportunities in order benefit their families. Such choices often affect women's capabilities and diminish their lives; their choices and preferences have a disproportionately damaging effect on their capabilities.

Women are not self-aware and do not understand the 'real motive forces ' pushing them to act in ways that diminish their capabilities (Ashima Goyal, 2007). So it is better to look at potential 'being' and 'doing' rather than who chooses to do what.

Every individual faces trade-offs, 'women or men' whether rich or poor, who choose to devote time to children or to old, must give up some valuable alternative roles/ activities in order to do so (Ashima Goyal). Personal time is a non-recoverable resource. Developing others capabilities may impose a loss of capabilities. But she values both of what a woman chooses to give up certain valuable personal activities for the sake her children will be lowering her personal well being unless she gives high weightage to her children's welfare 21ST centuary women are capable of multiple roles. Women having multiple roles are more independent, confident and tolerant. They are having high self esteem and positive attitude towards multiple roles (Mathur, 1996). But women are hesitant to take part in politics. There is gender inequality in our society. Males are considered as dominate and females are sub ordinate (Jean Baker Miller, 1976). Because women are considered subordinate group of the society they develop characteristics such as passivity and dependency, and to cope with this status on the basis of relationship of dominance and subordination, women differ from men in their orientation to power. Thus the distinctive psychology arises from their position of inequality. A distinguish psychologist Jean Baker Miller (1976) has noted that there is no language to describe the structuring of women's sense of self, which is organized around being able to make and maintain affiliation and relationship. This difference is conceptualized as holding the potential for more co-operating more affiliating ways of living. All these distinctive qualities give rise to a new 'psychology of women ' that would recognize that women have a different starting phase for their development that they stay with, build on and develop in the context of attachment and affiliation with others (Miller 1976). There are so many causes of gender inequality in our society.

Different Socialization Process

Women and men are socialized differently in our society as we eye gender role expectation begin to influence human developed from the moment a child is born. These expectation are strongly embedded in the fabric of the society. It is internalized the dynamic organization of the child that has a a profound impact on the adult personality.

Gender role socialization has been defined as a multifaceted process occurring across the life span, of reinforcing specific belief and behavior that a society considers appropriate based on biological sex (Remer, Rostosky and Wright, 2001). This process has limiting effect on both men and women, for example the myth and stories which we tell our children abound with sex role stereotypes and send subtle but powerful messages that men are strong, clever and resourceful while women are passive, weak , depended and helpless. There are lifelong consequences for growing girls who learn that feminism, is incompatible with strength, assertiveness, competence and boys who learn that masculinity is incompatible with expression of fear, dependency, emotionality or weakness (Lerner, 1988).

Mother-Child Relationship

Nancy Choudhary (1978) attributed the difference between women and men primarily due to early child care. A girls identity formations occurs in the context of ongoing relationship. Girls are supposed to be like their mothers and boys are supposed to be like their fathers. Attachment that is encouraged in girls and separation from mother is essential to the development of the boys. It is because masculinity is defined through separation where as femininity is defined through attachment .Male gender identity is threatened by intimacy while female identity is threatened by separation (Gillian, 1982).

According to Ellyn Kaschak, gender is the organizing principle in people's life, she focuses on the societal impact on gender role development. Masculine defines the feminine; that is men determine the roles that women's play. It is because women are socialized to feel rather than to act and because society values action more than feelings so women are places in a subordinate roles.

Women leaders who dare to enter politics today are typically found in one of three dilemma.Firstly, in order to compete with men is attaing or holding a leadership position , they may belive that it is necessary for them virtually to deny their sex. They may try to turn their back up on it , ignore it and 'rise above it'. They may think they are successful when they evoke the comment 'she is just like a man.'

Secondly they may use their position as leaders as compensation for an inability, however caused to function sexually and physically as woman. They may their do this both repressively and with violence. Their true nature, or by a process of sublimation which can under a well disciplined self control afford an adequate outlet for the whole person through socially beneficent channels Thirdly, they may try to be both women and leaders, lover and mothers and worker in the world . But under present economic arrange ment they are in danger of finding this an exceeding by demanding challenge and ultimately perhaps experience a weariness of flesh so profound that successful attainment is denied in both direction.

A lack of option forces women to make a conscious choice in favour of 'less', but they are not aware of injustice and inequality and are quick to use institution that respect their choices and special abilities. Opportunities created for women need to be suited to women's and to improve the tradeoffs they face. ICT is naturally suited to these neds and should be encouraged for women. While women have developed special talents roles and activities, understand and lack of experience in the world outside the world require policy intervention. The quick success of much special institution suited to their needs and abilities suggest that women are both self aware and ready for change. If there is scope for responsible choice with self awareness, change can be fast; if it builds on the higher social capital such choices create, it can be more efficient. Our analysis brings out the power and usefulness of the focus on the state of the individual pioneered by capability approach, but shades it by suggesting that a choice in favour of less has to be respected in order to lead to more. (Ashima Goyal).

The True source of women's power as leaders seems to lie close to their deep concerns as women. When this is ignored and women assume posts of responsibility which artificially force their loyalty-as is true for example, in many business position of execution leadership the results both in the effect over in the women personality and on the quality of leadership is likely to be the unwholesome and ugly. Certain hardness develops; a protective shell of impersonality, which is neither masculine nor feminine, becomes encrusted over the individual.

The woman who is going to realize her selfhood, as a leader should look well to it that the cause she serves is worthy-if it appeals to her and does not involves her real interests and desires. Nothing is more deeply disruptive and fatiguing to the spirit them the effort to realize objectives which seem remote, unreal or false to ones nature.

These are certain attributes which more manifest is women than in women. The combination of energetic, enthusiastic, resourcefulness with warmth of fellow feeling and desire for the follower's cooperative participation in a unified effort, which is the mark of the good leader as in fact a bringing together of those traits popularly characterized as masculine and feminine. Both kinds of qualities are essential and both are present is differing proportion in every man and woman.

There is need of womanliness in woman political leaders. The good woman leader is the womanliest person. She follows her natural impulse to woo those she leads through her sympathies and enthusiastic.

The good woman leader will know that in her grasp of every problem. She naturally tends to give an emphasis to certain aspects which men may be inclined to slight. If, from a superficial point of view this is her limitation, it is also her glory and strength.

Reference

Chodorow , Nancy (1978), The Reproduction of Mothering: University of California Press.

Blondel, Jean (1987), Political Leadership; Issues in Concept and Analysis, Sage Publication India, New Delhi.

Elliot, J. M. (1999), Feminist Therapy in G. Corey (ed); Theory and Practice of Counseling and Psychotherapy (7th edition , p. 380-381).

French, J. R. P. and Raven, B. M. (1958), Group Support, Legitimate Power, Social Influence, J. Press 26, (p. 400-409).

George, Simmel (1902) and Pigeons (1935), The Number of the Members as Determining the Sociological form of the Group, *Amer., J. Social,* 8 (p. 1-46).

Goyal, Ashima (2007), Woman Making Choices: Masked but Aware? *Indian Journal of Gender Syudies,* 14:3 (2007), p. 409-437.

Gilliyan (1982), In a Different Voice, Cambridge M.A: Harvad University Press.

Hershely and Corey (2005), Feminist Therapy in G. Corey, Theory and Practice of Counselling and Psychotherapy, 7th edition, p. 380-381.

Jennings Hall Helen (1943), Leadership and Isolation, A Study of Personality an Interpersonal Relations, New York: Mekey, 240. p. 349-426.

Mathur (1996).

Miller (1976), Toward a New Psychology of Women: Boston: Beacon Press.

Mishra, S. N. (1977), Pattern of Emerging Leadership in Rural India, Patna, Associate Book Agency.

Remer *et. al* (2001), Counseling; Women from a Feminist Perspective.

Sanderson, (ed); Leadership for Rural Life, New York .Wiley ,1940 (i) B. M. Kreithlow, E . W. Aiton and A.P. Torrence, Leadership for Action in Rural Communities, Illinois, Interstate Publication; E. F. Borgatta *et. al.* ''Some Findings Relevant to Greatman Theory of Leadership'', *American Sociological Reviews*, Vol. X:X, 1954.

Sharf (2000), Theories of Psychotherapy and Counselling.

Verma, R. K. (1991), Rural Political Leadership: A Study of Social Structure and People's Perception: Amar Prakash, 1991.

Verma, R. K. (1996), "Political Leadership: Issues in Concept and Approaches", *Journal of Social and Economic Studies*, Combined Volume 13.

24

महिलाओं का राजनीतिक सशक्तिकरण

एलविन बखला

हमारे संविधान में महिलाओं को हरेक क्षेत्र में प्रगति और विकास के लिए समान अवसर देने का प्रावधान है किन्तु आजादी के 62 वर्ष बाद भी भारतीय महिलाओं को राजनीति में समान अवसर नहीं मिल पाया है। कुछ लोग तो आज भी ऐसे हैं जो महिलाओं की राजनीति में भागीदारी को ही उपेक्षित निगाह में देखते हैं। परन्तु आज की नारी ने अपनी प्रतिभा और काबिलियत से राजनीति में अपना महत्वपूर्ण स्थान बना लिया है। लेकिन यह भी सच है कि जो महिलाएं राजनीति में आई हैं वे या तो राजनीतिक पारिवारिक पृष्ठभूमि से हैं या फिर अपने पिता या पति के विरासत को आगे बढ़ाने के लिए आगे आई है। इनमें कांग्रेस की भूतपूर्व प्रधानमंत्री स्व. श्रीमती इंदिरा गाँधी, सोनिया गाँधी, राजिन्दर कौर भट्ठल, शीला दीक्षित, सुचेता कृपलानी, नन्दिनी सत्पथी, अनवरा ताईमुर, भाजपा की सुषमा स्वराज, उमा भारती, वसुंधरा राजे सिंधिया, स्व. विजया राजे सिंधिय, तृणमूल कांग्रेस की ममता बनर्जी, बी.एस.पी. की मायावती, ए.डी.एम.के. की जयललिता, जानकी रामचन्द्रन, राजद की राबड़ी देवी आदि प्रमुख है। लेकिन यह सच है कि राजनीति में आम महिलाओं की भागीदारी बहुत कम है।

राजनीति में महिलाओं के प्रतिनिधित्व को लेकर दो बातें सामने आती है– प्रथम, क्या उन्हें राजनीति में पर्याप्त प्रतिनिधित्व मिलना चाहिए और यदि हाँ तो क्यों? द्वितीय, क्या उन्हें राजनीति में पर्याप्त प्रतिनिधित्व की आवश्यकता नहीं है

और यदि नहीं तो क्यों? इस संदर्भ में ध्यातव्य है कि वर्तमान समाज में दो वर्ग है– सुधारवादी या विकासवादी तथा रूढ़िवादी। सुधारवादी वर्ग द्वारा ऐसा कहा जा रहा है कि महिलाओं को राजनीति में भी पर्याप्त प्रतिनिधित्व मिलनी चाहिए क्योंकि ऐसा नहीं होने से हमारे समाज में पर्याप्त विकास असंभव है। दूसरी ओर, रूढ़िवादियों का मानना है कि महिलाओं के घर से बाहर आ जाने के बाद उसका बुरा प्रभाव परिवार पर पड़ेगा। ऐसा इसलिए कि हमारी पारिवारिक व्यवस्था में घर संभालने का सम्पूर्ण दायित्व महिलाओं पर है और उनके घर से बाहर आने से यह व्यवस्था टूट जाएगी तथा समाज के विकास की नीव कमजोर हो जायेगी ।

यदि गहनतापूर्वक अध्ययन किया जाय तो ऐसा प्रतीत होता है कि सुधारवादियों और रूढ़िवादियों, दोनों के तर्क में सत्यता है, परन्तु विचार करने योग्य तथ्य यह है कि क्या महिलाओं को सदैव चहारदीवारी के भीतर ही कैद करके रखा जाय? हमारे समाज में ऐसे अनेक उदाहरण है, जब महिलाओं ने पारिवारिक दायित्वों को संभालते हुए भी राजनीति में सक्रिय होकर अपना महत्वपूर्ण योगदान दिया है। भारतीय सभ्यता के इतिहास में सर्वाधिक विकसित समाज ऋग्वैदिक काल में ही था। इस समय समाज में महिलाओं को प्रत्येक क्षेत्र में पुरुषों के समान अधिकार प्राप्त थे शिक्षा से लेकर राजनीतिक क्षेत्र तक। इस काल में महिलाएँ 'सभा' एवं 'समिति' जैसी सर्वोच्च राजनीतिक संस्थाओं में अपनी सशक्त उपस्थिति दर्ज करवाती थी लेकिन दुर्भाग्यवश उत्तर वैदिक काल में महिलाओं की राजनीति के क्षेत्र में सक्रियता कम होती चली गयी। धीरे-धीरे मध्यकाल तक आते-आते उनके सभी अधिकार छीन लिए गये। उन्हें पुरुषों का भोग्य बना दिया गया तथा मध्यकाल में पर्दा प्रथा के प्रचलन के पश्चात् से उनकी स्थिति और भी बदतर हो गयी। वे अपने अधिकारों के लिए किसी प्रकार से आवाज नहीं उठा सकती थी। आवाज उठाने पर उन्हें विविध प्रकार से सताया जाता था। लेकिन आधुनिक काल में पश्चात्य शिक्षा के विकास के बाद महिलाओं का हर क्षेत्र में भागीदारी बढ़ी है। लेकिन राजनीति के क्षेत्र में अब भी पीछे है। उन्हें ऐसा महसूस हो रहा था कि राजनीति में पर्याप्त प्रतिनिधित्व के बिना उनके लिए अनुकूल वातावरण उपस्थित हो ही नहीं सकता। अतः अब महिलाओं द्वारा राजनीति में अपने पर्याप्त प्रतिनिधित्व की मांग की जाने लगी है।

महिला आरक्षण की आवश्यकता

संवैधानिक दृष्टि से भारत के सभी नागरिक बराबर है। इस दृष्टि से देखा जाय तो आरक्षण की आवश्यकता ही नहीं है। लेकिन भारतीय संविधान निर्माताओं ने

माना कि समाज के कुछ वर्गों के लोग काफी पिछड़े हुए हैं और जब तक उन्हें आगे बढ़ाने के लिए विशेष कदम नहीं उठाये जायेंगे तब तक वे पिछड़े के पिछड़े ही रहेंगे। इसी आधार पर अनुसूचित जातियों एवं जनजातियों के लिए सरकारी नौकरियों और शिक्षण संस्थाओं में आरक्षण की व्यवस्था की गयी। अन्य पिछड़े वर्गों में भी मण्डल आयोग की सिफारिश के आधार पर 27 प्रतिशत आरक्षण देने की व्यवस्था की गयी। इसी प्रकार महिलाओं को भी इस पुरुष प्रधान समाज में राजनीति के क्षेत्र में आगे बढ़ने में अनेक कठिनाईयों का सामना करना पड़ रहा है। यह तो सच है कि यदि महिलाओं के लिए राजनीतिक आरक्षण की व्यवस्था नहीं की गयी तो वे अपने बलबूते विधानसभाओं तथा संसद में पर्याप्त संख्या में नहीं पहुंच सकेगी। इसलिए महिलाओं को राज्य विधानसभाओं एवं संसद में 33 प्रतिशत आरक्षण दिया जाना आवश्यक है क्योंकि सही अर्थ में समानता तभी प्राप्त की जा सकती है जब महिलाओं को देश की निर्णय प्रक्रिया में महत्वपूर्ण भूमिका मिले।

महिला आरक्षण की दिशा में उठाये गये कदम

शुरू में 1974-75 में 'कमेटी ऑन स्टेटस ऑफ वीमेन' (महिलाओं की स्थिति पर समिति) ने महिलाओं के लिए संसद एवं विधानसभाओं में सीट आरक्षित करने की अनुशंसा पर असहमति जताई। आजादी के पूर्व केन्द्रीय विधायिका में महिलाओं के लिए 33 प्रतिशत आरक्षण था। 1952 में संसद में 4 प्रतिशत सीटें महिलाओं के लिए निर्धारित थी। समिति ने ग्राम स्तर पर वैधानिक 'महिला पंचायत' गठित करने का सुझाव दिया जो पंचायती राज व्यवस्था का अंग होगा। यह अस्थायी व्यवस्था तब तक के लिए होगी जब तक कि महिलाओं की समुचित भागीदारी राजनीतिक प्रक्रिया में न हो जाय। लोकसभा एवं विधानसभा के लिए प्रत्येक दल 15 प्रतिशत महिला उम्मीदवारों को टिकट दें लेकिन महिला आरक्षण का विरोध किया गया।

इसके बाद सन् 1988 में 'नेशनल पर्सपेक्टिव प्लान' (राष्ट्रीय दृष्टिकोण योजना) ने महिलाओं के लिए पंचायत समितियों, जिला परिषदों तथा स्थानीय नगर निकायों में 30 प्रतिशत सीटें आरक्षित करने की अनुशंसा की। सन् 1989 में भोपाल सम्मेलन में कांग्रेस ने पंचायती राज संस्थाओं तथा स्थानीय नगर निकायों में 30 प्रतिशत सीटें महिलाओं के लिए आरक्षित करने का संकल्प पारित किया। 1989 में लोकसभा चुनाव में अधिकांश राजनीतिक दलों ने अपने घोषणा पत्रों में

महिलाओं का प्रतिनिधित्व बढ़ाने की बात कही। संसद एवं विधानसभाओं में महिलाओं के लिए आरक्षण के पक्ष में निम्न तर्क दिये गये, जो सार्थक है–

1. महिलाओं का प्रतिनिधित्व संसद एवं विधान मंडल में नगण्य है, इसका कारण राजनीतिक दलों की संकीर्णता के कारण टिकट नहीं दिया जाना है।
2. न्याय का तकाजा तो यह है कि महिलाओं की आधी आबादी के कारण आधी सीटें आरक्षित हो फिर भी प्रथम चरण में एक तिहाई सीटें ही आरक्षित हो।
3. कुछ संकीर्ण विचार वाले व्यक्तियों, दलों एवं संगठनों का यह भ्रम कि महिला आरक्षण से 'बॉब कट' महिलाओं और ऊँची जाति की महिलाओं का सदन में बाहुल्य हो जाएगा पूर्णतः निराधार है क्योंकि अधिकतर प्रतिनधि स्वतंत्र उम्मीदवार की अपेक्षा राजनीतिक दलों के टिकटों पर ही चुने जाते हैं सो सामाजिक न्याय वाली पार्टियां यदि पिछड़ी या दलित जातियों की महिलाओं की टिकट देगी तो उनके पुरुष सदस्यों की जगह महिला प्रतिनिधि बनेगी।
4. अभी भी महिलाओं की साक्षरता कम है जबकि दो तिहाई पुरुष शिक्षित सो महिलाओं को संसद एवं विधानमंडल में आरक्षण देकर उमकी चेतना का शीघ्र विकास किया जाएगा।
5. जब संविधन में 73वीं तथा 74वीं संविधन संशोधन करके महिलाओं को क्रमशः पंचायती राज संस्थाओं और नगर निकायों में एक तिहाई आरक्षण दिया जा चुका है तो उसका विस्तार राज्य विधानमंडल और केन्द्रीय स्तर तक क्यों नहीं किया जा सकता है।

इस बार भी महिला आरक्षण विधायक को लेकर सदन में जोरदार हंगामा हुआ लेकिन नतीजा वही ढाक के तीन पात।

23 अप्रैल 1993 भारतीय महिलाओं के लिए एक सुखद दिन था जब भारतीय संविधान के 73वें संविधान संशोधन में पंचायतों में 33 प्रतिशत स्थान उनके लिए आरक्षित कर दिया। देश के त्रिस्तरीय पंचायतों में महिलाओं के लिए की गयी आरक्षण की व्यवस्था एक क्रांतिकारी कदम है। संविधान के 73वें व 74वें संशोधन के परिणामस्वरूप देश की ग्रामीण व नगरीय पंचायतों में महिलाओं की भागीदारी बढ़ी है। त्रिस्तरीय पंचायत व्यवस्था में एक तिहाई स्थान महिलाओं के

लिए आरक्षित किये जाने की वजह से करीब 14 लाख महिलायें जनप्रतिनिधि के रूप में 1,63,000 पंचायत के विभिन्न पदों पर व 10,000 सरपंच के रूप में सत्ता में शरीक हुई हैं। शेष जिला परिषद सदस्या व पंचायत समिति के सदस्या के रूप में चुनकर आई है। इसके अलावे देश की एक तिहाई ग्राम पंचायतों, पंचायत समिति, जिला परिषद्, नगर क्षेत्र समितियों समेत नगरपालिका आदि में शासन की बागडोर इन महिलाओं के हाथ में है।

1993 में 73वें और 74वें संविधान संशोधन के बाद जो विभिन्न राज्यों में त्रिस्तरीय पंचायत चुनाव हुए उनमें सर्वाधिक संख्या महिला पंचायत प्रतिनिधि उत्तरप्रदेश से चुनकर आई। दूसरा स्थान मध्यप्रदेश तथा तीसरा स्थान आन्ध्र प्रदेश का रहा। ग्रामीण पंचायती राज व्यवस्था की सर्वोच्च संस्था जिला परिषद् में भी सर्वाधिक महिला सदस्य उत्तर प्रदेश से ही चुनकर आयी। द्वितीय स्थान पर आन्ध्र प्रदेश, जबकि तृतीय स्थान पर कर्नाटक रहा। सरपंच व ग्राम प्रधान के पद पर भी सर्वाधिक महिला प्रतिनिधि उत्तर प्रदेश से ही निर्वाचित हुई। आंध्र प्रदेश द्वितीय स्थान पर रहा। बिहार में भी हुए 2001 के त्रिस्तरीय पंचायत चुनाव में बड़ी संख्या में महिलाएं वार्ड सदस्य उपमुखिया, मुखिया, पंचायत समिति सदस्या, ब्लॉक उपप्रमुख-प्रमुख समेत जिला परिषद् प्रतिनिधि के रूप में निर्वाचित हुई।

पंचायती राज संस्थानों की तरह ही संसद व राज्य विधानमंडल में भी एह तिहाई आरक्षण की व्यवस्था महिलाओं के लिए किये जाने की आ्वयकता है। महिला आरक्षण बिल जिसे 81वें संविधान संशोधन के तहत् प्रस्तावित किया गया, उसका 1996 तथा 1998 में पुरुष सांसदों द्वारा घोर विरोध किया गया लेकिन बाद में यह मुद्दा फिर उठा और देश के विधानमंडल व संसद की राजनीति में महिलाओं की भागीदारी की अद्यतन स्थिति का अवलोकन व विश्लेषण करने पर महिलाओं की भागीदारी पुरुषों के भुकाबले काफी कम पायी गयी है। अतः वहाँ भी 33 प्रतिशत आरक्षण विधायक अब विवाद का मुद्दा बन गया। लेकिन महिलाओं ने इसके समर्थन में व्यापक रैली एवं धरना प्रदर्शन कर सरकार द्वारा 33 प्रतिशत आरक्षण बिल पास कराकर ही दम लिया। कांग्रेस अध्यक्ष श्रीमती सोनिया गाँधी भी इसके समर्थन में आगे आई। यह विधेयक जब संसद में पेश किया गया तो भाजपा के गठबंधन सरकार सत्ता में थी। भाजपा द्वारा प्रस्तुत इस विधेयक का स्वरूप कुछ भिन्न और विचित्र हो गया। लेकिन महिला आरक्षण विधेयक के विरोधियों ने लोकसभा में तो यह विधेयक पेश ही नहीं होने दिया। लोकसभा और विधनसभाओं में महिलाओं को 33 प्रतिशत आरक्षण प्रदान करने का मुद्दा राजनीतिक

दलों के बीच तीव्र मतभेद के कारण एक बार पुनः टल गया। भाजपा के नेतृत्व वाली गठबंधन सरकार ने अंततः अपने प्रयास में महिला आरक्षण विधेयक को सदन में प्रस्तावित करने में सफलता प्राप्त कर ली। इस बार विपक्ष की सबसे बड़ी पार्टी कांग्रेस ने विधेयक के प्रति सकारात्मक रूख अपनाया जिससे लगने लगा कि परिस्थितियाँ अनुकूल रही तो विधेयक अधिनियम का रूख ले लेगा लेकिन कांग्रेस गठबंधन सरकार के गठन के बाद भी यह मुद्दा संसद में लटका ही रहा।

महिला आरक्षण विधेयक के प्रावधान

सर्वप्रथम यह जानना आवश्यक है कि, विवादास्पद महिला आरक्षण विधेयक का आखिरकार प्रारूप है क्या? तो इस संदर्भ में कहा जा सकता है कि अटल बिहारी वाजपेयी के नेतृत्व वाली भाजपा सरकार द्वारा निर्मित महिला आरक्षण सम्बन्धी 84वें संविधान (संशोधन) विधेयक के कुछ प्रावधान इस प्रकार है :

(1) संविधान के अनुच्छेद-330 के खण्ड (1) में लोकसभा में महिलाओं के लिए स्थान आरक्षित होंगे।

(2) अनुच्छेद-330 खण्ड (2) के अधीन आरक्षित स्थानों की कुल संख्या के, जहाँ तक सम्भव हो, एक तिहाई स्थान यथास्थिति अनुसूचित जातियों अथवा अनुसूचित जनजातियों की महिलाओं के लिए आरक्षित होंगे।

(3) किसी राज्य अथवा संघ राज्य में लोकसभा के लिए प्रत्येक चुनाव द्वारा भरे जाने वाले स्थानों की कुल संख्या के जहां तक सम्भव हो एक-तिहाई स्थान, जिनके अन्तर्गत अनुसूचित जातियों एवं अनुसूचित जनजातियों की महिलाओं के लिए आरक्षित स्थानों की संख्या भी है, महिलाओं के लिए आरक्षित रहेंगे और ऐसे स्थान उस राज्य अथवा संघ राज्य क्षेत्र में भिन्न-भिन्न चुनाव क्षेत्रों को चक्रानुक्रम द्वारा आवंटित किए जा सकेंगे।

(4) जहाँ ऐसे नाम-निर्देशन लोकसभा के लिए तीन साधारण निर्वाचनों से मिलकर बनने वाले प्रत्येक ब्लॉक के सम्बन्ध में किए जाते हैं, वहां एक स्थान प्रथम दो साधारण निर्वाचनों के पश्चात् गठित की जाने वाली प्रत्येक लोकसभा के लिए आंग्ल-भारतीय समुदाय की महिला के नाम-निर्देशन के लिए आरक्षित रहेगा और तीसरे साधरण निर्वाचन के पश्चात् गठित की जाने वाली लोकसभा में उस समुदाय की महिला के लिए कोई स्थान आरक्षित नहीं रहेगा।

(5) अनुच्छेद-332 (क) प्रत्येक राज्य की विधानसभा में भी महिलाओं के लिए स्थान आरक्षित होंगे।

(6) इस अधिनियम द्वारा संविधान में किए गए संशोधनों से लोकसभा, किसी राज्य की विधनसभा अथवा दिल्ली की विधानसभा में किसी प्रतिनिधित्व पर तब तक प्रभाव नहीं पड़ेगा, जब तक इस अधिनियम के प्रारम्भ में विंद्यमान (यथास्थिति) लोकसभा, किसी राज्य अथवा दिल्ली की विधानसभा का विघटन नहीं हो जाता।

जहाँ तक वैश्विक स्तर पर राजनीति में महिलाओं की सहभागिता का प्रश्न है, तो वर्तमान समय में न केवल विकासशील देशों में अपितु विकसित देशों में भी इनकी स्थिति दयनीय है अपितु कहा जा सकता है कि विश्व के सर्वाधिक विकसित देशों में महिलाओं की स्थिति सबसे अधिक दयनीय है।

भारत में महिलाओं को आरक्षण दिए जाने की मांग 80 के दशक से उठाई जा रही है, परन्तु विश्व में इससे पहले महिला आरक्षण की बात की जा चुकी थी। यहां तक कि रूस द्वारा इसका प्रयोग भी किया गया, परन्तु वह विफल रहा और इस विधेयक को ही भंग कर देना पड़ा।

भारत में महिला आरक्षण को लेकर जिस प्रकार का विवाद बार-बार खड़ा किया जाता रहा है, उससे यह स्पष्ट हो जाता है कि यह एक चुनावी मुद्‌दा बन गया है और इसे निकट भविष्य में सुलझा पाना मुश्किल है। अच्छा तो यह होगा कि विधायिका में आरक्षण देने के स्थान पर महिलाओं को शैक्षणिक एवं आर्थिक क्षेत्र में विकास के पर्याप्त अवसर प्रदान किए जाएं और समाज में ऐसा वातावरण निर्मित किया जाए कि महिलाएं स्वयं को निर्भीक और स्वतंत्र अनुभव कर सकें तथा देश के विकास में सहभागी बन सकें।

संदर्भ सूची

सिंहल, डॉ. एस. सी. (2007), समकालीन राजनीतिक मुद्दे, लक्ष्मी नारायण अग्रवाल पब्लिकेशन, आगरा, पृ. 160-169।

राजाराम, कल्पना (2008), भारत का संविधान और भारतीय राजनीतिक व्यवस्था, स्पेक्ट्रम बुक्स प्रा. लि., जनकपुरी, पृ. 419-422।

गुप्ता, सरोज कुमार (2007), भारतीय नारी कल, आज और कल, प्रकाशन संस्थान, नयी दिल्ली, पृ. 330-361।

फाड़िया, डॉ. बी. एल. (2007), समकालीन राजनीतिक मुद्दे, साहित्य भवन पब्लिकेशन, आगरा।

गोपाल, डॉ. शर्मा, क्षवी कविता वाचक, स्त्री सशक्तिकरण के विविध आयाम।

स्वप्निल सारस्वत, डॉ. सिंह निशांत, समाज, राजनीति और महिलाएं, दशा और दिशा, नमन प्रकाशन, नई दिल्ली।

के. एम. मात्यु (2001), मनोरमा ईयर बुक।

डॉ. रेणु दिवान (2007), नारी संवाद मार्च-जून।

25

राजनीति में महिलाओं की भूमिका

हरिनारायण प्र. चौरसिया

महिला आंदोलनों की सफलता तब तक नहीं मानी जाएगी जब तक "नारी तुम केवल श्रद्धा हो" जैसे विचारों को सामाजिक धरातल पर उतार न लिया जाए। किसी भी सभ्य समाज की परिकल्पना तभी की जा सकती है,जब उस समाज की महिलाओं की वास्तविक स्थिति, मूलभूत संसाधनों तक पहुंच तथा राजनीतिक, सामाजिक नीति निर्माण की प्रक्रिया में सहभागिता को सुनिश्चित किया जाए। महिलाओं का सशक्तिकरण एक लगातार चलने वाली अनवरत गतिशील प्रक्रिया है। यही वजह है कि समाज एवं राष्ट्र की प्रगति के लिए महिलाओं का विशेष महत्त्व होता है। इसलिए कहा जाता है कि, 'नारी स्वयं एक शक्ति ही नहीं एक जननी भी है।'

अधिकार ही मनुष्यों के व्यक्त्वि को प्रबलता प्रदान करता है, इसी श्रृंखला में महिला अधिकार भी एक धारा है, जिसके सहारे महिला अबला से सबला बनने तक की यात्रा करती है। आजादी के पूर्व महिलाओं की स्थिति अत्यन्त शोचनीय थी, वह शोषण, तिरस्कार एवं कुप्रथा जैसी कुसंस्कृतियों की शिकार थी। समाज में कई प्रकार की रूढ़ियां व्याप्त थी, जिनमें बाल विवाह, सती प्रथा तथा विधवा तिरस्कार आदि अन्य प्रथाएं प्रमुख थी, जिनका कारण तात्कालिक सामाजिक विचार का पिछड़ापन तथा महिलाओं की अज्ञानता के बंधन में जकड़ी लोहे की बेड़ी थी। आजादी के बाद से महिलाओं को विकास तथा समाज की मुख्य धारा में लाने का प्रयास किया जा रहा है।

महिलाओं की स्थिति में निरन्तर परिवर्तन समाज में क्रांतिकारी परिवर्तन, आधुनिक शिक्षा, विधायी, व्यवस्था, राजनैतिक आदर्श, सामाजिक एवं सांस्कृतिक मूल्यों में परिवर्तन, औद्योगीकरण, नगरीकरण इत्यादि कारणों से है। महिलाओं का शोषण पुरुषों से ज्यादा होता रहा है। जहाँ अल्प आयु में ही बाल श्रमिकों के रूप में वे आर्थिक क्षेत्र में प्रवेश करती हैं, साथ ही साथ कम आयु में ही वैवाहिक और पारिवारिक उत्तरदायित्त्व के कारण उनके शारीरिक, मानसिक और बौद्धिक विकास में बाध आती रही है। कृषि कार्यों में महिला श्रमिकों का अत्यधिक शोषण होता है, भू स्वामियों द्वारा कमजोर आर्थिक वर्ग की महिला और पुरुष दोनों अशिक्षा एवं अज्ञानता के कारण आजीवन उपेक्षा के शिकार बने रहते है। ग्रामीण क्षेत्रों की महिलाओं में राजनैतिक अधिकारों के प्रति जो अज्ञानता है, उसका कारण सामाजिक संरचना और सामाजिक आदर्श है, जो आज भी बाध डालने का कार्य करते हैं। विभिन्न सर्वेक्षणों एवं अनुसंधानों से पता चलता है कि ग्रामीण महिलाओं को अपने अधिकारों की जानकारी मुख्य रूप से अनैपचारिक साधनों जैसे पारिवारिक सदस्यों, मित्रों एवं पड़ोसियों से प्राप्त होती है। भारतीय ग्रामीण समाज जाति धर्म, क्षेत्रीयता तथा सम्प्रदाय पर आधारित होता है जिसके कारण भारतीय महिला एक सामाजिक वर्ग के रूप में निकसित नहीं हो पाती। महिलाओं पर परम्परागत व्यवस्था का प्रभाव बना रहता है।

भारतीय महिलाओं की सामाजिक स्थिति और भूमिका बहुत कुछ समाज के स्वरूप और विशेषताओं पर निर्भर करती हैं उसमें समाज की परम्पराएँ कैसी हैं, वह समाज आधुनिक है अथवा परम्परागत यह सब सामाजिक परिस्थितियों के रूप को प्रभावित करते हैं, साथ ही साथ समाज का आकार और संरचना भी महिलाओं की सामाजिक स्थिति का निर्धारण करते हैं। समाज में होने वाले विकास जैसे-नगरीकरण, जनसंख्या वृद्धि, औद्योगीकरण, यातायात के साधन इत्यादि भी महत्त्वपूर्ण भूमिका अदा करते हैं। वर्त्तमान परिवेश में पुत्रियों का धीरे-धीरे महत्त्व बढ़ रहा है। उनको सामाजिक सम्मान पुरुषों की भांति मिल रहा है। अब पुत्रियाँ परिवार में अधिक स्वतंत्रता महसूस कर रही हैं। परिवार भी पुत्रियों के प्रति जागरूक हो गए है। शिक्षित माताएँ बच्चों के प्रति अधिक सक्रिय हैं। मताधिकारों ने पुरुष-महिला की स्थिति को समान कर दिया है। शहरी और ग्रामीण महिलाओं के विचारों में भी परिवर्तन आया है और समाज के प्रतिमानों, मूल्यों के प्रति उनका दृष्टिकोण बदल रहा है। शिक्षित महिलाओं में भी व्यक्तिगत आधुनिकता आ रही है। उनकी आधुनिकता से भी सामाजिक गतिशीलता मिलेगी।

ये शिक्षित महिलाएँ यह समझ रही है कि मेरी दयनीय स्थिति के लिए अशिक्षा, अंधविश्वास रूढ़िवादिता, परम्परागत मान्यता तथा समाज का पुरुष प्रधान होना जिम्मेवार है। आज की महिलाएँ चाहती हैं कि वे अपने अधिकारों के साथ-साथ बौद्धिक जागरूकता एवं आत्मनिर्भरता भी प्राप्त करें। वे अपने पैरों पर खड़ा होने की इच्छा ही नहीं, बल्कि एक प्रबल क्षमता भी रखती हैं।

महिलाओं के प्रति भेदभाव के लिए निरक्षरता भी एक प्रमुख कारण है। महिलाओं की साक्षरता 1951 में 8.66% थी वही आज के सुधरे परिवेश के कारण महिलाओं की साक्षरता दर 2001 की जनगणना के अनुसार 54.16 प्रतिशत हो गई है। श्रमिक महिलाएॅ घरेलू उद्योगों, छोटे-छोटे व्यवसायों और नौकरी तथा भवन निर्माण जैसे असंगठित क्षेत्रों में भी काम कर रही है।

भारतीय महिलाओं को प्रोत्साहित करने एवं विकास की ओर ले जाने के लिए केन्द्र तथा राज्य सरकारों ने विभिन्न प्रकार के महिला कल्याण कार्यक्रम, पुरस्कार आदि प्रारंभ किए हैं। बहुत से अधिनियमों को कानूनी अमली जामा पहनाया गया है। केन्द्र एवं राज्य सरकारों द्वारा चलाये जा रहे महिला कल्याण कार्यक्रम संबंधी कुछ अधिनियमों की सूची इस प्रकार है–

1. विशेष विवाह अधिनियम, 1954
2. हिन्दू विवाह अधिनियम, 1955
3. वेश्यावृत्ति निवारण अधिनियम,1956
4. स्त्री-बालक संस्था अधिनियम, 1956
5. दहेज निषेध अधिनियम, 1961
6. प्रसूति लाभ अधिनियम, 1961
7. समान पारिश्रमिक अधिनियम, 1976
8. कुटुंम्ब न्यायालय अधिनियम, 1984
9. मुस्लिम स्त्री (विवाह विच्छेदन) अधिनियम, 1986
10. सती निवारण अधिनियम, 1987
11. प्रसव पूर्व निदान तकनीकी अधिनियम, 1994
12. कस्तूरबा गाँधी शिक्षा योजना, 1997
13. स्त्री शक्ति पुरस्कार योजना, 2000

14. महिला स्वाधार योजना, 2001
15. राष्ट्रीय पोषाहार मिशन योजना, 2001
16. जीवन भारती महिला सुरक्षा योजना, 2003
17. जननी सुरक्षा योजना, 2003
18. महिला स्वयंसिद्ध योजना, 2004
19. बंदेमातरम् योजना, 2004
20. कस्तूरवागॉधी विद्यालय योजना, 2004
21. घरेलू हिंसा से संरक्षण विधेयक, 2005

इसके अतिरिक्त 218 महिला औद्योगिक प्रशिक्षण संस्थान खोले गए। 582 महिला स्कंध सामान्य शिक्षण संस्थानों और निजी औद्योगिक प्रशिक्षण संस्थानों को प्रारंभ किया गया, जो राज्य सरकारों के नियंत्रण में है। महिलाओं के सामाजिक और आर्थिक विकास के लिए स्वयंसिद्ध योजना, स्वाशक्तियोजना, स्वाधार योजना, तथा अल्पावधि प्रवास गृह योजना, घरेलू हिंसा कानून जैसे संरक्षणात्मक कदमों की शुरुआत की गई है, जो महिलाओं के लिए सर्वोत्तम है।

महिलाओं के संबंध में एक बड़ी घटना तब हुई, जब उच्चतम न्यायालय ने 13 अगस्त, 1997 को विशाखा तथा अन्य बनाम् राजस्थान सरकार और अन्य के मामले में दिए गए ऐतिहासिक पफैसले में काम के स्थान पर महिलाओं का यौन शोषण या उत्पीड़न रोकने के लिए व्यापक दिशा-निर्देश और मानक भी निर्धारित किए, जिसे बाद में संविधान के प्रावधानों के अन्तर्गत कानूनी रूप दिया गया। संविधान में 73वें एवं 74वें संशोधन द्वारा महिलाओं को पंचायत तथा शहरी निकायों में प्रतिनिधित्व हेतु एक-तिहाई स्थान आरक्षित किए गए है। यही नहीं, इन संस्थानों में प्रधान और अध्यक्ष के एक-तिहाई पद भी महिलाओं के लिए आरक्षित किए गए है, ताकि उन्हें केवल प्रतिनिधित्व ही नहीं नेतृत्त्व करने का भी अवसर मिले। 'हिन्दू उत्तराधिकार संशोधन अधिनियम 2005 पारित किया गया, जिसमें महिलाएं पैत्रिक सम्पति में अपने हक का कानूनी दावा कर सकती है।

महिलाओं का मान सम्मान बढ़ाने के लिए पुरस्कार/दिवस मनाया गया। इसी कड़ी में 1975 को 'अन्तर्राष्ट्रीय महिला वर्ष घोषित किया गया। 2001 में भारत में 'महिला सशक्किरण वर्ष' घोषित किया गया। इसके साथ ही 31 जनवरी, 1992 में 'राष्ट्रीय महिला आयोग का गठन' हुआ। 'स्त्री शक्ति पुरस्कार' भारत

की पांच महायशस्विनी महिलाओं के नाम से दिया जाता है, ये— है-कालगी, माता जीजा बाई, देवी अहिल्या बाई, झांसी की रानी लक्ष्मी बाई तथा रानी गौन्डिल्यू। ये पुरस्कार 8 मार्च को अन्तर्राष्ट्रीय महिला दिवस पर दिए जाते हैं।

जनसंख्या के हिसाब से राजनीति में महिलाओं की भूमिका बहुत कम हैं हालांकि महिलाओं में पहले की तुलना में काफी जागृति आई है। आज हर क्षेत्र में महिलाएं पुरुषों के साथ कदम से कदम मिलाकर चल रही है। उनकी आर्थिक, सामाजिक एंव राजनीतिक सभी क्षेत्रों में उत्थान हुआ है। बिहार में पंचायती राज संस्थाओं, नगर निकाओं के चुनावों में और शिक्षकों तथा न्याय-मित्रों की नियुक्ति में महिलाओं को 50% आरक्षण देकर सरकार ने राजनीति एवं सामाजिक क्षेत्रों में उनकी भूमिका बढ़ा दी है। लोक सभा एवं राज्य की विधान सभाओं में भी महिलाओं को आरक्षण देने की मांग उठ रही है जिसे दबाना अब किसी के बूते की बात नहीं है।

कई राजनीतिक पार्टियों एवं संगठनों द्वारा आलोचना की जाती है कि महिलाओं को आरक्षण देने से कार्यों में कुशलता का ह्रास हुआ है और महिलाएँ सब काम पुरुषों के माध्यम से ही करती है। सारे निर्णय उनके पति या भाई के रूप में पुरुष ही करते हैं। इन आलोचनाओं में थोड़ा दम जरूर है, लेकिन आने वाले दिनों में जैसे-जैसे महिलाएं शिक्षित और प्रशिक्षित होती जाएंगी उनके कार्यों में निखार होता जाएगा। राजनीतिक दलों और संगठनों को इस दिशा में प्रयास करना चाहिए।

बिहार सरकार ने महिलाओं के आर्थिक, राजनीतिक और सामाजिक उत्थान के लिए काफी प्रयास किया है। मुख्यमंत्री कन्या विवाह योजना के अन्तर्गत वर्ष 2008-09 में कुल 20 करोड़ रुपये स्वीकृत हुआ है। मुख्यमंत्री कन्या सुरक्षा योजना अन्तर्गत प्रतिलाभुक 2 हजार रुपयें का बॉण्ड देने हेतु यू.टी.आई. के साथ एम.ओ.यू. हस्ताक्षरित और वर्ष 2008-09 में इस योजना हेतु कुल 26 करोड़ रुपये स्वीकृत हुआ है। मुख्यमंत्री नारी शक्ति योजना प्रारंभ हुआ एवं इस योजना अन्तर्गत 5600 नये स्वयं सहायता समूहों का गठन और 1391 समूह साधन सेवियों का चयन हुआ है। महिलाओं के आर्थिक शक्तिकरण हेतु 32 फेडरेशनों को 2.50 लाख रुपये प्रति फेडरेशन की दर से निवेश-कोष में अनुदान-राशि का वितरण हुआ है। 16 जिलों में महिलाओं के लिए हेल्पलाईन स्थापित एवं 22 जिलों में नये हेल्पलाईन की स्थापना कार्य प्रगति में है। महिला आरक्षण से संबंधित कानूनों की जानकारी हेतु सामाजिक जागरूकता कार्यक्रम अन्तर्गत 10 जिलों के 121 पंचायतों

में 363 नुक्कड़ नाटक आयोजित किए गए। महामहिम भारत के राष्ट्रपति श्रीमती प्रतिभा देवी सिंह पाटिल ने अपना उद्‌गार व्यक्त करते हुए कहा है, "**महिलाओं को शैक्षण्कि सामाजिक और आर्थिक रूप से आत्मनिर्भर बनाने की दिशा में यहां नई पहल हुई है। निश्चित रूप से यह राज्य अब पूरे देश को महिला सशक्तिकरण के क्षेत्र में नई दिशा दिखाएगा।**"

समय की मांग यही है कि ठोस कार्यक्रम के जरिये ऐसा माहौल बनाया जाए जिसमें समाज में प्रत्येक सदस्य को जाति, वंश या लिंग के भेदभाव के बिना समाज के उत्थान के लिए कार्य करने वाले बराबरी के सहयोगी की तरह देखा जाए। महात्मा गाँधी ने जिस बात का स्वप्न देखा था, वह समान अधिकारों, समान अवसर और समान भागीदारी वाली अधिक न्यायोचित और मानवीय दुनिया की दिशा में की जा रही यात्रा का एक कदम भर है, **क्योंकि जब किसी महिला का विकास होता है तो उसके परिवार का भी विकास होता है। जब परिवारों का विकास होता है तो समाज फलते-फूलते है, जिसका लाभ राष्ट्र को मिलता है। इसलिए जब स्त्री या पुरुष में किसी एक को शिक्षित करने की बात आए, तो यह हक सर्वप्रथम एक नारी को मिलना चाहिए।**

निष्कर्ष के रूप में कहा जा सकता है कि आज भारतीय महिलाओं के कल्याण और सशक्तिकरण के लिए राजनैतिक, आर्थिक तथा समाजिक पोषण मिला है। महिलाओं की स्थितियों में सुधार तथा विकसित समाज की मुख्य धारा में जोड़ने के लिए विधायी उपाय, कल्याणकारी योजनाएँ तथा विकास कार्यक्रमों का संचालन किया जा रहा है। महिलाओं को अपने अधिकार एवं दायित्वों के प्रति सजग करने के लिए शिक्षा के समुचित अवसर उपलब्ध कराये गए हैं जिससे महिलाओं में स्वावलम्बन और आत्मनिर्भर की भावना जागृत हुई। जब महिलाओं को समान अवसर या अधिकार देंगे तभी हम कोई सामाजिक परिवर्तन, आर्थिक उपलब्धि, राजनैतिक सत्ता, समाज में शांति, सुरक्षा तथा विकास की नींव डाल सकेंगे। आज आवश्यकता है नारी के प्रति पुरुषों को अपनी नकारात्मक पुरानी सोंच बदलने की।

26

महिला सशक्तिकरण–
राजनैतिक वैधानिक प्रावधान : एक समाजशास्त्रीय समीक्षा

गजनफर आलम

महिला सशक्तीकरण में सामाजिक सुविधाओं की उपलब्धता, राजनैतिक और आर्थिक नीति निर्धारण में भागीदारी, समान कार्य के लिए समान वेतन, कानून के तहत सुरक्षा एवं प्रजनन अधिकारों आदि को सम्मिलित किया जाता है। दूसरे शब्दों में हम कह सकते हैं कि महिला सशक्तीकरण का मतलब हर क्षेत्र में उनकी उपस्थिति या भागीदारी को सुनिश्चित कराने से है। सरकार ने समाज में लिंग आधारित भिन्नताओं को दूर करने की यात्रा एक तरह से सन् 1953 में महिला कल्याण की नीति अपना कर शुरू की थी। बाद में यह यात्रा महिला विकास तक पहुंची और अब महिला सशक्तीकरण का नारा सामने आया है। महिला सशक्तीकरण का राष्ट्रीय नीति का उद्देश्य महिलाओं की प्रगति एवं विकास को सुनिश्चित करना तथा आत्मशक्ति को बढ़ाना है। पूर्व में महिला सशक्तीकरण के लिए उठाये गये कदम।

महिला और बाल विकास विभाग

1985 में देश भर की महिलाओं और बच्चों की स्थिति सुधारने हेतु महिला और बाल विकास विभाग की स्थापना की गई। यह सरकारी तथा गैरसरकारी संगठनों में तालमेल रखते हुए नीति, योजनाएँ तथा कार्यक्रम बनाता है। महिला और बाल

विकास विभाग के अन्तर्गत एक संवैधानिक संस्था-राष्ट्रीय महिला आयोग तथा तीन स्वायत्त संगठन कार्य करती है। जो है, राष्ट्रीय लोक सहायता तथा बाल विकास संस्थान, केन्द्रीय समाज कल्याण बोर्ड तथा राष्ट्रीय महिला कोश। महिला एवं विकास विभाग महिलाओं के लिए दो प्रमुख रोजगार एवं प्रशिक्षणोन्मुख कार्यक्रमों पर अमल कर रहा हैं वे हैं–

(1) प्रशिक्षण तथा रोजगार कार्यक्रम (स्टेप)

(2) स्वावलम्बन

स्टेप कार्यक्रम 1987 में शुरू हुआ जिसका उद्देश्य कृषि, पशुपालन, डेयरी, मछली पालन, हस्त शिल्प आदि महिलाओं की प्रधानता वाली परम्परागत कार्यों में गरीबी व बदहाली में जीवन यापन करने वाली महिलाओं को रोजगार के अवसर उपलब्ध कराने के लिए हुनर एवं उत्पादकता में सुधार लाना।

महिला सशक्तीकरण की शुरूआत संयुक्त राष्ट्रसंघ द्वारा 08 मार्च 1975 को अन्तर्राष्ट्रीय महिला दिवस से माना जा सकता है। पुनः महिला सशक्तीकरण की पहल 1985 में महिला अन्तर्राष्ट्रीय सम्मेलन नौरोबी में की गई। भारत ने भी महिला सशक्तीकरण के लिए अनेक कदम उठाएं। 31 जनवरी 1992 को राष्ट्रीय महिला आयोग का गठन हुआ जिसके माध्यम से सदियों से पिछड़े, शोषित एवं उपेक्षित नारी वर्ग के विकास हेतु विशेष ध्यान दिया जा रहा है। वर्ष 2001 में भारत सरकार ने ''महिला सशक्तीकरण वर्ष घोषित किया तथा राष्ट्रीय महिला शक्ति सम्पन्न नीति 2001 की घोषणा की। जिसके लक्ष्य निम्नलिखित हैं–

(1) महिलाओं की पूर्ण क्षमता की प्राप्ति एवं पूर्ण विकास हेतु सकारात्मक आर्थिक तथा सामाजिक नीतियों के माध्यम से वातावरण का सृजन करना।

(2) राजनीतिक, आर्थिक, सामाजिक, सांस्कृतिक तथा सिविल सभी क्षेत्रों में पुरुषों के साथ समान आधार पर महिलाओं द्वारा समस्त मानवाधिकारों तथा मौलिक स्वतंत्रताओं का सैद्धान्तिक तथा वस्तुतः उपयोग करना।

(3) राष्ट्र के सामाजिक, राजनैतिक तथा आर्थिक जीवन में महिलाओं की भागीदारी तथा निर्णय स्तर पर समानता लाना।

(4) सभी स्तरों पर स्वास्थ्य, देखभाल, स्तरीय शिक्षा, जीविका, व्यवसायिक मार्गदर्शन, रोजगार, समान पराश्रमिक, सुरक्षा तथा सार्वजनिक पदों इत्यादि में महिलाओं की समान पहुँच।

(5) महिलाओं के साथ होने वाले सभी प्रकार के भेदभावों के उन्मूलन के उद्देश्य से कानूनी प्रणालियों की सुदृढ़ीकरण।

(6) पुरुषों तथा महिलाओं दोनों की सक्रिय भागीदारी द्वारा सामाजिक रवैये और प्रथाओं में परिवर्तन।

(7) विकास प्रक्रिया में महिला परिप्रेक्ष्यों में शामिल करना।

(8) महिलाओं तथा बालिकाओं के साथ होने वाली हिंसा के सभी रूपों तथा भेदभावों का उन्मूलन।

(9) सिविल समाज, विशेषकर महिला संगठनों के साथ भागीदारी बनाना तथा उसका सुदृढ़ीकरण आदि।

हमारे देश में विभिन्न महिला संगठनों द्वारा विधायिका में महिलाओं को आरक्षण दिए जाने की बात की जाती है। इसी क्रम में 1996 में तत्कालीन प्रधानमंत्री एच.डी. देवगौड़ा के शासनकाल में व्यवस्थापिका में महिलाओं को आरक्षण दिए जाने वाले विधेयक को पहली बार सांसद में प्रस्तुत किया गया। उसके बाद भी इस विधेयक को कई बार लाया गया लेकिन अभी तक यह पारित नहीं हो सका है। 84वें संविधान संशोधन विधेयक 1998 के रूप में लम्बित इस विधेयक द्वारा संविधान के अनुच्छेद 330 एवं 332 में संशोधन किया जाना प्रस्तावित है। विधेयक के प्रावधानों के अनुसार लोकसभा एवं राज्य विधानसभाओं में कुल स्थानों का 33% स्थान महिलाओं के लिए आरक्षित रहेगा तथा राज्य अथवा संघ राज्य क्षेत्रों में लोकसभा के लिए होने वाले निर्वाचन में जहां तक संभव हो एक तिहाई स्थान महिलाओं द्वारा भरे जायेंगे जहां निर्वाचन क्षेत्रों की संख्या तीन अथवा तीन से कम है वहां आरक्षण की व्यवस्था चक्रानुक्रम द्वारा लागू की जायेगी। प्रस्तावित इस विधेयक को पास कराने हेतु सभी राजनैतिक पार्टियों में आम राय बनाने की कोशिश की गयी तथा इसको पास कराने का भरसक प्रयास किया गया। यद्यपि यह विधेयक कुछ राजनैतिक पार्टियों के द्वारा विभिन्न वर्गों और जातियों की महिलाओं के लिए अलग-अलग आरक्षण की व्यवस्था करने के लिए विरोध प्रदर्शन के कारण पास नहीं हो सका है। उल्लेखनीय है कि इससे पूर्व सांसद द्वारा 73वां एवं 74वां संविधान संशोधन अधिनियम 1993 पारित किए गए। इस संशोधन द्वारा ग्राम पंचायतों तथा नगर पालिकाओं में क्रमशः अनुच्छेद 243(घ) तथा अनुच्छेद 243(न) द्वारा आरक्षित एवं अनारक्षित वर्ग की महिलाओं हेतु 33% की आरक्षण की व्यवस्था की गयी है। इस व्यवस्था के क्रियान्वयन से

देश के सभी प्रान्तों में ग्रामीण और शहरी पंचायतों के सभी स्तरों पर कई महिलाएं जनप्रतिनिधियों के रूप में अहम् भूमिका का निर्वाह कर रही है। इसी प्रकार की व्यवस्था "महिला आरक्षण विधेयक" के माध्यम से संसद और राज्य विधान मण्डलों में प्रस्तावित की गयी है। इसके प्रमुख प्रावधान निम्नलिखित हैं–

- संविधान के अनु. 330 के खण्ड (1) में लोकसभा महिलाओं के लिये स्थान आरक्षित होंगे।
- संविधान के अनुच्छेद 330 के खण्ड (2) के अधीन आरक्षित स्थानों की कुल संख्या के जहाँ तक संभव हो, एक तिहाई स्थान यथास्थिति एस. सी./एस.टी. की महिलाओं के लिए आरक्षित होंगे।
- जहाँ ऐसे नाम निर्देशक लोकसभा के लिये तीन साधारण निर्वाचनों से मिलकर बनने वाले प्रत्येक ब्लॉक के सम्बन्ध में किये जाते हैं, वहाँ एक स्थान प्रथम हो, दो साधारण निर्वाचनों के पश्चात् गठित की जाने वाली प्रत्येक लोकसभा के लिए एंग्लो-इंडियन समुदाय की महिला के नाम निर्देशन के लिए आरक्षित रहेगा और तीसरे साधरण निर्वाचन के पश्चात् गठित की जाने वाली लोकसभा में उस समुदाय की महिला के लिये कोई स्थान आरक्षित नहीं रहेगा।
- संविधान के अनु. 332क(1) प्रत्येक राज्य विधानसभा में भी महिलाओं के लिए स्थान आरक्षित रहेंगे।
- किसी भी राज्य या संघ राज्य क्षेत्र में लोकसभा के लिए प्रत्यक्ष चुनाव द्वारा भरे जाने वाले स्थानों की कुल संख्या के जहाँ तक संभव हो एक तिहाई स्थान जिनके अन्तर्गत अनुसूचित जातियों/अनुसूचित जनजातियों की महिलाओं के लिए आरक्षित रहेंगे और ऐसे स्थान उस राज्य या संघ राज्य क्षेत्र में भिन्न-भिन्न चुनाव क्षेत्रों को चक्रानुक्रम द्वारा आवंटित किए जा सकेंगे।
- इस अधिनियम में किये गये संशोधनों से लोकसभा, किसी राज्य की विधानसभा या दिल्ली की विधानसभा में किसी प्रतिनिधित्व पर तब तक प्रभाव नहीं पड़ेगा जब तक कि इस अधिनियम के प्रारम्भ पर विद्यमान लोकसभा, किसी राज्य की विधानसभा या दिल्ली की विधानसभा का विघटन नहीं हो जाता है।
- जहाँ निर्वाचन क्षेत्रों की संख्या तीन अथवा तीन से कम है वहाँ आरक्षण की व्यवस्था चक्रानुक्रम द्वारा लागू की जायेगी।

संसद एवं विधानसभाओं में महिलाओं के लिए आरक्षण के पक्ष में दिए जाने वाले तर्क–

- महिलाओं का प्रतिनिधित्व संसद एवं विधान मंडल में नगण्य है। इसका प्रमुख कारण है राजनैतिक दलों की संकीर्णता एवं अदूरदर्शिता के कारण महिलाओं को समुचित संख्या में टिकट नहीं दिया जाता है।
- महिलाओं की आधी आबादी के नाते नीति निर्धारण में उन्हें समुचित भूमिका निभाना आवश्यक है यानि न्याय का तकाजा तो यह है कि महिलाओं के लिए आधी सीटें आरक्षित हो।
- महिलाओं के विरुद्ध नाना प्रकार के अपराध एवं हिंसात्मक प्रताड़नाएं घर से सड़क तक होती रहती है, उन्हें विभिन्न सामाजिक कुरीतियों का शिकार होना पड़ता है और उन्हें दीन एवं दोयम दर्जे का नागरिक समझा जाता रहा है, प्रतिनिधित्व मिलने अथवा दिए जाने से उन्हें आत्म-सम्मान मिलेगा।
- प्रतिनिधित्व से लड़कियों के समक्ष एक नया रोल मॉडल पेश हो सकेगा और इसका सकारात्मक प्रभाव महिला सशक्तीकरण के रूप पर पड़ेगा।
- महिलाओं में निरक्षरता का प्रतिशत पुरुषों की तुलना में काफी ज्यादा है। अभी शेष महिलाओं को साक्षर बनाने में कई दर्शक लग जायेंगे। इसीलिए महिलाओं को संसद व विधानमंडल में आरक्षण देकर उनकी चेतना का शीघ्र विकास किया जा सकता है।
- जब संविधान में 73वां और 74वां संशोधन करके महिलाओं को क्रमशः पंचायतीराज संस्थाओं और नगर निकायों में एक तिहाई आरक्षण दिया जा चुका है, तो उसका विस्तार राज्य-स्तर और केन्द्र स्तर तक क्यों नहीं किया जा सकता है?
- पुरुष के प्रभुत्व के चलते राजनैत्रिक दल चुनाव में अधिक महिलाओं को खड़ा नहीं करते। आरक्षण से दलों द्वारा महिला उम्मीदवारों को चुनाव के लिए समर्थन करना सुनिश्चित होगा।
- दलित महिलाएं भी S.C./S.T. की तरह एक वंचित श्रेणी है। वे सैकड़ों वर्षों से पितृसत्तात्मक सामाजिक व्यवस्था में उत्पीड़न एवं अन्याय की शिकार रही है। अतः दलित महिलाओं को उसी श्रेणी में आरक्षण देकर उनका प्रतिनिधित्व बढ़ाना चाहिए।

- पर्याप्त प्रतिनिधित्व के अभाव में महिला सदस्य कानून बनाने की प्रक्रिया में प्रभावशाली हिस्सा लेने तथा महिलाओं के पक्ष में कानून लागू कराने में असफल रहती है जिसका महिलाओं के हितों पर उल्टा प्रभाव पड़ता है।

पंचायती राज एवं महिला सशक्तीकरण

राजधानी दिल्ली में पंचायती राज व्यवस्था के 15 वर्षों के उपलब्धियों तथा स्थानीय लोकतंत्र को अधिक सशक्त बनाने के मुद्दे पर आयोजित राष्ट्रीय सम्मेलन में प्रधानमंत्री डॉ. मनमोहन सिंह ने कहा कि पंचायती राज की सबसे बड़ी सफलता यह है कि इसने महिलाओं का राजनीतिक एवं सामाजिक सशक्तीकरण किया है। सम्पूर्ण निर्वाचित पंचायत सदस्यों में 9 लाख 75 हजार महिला प्रतिनिधि हैं। एक तथ्य यह भी है कि निर्वाचित पंचायत महिला प्रतिनिधियों की यह संख्या विश्व में कुल निर्वाचित महिला प्रतिनिधियों से भी ज्यादा है। बिहार, राजस्थान, मध्य प्रदेश, छत्तीसगढ़, हिमाचल प्रदेश, उत्तराखंड में 50 प्रतिशत आरक्षण दिए गए हैं। इन राज्यों में महिलाओं ने कई कीर्तिमान स्थापित किए हैं–

- गाँव गुआरा का कालौल की जमूरी बाई दो माह तक अकेले काम करके दो बीघा जमीन में तालाब खोद कर गाँव का जल संकट दूर किया उसके बाद सारा गाँव उसे भागीरथी कहकर सम्मान देने लगा।
- मुझे पति एवं सरपंच में से एक को चुनने के लिए मेरे पति ने कहा लेकिन मैंने सरपंच को चुना। अतः मेरा तलाक हो गया- 21 वर्षीय सरपंच सावित्री देवी (कनार्टक)
- मैं कभी सोच भी नहीं सकती थी कि इस उच्च जाति के पंचायत में मैं मुखिया बन सकती हूँ– नगीना मोची मधुबनी (बिहार)
- रेवाड़ी ब्लॉक (हरियाणा) की महिला सरपंच ने अपने इलाके से शराब की दुकान हटवायी।
- राजस्थान के अलवर जिला के निम्मुचाना गांव की सरपंच कोयली देवी ने अपने ही ससुर एवं पति पर अधिसूचना जारी कि कि वे बतायें कि पंचायत की जमीन हड़पने की वजह से उनके खिलाफ कार्रवाई क्यों न की जाये?
- हरियाणा के ही अन्य ब्लॉक के बेट्टा-पट्टी की ग्राम पंचायत की सरपंच ने वहां पानी की समस्या का समाधान करवाया।

- केरल के कोझीकोड जिले की महिलाओं ने जिले के पहाड़ी इलाका में पानी की समस्या हल करने का संगठित प्रयास किया।
- नरपत नगर ग्राम पंचायत की सदस्य चमेली देवी ने बताया कि करोड़ों रूपये की बात छोड़िये एक हैंड पम्प लगवाने के लिए हम महिलाओं को कितना पसीना बहाना पड़ता है, इसका अन्दाजा ए.सी. वाले कमरे में बैठकर नहीं लगाया जा सकता है।
- बिहार के पूर्वी चम्पारण जिले के डिन्जी भिरखिया-छिपुलिया गांव की मुसहर जाति की महिला गिरजा देवी को संयुक्त राष्ट्रसंघ ने महिला विकास प्रकोष्ठ और आर्थिक एवं सामाजिक मामले के विभाग के 15वें सत्र के भाषण देने के लिए न्यूयार्क आमंत्रित किया गया।
- महिला सशक्तीकरण में सकारात्मक भूमिका निभाने के लिए मधुबनी जिले के लखनौर पंचायत समिति की सदस्य तिलिया देवी को वर्ष 2006 के नोबेल शांति पुरस्कार के लिए नामित किया गया था।
- कटिहर जिले के बलरामपुर प्रखण्ड के किरोरा ग्राम की हलिमा खातून ने पंचायत प्रमुख का चुनाव जीता। हलीमा अपनी पेट की आग बुझाने के लिए भीख मांगा करती थी आदि।
- पिपरा बिलाई गांव में झण्डा फहराने के कारण दबंग लोगों ने मारा-गुंदिबाई के शब्द।
- मैं चुनाव लड़ी तो लोग मुझे कहने लगे कि तुम्हें पुरुषों की कमी में रहना चाहिए– श्रीमती नाथू बेगम (देहरादून)
- पंचायत के लिए नियमित चबूतरे पर गुन्दीबाई बैठ नहीं सकती। उन्होंने कहा कि मुझे चबूतरे से नीचे खड़ा रहना पड़ता है क्योंकि कुछ ऊंचे वर्ग के लोग यही चाहते हैं।
- मेरा उपाध्यक्ष कभी पंचायत सभा में नहीं आता क्योंकि उसे एक नीची जाति की अध्यक्षता में बैठना मंजूर नहीं है। - जिला बंगलोर की श्रीमती अस्थमा नारायण रेड्डी।

पंचायतों में आरक्षण के फलस्वरूप जो महिलाएँ चुनकर आयी है। वे इस सत्य को उजागर कर रही है कि महिलाएँ निष्क्रिय एवं निःसहाय नहीं है। आरक्षित सीटों के अलावा अन्य सीटों पर चुना जाना इसका संकेत है। चुनाव

परिणाम यह साबित किया है कि स्वर्ण जाति के साथ-साथ अनुसूचित जाति एवं अनुसूचित जनजाति की महिलाएँ भी अब पंचायत में प्रतिनिधित्व कर सकती हैं। साथ ही पंचायत के प्रतिनिधि बनने के लिए शिक्षित होना अनिवार्य नहीं है।

13 जुलाई 1998 को लोकसभा और राज्य विधानसभाओं में महिलाओं को 33% आरक्षण दिये जाने से सम्बन्धित 84वां संविधान संशोधन विधेयक पेश करने का प्रयत्न किया गया था, परंतु विपक्षी दलों ने उन्हें ऐसा नहीं करने दिया। इसके पीछे विपक्षी दलों का तर्क यह था कि इस बिल द्वारा आरक्षण की जो व्यवस्था की गयी है, इसके मुस्लिम एवं अन्य पिछड़े वर्गों की महिलाओं को कोई पफायदा नहीं होगा। इसलिए एक नया विध्येयक .पेा किया जाना चाहिए, जिसमें मुस्लिम व अन्य पिछड़े वर्गों की महिलाओं को भी महिलाओं के लिए निर्धारित स्थानों में आरक्षण प्राप्त हो। बिल पेश नहीं किये जाने के अन्य दूसरे कारणों में बिल में प्रस्तावित महिलाओं के लिए प्रत्येक निर्वाचन क्षेत्र में एक के बाद एक आरक्षण देना, इसके बारे में सभी दलों में सहमति नहीं होना। विपक्षी दलों के साथ-साथ सरकार के सहयोगी दलों द्वारा भी बिल का विरोध करना, सरकार दलों द्वारा आम सहमति करने का प्रयास नहीं करना और लोकसभा में सत्तारूढ़ दल को पूर्ण बहुमत प्राप्त नहीं होना आदि शामिल है।

भारत के पंचायतों में महिलाओं को 33% आरक्षण तो मिल गया है लेकिन विधानसभा और संसद के गलियारों में महिलाओं की अपेक्षित भागीदारी सुनिश्चित करने में राष्ट्रीय राजनीतिक दल ईमानदारी नहीं दिखा रहे हैं। हमारे यहां संसद में महिलाओं का प्रतिशत पाकिस्तान, नेपाल और इराक से भी कम है। अन्य देशों की तुलना की जाए तो इस मामला में रवान्डा सबसे ऊपरी पायदान पर है। यहाँ लोअर हाउस में 56.30 प्रतिशत महिलाएँ हैं।

आजादी के 60 साल बाद भी लोकसभा के आधी आबादी का प्रतिनिधित्व करने के लिए लगभग 50 महिलाएँ ही पहुँची है। ये शर्मनाक आंकड़े तब और अखरते हैं जब हम याद करते हैं कि अगर पिछले आम चुनाव में पहले उक्त विधेयक पारित कर दिया गया होता तो आज लोकसभा में कम से कम 179 महिलाएं होती यानि मौजूदा संख्या से 129 अधिक।

अमरीकी संसद में निर्वाचित महिलाओं की संख्या 16.8% है। जिस अफगानिस्तान को अमेरिका लोकशाही का पाठ पढ़ा रहा है उसने भी अपनी संसद में औरतों को 33% आरक्षण दिया है। बंग्लादेश और मोरक्को में 15%, पाकिस्तान

रैंक	*देश*	*लोअर हाउस में महिलाओं का प्रतिशत*
1.	रवांडा	56.30 प्रतिशत
2.	स्वीडन	47.00 प्रतिशत
3.	क्यूबा	43.20 प्रतिशत
4.	फिनलैंड	41.50 प्रतिशत
5.	अर्जेंटीना	40.00 प्रतिशत
6.	नीदरलैंड	39.30 प्रतिशत
7.	डेनमार्क	38.00 प्रतिशत
15.	नेपाल	33.20 प्रतिशत
45.	पाकिस्तान	22.50 प्रतिशत
52.	चीन	21.30 प्रतिशत
71.	अमेरिका	16.80 प्रतिशत
83.	रूस	14.00 प्रतिशत
108.	भारत	08.20 प्रतिशत
112.	भूटान	08.10 प्रतिशत

के संसद में 22%, दक्षिण अफ्रीका में 30%, अर्जेन्टीना संसद में 30% आरक्षण लागू है। दुनिया में सबसे अधिक निर्वाचित महिलाएं रवांडा, स्वीडन, डेनमार्क, फिनलैंड में हैं। फिनलैंड की सरकार ने यह कानून बनाया है कि हर निर्णायक संस्था में कम से कम 40% महिलाएं होनी चाहिए। शर्म की बात यह है कि अफ्रीका का एक छोटा सा देश रवांडा भी महिला आरक्षण कानून पारित कर चुका है और वहां के सांसद में 56.30% सीटों पर महिलाएं निर्वाचित हो चुकी है। पड़ोसी देश नेपाल भी महिलाओं को 33% आरक्षण देने का कानून पारित करने वाला है। हमारे देश में ऐसे आरक्षण के विरोधियों का कहना है कि पिछड़ी जाति की महिलाओं के लिए अलग से कोटा दिया जाए।

विधायिका में महिला आरक्षण के मामले पर सभी गतिरोधों को समाप्त करने के लिए एक नया प्रस्ताव सरकार के पास विचारधीन है। इस प्रस्ताव के अन्तर्गत महिलाओं को समुचित प्रतिनिधित्व देने के लिए संसदीय एवं विधान सभाई सीटों की वर्तमान संख्या में एक तिहाई की वृद्धि कर उसे महिलाओं के लिए आरक्षित करने की योजना है। महिलाओं को इस प्रकार से आरक्षण देने के लिए संविधान में संशोधन करना होगा, क्योंकि संविधान के वर्तमान प्रावधानों के अनुसार निर्वाचन क्षेत्रों की संख्या में वर्ष 2026 तक कोई परिवर्तन नहीं किया जा सकता है।

लोकसभा में महिलाओं का प्रतिनिधित्व				राजसभा में महिलाओं का प्रतिनिधित्व			
वर्ष	*कुल सदस्य संख्या*	*महिला सदस्य संख्या*	*महिला सदस्यों का %*	*वर्ष*	*कुल सदस्य संख्या*	*महिला सदस्य संख्या*	*महिला सदस्यों का %*
1952	499	22	4.4	1952	219	16	7.3
1957	500	27	5.4	1957	237	18	7.5
1962	503	34	6.8	1962	238	18	7.6
1967	523	31	5.9	1967	240	20	8.3
1971	521	22	4.2	1971	243	17	7.0
1977	544	19	3.3	1977	244	25	10.2
1980	544	38	5.2	1980	244	24	9.8
1984	544	44	8.1	1984	244	28	11.4
1989	517	27	5.2	1989	245	24	9.7
1991	544	39	7.2	1991	225	38	15.5
1996	543	39	7.1	1996	223	20	9.0
1998	543	43	7.9	1999	237	22	8.2
1999	545	49	8.6	2004	238	20	8.5
2004	539	44	8.2				
औसत	529.21	34.14	6.2	औसत	218	22.30	9.3

नारी सशक्तीकरण की वास्तविक उपलब्धि यह है कि वह स्वयं पर विश्वास रखकर अपने नारीत्व पर गर्व करे। अपने शर्तों पर जिन्दगी जीने का उसमें साहस हो। यह काम महिला आरक्षण जैसे– आन्ध्र प्रदेश के छोटे से गांव कलवा का सरपंज फातिमा बी जिसे संयुक्त राष्ट्रसंघ की पूर्व महासचिव कोफी अन्नान ने पंचायत में महत्वपूर्ण काम करने के लिए स्वयं सम्मानित किया। गांव गुआड़ा कालौल की मंजूरी बाई ने दो महीने तक अकेले काम करके दो बीघा जमीन में पोखरा खोदकर गांव के जल संकट को दूर किया। यह उदाहरण महिला सशक्तीकरण को दर्शाता है। अतः पंचायत से लेकर संसद तक सभी स्तरों पर निर्णय प्रक्रिया में समान अधिकारों और स्थान के लिए महिलाओं की सशक्तीकरण का प्रश्न राजनैतिक रूप से हल करना होगा। सभी राजनैतिक दलों के नेता को चाहिए कि आपस के मतभेदों को भुलाकर तथा पुरुष मानसिकता से निकल कर इस बिल पर आम सहमति बनावें तथा महिला सशक्तीकरण की प्रक्रिया को तीव्रता दें।

निष्कर्ष

उपरोक्त विश्लेषणों से स्पष्ट है कि महिला विकास का सवाल मुख्यतः एक राजनैतिक सवाल है और जब तक इसे राजनीतिक सवाल के रूप में नहीं देखा जायेगा और देश की राजनीति एवं सत्ता में महिलाओं को समान भागीदारी नहीं दी जायेगी, जब तक महिलाओं की प्रगति अधूरी ही रहेगी। महिला आरक्षण एक अस्थायी आन्तरिक व्यवस्था ही हो सकती है। यह सच्ची लोकतांत्रिक प्रक्रिया और आम महिलाओं की मुख्यधारा में भागीदारी का विकल्प नहीं हो सकता परन्तु उस दिशा में एक सही कदम है। अन्ततः महिलाओं में सकारात्मक चेतना तथा समान अवसर व सुविधाएं दिया जाना चाहिए परन्तु उन्हें अपने पैरों पर खुद खड़ा होना होगा और जीवन के विभिन्न क्षेत्रों में अपनी क्षमता, योग्यता, विवेक तथा परिश्रम से आगे बढ़ना होगा।

संदर्भ सूची

भारतीय समाज की संरचना– एन.सी.ई.आर.टी.

द चेंजिंग पोजीशन ऑफ इंडियन वूमेन– एम.एन. श्रीनिवास

रिजर्वेशन एज ए स्ट्रेडजी फोर पोलिटिकल एम्पावरमेंट– रचना सुचिनमयी।

आल्टरनेट मॉडर्नीटिज रिजर्वेशन्स एण्ड वीमेन्स मूवमेंट इन 20वीं सेंचुरी इंडिया– मेरी जॉन।

भारतीय महिलाएँ : दशा एवं दिशा– सुभाष शर्मा।

वीमेन एण्ड सोसायटी इन इंडिया– नीरा देसाई।

वीमेन वेलपफेयर एंड डेवलपमेंट– डी. चौधरी।

कुरुक्षेत्र– दिसम्बर 2000 एवं दिसम्बर 2007।

योजना– मार्च 2004 व अक्टूबर 2008।

27

Women's Political Development in India

Madhu Singh

Women in India have always had a raw deal in social, economic, political and educational opportunities. To achieve sustainable development and create a balanced society gender equality has to be made a national agenda. Women constitute almost half of the world population. Their contribution to the social and economic development of societies is also more than half as compared to that of men by virtue of their dual roles in the productive and reproductive spheres. Through we know that in India, Women have played an important role politically eg. Rani Ahayla Bat, Raml Laxmi Bat, Rajia Sultan and of course Indira Gandhi who have brought Into the political domain strength and wisdom. However through much of the world women's equality is undermined by the historical imbalances in decision making power and access to resources, rights and entitlement for women. Women's participation in formal political structures and processes, where decisions regarding the use of societal resources generated by both men and women, remains insignificant. Presently, women's representation in legislatures around the world is 15 per cent. Despite the pronounced commitment of the international community to gender equality and to bridging the gender gap in the formal political arena, which was reinforced by the Convention on Elimination of All forms of Discrimination Against Women (CEDAW) and the Beijing Platform of Action. There are only 12 countries where women hold 33% or more seats in the parliaments.[1] We can say that it is very glaring "Women represent 50% of the population of which 30% forms the official labour force, 60% of the total working hours are performed by women but receive only 10% of the worlds income. This is the awful economic profile of income in the world. This is also true of Indian women and very much true of rural women.[2]

Women are in no way inferior to men, they do not get enough opportunities to excel in their work. The value of women as a national resource remains unrecognised. To fight the above inequalities we have to think very sincerely and innovatively. Political power seems to be the strongest tool to eradicate the above inequalities.

With an increasing recognition about women's historic exclusion from structure of power a global commitment has been made to redress gender imbalances in politics. Women's enhanced participation in governance structures is viewed as the key to redress gender inequalities in society. The global debate on the promotion of women's political participation/ representation has been surrounded by intrinsic instrumentalist argument. The former argues for equal participation of women in politics from the human rights perspective. Since women constitute half of the world population so they should have equal participation and representation in world democracies. Instrumental argument pushed for women's greater participation on the essential ground that men and women are different. Women have different vision and concepts of politics owing to their sex and their gender roles as mothers. Therefore, it is assumed that women in politics will bring a special caring and focus on female values in politics. It is very true that women must be included in politics - whatever the argument may be.

The challenge facing all advocates of gender equality in politics is the wide gap between shared values reflected in the national and international policies and practices. eg. The Indian Constitution is one of the most progressive in the world and guarantees equal rights for men and women, however Indian women are still anxiously waiting for their dreams of equality to be translated into reality. To fight the above inequalities, we have to think very sincerely and innovatively. Since political power is the strongest tool to eradicate inequality. For promoting wormers political participation we should first understand the structural imperatives of a society in which women's political participation is instituted.

Women's historic exclusion from political structures and processes is the result of multiple structural, functional and personal factors that vary in different social contents across countries. Beyond these differences in national and local contents, there are general issues in women's political participation that relates to the wider content of national and international politics, liberal democracy and development. Democracy as well as development poses limitations on women's effective political participation. People have gained in terms of education, health and income because of development but development has not borne the same fruit to women. Leacock has also said ".....within an equalitarian world order, so called development could not release women from oppressive social, economic and political institutions; it merely defines 'new conditions of constraints."[3] Women's mere participation is mainstream development does not lead to their advancement and gender equality; it is only if the contradictions in development is eliminated that they will develop. The level and nature of participation is equally important to determine whether women are able to share development gains.

If we examine women's participation in democracy we see that democracy has historically served men better than women right from the Greek to modern times. It built the public—private dichotomy and included women from citizenship. Women have been kept outside the public domain as most of the political thinkers and philosophers such as Plato, Aristotle, Rousseau, John Lock, Thomas Hobbes and Hegel considered women fit only for domestic roles in the private sphere, they maintained that there was no place for women in politics because of their suitability in carrying roles as mothers and wives. This public-private domain has been the foundation of the various forms of world democracies. The ancient and modern democracies have failed to recognise women as citizens. It is only the liberal political philosophy of the 19th century that promoted the idea of free and rational individual which was used by suffragists to demand for the right to vote. However the liberal theory also perpetuates patterns of patriarchy and ignores gender subordination in both polity and society. This is why despite having struggled to get the right to vote women have not been able to impact public policy and could not being the private sphere in the preview of the public.

Issue of Women's Reservation

Also after 60 years of Independence gender equality is still far from being a reality. Inequalities remain persistent in such basic issues as right to education, the right to basic amenities and access to political power.

The extent of political participation of women in India is still marginal and obstacles to it abound. Democracy implies popular control of policy makes through free elections and becomes vibrant through voluntary activities occurring in between elections. "Measures are called for to encourage taking of such steps which encourage full participation of all women and discourage non-participation or apathetic conduct towards politics, elections and voluntary activities."[4]

The issue of women's reservation is a very controversial issue. Though constitutionally as mentioned before equal rights have been given, this has not helped women to develop. They are still socially and culturally exploited. Gandhiji had declared in 1931 during the 2nd round table conference: "I would boycott the legislature which will not have the proper share of women members."

There is a clear consensus in literature that gender quota is an effective tool in addressing women's exclusion and ensuring their presence in formal structure of politics. However, there is a controversy as to the extent of women's presence is political structures. This has raised the issue oil the nature and modalities of bender quotes and its limitation to empower women in politics.

The 73rd and 74th amendment ensured 1/3rd of the total seats for women in all, elected offices of the local bodies. This has helped to strengthen the position of women in the states which implemented this. In the beginning the women representatives faced difficulties, not that this does not continue. However their position has improved from before, mainly because of the boldness of some of these women. Women are better managers and if able to participate actively, they will be more successful in bringing about development, as they can get work done with the scarce resources which are available. This is because they have experience in the field of managing household expenses.

Till data 33% of reservation for women in legislatures has not been implemented. "The controversy engulfing the issue of women's reservation has made the Women's Reservation Bill one of the most controversial and debatable bills in the history of Indian Parliament." The bills fate has been jinxed with its oppositions clamouring for quotas in the bill for women belonging to the SC, ST and OBC's and minorities this is an insidious attempt to stall the bill. The Women Reservation Bill is so controversial because, it firstly, treats women as a homogenous group for affirmative action. Secondly, there is no reservation of seats for OBC and minority women. Thirdly, there is a lack of capable women candidates and women elected are mere 'proxies' for male politicians and fourthly, the silence of the government on the women's reservation bill, about reservation of women in Rajya Sabha.[5]

The basis of this bill lies in the mission of social justice. This is based on the concept of welfare state as asserted in the preamble of the constitution. This has been justified as a means to put an end to oppression of women. Therefore, reservation for women is to fulfill the promise of equality enshrined in the founding text of independent India. 33 per cent reservation is sought as it is a proportion at which a minority constitutes a critical mass, and will have an impact on the decision of the assembly. A strong presence of women in political assemblies would help women to deal with issues concerning women. "The expectation that reservation for women in legislatures will lead to better governance is based in the theory that women will look after womens welfare better than man Will."[6]

Though there are many leaders and parties who are against the Bill, equally there are parties and people who are vociferously supporting the Bill. Supporters of the Bill feel that women will make parliament sober and that men alone cannot decide the future of the country. Women's Reservation Bill more than correcting gender injustice will enhance the participatory character of Indian democracy significantly. "Women's participation in politics is necessary for holistic development. Women have better perspectives oil vial issues as environment health care and education."[7] Another merit will be that political assembles with women would make political life more peaceful, honest and sincerely developed to common good.

The Women's Reservation Bill strives, to facilitate women's empowerment and create a gender just society. However there is much more to this issue is multi-dimensional and linked with modern man. The gender gap is politics cannot be redressed simply by bringing more women in the system. Unless supportive mechanisms are put in place and women are provided with an enabling environment participation will be not be useful. The quota system is central to affirmative action measures experience shows that quota modalities must be direct, empowering and enable women to develop their constituency. The truth is that within the patriarchal context of modem democracies when women enter politics through gender quotas, they are unable to transform the sexual politics in the state institutions. Rather they are forced to play on males terms. Therefore without the transformation of the wider politics gender quotas cannot lead to women's political empowerment.

Factor's Hindering Women's Political Participation

Women's participation and access to formal political power structures vary across countries. The structural and functional constraints faced by women are shaped by social and political relations in a society. The common patterns of women's political exclusion stein from (a) social and political discourses (b) political structures and institutions (c) the socio-cultural and functional constraints that put limits on women's individual and collective agency.

Ideological Factors

Patriarchy as a system of male domination shapes womens relationship in politics. It transforms male and females into men and women and constructs the hierarchy of gender relations where men are privileges. Andrienne Rich defines patriarchy as 'A familial-social, ideological, political system in which men by force, direct pressure or through ritual tradition, law and language, customs etiquette, education, and the discussion of labour, determine what part women shall or shall not play in which the female is everywhere subsured under the male."[8] The gender role ideology is used as an ideological tool by patriarchy to place women within the private arena of home as mothers and wives and men in the public sphere. This is one of the vital factors that shape the level of womens political participation globally. However this ideological divide is not reflective of the reality as boundaries between public and private are often blurred in the daily lives of women. Nonetheless, domestic domain continues to be perceived in the north as well as in the south as the legitimate space for women, while public space is associated with men. Women have to negotiate their entry into and claim on public space according to the discussing and material opportunities available in a given culture and society. Although the gender role ideology is not static rather remained in a MIX While intersecting with economic social and political systems of a particular society, women continue to be defined as private across countries which resulted in their inclusion from politics.

Political Factors

The nature of politics as an important factor for the inclusion or exclusion of women is politics. Vicky Randall defines politics as an "articulation, or working out of relationships within an already given power structure." This is in contrast with the traditional view of politics that defines it as an activity, a conscious, deliberate participation in the process by which resources are allocated among citizens. This conception of politics restricts political activity only in public arena and the private sphere of family life is rendered as apolitical. This public—private dichotomy in traditional definition of politics is used to exclude women from public political spheres and even when women are brought into politics they enter as mothers and wives.

Male domination of politics, political parties and culture of formal political structures is another factor that hinders womens political participation. The male dominated political parties have male perspectives on issues of national importance. Women are usually not elected to positions of power within the party structure because of gender biases of male leadership. Meetings of councils or parliamentary session are held in odd timing conflicting with women's domestic responsibilities.

The level of democratisation also impact women's political participation. The developing countries have created more space for women's participation in politics as compared to countries where religious orthodoxy has been shaping politics and democracy.

Socio-cultural Factors

Socio-cultural factors the subordinate status of women vis-a-vis men is an universal phenomenon though there is a difference in the nature and extent of subordination across countries. Socially we see that females are valued less than male because of their socially ascribed roles in reproductive sphere. This gender states quo is maintained through low resource allocation to women's human development by the state, society and the family. This is reflected in the social indicators like education, health, employment, ownership of productive resources and politics in all countries. The socio-cultural dependence of women is one of the key detrimental factor to their political participation in public political domain.

Women also find it hard to participate in politics due to limited time available to then because of their dual roles in the productive and reproductive spheres. With their primary roles as mothers and wives and completing domestic responsibilities and care work, they are left little time to. participate in politics. They also face cultural constraints on their mobility. The mechanisms of Sex Segregation and Purdah are used to restrict their mobility.

Economic Factors

Politics is increasingly becoming commercialised. More and more money is needed to participate in politics. Women lack access to and ownership of productive resources, limiting the scope of their political works.

Lack of Social Capital and Political Capacities

Women often lack social capital because they are often not head of communities, tribes or kinship groups, resulting in the absence of constituency base for them and means of political participation, such as political skills, economic resources, education, training and access to information.

To ensure the political representation and empowerment that has long been promised requires organized and concerted action. Although India has been inching towards increased empowerment for women, there is still a long way to go. Today women only account for a dismal 3% of the current administration and 8% of India's political representation. The formation in the early 1990's of the national commission for women has been an important step forward.

Women's reservation in Panchayati Raj institutions has provided an opportunity for leadership and participation. To a certain extent they have been successful. However women leaders need to articulate the needs and priorities related to rights, entitlements and basic services provision of their constituency. They should participate in social planning and policy development and act upon them. One finds that women elected representatives are unable to exercise their leadership. They do not participate effectively in meeting. They are unable to articulate the priorities of their constituency and influence decision making. Mostly their voices are silent.

Increasing Womens Awareness

Therefore it is clear that political empowerment is not wholly sufficient for women to exercise their leadership. They need skills, knowledge and information to articulate their concerns and influence the decision making as per their concerns. Without academic and social education, political empowerment of women in certain parts of the country have proved fertile. The uneducated women who are elected are puppets in the hands of their male family members and are also subjected to exploitation at the hands of government machinery. Therefore efforts has to be made towards all around development of each and every section of Indian women. Social perception about women leadership in governance needs to be changed through gender sensitisation.

The main concern should be to strengthen women leadership by promoting opportunities for systematic learning, to provide their a curriculum for political empowerment and self-development. To build their awareness power and capacities so that their political participation is meaningful. 'Women leadership and empowerment can be made more effective if the male elected representatives, government officials, family members as well as other women are made aware of gender issues. It is right time that India women got their due share. Without removing these inequalities, no progress and development could be achieved. Democracy is not achieved solely by bringing in the most people friendly political manifesto guaranteed to work wonders but through consensual political and tolerance for diversity.

The responsibility to create supportive environment for gender equality and advancement of women's shared responsibility falls equally on the national and international communities. The socio-cultures, political and economic structural barriers at the national and international levels, have to be transformed or else the goal of gender equality as women's equal participation in politics and development will remain impossible to attain. Government should also be participative and decentralised as this creates space for greater interaction between the state and the society. Human capacities are dependent on the availability of resources such as education which we have discussed earlier, health and employment, this is directly liked with women's ability to create space for themselves in politics and development. Women's consciousness of their political rights is another condition for their individual and collective development as this will transform politics and development in a sustainable manner.

A strong women's movement and civil society is another condition which will influence the direction of politics and development in favour of women. It is only then can there be a major change in women's political empowerment. All these steps if taken will improve position of women is society. They will get their due according-to their capacities and not be relegated to the background as we see that women in politics are sidelined the important ministries always go to the values in males in India. If the steps motioned above are taken women will be able to contend equally with their male counterparts on the political front and this will lead to their development.

Notes

1. Farzana Bari, "Women's Political Participation: Issues and Challenges", EGMAVPD-EE/2005/EP. 12.
2. Manimekalai, "Economic Empowerment of Women Through Self Help Groups." Third Concept, Feb. 2004.
3. Leacock, 1977; 320.
4. L. N. Sharma and Sushmita Sharma, "Womens Political Participation: Propitiators and Impediments." Human Rights, edited by L.N. Sharnia, G. P. Ojha and N1. M. Pathak, Research Publication, 1999.

5. Bisnuta Das, "Issue of Women's Reservation: A Theoretical Perspective" Third Concept, August 2002.
6. A. Thanikadi and M. Sugirtha, "Imperatives of the Political Empowerment of Indian Women, Third Concept, April 2007.
7. Indira Sen, P. V. Is Reservation Good for Women? *Hindu*, 27 Dec. 1996.
8. Rich Andrienna 1977, 57.

28

Women's Empowerment: The Efforts Towards the Reservation of Seats in Parliament

Ram Prakash & Mrs. Ratna

It is an established fact that women constitute the depressed and oppressed class of the Indian society. It is largely felt that state institutions fail to deliver on promises of equality and justice for women as guaranteed in the constitution and other legal codes. This in fact has resulted in deterioration in the condition of women in many respects—women are angry and agitated over the continued oppression of the working population in the cities and villages. Hence the periods of the 1970s, 1980s and the early 1990s witnessed Indian women's movement and the demand for reservation of seats in the parliament. This demand got momentum in these decades due to growing communal violence, criminalization of politics and economic reforms under the liberalization and privatization programmes and the resulting social and economic insecurities in womenfolk.

The women's organizations were of the view that if women were adequately represented in the legislatures the oppression of women in the society would come to an end. The underlying assumption was that women in sufficient numbers in parliament would make appropriate laws to ensure their rights and dignity often vulnerable in a male dominated society.

A study reveals that women are not properly and proportionally represented in our resent Lok Sabha. There are total 545 seats in the House of the People out of which women occupy a meager strength of 44 seats which is about 8% of the total strength. In Scandanavian countries, a high representation of women is visible in parliament. In Sweden, it is as high as 45 per cent, in Denmark and Finland it is 38 per cent each and 36 per cent in Norway. A recent report of the United Nations Development Fund for Women (UNIFEM) shows that by 2002, only 11 countries had reached the 30 per cent bench mark and they included Sweden, Denmark, Germany, Finland, Norway, Iceland, the Neatherlands, South Africa, Costa Rica, Argentina and Mozambique. All these countries have used quotas in some form or the other. In Sweden, the major parties have 50 per cent quota for women which in other words can be illustrated that there is 50 per cent quota for men in the major political parties.

An interesting fact however to note is that women's political participation is not low only in the poor or developing countries. The UNIFEM report says that in many "wealthy countries, women's political participation is well below that achieved in many developing nations". The US, France and Japan, where women's share of parliamentary seats is 12 per cent, 11.8 per cent and 10 per cent respectively, lag behind 13 developing countries in sub-saharan Africa, which is experiencing the greatest regional poverty in the world. In South Africa and Mozambique, women's share of seats is 30 per cent, while Rwand and Uganda have 25.7 per cent and 24.7 per cent respectively.

To Quote UNIFEM report in this context, "Though the demand has been repeatedly made in the last few years from international plateforms about the need to have at least 30 per cent representation of women in key decision-making positions.. women are still, on the whole, largely absent from parliaments. They account for about 14 per cent of the members in 2002, overall".

It is worthwhile to mention here that celebrated women leaders like Sarojini Naidu have been against preferential treatment to women. In particulars, they have vehemently opposed reservation for women in the legislature and very vocal about it. When asked about this issued, this is what Sarojni Naidu had to say, "Why do you want to make women realize that they are not at par with men? Why reservation for them when they can do equally well or even better than men in many spheres of life? Why this discrimination. Let them gain confidence and allow them to be proud of their achievements. Let them feel that what they are today is only because they deserved it and not because they were given any special treatment or they enjoyed any special privileges."

In their letter to the premier and chairman Minorities committee on the status of women in the proposed new constitution (Govt. of India Act, 1935), the three prominent organizations of that time (namely All India women's conference, women's Indian Association and the Central Committee for the National Council of women in India) demanded complete and immediate recognition of women's political status. However, they insisted that no reservation be made for women in Legislature. To quote the memorandum in this context.

"We are enjoined to resist any plea that may be advanced by small individual groups of people of any kind of temporary concessions of adventitious methods of securing the adequate representation of women in the legislatures in the shape of reservation of seats, nomination or co-option whether by statute, convention or at the discretion of the provincial and central governments. To seek any form of preferential treatment would be to violate the Integrity of the universal demand of Indian women for absolute equality of political status." This memorandum with the title 'status of women in the proposed new constitution" was jointly prepared and written by Sarojni Naidu and Begum Shah Nawaz in Nov. 1931.

However, what the great women leaders of yester years saw as a threat to the integrity to the cause of women, is something that the new brand of feminist leaders vehemently espouse. Critics opine that the call or demand for quota system in legislatures in the name of women empowerment is nothing else but a naked greed for power in the name of one's gender.

Unfortunately very few political parties in India have the will power and determination to serve the best interests of the nation. The political parties have consistently sacrificed the nation's interest for their own political agendas, Reservation on caste and religion and caste politics to divide the nation was bad enough. Now, gender based politics sums to be the new frontier.

In 1990s several woman organizations demanded that political empowerment will be feasible only if they are provided 33 per cent reservation in the legislative bodies. This was the only possible road which could lead to their emancipation. They demanded power to decide matters that affect their lives and their families. Political parties and mass organization played a significant role in developing this discussion which ultimately resulted in introducing the women's Reservation Bill or the 81st constitutional Bill which was first introduced in September 1996. It was introduced by the then United Front Government. But the bill was promptly sent for 'cold storage' as it was sent to a parliamentary committee after stiff and loud opposition of the MPS from the Samajwadi Party and Rashtriya Janata Dal. Since then this bill has been brought in Parliament twice or thrice but it has been shelved on one pretext or other due to the reluctance of the legislators. In fact BJP came out with the improbable suggestion that one-third of the Lok Sabha constituencies should have two MPS one male and one female! i.e. there should be a provision for dual representation. The net result is that Indian Parliament is still dilly-dallying on this crucial issue.

In response to this demand of the women's organizations, at the beginning of the ninetees, the government introduced legislation to allow reservation for women in local bodies i.e. the elected panchayats, municipal corporation and boards. Many women did come forward aspiring to participate in the decision making for their community. However very soon, the illusion of empowerment of women at the local level was broken. The local governments have very limited power to make decisions and very little financial means to implement any community determined programme. The Bill for 33% reservation for women in the Parliament and state legislature was only the advance response of the govt. towards achieving the aspirations of political empowerment of women.

The supporters of the Bill felt that women have no future under the present political system. There is a shocking low representation of women in legislative bodies i.e. about 8 per cent. The reason is that the existing system of democracy and its political process are designed to exclude a vast majority from power. They are designed to maintain and defend an economic and social order based on ruthless exploitation and oppression of the people by a small minority of exploiters. The supporters of the Bill were of view that the sufferings of women can only be ended and mended when they will be in a position to decide matters that affect their liver and families.

However, the policy of reservation for women in legislatures was criticized vehemently by a section of intellectuals on several counts. Firstly, reservation systems sacrifice merit for mediocrity. Right from the birth of India as a republic, leaders have spoken out against the reservation system. In a letter to all chief ministers on June 27, 1961 Pandit Nehru wrote" I have referred above to efficiency and to our getting out of our traditional ruts. This necessitates our getting out of the old habit of reservations and particular privileges being given to this caste or that group." Secondly, the basic assumption behind the bill that women vote only for women is deeply flawed and against the fundamental principles of democracy. The members elected in the parliament have been chosen by both male and female voters and represent the people of their constituencies both men and women. Ironically, reserving 33% seats for women would limit the choices of other women for electing their chosen representative. Thirdly, it is a wrong assumption that' more women is legislature will empower women'. Women have made great strides in all spheres of life and today they are empowered like never before.

In the elections of 2004, about 53.37% of women exercised their franchise and sent their representatives to the legislature. An employment data available from the Labour Bureau reveals that the rate of employment of women has risen by more than 100%, while the rate of employment of men has decreased by a few percentage points. The rate of employment of women is rural areas has increased by an even greater margin (132%) since 1970.

Today numerous laws have been enacted in favour of women and equal opportunities abound. Women lead major political parties today and hold key positions in others. This all was achieved with the representatives in the legislature that were democratically elected and not by reservation. Since the purpose of legislation is to enact laws, one wonders what new laws can by enacted by artificially increasing the number of women law makers is an undemocratic fashion.

The opponents of the quota system for women in legislatures felt that women reservation Bill is a myopic piece of legislation. It furthers vested interests and ideologies. It is discriminatory, undemocratic and might even be unconstitutional. Limiting the available representatives based on religion, gender or caste is completely antagonistic to the fundamental principles of our democracy and constitution.

Today women in Indian society are no more unsafe IPC has around 30 women specific provisions only to help women e.g. (a) 304B-Dowry death, (b) 498A - Dowry harassment, (c) 376- Rape , (d) 497 - Adultry, (e) 509 - Indecent representation of women, (f) Outraging the modesty of women (g) Domestic violence against women law etc. We do not need more women specific laws which women parliamentarians would be expected to do in the name of women empowerment. We do not need more laws. What we need is the proper social awareness and implementation of these laws and uplifting their status. 33 per cent quota system for women would be totally counter productive.

Women's reservation in the parliament may ultimate prove to be restorative step. It is very surprising that the English media which is opposed to the caste based reservations is very supportive to the gender based reservations.

Our constitution provides for equality before law and equal protection of laws. It also provides equal opportunities to all and everybody enjoys the same right to education and work. Our political system has produced dynamic women towering political leaders like Smt. Indira Gandhi, Mayawati, Jayalalitha, Sushma Swaraj etc. without any sort of reservation. Hence, there is probably no need to resort to quota system for women which tantamount to women activism. A deserving man or woman would definitely claim his or her share is running the society or the country but "let the natural leadership flower by virtue of one's prowess rather than the gender".

PART–5

Vivid Dimensions of WPL

29

Electoral Violence Hindering Women's Political Participation

Shefali Roy

> *"Intolerance is itself a form violence and an obstacle to the growth of true democratic spirit"* **—M. K. Gandhi**

Political participation is an essential ingredient of democracy. It is involvement of individuals or group of individuals in taking decisions or influencing decision making process. It promotes stability and order is administration by giving every one the opportunity to express his own interest. It secures greatest good of greatest numbers. Political participation results from changes in traditional structure, attitudes and behavioural patterns, by encouraging mass participation in the public affairs. Participation benefits the participants as well as the larger community. It provides citizens a sense of dignity and value and facilitates broader political understanding. It is therefore a necessity to have equal participation of women who constitute almost half of the population (through sex ratio is declining) in the democratic process.

UNDP enunciated following indicators in regard to political participation:

- Freedom of association or assembly.
- Free and fair elections.

- Continuity of democratic system.
- Community of local decision making.

The term political participation denotes empowerment of citizens and conferring of political rights on them. Democracy, adult suffrage and Acts of decentralization (73rd and 74th Amendments to constitution) are enough evidences of political rights of the people in India. But participation in the sent of voluntary involvement is a far cry. Women's participation is till worse[1].

In a democratic set up of India, women enjoy political rights at par with men. These rights were granted to them as gift by the makers of the Indian Constitution. Women of India, particularly of Bihar which is semi agrarian feudal society, laden with orthodoxies, do not accrue the benefits generated by Affirmative Action in the political arena more specifically in local self government.

Women remain marginalized in decision making bodies, at times almost invisible leading to lack of feminist perspective. Women have been unable to find or create a space for themselves in power sharing structure. If we analyze the indicators we derive the conclusion that women alienate themselves from political affairs. They lack adequate awareness of political events, issues and efficacy. They hold negative attitude towards politics, regarding it a masculine affair. Very few women have been successful in subverting boundaries of gender and getting their voice heard in the political process of the government. The unequal participation at local, state and national level reflects structural, attitudinal and cultural barriers prevailing in all societies. This eventually results in apathy, alienation and anomie (rootlessness of values) which damages the fabric of democratic edifice. In pre independence days women could play more effective role because attitudes of family and society were quite favourable. Pol. Participation was confined to liberation of the nation charged with patriotic fervour but with independence, power politics emerged, confining women to the four walls of the house.

In course of analyzing constraints in the path of Pol. Participation, one found that a major factor in restraining the speed of political participation is violence and criminal political nexus.

Violence seems almost inevitable as it has become rule to service and conquer. It is the way through which powerful keeps its hold over powerless. In this wild situation, those who are at lowest strata in the power structure are those who suffer the most. Women therefore for most obvious reasons are the vulnerable lot. If we want to assess the situation today we can categories violence against women in following manner [2].

Violence within family (Domestic) comprises of wife beating marital rape, dowry death, unwanted pregnancy, sexual abuse of girl child, infanticide and female foeticide and even alcoholism. As charity begins at home, so does violence. Though there is a domestic violence Act modified in 2005 but the result is not tangible because of lack of awareness. From family, violence finds a larger stage within community where violence takes the form of trafficking, rape, forced prostitution, sexual abuse at work place, intimidation at work, sharing of women, passing derogatory remarks. Women are so brought up in Society that they become easy prey to acts of violence. Such weak and insecured women can never think of taking part in politics which is replete with examples of diversified violence. Women become worst victims of violent aggression, discrimination and exploitation. In the country paper of India in 1995 in the fourth world conference on women held in Beijing—violence against women has been defined as one of the most crucial mechanism by which women are forced into a subordinate position. It is a manifestation of unequal power relation which has led to men's domination over the discrimination against women. The platform for Action document of Beijing conference holds that violence against women means any act of gender based violence that results in or likely to result in physical, sexual or psychological harm or suffering to women including threats of such acts, coercion, or arbitrary deprivation of liberty whether occurring in public or private life [3].

The situation is same across states in varying degree. The situation of law and order is not very satisfactory in Bihar so violent acts become regular feature of the day. Bihar suffers from combined process of politicization of crime and criminalization of politics. Politicians make full use of anti-social elements, violence, and intimidation by hired criminals for electoral gains. One of the most disturbing features of post independence election arena is reckless use of muscle power by political parties. Earlier goondas helped in conducting (winning) elections by scientific rigging, booth capturing and terrorizing electorate. Later they realized that if they can help in winning election why can't they contest elections themselves and win by bullet power rather than ballot paper. Once this idea was mooted, there was sudden rise of goons in political battlefield. Candidates with criminal moorings got ticket and they contested elections fearlessly. Not only that, many of them even won elections and gradually it was found that many Lok Sabha and states assemblies Members were under trials. Bihar was not an exception gauging the situation, The Patna High Court Bench of Chief Justice R. S. Dhawan and Justice Shashank Kumari Singh had on April 30, 2004 asked the Election Commission to act fast in preventing the entry of de-franchised candidates in Parliament [4]. The Times of India (Patna Ed.) May, 7 2004 p- I. But the Supreme Court on 6th May 2004 stayed the Patna High Court directive to Election Commission to Consider the countermanding of poll in the constituencies from where the under trials were contesting for Lok Sabha or State Assemblies till the electoral process is complete. It gave of course a sigh of relief to politician of criminal background but Apex Court emphasized on candidates having clear background. Such directives cannot eliminate political Criminal nexus. Stringent laws and its implementation can only soothe the frustration. The election time appears to be a profitable season for criminals. Once the election is over, criminals return to normal task of murder, loot, dacoity, kidnapping etc. The Times of India in its May 8, 2004 (Pat. Ed) on its first page wrote "Polls over, criminals back in Dhandha"[5].

This is an undisputed fact as Vohra committee Reported in 1995 laid before the Parliament, that criminal gangs enjoy the patronage of local level of politician, cutting across party lines, more so in states like Bihar, U.P. Haryana. At the local level, the situation is alarming. Hence well qualified and gentlemen of society refrains from joining politics, it really not possible for women to participate, under such circumstances.

If we cite the example of Bihar, we see that Panchayati Raj elections were held in Bihar after 23 years and 8 years after passing the Panchayati Raj Act in 1993. Violence was witnessed in PRI elections in 2001. It was dreadful. As soon as nomination process began, the reports of violence started appearing in the local newspapers. It claimed lives of 129 people, including 50 candidates who were killed in pre poll violence[6]. In 2006 elections 42 cases of murder came up. 25 cases were investigated and finding was gender bias of all castes be OBC, UC or dalit. Even some criminals have put their women in PRI elections. Police failed to prevent spread of violence though 40,000 people with criminal record were arrested.

The problem does not end here. Some women who join politics face post electoral violence. They face problem in decision making. They work under pressure and therefore cannot develop critical thinking of their own. Lack of awareness on the part of their rights and duties further make them weak. Nitish government provided 50% reservation of seats for women in PRI and as a result women held 50% posts but in many cases it was proxy rule by their male counter parts. This was a new dimension of post electoral violence. This gave birth to Mukhiya patis and sarpanch patis or even gungi guarya's, former took vertual decisions and latter worked as an appendage. Women therefore suffered mental agony above all women representations are not respected and electorate do not response faith in women leadership.

In fine, we can assert strengthening of law enforcement machinery, local self government and timely intervention and community action can prove to be most effective deterrent to violence against women. Criminalization of politics should be minimized. No Reservation can empower women until and unless there is free and fair feasible election environment. Fast track court should continue with its operation. The election commission and representation of proper Act must debar convicted candidates from contesting elections. Media awareness campaigns must take place along with PRI women representatives' orientation and training programmes for their capacity building.

No reformatory law can transform the society. Women can no longer remain recipient of change; she has to become an instrument of change. That she can do with the power of 'Non Violence'.

Notes and References

1. S. K. Singh Vaishali Saxena (2000), Human Rights Indicators: Some Issues Anamika Publishers, New Delhi, p. 6.
2. Promilla Kapoor (2001), Empowering the Indian Women, Publication Division, Ministry of Information and Broadcasting, Govt. of India, p. 37.
3. Advancement of Women in India, 1995-1999 A Draft Report from Women's Movement, August, 1999, p. 62.
4. *The Times of India,* Patna Edition, May-7, 2004, p. 1.
5. *Times of India,* Patna Edition, May-8, 2004, p. 1.
6. A Report of Ashish Bhat, *Economic and Political Weekly,* May-19, 2001, pp-683-84.
7. Abhay Kumar (1999), Electoral Violence, Kanishk Publishers, New Delhi.
8. McCorna Thelma, Development with Equity with Women, Sage Publications.
9. "Women Political Participation and Good Governance 21st Century Challenges UNDP Report 2000.

30

Role of Women in Ecological Development

Indira Sinha

From Eco-religion to Political Ecology

From time immemorial there has been a subtle relationship between women and the environment. In fact she is looked upon as a part of nature. But in this garb of development, industrialization, modernization, both women and environment are being neglected. The natural resources, which are getting degraded, is interfering with women's responsibilities towards domestic sphere which has a negative impact on women psychologically and physically.

Women and Environment

The interdependence of women with nature can be understood from the following observations:

1. They are having base and skills for natural resources management.
2. They are better managers for natural resources.
3. They have sensitiveness towards environment.
4. They have high ecological consciousness.

Natural resource reduction and environmental degradation has direct consequences for women's time, income, health and social support system. The knowledge of women regarding the forest produces which have high herbal and medicinal value gained through long experience is disappearing with deforestation. Traditionally women have been responsible for subsistence and survival economics and culturally accepted division of labor within the family. Due to task to obtain and women have to spend more and more searching for them, other household work like cooking, child rearing, agricultural work and caring of animals has to be done in addition. Women have played a significant role in effecting the transformation of religion to a political ecology in which sustainable development will be the touchstone of the development. This paper will focus on women's interventions and activism to mainstream sustainable environment in the context of the emerging political ecology in India. This paper also highlights the case of the Narmada Bachao Andolan against big dams spearheaded by a great environmentalist, 'Medha Patkar.

Eco-religion in India

Ancient Indian developed many ideas, attitudes and practices which favored the maintenance of ecological balance for the welfare of all. These views are reflected in several philosophical and religious texts of the Vedas and Puranas which form the basis for an environmental ethics ancient Indian advocated an integrated approach to progress without undue exploitation of natural resources. They laid down traditions, customs, rituals to ensure that the complex, abstract principles they had developed could be put into practice, overtime these practices developed agricultural technology, methods of environmental protection, and knowledge of medicinal properties of trees. About ten percent of the indigenous tribal population in India, a total area of about 50 lakhs hectares over 15 states, is covered by the shifting cultivation in India. The land is not ploughed in this type of farming and neither is there any need for domesticating animals. The cultivators have total confidence in the generative power of the earth and see no need to resort to eco-destructive methods.

Women Spearhead Movements in Political Ecology

The fast growing of cities in India has led to deforestation and conversion of highly productive lands to meet the demands of industrialization and urbanization. Deforestation has a direct bearing on women's daily lives; women find it harder to secure domestic fuel and fodder in rural areas as well as other products used within the household. A study conducted in a Himalayan village in Chamoli district of UP revealed that each household spends between six to ten hours every day on collecting fuel and fodder.

Women in the rural areas depend on forests not only for meeting their subsistence needs, but also for income and employment. This includes activities such as making rope from different types of grasses, weaving basket, rearing tassar silk cocoons lac cultivation, making products from bamboo and oil extraction, selling sal seeds and Tendu leaves. Thus deforestation also results in job losses for the poor women especially when they are self employed. Rural women have realized that the key to economic progress should be ecologically sustainable and satisfy the basic needs of the community. Women's activism to address this development gap has historical roots in the struggles for nationalism, worker's rights and peasant struggles. These struggles have been given rise to several grass roots people's movements in which women are actively involved' to protect the environment in a bid to conserve local resources. In the Himalayan hills of UP people collectively rose to defend local interests against timber logging by contractors and private agencies that has jeopardized ecological stability and reduced local people's opportunity to benefit from sound forest exploitation. The Chipko movement, which originated in the hills of UP, was spearheaded by women who protected the trees from felling trees from felling by hugging them. The Appiko movement similarly originated as a forest protection movement in Karnataka. Both movements led by women drew inspiration from the Bishnoi eco-religious philosophy of harmonious living blended with environment conservation. Women are beginning to transform this environmental philosophy into a political one where policymakers have often needed women's interventions in forest protection and ordered to the large- scale felling of trees. Against this backdrop' it is interesting to examine the case of the Narmada anti dam movement spearheaded by Medha Patkar an extraordinary women' over a period of two decades and its entry into the realm of political ecology.

The Narmada Bachao Andolan

Medha Patkar is well known the world over as a powerful of the voiceless poor and oppressed people. Medha Patkar' founder of the Narmada Bachao Andolan and the National Alliance of People's Movement is immersed in the tribal and peasant communities in Maharashtra, MP and Gujarat which she eventually organized as the Narmada Bachao Andolan. The NBA began as a fight for information about the Narmada Valley Development Projects and continued as a fight from 1990-91 for the just rehabilitation of lakhs of people ousted by the Sardar Sarovar Dam. The SSD was a project that would displace upon completion 320,000 tribes and submerge over 37,000 hectares land. Medha Patkar has been a central organizer and strategist of NAPM a people's movement organized to stop the constructions of a series of dams planned for India's largest westward flowing river, the Narmada. For 19 years Medha Patkar has led the struggle for the people affecting by the controversial SS Project on the Narmada River in four states. A few years ago, she formed the NAPM with other activists against globalization without a human face. From the NAPM has emerged the people's political front in 2006. In an interview' Medha Patkar threw light on the larger issues involved in the formation of the PPF and electoral politics. She believes that people's movements are inevitable in any democracy to keep the democratic process alive and in raising and setting the conflict between the state and the people on people's issues. According to her it is necessary to challenge the changed culture of politics, which is communal and criminal to a large extent .....we will not start calculating our probable successes and failures only with numbers, but would rather exhibit alternative ways of not only contesting elections' but also of politics. Medha considers politics as a kind of movement. She says just as we address the issues of livelihood and economic policies in our struggle, here we have to address the issues of political degradation,. Regarding the PPF's agenda she says " we are for a secular state. We are not for allying with any party, but if any party supports the candidates emerging from PPF, nothing wrong with it. We know everything cannot be achieved in one election. The process between two elections is also going to be vital. She has now launched a yatra named "POL KHOL YATRA"to expose fallacious claims made by various government on rehabilitation of tribes displaced by the Sardar Sarover Dam in Narmada valley.

The Silver Lining

Women who are neglected at large in the development process have been awakened by national environmental movements like the NBA owing to the networking with the NBA women in the local collectiveness/federations have increased contact with the bureaucracy in the govt. office.

Recommendation

1. The protection of women decision maker's, advisors and manager's related to environmental protection should be increased.
2. Environmental education should be expanded in rural areas.
3. The potential of science and technology should be utilized to solve environmental related problems and ease women's workload inside and outside the home.
4. The central govt. should developed a strategy to eliminate various obstacles- constitutional, legal, administrative, social and economic in nature to women's full participation in sustainable development.
5. The government, non governmental organizations, environmental conservation agencies and the common

man should recognize and mobilize women as active participants to protect and enrich the natural resources that sustain us.

6. In spite of all these aspects there must be promotion of disseminating the gender relevant knowledge and valuation of women's role through formal non -formal education.

References

Environmental issues – Zahid Hussain

Environmental pollution – P. R. Trivedi

Environmental protection – Arvind Kumar

Forest protection force – *The Hindu*

31

नारी नेतृत्व : भारतीय संदर्भ में ऐतिहासिक विश्लेषण

बिनोद शंकर झा

प्राचीन भारत में रचे गये ग्रन्थों का महत्व इस बात से भी है कि उसमें महिलाओं के बारे में कुछ न कुछ जानकारी अवश्य मिलती है। *ऋग्वैदिक युग* में स्त्रियों की समाज में सम्माननीय स्थिति थी। पत्नी का यज्ञ के समय उपस्थिति अनिवार्य होना, इसका स्पष्ट प्रमाण है। उन्हें द्विज बनने का भी अधिकार था। स्त्री गृह स्वामिनी होती थी तथा घर के समस्त कार्य उसी के देखरेख में होते थे। स्त्रियों की शिक्षा पर पर्याप्त ध्यान दिया जाता था। सतपथ ब्राह्मण में स्पष्ट रूप से वर्णित है कि स्त्रियाँ उच्च शिक्षा प्राप्त हुआ करती थी। वेदों का उन्हें पूर्ण ज्ञान था। पुरूषों के समान स्त्रियाँ भी मंत्र रचना किया करती थीं। आठ विदुषी महिलाएँ जो वेद के मंत्र रचना में सहायक बनीं वे थीं-अपाला, इन्द्राणी, काक्षावती, घोषा, सूर्या, सावित्री, दक्षिण प्रजापति, अभिरणी और रात्रि भारद्वाज। ऋगवैदिक युग में स्त्रियों में पर्दे की प्रथा नहीं थी। फलतः उन्हें घूमने, यज्ञ, त्योहार एवं उत्सवों में भाग लेने की स्वतंत्रता थी।

उत्तरवैदिक काल में स्त्रियों की दशा में आश्चर्यजनक परिवर्तन हुआ एव उनकी स्थिति सोचनीय हो गयी। अब उनका *ऋगवैदिक काल* की तरह सम्मान न रहा। स्त्रियों को जुआ एवं सुरा की श्रेणी में रखा जाने लगा। स्त्रियों द्वारा सभाओं एवं परिषदों में भाग लेने पर प्रतिबंध लगा दिया गया। यद्यपि शिक्षित नारियों के अनेक उदाहरण इतिहास में मिलते हैं। गार्गी एवं मैत्रेयी इस युग की अत्यन्त

विदुषी स्त्रियाँ थीं। *वृहदारण्यक उपनिषद्* में वर्णित है कि जनक के दरबार में गार्गी के प्रश्नों से परेशान याज्ञवल्क्य ने कहा कि हे गार्गी अब तुम मुझसे अधिक जिज्ञासा न करो। इस प्रकार विदुषी महिलाएँ विभिन्न सभाओं में भी भाग लेती थीं एवं विद्वानों को प्रभावित करती थीं।

'*रामायण*' एवं '*महाभारत*' में भारत के दो प्रमुख महाकाव्य हैं। भारतीयों के जनजीवन को उत्साहित करने में इन दोनों महाकाव्यों का विशेष योगदान है। इस युग में स्त्री का स्थान सामान्यतः ऊँचा था। महाकाव्यों में कहा गया है कि जिस घर में स्त्री नहीं होती वह जंगल के समान है। पत्नी ही धर्म, अर्थ एवं काम की संरक्षिका मानी गई है। इस काल में कन्या का जन्म अशुभ माना जाता था। तथापि कन्याओं की शिक्षा का उचित प्रबन्ध था। कुछ राज परिवारों को छोड़कर सामान्यतः स्त्रियों में पर्दे की प्रथा न थी तथा वे स्वतंत्रतापूर्वक घूम सकती थी एवं उत्सवों एवं समारोहों में भाग ले सकती थी।

प्राचीन भारतीय सभ्यता के संबंध में 'धर्मशास्त्र' अत्यधिक प्रकाश डालते हैं। इस युग में मुख्य ग्रन्थ मनु, विष्णु, याज्ञवल्क्य तथा नारद रचित स्मृति ग्रन्थ है। मनुस्मृति में स्त्रियों की स्थिति के विषय में पर्याप्त उल्लेख है। मनु ने यद्यपि एक स्थान पर स्त्रियों का आदर करने के लिए लिखा है 'जहाँ स्त्रियों की पूजा होती है वहाँ देवता रमण करते हैं तथा जहाँ उनका अनादर होता है वहाँ के सारे यज्ञ अनुष्ठान एवं धार्मिक क्रियाएँ निष्फल हो जाती है।'' किन्तु मनुस्मृति में अन्य स्थानों पर नारी को बुराई की जड़ एवं आदमियों को दूषित करने वाला कहा गया है। मनु के अनुसार स्त्रियों को कभी भी स्वतंत्र नहीं रहना चाहिए। वाल्यावस्था में पिता के, युवावस्था में पति के तथा वृद्धावस्था में पुत्र के अधीन रहना चाहिए। धर्मशास्त्र काल में संभवतः सती एवं पर्दाप्रथा प्रचलित नहीं थी। परन्तु वैदिक काल की तुलना में स्त्री को अधिकार कम हो गये थे तथा उनकी दशा ह्रास की स्थिति में था।

छठी शताब्दी से पूर्व मिथिला में स्त्रियों की दशा सुदृढ़ थी। यहाँ के लोग शिक्षित एवं कुलीन थे। स्त्रियाँ भी शिक्षित थीं। अतः दूरस्थ प्रदेश के राजा भी यहाँ के राजकुमारियों से विवाह करने को उत्सुक रहते थे।

मौर्यकाल में एवं गुप्त काल में स्त्रियों की स्थिति कोई विशेष अच्छी नहीं थी। स्त्रियों को घर से बाहर जाने की अनुमति नहीं थी तथा पति की इच्छा के विरुद्ध वे कोई कार्य नहीं कर सकती थी। मौर्य युग के अनेक ऐसी स्त्रियों का भी उल्लेख मिलता है जो पारिवारिक जीवन व्यतीत नहीं करती थी बल्कि गणिका अथवा

वेश्या की जीवन-यापन करते हुए राजा का मनोरंजन करती थी। स्त्रियों से गुप्तचरों का कार्य भी लिया जाता था। राजमहल में भी स्त्रियाँ सैनिक के रूप में कार्य करती थीं। मौर्यकाल में सती-प्रथा का प्रचलन नहीं था। कौटिल्य ने सती होना आत्महत्या करने के समान घृणित व दण्डनीय बताया है। याज्ञवल्क्य स्मृति में कहा गया है कि कन्याओं का उपनयन संस्कार नहीं किया जाता था। अब उन्हें वैदिक शिक्षा भी नहीं दी जाती थी। पारिवारिक सम्पत्ति में कन्याओं का कोई अधिकार नहीं होता था। विधवाओं की स्थिति कष्टप्रद थी। सती प्रथा के उदाहरण गुप्तयुग में मिलते हैं।

यूनानी लेखकों के वर्णनों से ज्ञात होता है कि राजघराने के स्त्रियाँ आवश्यकता होने पर शासन सूत्र भी अपने हाथों में ले लेती थीं। मेगास्थनीज के वर्णन से ज्ञात होता है कि स्त्रियों को भी शिक्षा की सुविधा उपलब्ध थी। पुरुष छात्रों के समान ही स्त्रियाँ भी शिक्षा प्राप्त करती थीं तथा उस काल में ब्रह्मचर्य का जीवन व्यतीत करती थीं।

ह्वेनसांग ने भारत वृतांत में लिखा है कि भारत में अंतर्जातीय विवाह प्रचलित नहीं थे। स्त्रियों का पुनर्विवाह नहीं होता था। तत्कालीन समाज में सती प्रथा प्रचलित थी। स्त्री-पुरुष दोनों की ही शिक्षा पर ध्यान दिया जाता था।

12वीं शताब्दी के आस-पास पुत्री की स्थिति पुत्र की अपेक्षा बहुत गिर गयी थी एवं पुत्री दुःख का प्रतीक मानी जाती थी (कथा सरित्सागर)। इस काल में विधवा स्त्रियों की स्थिति अत्यन्त सोचनीय थी। उनपर अनेक प्रतिबंध लगा दिये जाते थे। राजपरिवारों तक सती प्रथा का प्रचलन था। सती प्रथा के अतिरिक्त कई जगह पुत्री के जन्म होने पर तत्काल उसकी हत्या कर दी जाती थी। राजपूत काल में जौहर की प्रथा का भी प्रचलन था। इस प्रथा के अनुसार जब दुश्मन की युद्ध में विजय होने लगती थी तथा रक्षा का कोई रास्ता नहीं रहता था तो राजपूत स्त्रियाँ अपने सतीत्व की रक्षा के लिए सामूहिक रूप से अग्नि में अपनी आहुति दे देती थी।

नारी नेतृत्व के संदर्भ में 1236 ई. में रजिया सुल्तान का दिल्ली की शासिका बनना एक बहुत बड़ी ऐतिहासिक घटना है। भारत में तुर्क शासन के इतिहास में वह पहली स्त्री शासिका थी। रजिया ने प्रशासनिक व्यवस्था को चुस्त बनाने के लिए कई परिवर्तन किये। रजिया ने स्वयं पर्दा छोड़ दिया और पुरुषों के वस्त्र धारण करने लगी। वह एक चतुर राजनीतिज्ञ एवं कुटनीतिज्ञ के रूप में अपनी पहचान बनाई।

सैनिकों को नेतृत्व करने की कला में रानी पद्मावती का नाम भी विशेष तौर पर याद किया जाता है। 1540 ई. में जायसी ने लिखा है कि अलाउद्दीन द्वारा चितौड़ पर आक्रमण का मुख्य कारण राजा रतन सिंह की सुन्दर पत्नी पद्मिनी को प्राप्त करना था। जब उलाउद्दीन ने पद्मिनी की सुन्दरता की चर्चा सुना तो उसने राणा रतन सिंह से पद्मिनी को उसके पास भेजने के लिए कहा। ऐसा नहीं होने पर धोखे से उसने राणा रतन सिंह को बुला बंदी बना लिया तथा पद्मिनी के बदले उसे मुक्त करने का प्रस्ताव राजपूतों के समक्ष रखा। पद्मिनी लगभग 1600 राजपूतों, जो पालकी के बाहक के रूप में थे, दिल्ली गयी एवं राणा को छुड़ा लायी।

16वीं सदी में स्त्रियों को विजयनगर में उच्च स्थान प्राप्त था। ऐसा विदेशी यात्रियों के लेखों से पता चलता है। उन्हें विद्या प्राप्त करने की सुविधा मिली हुई थी। राज्य के उच्च पदों पर स्त्रियों को रखा जाता था। पर्दा प्रथा का प्रचलन नहीं था। स्त्रियाँ पुरुषों के साथ सामाजिक उत्सवों तथा युद्ध में भाग लेती थीं। साहित्य के निर्माण में भी स्त्रियों का विशेष योगदान था। 'बरदाम्बिका परिणय' तथा 'मथुरा विजय' नामक ग्रन्थ की लेखिका क्रमशः तिरूमलम्बादेवी तथा गंगा थी। परन्तु बाल-विवाह तथा विवाह में दहेज संबंधी कुरीति का प्रचलन भी था।

सल्तनकालीन शासन 1206 से 1526 तक माना जाता है। इस काल में स्त्री का स्थान पुरुष की अपेक्षा निम्न समझा जाता था। मुस्लिम शासन काल में भारतीय नारियों के ऊपर अत्याचार अपनी चरम सीमा पर पहुँच गया था। वे आध्यात्मिक उत्तरदायित्व से भी हीन थीं। इस प्रकार स्पष्ट है कि मध्यकाल आते-आते स्त्रियों की स्थिति दयनीय हो गयी। अशिक्षा, अज्ञानता और रूढ़िवादिता ने इस काल में स्त्रियों को उबरने नहीं दिया। मध्ययुगीन समाज सुधारकों में नानक, कबीर, बल्लभाचार्य आदि का नाम विशेष रूप से उल्लेखनीय है। नानक ने हिन्दू जाति में उपेक्षित नारी को गौरव के आसन पर प्रतिष्ठित करने की चेष्टा की। नानक के अनुसार, "हम स्त्री के गर्भ से जन्म लेते हैं। उसी से हमारी जीवनपर्यन्त मैत्री है। उसी से सृष्टि कर्म चलता है। स्त्री हमें सामाजिक बन्धन में रखती है। फिर हम उस स्त्री को मन्द क्यों कहें जिससे महान पुरुष जन्म लेते हैं।" कबीर मानवतावादी विचारधारा के प्रति आस्थावान थे। हिन्दू समाज में नारी वर्ग का नैतिक अवमूल्यन एवं बाल-विवाह से वे व्यथित रहते थे। अपनी ओजस्वी वाणी के द्वारा उन्होंने समाज में स्त्रियों की दशा को उच्च करने का प्रयास किया। स्त्रियों के प्रति वल्लभाचार्य का दृष्टिकोण वैदिक कालीन व्यवस्था के अनुसार था।

उनकी दृष्टि में स्त्री पुरुष में कोई भेद नहीं है क्योंकि उनकी आत्मा समान हैं। उन्होंने अंतर्जातीय विवाह को भी प्रोत्साहन दिया।

ब्रिटिश शासन काल में सम्पूर्ण भारतवासी ही गुलामी के बेड़ियों में जकड़े हुए थे, फिर स्त्रियों की स्वतंत्रता का प्रश्न ही नहीं था। लेकिन स्वतंत्रता संग्राम में पुरुषों के साथ-साथ देश की नारियों ने भी हिस्सा लिया। 19वीं सदी के मध्य ब्रिटिश शासन के खिलाफ अपने बहादुरों के साथ झांसी की रानी खूब लड़ीं। वह विश्व इतिहास में युद्धों की रानी के रूप में जानी जाती है। महिलाओं को राष्ट्रीय स्वतंत्रता संग्राम में आसानी से आने की स्वीकृति कैसे मिली जबकि उन्हें किसी भी राजनीतिक या सार्वजनिक गतिविधि में भाग लेने की अनुमति नहीं थी। परन्तु तनिका सरकार के अनुसार महिलाओं का राष्ट्रीय राजनीति में सामंजस्य इसलिए हो सका क्योंकि गाँधी जी को एक संत एवं देवता तथा देशभक्ति के आंदोलन को धर्मयुद्ध माना गया। गाँधीजी की सोच यह थी कि गर्भधारण और मातृत्व के अनुभवों से गुजरने के कारण महिलाएँ शांति और अहिंसा का संदेश फैलाने के लिए ज्यादा उपयुक्त हैं। गाँधी जी महिलाओं को सार्वजनिक जीवन में एक नया आत्मसम्मान, एक नया विश्वास और एक नई छवि दिलाई। सन 1920-22 में जब असहयोग आन्दोलन शुरू हुआ तो पहली बार महिलाएँ भारी संख्या में आंदोलन से जुड़ गयीं। 1921 के कांग्रेस सम्मेलन में 144 महिला प्रतिनिधियों ने भाग लिया। मुंबई में महिलाओं ने राष्ट्रीय स्त्री सभा का गठन किया जो बिना पुरुषों की मदद से चलाये जाते थे। इसके दो उद्देश्य थे-स्वराज और महिलाओं का उद्धार एवं उत्थान। असहयोग आंदोलन में महिलाओं की भागीदारी से उन्हें अपने लिए एक जगह मिली। सविनय अवज्ञा आन्दोलन से राष्ट्रीय आन्दोलन में महिलाओं की भागीदारी का एक नया चरण शुरू हुआ एवं गुणात्मक एवं संख्यात्मक दोनों रूपों से उनकी भागीदारी में काफी वृद्धि हुई। हजारों महिलाओं ने नमक सत्याग्रह आंदोलन में नमक बनाने से लेकर बेचने तक काम किये। उस समय राष्ट्रीय आन्दोलन में हर तबके की महिलाएँ आंदोलन में भाग लीं। एनी बेसेन्ट, सरोजनी नायडू, कजिन्स, कमला देवी चट्टोपाध्याय आदि ने महिलाओं को नेतृत्व प्रदान किया।

1930 के दशक में महिलाओं को प्रथम बार पुलिस दमन का सामना करना पड़ा। महिलाओं के जुलूसों पर भी लाठी चार्ज किया जाने लगा। इस तरह की घटनाओं से जनता में काफी आक्रोश फैला और आंदोलन ने और जोर पकड़ा। 1930 में मुंबई में चुनाव के खिलाफ धरने पर बैठी 400 महिलाओं को एक साथ गिरफ्तार किया गया। 1930-33 के बीच 20 हजार महिला सत्याग्रही जेल भेजी

गई। आंदोलन में महिलाओं की भूमिका सुनिश्चित की जा सके इसके लिए देश सेविका संघ, नारी सत्याग्रह समिति, महिला राष्ट्रीय संघ, लेडिज पिकेटिंग बोर्ड, स्त्री स्वराज संघ, स्वयंसेविका संघ आदि बने।

ज्यों-ज्यों आंदोलन में तेजी आयी एवं उसमें महिलाओं की भागीदारी बढ़ी, महिलाओं के मुद्दे भी सार्वजनिक चर्चा में आये। 1926 में स्थापित ऑल इण्डिया वूमेन्स कान्फ्रेंस के कार्यों में भी विस्तार होता चला गया। इसका उद्देश्य मुख्य रूप से यह हो गया कि महिलाओं का शैक्षिक स्तर बढ़ाया जाय जिससे पुरूषों के समान महिलाओं की भूमिका को सुनिश्चित किया जा सके। पहले इसकी अध्यक्ष केवल नाम के वास्ते होती थी और अब चूंकि संस्था एक एक्टीविस्ट संस्था बन गई थी अतः इसकी अध्यक्षा 1931 में सरोजनी नायडू चूनी गयी।

जब भारत में 1950 में प्रजातांत्रिक संविधान को अंगीकार किया गया तो प्रत्येक भारतवासी का, जिसमें निःसन्देह स्त्री भी शामिल हैं, राजनीति और निर्णय लेने की हर प्रक्रिया के स्तर पर सहभागिता के अधिकार को बिना किसी भेदभाव स्वीकार किया गया। इसके बावजूद सार्वजनिक जीवन में महिलाओं की भागीदारी में कोई विशेष हिस्सेदारी नहीं हुई। स्वतंत्रता के बाद राजनीतिक प्रक्रिया में महिलाओं की भूमिका और उनकी स्थिति पर 'कमिटी ऑन द स्ट्रेटस ऑफ वूमेन ऑफ इण्डिया' (1975) के अपने रिपोर्ट में कहा था, ''समाज और राजनीति में महिलाओं की स्थिति बताती है कि संविधान में उन्हें पुरूषों के समकक्ष दर्जा देकर जिस क्रान्ति की आशा की गई थी, वह अब भी बहुत दूर है। अब तक शक्तिशाली पदों पर स्त्रियों का पहुँचना संयोग ही था। केन्द्र में इन्दिरा गाँधी, राज्य में सुचेता कृपलानी, नन्दिनी सत्पथी, जे. जयललिता, मायावती, राबड़ी देवी, सुषमा स्वराज, शीला दीक्षित, उमा भारती, वसुन्धरा राजे जैसी महिला नेतृत्व दे चुकी है। भारत के राष्ट्रपति के पद पर अभी एक महिला श्रीमति प्रतिभा पाटिल विराजमान हैं। महिलाओं की राजनीतिक सहभागिता की संस्थागत स्वरूप प्रदान करने का श्रेय 73वें संविधान संशोधन विधेयक को जाता है। देश के इतिहास में प्रथम बार पंचायत व्यवस्था के प्रत्येक स्तर पर महिलाओं के लिए 33 प्रतिशत स्थान आरक्षित किये गये हैं। इसके परिणामस्वरूप सम्पूर्ण देश में सरपंच, मुखिया, प्रमुख एवं जिला प्रमुख इत्यादि पर महिलायें भी पदासीन हुई हैं। आरक्षण के इस क्रान्तिकारी कदम के पीछे यही उद्देश्य है कि इससे महिलाओं में राजनीतिक जागृति आयेगी। अपने अधिकार के प्रति उनमें चेतना पैदा होगी, इस प्रकार क्षेत्र एवं देश के कल्याण कार्यों में भाग लेने के लिए वे सक्षम होंगी।

स्त्रियों को आरक्षण मिलने की वजह से शनैः-शनैः महिलाएँ विभिन्न उत्तरदायित्वों को संभाल रही हैं। परन्तु, भारत में नारी नेतृत्व के मार्ग में अभी भी सबसे बड़ी बाधा अधिकांश महिलाओं का शिक्षा से वंचित होना है। कोई भी राष्ट्र अपनी प्रगति और सम्पन्नता के पथ पर अग्रसर होना चाहता है तो इसके लिए आधी जनसंख्या महिला का शिक्षित होना अनिवार्य है जिससे उनकी क्षमता का भी लाभ राष्ट्र को प्राप्त हो सके।

संदर्भ-सूची

Kapur Promila, Empowering the Indian Women, Publication Division, Ministry of Information and Broadcasting, Govt. of India.

ए. के. मित्तल, भारत का राजनीतिक एवं सांस्कृतिक इतिहास, साहित्य भवन पब्लिकेशन, आगरा।

साधना आर्य, निवेदिता मेनन, जिनी लोकनीता (संपादक), नारीवादी राजनीति : संघर्ष एवं मुद्दे, हिन्दी माध्यम कार्यान्वयन निदेशालय, दिल्ली विश्वविद्यालय, नई दिल्ली।

A. S. Altekar, The Position of Women in Hindu Civilization.

R. C. Dutt, "A History of Civilization in Ancient India".

आर. पी. जोशी एवं डॉ. रूपा मंगलानी (संपादक), भारत में पंचायती राज, राजस्थान हिन्दी ग्रन्थ अकादमी, जयपुर।

32

बिहार पंचायती राज व्यवस्था में महिला सशक्तिकरण

मुखलाल राय

वेदों में नारी का जो वर्णन हुआ है उससे ज्ञात होता है कि उस समय समाज में नारी को समानता का अधिकार प्राप्त था। नारी पुरुष की सहभागिनी और सहायिका थी। स्त्री-पुरुष के साथ यज्ञ में बैठती थी और उसे यज्ञ करने का अधिकार था। वह युद्ध में पुरुषों के साथ जाया करती थी और युद्ध कार्यों में भाग लेती थी। ब्राह्मण ग्रंथों व उपनिषदों में नारी को पति की अर्द्धांग्नि बताया गया है। आपस्तम्ब धर्म सूत्र ने पति-पत्नी को धार्मिक कृत्यों में समान माना है। नारी की ज्ञान और संपत्ति का पुंज मानते हुए कहा गया है कि "यत्र नार्यस्तु पूज्यन्ते, रमन्ते तत्र देवता।" प्राचीन समय में स्त्रियों भी शिक्षा संबंधी व्यवस्था बहुत उन्नत थी। बहुत सी नारियों ने वैदिक ऋचाएँ तक रची है। बधु को यह आशीर्वाद दिया जाता था कि वह सभा में आत्मविश्वास से बोले। अतः नारी को सभी में बोलने की स्वतंत्रता प्राप्त थी। किन्तु धर्मशास्त्र परंपरा के स्मृति युग में नारी की स्वतंत्रता का हनन हुआ। स्मृति ग्रंथों के अध्ययन से स्पष्ट होता है कि स्मृति काल में स्त्रियों की दशा उत्तम नहीं रही। स्त्रियों को शूद्रों की श्रेणी में रखा गया और उन्हें वेद आदि की अध्ययन से वंचित किया गया तथा मनु, गौतम आदि ने स्त्रियों को अस्वतंत्र माना। भारत में मुस्लिम काल एवं ब्रिटिश काल में भी स्त्रियों की स्थिति दयनीय रही। कुछ विद्वानों की मान्यता यह है कि भारतीय परंपरा जो मूलतः धर्मशास्त्रों पर आधारित है इसमें भी नारी

को दोयम दर्जा दिया गया है और यह परंपरा ही नारी की वर्तमान स्थिति के लिए उत्तरदायी है।

वर्तमान समय में नारी अधिकार अंतर्राष्ट्रीय चर्चा का विषय बना हुआ है। नारी की पराधीनता एवं पिछड़ी सामाजिक दशा हमारे वर्तमान समाज की प्रमुख समस्याओं में से एक ज्वलन्त समस्या है। नारी अधिकारों के हनन का मुख्य कारण भी नारी अधिकारों का प्रकाश में नहीं आना है एवं धार्मिक परम्पराएं हो सकती है क्योंकि किसी देश की सामाजिक, राजनैतिक एवं सांस्कृतिक चेतना को उसकी सामाजिक परम्पराएं प्रभावित करती है। ऐसी स्थिति में नारी अधिकारों पर विचार-विमर्श करना आवश्यक हो जाता है। वैश्विक स्तर पर महिला सशक्तिकरण का प्रारम्भ पाश्चात्य देशों में वैयक्तिक स्वतंत्रता के समर्थकों द्वारा लोकतांत्रिक शासन प्रणाली को अपनाये जाने के रूप में हुआ लेकिन एक आन्दोलन के रूप में महिला सशक्तिकरण की शुरूआत 8 मार्च 1975 को अंतर्राष्ट्रीय महिला दिवस से मानी जा सकती है। 1974 को महिला सशक्तिकरण वर्ष एवं 1975 से 1985 के दशक को महिला दशक के रूप में मनाया गया। महिला सशक्तिकरण की पहली महिला अंतर्राष्ट्रीय सम्मेलन नैरोबी में 1985 में हुई। एशिया एवं प्रशांत में महिलाओं के उच्चीकरण हेतु जकार्ता घोषणा पत्र 1994 तथा बीजिंग घोषणा पत्र तथा कार्यान्वयन हेतु प्लेटफार्म (1995) ने महिला सशक्तिकरण को नए आयाम दिए। सशक्तिकरण का अर्थ किसी कार्य को करने या रोकने की क्षमता से है जिसमें महिलाओं को जागरूक करके उन्हें आर्थिक, सामाजिक, राजनैतिक, शैक्षिक और स्वास्थ्य संबंधी साधनों को उपलब्ध कराये जाने से है ताकि उनके लिए सामाजिक न्याय और पुरुष महिला समानता का लक्ष्य हासिल हो सके। महिला सशक्तिकरण की राष्ट्रीय नीति का उद्देश्य महिलाओं की प्रगति, विकास एवं आत्म शक्ति को सुनिश्चित करना है।

जहाँ तक भारत में महिला सशक्तिकरण के प्रयासों का प्रश्न है तो इसका बीजारोपण भारतीय संविधान का निर्माण करते समय ही हो गया। महिलाओं को पुरुषों के समकक्ष मानते हुए उन्हें विधिक, राजनैतिक, सामाजिक तथा आर्थिक समानता प्रदान की गई। महिलाओं के सशक्तिकरण की प्रक्रिया में चौथी पंचवर्षीय योजना के बाद से उल्लेखनीय रूप से परिवर्तन आया। ''महिलाओं का विकास का मुद्दे का स्थान महिलाओं का सशक्तिकरण ने लिया। संविधान के 73वें एवं 74वें संशोधन द्वारा पंचायती राज संस्थाओं तथा स्थानीय नगर निकायों के एक तिहाई पद महिलाओं के लिए आरक्षित कर दिया गया। यह इस दिशा में सर्वाधिक

क्रांतिकारी कदम था। 31 जनवरी 1992 को राष्ट्रीय महिला आयोग का गठन हुआ जिसके माध्यम से सदियों से पिछड़े, शोषित एवं उपेक्षित नारी वर्ग के विकास पर विशेष ध्यान दिया जा रहा है। वर्ष 2001 में भारत सरकार ने महिला सशक्तिकरण वर्ष घोषित किया तथा राष्ट्रीय महिला शक्ति सम्पन्नता नीति 2001 घोषित किया था। डा. अम्बेडकर ने कहा है कि "भारतीय नारी श्रम से नहीं घबराती किन्तु आंसुओं की चिन्ता करते हुए वह रोटी, असमान व्यवहार, अपमान, शोषण से अवश्य डरती है।" दूसरी ओर स्वामी विवेकानन्द ने कहा है कि 'स्त्रियों की अवस्था में सुधार लाए बिना विश्व कल्याण असंभव है जैसे कि एक पंख से उड़ान भरना।' प्रो. अमर्त्यसेन ने लिखा है कि "महिला सशक्तिकरण से न केवल महिलाओं के जीवन में निश्चित रूप से सकारात्मक असर पड़ेगा बल्कि पुरुषों और बच्चों को भी इससे लाभ होगा।

इक्कीसवीं सदी के प्रथम दशक में महिलाओं की भागीदारी के लिए त्रिस्तरीय पंचायत राज संस्थाओं में 50 प्रतिशत स्थान आरक्षित कर बिहार ने महिला सशक्तिकरण की दिशा में एक महत्वपूर्ण शुरुआत की है। इस प्रणाली को जनवरी 2006 में एक अध्यादेश द्वारा लागू किया गया। इसके अमल में आने से राज्य में बिहार पंचायती राज अधिनियम 1993 निरस्त हो गया। इस अध्यादेश से पंचायती राज में महिलाओं को पुरुषों के बराबर आधे स्थान पर भागीदारी के प्रावधान से लोकतंत्र में 'समानता' की अवधारणा और मजबूत हुई है। आज लोकतंत्र में महिलाओं की बढ़ती हुई आबादी को विकास का भी घोतक माना जाता है। महिला सशक्तिकरण की दृष्टि से यह महत्वपूर्ण है कि बिहार की नई प्रणाली की तर्ज पर हिमाचल प्रदेश, राजस्थान और उत्तराखंड की राज्य सरकारों ने भी पंचायती राज संस्थाओं में महिलाओं हेतु 33 प्रतिशत से बढ़ाकर 50 प्रतिशत स्थान का आरक्षित करने की घोषणा की है। स्त्री-पुरुष की समान भागीदारी हेतु पंचायत राज अधिनियम 2006 में यह प्रावधान है कि आरक्षित स्थानों में से आधा महिलाओं के लिए आरक्षित होगा। अतः अनुसूचित जाति, अनुसूचित जनजाति और पिछड़े वर्गों के सदस्यों और पदाधिकारियों के लिए आरक्षित स्थानों में से आधा स्थान महिलाओं के लिए निर्वाचन के लिए आरक्षित है। इस भांति हर स्तर की पंचायत इकाई के अनारक्षित स्थानों में से भी आधा स्थान महिलाओं के लिए आरक्षित होगा।

यह एक विचारणीय मुद्दा है कि आरक्षण की सुविधा के बिना क्या महिलाएं पंचायती राज संस्थाओं के चुनाव में पर्याप्त स्थान ग्रहण कर पायेगी। 2001 के

पंचायत चुनाव में महिलाओं को विजयी होना कठिन था। यदि 2001 पंचायत चुनाव की आंकड़ा को देखें तो पाएंगे कि बिहार ग्राम पंचायत में 8463 मुखिया पदों पर 78 महिलाएं, 531 प्रखंड प्रमुख पदों पर 54 तथा जिला परिषद अध्यक्ष पद पर मात्र 9 महिलाएं विजयी रही। वर्ष 2006 में जब पंचायती राज अधिनियम में बदलाव लाया गया तो इस वर्ष के पंचायत चुनाव में 8463 ग्राम पंचायतों में 4435 मुखिया, 531 प्रखंडों में 292 पंचायत प्रमुख एवं 38 जिला परिषदों में 19 जिला परिषद् अध्यक्ष पर महिला उम्मीदवार विजयी हुई। यहाँ पर उल्लेखनीय है कि बिहार के कुल 4,60,20,000 मतदाताओं में महिला मतदाताओं की संख्या 2,12,60,000 से कुछ अधिक ही है, अर्थात् 50 प्रतिशत से कुछ कम है। 2006 की नई पंचायती राज प्रणाली में 50 प्रतिशत महिला आरक्षण के प्रावधान को चुनौती देने वाले सभी रिट याचिकाओं को पटना उच्च न्यायालय के तीन न्यायाधीशों की खण्डपीठ ने 19 मई 2006 को अपने एक फैसले के तहत खारिज कर दिया। खण्डपीठ ने सर्वसम्मति से 50 प्रतिशत महिला आरक्षण के प्रावधानों को 91 पृष्ठ के फैसले से सही ठहराया। इस पक्ष के समर्थन हेतु खण्डपीठ ने 73वें संशोधन अधिनियम 1992 के अनुच्छेद 243 डी. में उल्लिखित आरक्षण के प्रावधान को उद्धत किया था और महिला सशक्तिकरण के तत्व को वैधानिक शक्ति प्रदान किया।

बिहार पंचायती राज अधिनियम 2006 द्वारा बिहार में सामाजिक बदलाव का रेखाचित्र उभर रहा है जब गांवों के कमजोर वर्गों के निर्वाचित प्रतिनिधि की पंचायती राज संस्थाओं में महत्वपूर्ण भूमिका हो गई है। यह उल्लेखनीय है कि दलित महिलाएं भी आरक्षित स्थानों से निर्वाचित होकर त्रिस्तरीय पंचायत राज संस्थाओं के अध्यक्ष पद पर आसीन होकर विकास कार्यों का संचालन कर रही है और ग्राम कचहरी में सरपंच और पंच की हैसियत से महिलायें कुछ मुकदमों का फैसला भी करेगी। राज्य की अनुसूचित जातियों के सोलह प्रतिशत जनसंख्या के अनुपात में सोलह प्रतिशत स्थान पर 2006 के चुनाव में निर्वाचित महिलाओं ने स्थान ग्रहण कर लिया है। दलित महिला हेतु आरक्षण के प्रतिशत के आधार पर बिहार में पहली बार राज्य के 38 जिलों में से तीन जिलों की जिला परिषदों (पटना, गया, समस्तीपुर) में तीन दलित महिलाएं अध्यक्ष पद पर चुन कर आई है। यह पुरुष प्रधान सामंतवादी और ऊंच-नीच के आधार पर श्रेणीबद्ध ग्रामीण समाज में एक क्रांतिकारी परिवर्तन का द्योतक है। इस आयाम का लोकतंत्र और सामाजिक संरचना पर दूरगामी प्रभाव पड़ेगा क्योंकि चाहरदिवारी से औरतें आज चौपाल तक आ गई है।

राष्ट्रीय रोजगार गारंटी योजना के कार्यक्रमों में मजदूरों की कुल संख्या में कम से कम एक तिहाई महिलाओं को आवश्यक रूप से रोजगार प्रदान करने की व्यवस्था की गई है। पुरुषों के समान महिलाओं को भी 60 रुपये प्रतिदिन मजदूरी का भुगतान करना होगा। महिलाओं के आर्थिक उत्थान हेतु स्वयं सहायता समूहों का भी गठन अपरिहार्य है। कृषि, पशुपालन एवं डेयरी फार्म, खाद्यी, ग्रामीण एवं कुटीर उद्योग, खाद्य प्रसंस्करण आदि कार्यों के माध्यम से महिलाओं को रोजगार का अवसर मिलेगा। कई उद्यमों में कुशलता बढ़ाने के लिए प्रशिक्षण का भी प्रबंध करना होगा। आवश्यकता के अनुसार महिला उद्यमियों को बैंक से भी ऋण भी उपलब्ध कराना होगा। यह जाहिर है कि पंचायती राज संस्थाओं का 50 प्रतिशत आरक्षण राजनीतिक सशक्तिकरण का द्योतक है। इस राजनीतिक सशक्तिकरण के माध्यम से आम महिलाओं को सामाजिक और आर्थिक सशक्तिकरण की दिशा में आगे बढ़ाना होगा। इस कदम से महिला के साथ-साथ गांव का परिवार भी सम्पन्न होगा क्योंकि महिला परिवार की धूरी मानी जाती है।

पंचायत राज अधिनियम 2006 के आधार पर हुए चुनाव के बाद ऐसा लगा मानो क्रांति की बीज पड़ गए और अब नया सबेरा दूर नहीं है, लेकिन जब सत्य से साक्षातकार हुआ तो करूण कन्दन के अतिरिक्त और कुछ भी नहीं था। इसमें संदेह नहीं कि सत्ता का सूत्र महिलाओं के हाथों में थमा दिया गया है लेकिन सच में उनकी स्थिति रबर स्टांप की ही है। उपले थापने वाले हाथों में कलम तो जरूर पकड़ा दी गई है लेकिन उन हाथों को थामने वाले सशक्त बाजुओं की पकड़ से महिलाओं की मुक्ति का कोई उपाय नहीं है। सच यही है कि पंचायत चुनाव में चुने गये अधिकांश प्रतिनिधियों को नहीं पता है कि उन्हें वास्तव में करना क्या है। ऐसे में क्या होगा यदि सत्ता की सूत्रधार ये महिलायें अपने ही अधिकारों के लिए सजग नहीं हो। ऐसे में उनसे दूसरे के अधिकारों की बात करना या क्षेत्र के विकास की बात करना पानी पर डंडा पीटने के समान है। वर्तमान ग्रामीण परिदृश्य इस बात को दर्शाता है कि अभी भी महिलाएं समाज के हाशिए पर ही है। वे इतनी जागरूक नहीं हो पाई है कि ग्राम पंचायत के स्तर पर ग्राम सभा की बैठकों में भाग लेने के लिए तत्पर रहें। गांव की आम महिलाओं को शायद इस बात की भी जानकारी नहीं है कि अब ग्राम सभा को संवैधनिक दर्जा मिल गई है। ग्राम सभा में महिलाओं की सीमित भागीदारी के संभवतः निम्नलिखित कारण है– सामंतवादी दृष्टिकोण, पुरुष प्रधान ग्रामीण जीवन, पर्दा प्रथा और पंचायत के प्रति उदासीन भावना। ऐसे सामाजिक परिवेश में महिला आरक्षण से जुड़ी हुई महिला सशक्तिकरण

को चुनी हुई महिला सदस्यों और अध्यक्षों के साथ-साथ गांवों की आम महिलाओं तक ले जाना सहज कार्य नहीं है। पंचायतों में लिंग भेद अभी जारी है क्योंकि अधिकांश पंचायतों में महिलाओं को उतनी इज्जत नहीं दी जा सकती है या उनके निर्णयों को स्वीकार नहीं किया जा सकता है। अभी भी महिलायें घर के पुरुष सदस्य के कहने पर इसका सदस्य बनने के लिए तैयार होती है और महिलाओं के बदले उस परिवार के पुरुष सदस्य ही कार्य निपटाते हैं। दूसरे शब्दों में महिलाएँ स्वयं आगे नहीं आ रही है।

सुझाव के रूप कहा जा सकता है कि पंचायती राज संस्थाओं में अधिकांश महिलाएं अनपढ़ है। इसलिए ऐसी महिलाओं के बीच प्रशिक्षण शिविर चलाना आवश्यक है। इसके साथ चर्चा सभा और महिला सम्मेलन भी आवश्यक है। पारिवारिक कार्यों में महिला के साथ उसके पति का सहकार तथा भागीदारी जरूरी है ताकि महिला समय निकाल कर पंचायत के कार्यों को निबटा सके। राजनैतिक माहौल में अपराधीकरण, आतंकवाद, कालाधन, चरित्र लांछन जैसे दुर्गुण है जिनसे महिलायें सार्वजनिक रूप से अलग रहती है क्योंकि उन्हें सामाजिक प्रतिष्ठा का भय बना रहता है। इसलिए सरकार, राजनेताओं और राजनीतिक दलों द्वारा इस दुषित वातावरण में परिवर्तन लाना जरूरी है। पुरुष प्रधान रूढ़ीवादी सोच समझ बदलनी चाहिए। आर्थिक आत्मनिर्भरता, राजनीतिक सहभागिता एवं सक्रियता का प्रमुख आधार है। इसलिए महिलाओं की आत्मनिर्भरता बढ़ानी चाहिए। महिलाओं को मात्र कानूनी अधिकार दिये जाने से समान अधिकार का उपयोग नहीं कर सकती बल्कि सामाजिक परिवर्तन हो समाज का नजरिया बदले एवं महिलाओं के मन में पनपे हीन भावना का अंत हो। पहली बार महिलाएं सार्वजनिक जीवन में आई है इसलिए उनमें भय संकोच एवं ज्यादा घबराहट है। अतः उनमें साहस त्याग एवं आत्मविश्वास की भावना पैदा करना आवश्यक है। महिलाओं में शक्ति विकसित करने के लिए शिविरों, चर्चा सभा और ओरियेन्टेशन कोर्स की व्यवस्था होनी चाहिए। आम महिलाओं की सक्रिय भूमिका और उनकी सुरक्षा एवं कल्याण के लिए पंचायती राज के हर स्तर पर एक मजबूत महिला समिति का गठन आवश्यक है। प्रधानमंत्री मनमोहन सिंह ने 'बेटी बचाओ अभियान' द्वारा यह संदेश दिया है कि पंचायतों के अधिकारों में कन्या भ्रूण हत्या एवं बाल विवाह कार्यक्रम जोड़ना होगा। महिला आरक्षण की अवधि दस वर्षों का होना चाहिए। निष्कर्षतः कहा जा सकता है कि पंचायती राज व्यवस्था द्वारा बिहार में महिलाओं का कुछ हद तक सशक्तिकरण हुआ है पर इसमें बहुत कुछ किया जाना अभी बाकी है।

33

स्वेच्छावाद तथा महिलाओं का राजनीतिक नेतृत्व : एक समीक्षात्मक अध्ययन

सैयद शहनवाज इ. अजमेरी एवं मो. इरशाद अली

भूमिका

भारत में नारियों को प्राचीन काल से ही सम्मानजनक स्थान प्राप्त हुआ है। हड़प्पा काल में नारियों की पूजा की जाती थी तथा उस काल में कोई भी पुरूष अपनी पत्नी के बगैर किसी प्रकार का धार्मिक अनुष्ठान अथवा सामाजिक दायित्व का निर्वहन नहीं करता था। वैदिक काल में न ही पर्दा प्रथा विधमान था और न ही सति-प्रथा का प्रचलन था। समाज पितष्ट-सत्तात्मक था परंतु पुत्र के अभाव में पुत्री सम्पत्ति की उत्तराधिकारी होती थी। भारत में मुसलमानों के आक्रमण के पश्चात् नारी की जीवन की करूणा गाथा का इतिहास आरंभ होता है। मध्यकाल में नारियों को सम्मानजनक स्थान तो प्राप्त नहीं था किन्तु राजनीति पदार्पण भारतीय इतिहास में इसी काल में दर्ज हुआ जब इल्तुतमिष ने अपने सुयोग्य पुत्रों के न रहने के कारण सन् 1236 में अपनी पुत्री रजिया सुल्ताना को अपना उत्तराधिकारी नियुक्त किया। इसी के साथ ही भारत के इतिहास में महिला शासक का पदार्पण हुआ। हालांकि उस समय भी सम्राज्य के दूसरे सरदारों ने इसका विरोध किया तथा अंततः उनकी हत्या कर दी गई। इसी प्रकार अकबर के शासन काल में रानी दूर्गावती जैसी महान योद्धा की चर्चा भी इतिहास में दर्ज है। अंग्रेज के भारत में आगमन के पश्चात भारत में नारी चेतना जागृत हुई और

अनेक नारी संबंधी आंदोलन चलाये गये। इस सिलसिले में सती-प्रथा, बाल-विवाह, कन्या जैसी घृणित प्रथाओं को विविध कानूनों के माध्यम से रोकने के सतत्, प्रयास किया गया।

विश्लेषण

1973-75 में मूल्य वृद्धि आंदोलन को महाराष्ट्र के शहरी इलाकों में Communists और Socialist महिलाओं ने संगठित एवं संचालित किया। स्वतंत्रोपरांत महिलाओं द्वारा राजनीतिक क्षेत्र में अपना सक्रिय योगदान दिया जिसका इतिहास साक्षी है। गाँधीजी ने 30 के दशक में महिलओं की अजादी के लिए लड़ने वाली योद्धा मृदुला साराभाई से कहा था कि "मैंने भारतीय महिलाओं को रसोईघर से बाहर लाने का कार्य किया है, अब आपको (महिला कार्यकर्ताओं को) उन्हें वापस लौटाने से रोकने का काम करना है।" वास्तव में गाँधीजी का यह कथन भारतीय महिलाओं ने आने गांठ में बांध लिया और उसके अनुरूप सशक्त राजनीतिक इच्छाशक्ति का विकास किया तथा राजनीतिक क्षेत्र में अपनी विलक्षण प्रतिभाा एवं सक्रियता का उच्च स्तरीय प्रदर्शन किया। महिलाओं ने 60 के दशक के अंत और 70 के दशक के प्रारंभ में अनेक सामाजिक आंदोलनों एवं राजनीतिक आंदोलनों में सक्रिय भूमिका निभाई। इन आंदोलनों में मुख्यतः नक्सलपंथी आंदोलन, चिपको आंदोलन जे.पी. आंदोलनों, मूल्य वृद्धि आंदोलन इत्यादि संगणित किये जाते हैं। 1973-75 में इस दौरान जन-रैली निकाली गयी जिनमें हजारों गृहणियों ने भाग लिया जो आमतौर पर अपने घरों से बाहर नहीं निकला करती थी। महाराष्ट्र के धरिया जिले में शहदा आदिवासी क्षेत्र में एक अलग किस्म के आंदोलन की शुरूआत की गई। इसके शुरूआती दौर में गांधीवादी सर्वोदय कार्यकर्ताओं ने इसे चलाया। यह आंदोलन अकाल राहत तथा जमीन के लिए आरंभ हुआ जिसमें भील आदिवासी महिलाओं ने उल्लेखनीय भूमिका निभाई। तदोपरांत इसने शराब विरोधी आंदोलन का रूप धारण कर लिया जिसमें महिलाओं की सक्रियता देखी गई। मध्यप्रदेश के छत्तीसगढ़ इलाके में जो समप्रति एक पृथक राज्य के रूप में है, महिलाओं ने छत्तीसगढ़ खद्यान श्रमिक संघ में बड़ी ही सक्रिय भूमिका का प्रदर्शन किया। इस संगठन को सन 1977 में स्थापित किया गया जिसका मूल उद्देश्य भिलाई इस्पात कारखाना के मशीनीकरण नीति का प्रतिवाद करना था क्योंकि इसे महिलाओं के रोजगार के लिए अनुकूल नहीं माना गया। एक नवीन संगठन महिला मुक्ति की स्थापना भी की गई। 1979 में आज युवा संघर्ष वाहिनी द्वारा इस आश्य की मांग

की गयी कि महिलाओं के नाम से भी जमीन का निबंधन अमल में लाना अनिवार्य है, यह मांग बाद में एक वृहद आंदोलन के रूप में परिवर्तित हो गया। इसके परिणामस्वरूप कई राज्यों में जमीन के पट्टे तथा पेड़-पौधें से संबंधित पट्टे भी सरकार द्वारा महिलाओं के नाम से दिये जाने लगे। भोपाल गैस पीड़ित महिला संगठन ने गैस त्रासदी से प्रभावित व्यक्तियों को न्याय दिलाने के लिए एक अहम् भूमिका निभाई। इसी तरह 1977 के आपातकाल के दौरान दिल्ली में एक ऐसे महिला संगठन की संस्थापना की गई जो महिला आंदोलन के सुदृढ़ आंदोलन के सुदृढ़ संगठन के रूप में उभर कर सामने आया। 1979 में दहेज उत्पीड़न संबंधी विवाह प्रश्नों को लेकर एक विशाल आंदोलन का ही असर था कि केन्द्रीय सरकार द्वारा महिलाओं के कल्याणार्थ महिला आयोग की स्थापना 1990 में की गई। तत्पश्चात् अन्य राज्यों में भी महिला आयोग अस्तित्व में आये।

सनद रहे कि भारतीय संसद एवं राज्य विधान मंडल में महिलाओं का अनुपात एक समान नहीं रहा है। सरोजनी नायडू को स्वतंत्र भारत की प्रथम महिला राज्यपाल होने का गौरव प्राप्त हुआ और वह भी भारत के सबसे बड़े प्रांत उत्तर प्रदेश की। इसी प्रकार सुचिता कृपलानी भी स्वतंत्र भारत की प्रथम महिला मुख्यमंत्री बनी और वह भी इसी उत्तर प्रदेश राज्य की। यही नहीं बल्कि 24 जनवरी 1966 को श्रीमती इंदिरा गांधी भारत की प्रथम महिला प्रधानमंत्री बनी, जिन्होंने एक लम्बे समय तक विभिन्न अंतरालों में देश को एक कुशल नेतृत्व प्रदान किया। इसे पूर्णरूपेण स्वेच्छावाद तथा महिलाओं के राजनीति नेतृत्व का गौरव उदाहरण के रूप में पेश किया जा सकता है।

इस परिप्रेक्ष्य में यह तथ्य भी रेखांकित करने योग्य है कि भारतीय लोक सभा में महिलाओं की संख्या एक समान नहीं रही है। प्रथम लोकसभा में कुल 489 सदस्यों के विरुद्ध महिलाओं की संख्या जहाँ 22 थी वहीं दूसरी लोकसभा में यह 27, तीसरी में 34 और चौथी में घटकर 31 हो गई। इसी तरह 5वीं लोकसभा में इनकी संख्या 22 और छठी में घटकर 19 हो गई जो वस्तुतः अब तक महिलाओं की लोकसभा में न्यूनतम संख्या माना जाता है। इसके बाद महिलाओं की संख्या में वृद्धि हुई, सातवीं लोकसभा में 28 हो गई। इसके बाद महिलाओं की संख्या में कमी बढ़ोत्तरी होती रही और 13वीं लोकसभा में इनकी संख्या 49 तक पहुँच गई जो अब तक की लोकसभा में सर्वोच्च संख्या मानी जाती है। जबकी समप्रति 14वीं लोकसभा में महिलाओं की संख्या 44 है।

भारत में महिलाओं के स्वच्छतावाद तथा उनके राजनीतिक नेतृत्व के सुस्पष्ट एवं सुंदर उदाहरण भारत के कई राज्यों में उनके मुख्यमंत्री के पद पर पदासीन रहने के रूप में दृटव्य है। वर्ष 1990 के बाद कई राज्यों में महिला मुख्यमंत्री, सुश्री उमा भारती ने मध्य प्रदेश, कुमारी मायावती ने उत्तर प्रदेश, श्रीमति विजय राजे सिधिंया ने राजस्थान, श्रीमति शिला दीक्षित ने दिल्ली तथा श्रीमती राबड़ी देवी ने बिहार का नेतृत्व किया। इन दृष्टांतों से यह स्पष्टतः परिक्षित होता है कि हिन्दुस्तान की सियासत में महिलाओं ने मुख्यमंत्री जैसे गौरवमय पदों पर रह कर अपनी राजनीति सूझबुझ एवं सक्रियता को आलोकित किया है। श्रीमति शिला दीक्षित ने तो दिल्ली विधानसभा में तीन बार विजय हो कर भारत में कीर्तिमान स्थापित किया है।

महिलाओं के राजनीतिक नेतृत्व का एक अत्यंत सुंदर एवं ज्वलंत उदाहरण भारतवर्ष में श्रीमति सोनिया गांधी का ''संयुक्त प्रगतिशील गठबन्धन'' का अध्यक्ष होने को भी माना जा सकता है इस उच्चस्थ पद पर आसिन रहते हुए भी इन्होंने पूरुष प्रधान समाज की इस अवधारणा के मिथक को तोड़ा है कि महिलाएँ जटिल राजनीति नेतृत्व में अक्षम है क्योंकि यह जग जाहिर है कि संयुक्त प्रगतिशील गठबंधन की सरकार में अनेक राजनीतिक दलों के न्यूनतम साझा कार्यक्रम को अधिक संयुक्त रूप से कार्य कर रही है और इनमें समन्वय का उतरदायित्व एक महिला यथा श्रीमति सोनिया गांधी के सबल कंधों पर है। नेतृत्व की प्रभावशीलता प्रतीक इतना विशाल है कि समय-समय पर केन्द्र की सरकार के संचालन का आरोप भी उन पर विपक्ष के द्वारा लगाया जाता रहा है कहने का तात्पर्य यह है कि महिला अगर किसी कार्य को करना चाहे तो निश्चित ही वह पुरुष से किसी भी मायने में कम नहीं होती है, क्योंकि उसमें दृढ़ इच्छाशक्ति होती है। फोर्ब्स पत्रिका के द्वारा किये गये सर्वेक्षण के अनुसार विश्व की प्रभावशाली महिलाओं में श्रीमति सोनिया गांधी का स्थान छठा है। इस संदर्भ में यह कहना भी अप्रासांगिक न होगा की भारत के सर्वोच्च राजनीतिक पद (राष्ट्रपति) पर एक महिला (श्रीमति प्रतिभा पाटिल) पदस्थापित हैं।

इस दिशा में बिहार के संदर्भ में अध्ययन करने पर यह विदित होता है कि यहाँ महिलाएँ पूर्व से राजनीतिक रूप में सक्रिय रही हैं। स्वतंत्रता संग्राम में महिलाओं ने बढ़-चढ़कर हिस्सा लिया है। आजादी के बाद बिहार विधानसभा एवं बिहार विधान परिषद् में इनका सदैव प्रतिनिधित्व रहा है। समप्रति बिहार विधान सभा एवं बिहार विधान परिषद् में इनकी संख्या क्रमशः 25 एवं 7 है।

यह तथ्य गौरतलब है कि पंचायती राज व्यवस्था में महिलाओं के राजनीतिक

नेतृत्व का गहन अध्ययन करने पर अपनी राजनीति सक्षमता एवं प्रवीणता का बेहतर प्रदर्शन कर सकती हैं। ग्रामीन स्तर पर राजनीति प्रयोगशाला के रूप में पंचायत राज एक अहम् एवं आदर्श भूमिका निभा सकता है। ज्ञातव्य है कि बिहार पंचायती राज अधिनियम 2006 के अधीन महिलाओं को 50 प्रतिशत आरक्षण दिया गया है। गत पंचायत चुनाव में लगभग 65 प्रतिशत महिला प्रतिनिधियों के विजयी होने के फलस्वरूप पंचायती राज व्यवस्थ का जो अद्‌भूत स्वरूप निर्मित हुआ है। उसकी पृष्टभूमि में यह कहना पर्याप्त नहीं होगा की महिलाओं के सशक्तिकरण की दिशा में पंचायतों की भूमिका क्या है, अपीतु अब स्वयं पंचायतों के सशक्तिकरण की दिशा में महिलाओं की भूमिका क्या होने जा रही है– इसे अवलोकित करना काफी दिलचस्प होगा। उल्लेखनीय है कि पंचायतों में महिलाओं के अधिक निर्वाचित होने के कारण जिला प्रशासन और राज्य प्रशासन के लिए चुनौती एवं अवसर दोनों ही है, क्योंकि प्रशासन को किसी महिला बहुलय लोक संस्था के साथ कार्य करने का कोई अनुभव नहीं है और अवसर इसलिए है कि अब पंचायतों को प्रशासनोन्मुखी से लोकोन्मुखी बनाने में राज्य प्रशासन को बहुत अधिक कार्य करने की आवश्यकता नहीं होगी क्योंकि महिलाएँ अपनी इस भूमिका में किसी भी दायित्व का निर्वहन करने के पूर्व उसे अपने परिवार के साथ जोड़कर देखना नहीं भूलेंगी। महिलाएँ अपने राजनीति नेतृत्व का प्रदर्शन त्रिस्तरीय पंचायतों यथा ग्राम पंचायत, पंचायत समिति एवं जिला परिषद के माध्यम से कारगर एवं प्रभावी ढंग से कर सकती है। यह तथ्य सर्वोदित है।

34

महिला राजनीतिक प्रतिनिधित्व : साहित्य के झरोखे से

मधु प्रभा सिंह

> *The world can't arrive at amicable settlement unless the rights between men and women are divided equally by fifty-fifty.*

जार्ज बनार्ड शॉ का यह कथन स्त्रियों और पुरुषों के बीच असमानता की कहानी कहता है। अधिकारों की बात तभी उठती है जब किसी के अधिकारों का हनन हो। अशिक्षा और अज्ञानता के कारण विश्व का चाहे कोई कोना हो, स्त्रियां सदियों से दमित, उपेक्षित और हाशिये पर रही। इसी कारण उनकी स्थिति सुधारने के उद्देश्य से प्रबुद्ध वर्ग और विविध संस्थाओं द्वारा महत्वपूर्ण कदम उठाए गए।

संयुक्त राष्ट्रसंघ का इस दृष्टि से योगदान सर्वाधिक महत्वपूर्ण है। 1979 में Declaration on the elimation of all form of discrimination againt women के साथ ही स्त्री-पुरुषों के समानाधिकारों की स्वीकृति सभी राष्ट्रीय सरकारों की बाध्यता हो गयी। महिला सशक्तीकरण के उद्देश्य से 1975 के वर्ष को महिला वर्ष और 1976-85 दशक को महिला दशक के रूप में मनाया गया। 1995 में बीजिंग में आयोजित चौथे विश्व महिला सम्मेलन का उद्देश्य भी यही था। इन समस्त प्रयासों के बावजूद भी महिलाएं राजनीतिक प्रतिनिधित्व की दृष्टि से काफी पिछड़ी है।

राजनीति के क्षेत्र में भारतीय महिलाओं की भागीदारी बीसवीं शताब्दी के प्रारंभ से स्वाधीनता आन्दोलन, समाज सुधार संबंधी आन्दोलन में सहभागिता

तथा छः प्रांतों में बने कांग्रेस मंत्रिमंडल के विविध पदों पर सुशोभित होने के साथ ही शुरू हो गयी थी। इंदिरा गांधी का प्रधानमंत्री होना, प्रतिभा पाटिल का राष्ट्रपति होना तथा शासन-प्रशासन के विविध महत्वपूर्ण पदों पर उनकी उपस्थिति गौरव की बात है। परन्तु लोकसभा और विधानसभा में महिला प्रतिनिधित्व का चार से बारह प्रतिशत के बीच आगे-पीछे होना दुखद संकेत है। राजनीतिक क्षेत्र में महिला-प्रतिनिधित्व की नगण्यता के कारण ही 81वें संशोधन विधेयक द्वारा विधानसभा और संसद तक महिला आरक्षण की मांग शुरू हुई। परन्तु आरक्षण संबंधी यह विधेयक पक्ष-विपक्ष के चक्कर में आजतक पारित न हो सका।

आरक्षण संबंधी बहस के दौरान स्वतंत्रता के पश्चात गंदे राजनीतिक माहौल को राजनीतिक क्षेत्र में महिला सहभागिता न होने का कारण बताया गया। यह बात बहुत हद तक सत्य भी है। राजनीति की इस गंदगी पर साहित्यकारों ने भी अपनी लेखनी चलाई। मैत्रेयी पुष्पा के 'अल्मा कबूतरी' उपन्यास मजबूर और बेबस नायिका अल्मा कबूतरी डकैत रहे प्रदेश समाज कल्याण मंत्री की जबर्दस्ती अंकशायिनी बना दी जाती है। प्रतिशोध में मंत्री की हत्या का अरमान लिए पढ़ी-लिखी अल्मा अनिच्छा होने पर भी उसकी प्राइवेट सेक्रेटरी बनती है। मंत्री की हत्या हो जाने पर उसकी जगह विधानसभा की सीट के लिए सत्तारूढ़ पार्टी की ओर से उम्मीदवार बनती है। राजनीति में प्रवेश का यह ढंग सामान्य भारतीय स्त्रियों की मानसिकता के विपरीत है। परन्तु स्त्रियों को इससे घबड़ाने की बजाय अतिरिक्त साहस और योग्यता के साथ राजनीतिक क्षेत्र में अधिकाधिक संख्या में पदार्पण कर स्वच्छ और स्वस्थ माहौल तैयार करने के लिए कटिबद्ध होना पड़ेगा। क्योंकि समस्या से भागना समस्या का समाधान नहीं बल्कि उसका डटकर मुकाबला ही नई राह निकालता है।

संविधान द्वारा प्रदत्त ग्रामीण महिलाओं के लिए 33% के आरक्षण ने दस लाख ग्रामीण महिलाओं को मात्र राजनीति में आने का अवसर ही नहीं दिया अपितु एक नए आत्मविश्वास का संचार किया। परन्तु आरक्षण के बाद भी ग्रामीण स्त्री अधिकार के प्रथम दशक में अधिकतर स्त्री-पंचों को आगे आने के लिए न केवल संघर्ष करना पड़ा अपितु पितृ सत्तात्मक समाज की क्रूर यातनाएं भी झेलनी पड़ी। उन्हें शारीरिक या मानसिक यातना देनेवालों में उनके पिता, श्वसुर, पति, भाई आदि संबंधियों से लेकर सरकारी कर्मचारी तक का हाथ होता है। मैत्रेयी पुष्पा के उपन्यास 'चाक' की नायिका सारंग नैनी को ग्राम पंचायत चुनाव के दरम्यान इनसब कठिनाइयों का सामना करना पड़ता है। महत्वाकांक्षा पूर्ति की चाह में

अत्याचारी और अन्यायी लोगों की सोहबत में पड़कर सारंग का पति रंजीत नामांकन पत्र भरने पर उसे गद्दार, बदकार, छिनाल, साली की उपाधि से विभूति करता है। 'पेटीकोट-गवरन्मेंट', 'जनानाराज', 'ब्रुगाईराज' जैसी फब्तियां पुरुषों की घिनौनी मानसिकता का द्योतक है। 'चाक' की इन पंक्तियों से पुरुषों की विकृत मानसिकता का पूर्णरूपेण खुलासा हो सकता है– 'लुगाई राजनीति में आ रही है, बुरी बात क्या है इसमें? अरे तुम सीतापुर की सावित्री की मिसाल ले बैठते हो विध ावा औरत, नाथ न पगहा।' 'और असावरवाली कृष्णा कुमारी तो विधवा नहीं है? 'यार अधबूदी कुंआरी को कुंआरी मानते हैं लोग? टोका टाकी की छूट किसी को नहीं। हाँ, विसाहुली के बहु है प्रधान, देख लो उसका फायदा करीना की पर्चा भरने भी बाबू ही गया था। कह दिया कि राजपाट मिलेगा तब क्या बड़ों का लिहाज करना छोड़ देंगे? ऐसी त्यागमयी लिहाजदारी... सारंग ने धोकर रख दी। सारंग? बेशर्म और। हत्यारी! पति-द्रोहिणी।' स्पष्ट है कि पुरुषों की अधीनता के तहत नारी सुलक्षणी अन्यथा कुलक्षणी या न जाने क्या-क्या। परन्तु अब ग्रामीण स्त्रियां इन अन्यायों के खिलाफ एकजुट और अपने अधिकारों के प्रति जागरूक हो रही है। अतः आगामी दिनों में उन्हें उस हथियार की तरह इस्तेमाल नहीं किया जा सकता जिसकी मूंठ पुरुषों के हाथ में है।

निश्चय ही शोषित व दमित इन ग्रामीण महिलाओं को देश के शासकीय निकायों में सहभागिता की दृष्टि से प्रदत्त आरक्षण सकारात्मक सोच की उपज है जो स्वागत योग्य है। महिलाओं के प्रखर व्यक्तित्व के विकास के लिए अस्तित्व की महत्ता को नजरअंदाज नहीं किया जा सकता। इसलिए भारत सरकार को महिलाओं के लिए लोकसभा व विधानसभा में 33% आरक्षण की मांग को अविलंब स्वीकार कर देश को चतुर्दिक विकास की तरफ अग्रसर करने का कारगर कदम उठाना चाहिए।

35

समाज और राष्ट्र का प्रतिनिधित्व करती जयशंकर प्रसाद की नारियाँ

कुमार रजनीकांत रंजन

> 'नारी तुम केवल श्रद्धा हो विश्वास रजत नग पदतल में,
> पीयूष स्रोत सी बहा करो, जीवन के सुन्दर सममतल में।'

जैसी पंक्तियों के उर्दगाता, आधुनिक युग के सर्वश्रेष्ठ महाकाव्य के रचनाकार, अपनी बहुमुखी प्रतिभा से सम्पूर्ण हिन्दी जगत को एक नयी दिशा देने वाले महाकवि जयशंकर प्रसाद की रचनाओं में अधिकांश नारी पात्र अपने विचारों, भावनाओं, कार्यों और योजनाओं से पूरे समाज और राष्ट्र को एक नयी दिशा देती हुई नजर आती है।

प्रसाद जी ने एक साथ उत्तम कविताओं, कहानियों, नाटकों, उपन्यासों और निबंधों की रचना की है जो अपनी-अपनी विद्याओं में प्रतिनिधित्व करती हैं। सभी विद्याओं की रचना करते हुए प्रसाद जी का कवि रूप हर जगह विद्यमान रहता है और जहां कहीं भी उन्हें अवकाश मिलता है वे काव्य रचना करने लगते हैं। उनका काव्यलोक हो या नाटकों की दुनिया, कहानियों के पात्र हों या उपन्यासों की कल्पना, सबकी बुनावट में प्रसाद जी ने नारी के तारों को इस तरह पिरोया है कि उनका समग्र साहित्य जैसे नारिमय हो गया। बात नाटकों से प्रारम्भ करते हैं, उनके प्रसिद्ध नाटकों में ध्रुवस्वामिनी का नाम आता है जो नारी प्रधान रचना है। इस नाटक के नामकरण से ही जाहिर होता है कि इसमें सम्पूर्ण घटनाओं के मूल

में नारी ही रही होगी। नाटक के प्रारम्भ में ही ध्रुवदेवी यह विचार करती हुई नजर आती है कि पुरुष के पर्वत सदृश्य सीधा तने हुए व्यक्तित्व के पैरों तले लता सदृश्य नारियों को लिपटकर अपने भाग्य पर रोना ही चाहिए न। यहां से ध्रुवस्वामिनी के व्यक्तित्व का तार बुनता हुआ नाटककार प्रसाद जी उसके द्वारा सम्पूर्ण शासनतंत्र को झकझोरने का कार्य करते हैं और बतला देतें हैं कि वैसा शासक जो अपने देश की अस्मिता को अक्षुण्ण नहीं रख सकता, गृहलक्ष्मी पत्नी को भी समझौता के अनुसार दुश्मनों के शिविर में भेजने को विवश हो जाता है उसे सत्ता में बने रहने का कोई अधिकार नहीं है। हम देखते है कि जब ध्रुवस्वामिनी को शकराज के शिविर में भेजा जाता तब वह किस तरह कूटनीतिक सूझ-बूझ से शकराज का नाश करती है और देश की मिटती हुई अस्मिता की रक्षा करती है। इतना ही नहीं वैसे शासक को भी सत्ता से हटाने में अहम भूमिका निभाती है तथा वैसे पति राम गुप्त का परित्याग कर चन्द्रगुप्त का वरण करती है जो उसकी अस्मत की रक्षा करने में पूर्णतः अक्षम है।

अन्य प्रसिद्ध नाटक है 'चन्द्रगुप्त' इसमें भी अलका और कार्नेलिया जैसी स्त्री पात्रों की कल्पना की गयी है जो हर सामाजिक और राष्ट्रीय परिदृश्यों को प्रभावित करती है। कार्नेलिया, जो विदेशी लड़की है उसके मुख से भी प्रसाद जी गवाते हैं-

"अरूण यह मधुमय देश हमारा।
जहां पहुंच अनजान क्षितिज को मिलता एक सहारा।"

उनका यह गीत राष्ट्र की सीमाओं को लांघ जाता है और सम्पूर्ण मानव जाति को सन्देश देता है कि भारत भूमि सर्वश्रेष्ठ है। अलका दूसरी प्रधान स्त्री पात्र है जो आदि से अन्त तक नाटक के माध्यम से पूरे राष्ट्र को नयी दिशा देती नजर आती है और अंततः यह गीत गाते हुए पूरे समाज को जगाने का कार्य करती है जो निश्चिंत बैठे हैं–

"हिमाद्रितुंग श्रृग से, प्रबुद्ध शुद्ध भारती।
स्वयं प्रभासमुज्वला स्वतंत्रता पुकारती।"

इसके अतिरिक्त उनके नाटक 'अजातशत्रु' और 'स्कन्दगुप्त' में भी ऐसी अनेक नारी पात्रों की कल्पना की गयी है जो पूरे राष्ट्र को आन्दोलित करती है। कहने को तो ये सभी पात्र ऐतिहासिक घटनाओं को प्रभावित करते हैं परंतु व्याज से इनकी दृष्टि तत्कालीन और भावी राष्ट्रीय परिस्थितियों पर रही है और उन्हें नयी दिशा देती है।

जयशंकर प्रसाद की कहानी आंधी हो, पुरस्कार हो या आकाशदीप हो सबमें एक नारी पात्र है जो सम्पूर्ण परिस्थितियों को आन्दोलित और प्रभावित करती है। आकाशदीप की चम्पा तो एक द्वीप सदृश्य राष्ट्र की अधिठात्री ही बन जाती है और उस द्वीप का नामकरण ही चम्माद्वीप हो जाता है।

प्रसाद जी के काव्य साहित्य का दूसरा पक्ष उपन्यास है जिनकी संख्या तीन है, जिनमें दो का नामकरण ही 'तितली' और 'दूरावती' है जिससे स्पष्ट होता है कि इसमें सम्पूर्ण घटनाक्रम के केन्द्र में नारी ही रही है। और अंततः प्रसाद जी का काव्यालोक है जिसकी पराकाष्ठा पर पहुंचकर वे स्त्री नामवाची 'कामायनी' महाकाव्य की रचना करते हैं। यह केवल मनु और श्रद्धा की प्रेमगाथा नहीं है और न ही इसमें मन की गुह्य वृत्तियों और चेतना को रूपाकर प्रदान करना कवि का साध्य रहा है। इस महाकाव्य के माध्यम से समग्र राष्ट्र ही नहीं सम्पूर्ण मानवता को एक नयी दिशा देने का काम कामायनी अर्थात श्रद्धा करती है। उसके माध्यम से कवि ने यह संदेश दिया है–

"शक्ति के विद्युत कण जो व्यस्त विकल विखरे हैं, हो निरूपाय,
समन्वय उनका करे समस्त, विजयिनी मानवता हो जाय।"

श्रद्धा ने सबसे पहली मानवता का सृजन, पोषण, रक्षण और उसका दिशा निर्देशन किया है। सामाजिक विप्लव के प्रलय से क्लात राष्ट्र और समाज को एक संदेश दिया है और विज्ञान के सिद्धान्त के सहारे ऊर्जा को केन्द्रित कर संघर्ष करने की सीख दी है। उसने भटके और क्लांत मानवता को रागात्मक परिशांति प्रदान करने के लिए–

'तुमुल कोलाहल कलह में, मैं हृदय की बात रे मन'

जैसे गीत का गायन किया है। इतना ही नही श्रद्धा समाज राष्ट्र और सम्पूर्ण मानवता को ज्ञान, इच्छा और क्रिया के समन्वय के माध्यम से समरसता का मार्ग दिखाया है–

"ज्ञान दूर, कुछ क्रिया भिन्न है
इच्छा क्यों पूरी हो मन की।
एक दूसरे से न मिल सके
यह विडंम्बना है जीवन की।'

इस प्रकार प्रसाद जी ने नारी के माध्यम से सम्पूर्ण समाज, पूरे राष्ट्र और समग्र मानवता को उस लोक का दर्शन कराया है जो चैतन्य है, समरस है और परमानन्दमय है-

"समरस थे जड़ या चेतन सुन्दर साकार बना था,
चेतनता एक विलसती आनंद आखण्ड घना था।"

और निष्कर्षतः हम कह सकते हैं कि जिस प्रकार राम के पूर्व सीता है, कृष्ण के पूर्व राधा है, पिता के पूर्व माता है उसी तर पुरुष के मूल में नारी की सत्ता है जो जयशंकर प्रसाद के अनुसार सम्पूर्ण मानवता के मूल में है।

36

राष्ट्रीय राजनीतिक धारा में नारी का योगदान सुभद्रा कुमार चौहान के साहित्य के परिप्रेक्ष्य में एक अध्ययन

कविता कुमारी सिंह

नारी के क्रांति चरित्र और उसके साहस सहयोग की दृष्टि से विचार करें तो यह इतिहास सृष्टि के आदिकाल तक खिंच जायेगा। पौराणिक देवासूर संग्राम के समय राक्षसों को परास्त करने के लिए देवताओं को भी नारी सहयोग की जरूरत पड़ी थी, और उसने समय पर दुर्गा, काली, महाकाली बन-असुरों का बधकर देवताओं को उनकी स्वाधीनता बहाल की थी। इतिहास में देवताओं से भी ऊपर देव माँ, माँ दुर्गा, महाशक्ति, महाकाली के रूप प्रतिष्ठित हैं। महादेव शिव तक महाकाली की उपासना करते थे। तब से लेकर आजतक नारी के इस शक्ति रूप की पूजा अर्चना होती आई है, तो उसके इस क्रांति चरित्र के ही कारण, जो शांति काल में ममतामयी है तो आपद्काल में रक्षक एवं संहारक भी।

वातावरण और परिस्थितियों को समयानुकूल प्रकट करने की क्षमता एक साहित्यकार में होती है, और वह समय की पुकार को सर्वसाधारण के बीच रख सकता है। अपने देश में स्वतंत्रता आन्दोलन के समय देशभक्ति की भावना उत्प्रेरित करने में कई रचनाकार आगे आये, उनमें 'सुभद्राकुमारी चौहान' का नाम तनिक भी पीछे नहीं है।

राष्ट्रीयता की भावना ओर सपफल अभिव्यंजना करने वाली सुभद्रा जी की कविता 'झांसी की रानी' एक प्रसिद्ध वीरगीत है, उसमें रानी लक्ष्मीबाई की

स्वतंत्रता सेनानियों को आन्दोलन करने का सफल प्रयास किया है। लक्ष्मीबाई का सम्पूर्ण जीवन-चरित्र इस कविता में इतनी सफलता से गूंध गया है कि जैसे पाठक लक्ष्मीबाई से रू-ब-रू हो रहा हो, ऐसा प्रतीत होता है। काव्य के हर पंक्ति में ओज झलकता है। इतना ही नहीं– 'बुंदेलो हरबोलों के मुँह हमने सुनी कहानी थी, खूब लड़ी मर्दानी वह तो, झाँसी वाली रानी थी।' पंक्तियों का बार-बार पुनरावर्तन न केवल गेयता में बल्कि उत्साह भाव से भी अभिवृद्धि कर पाठक को रोमांचित कर देता है। प्रारम्भिक कविताओं में कवयित्री का राष्ट्रप्रेम उमड़ता है जो असहयोग आन्दोलन में इतना सारावोर होता है कि जीवन की वैवाहिक सुखमयी घड़ियाँ उन्हें काट खाने लगी। जब सारा देश वेदना की आग में झुलसता हो तो नारी की ममता अपनी भारत-माता के लिए मचल जाती है और वह असहयोग आन्दोलन में कूद पड़ती है। परन्तु उनकी आन्तरिक पीड़ा संसार के लिए प्रेम का संदेश देती रही ।

''मैंने न कभी रोई जीवन में रोता दिखा न यह संसार,
मृदुल प्रेम के ही गिरते हैं आँखों से आँसू दो-चार''

तत्कालीन समय में सम्पूर्ण देश अंग्रेजों के खिलाफ लड़ने को तत्पर था। आवश्यकता थी तो बस उस सुसुप्त जनमानस में एक नई चेतना, एक नया जोश भरने की। यह काम सुभद्रा जी ने अपनी कविताओं के माध्यम से बखुबी किया। इतिहास के गौरवमय पात्र की गौरवगाथा के माध्यम से उन्होंने जन-मन में क्रांति की चिंगारी सुलगा दी।

उन्होंने जालियाँवाला बाग में भीषण नरसंहार के दर्दनाक हादसे के बाद लिखी 'जालियाँवाला बाग में वसंत' नामक कविता में उन्होंने शासन की बर्बरता एवं क्रुरता को उद्घाटित कर अपनी राष्ट्रभावना की उदात्त अभिव्यंजना की है।

''यहाँ कोकिलनहीं, काक हैं शोर मचाते,
काले-काले कीट, भ्रमर का भ्रम उपजाते।''

सुभद्रा जी का हृदय स्वदेश-प्रेम की भावना से ओत-प्रोत है। मातृभूमि की करूण पुकार उनको व्यथित कर देती है। स्वदेश के लिए स्वयं को न्यौछावर करना तो अपना सौभाग्य समझती है। आत्म-बलिदान तथा देश-प्रेम की मार्मिक व्यंजना इन पंक्तियों में देखने योग्य है–

''न होने दूँगी अत्याचार, चलो, मैं हो जाऊँ बलिदान,
मातृ-मन्दिर में हुई पुकार, चढ़ा दो मुझको भगवान।''

सुभद्रा कुमारी चौहान की एक कविता 'झाँसी की रानी' ने वह काम किया जो कविता की कई किताबें मिल कर भी नहीं कर सकती। हिन्दी साहित्य में, मैथिलीशरण गुप्त की 'भारत-भारती' और सुभद्रा कुमारी चौहान' की 'झाँसी की रानी' करोड़ों युवकों के हृदय में देशभक्ति की भावना भरने में सफल हुई। सुभद्रा जी की यह कविता आधुनिक हिन्दी कविता में अकेला गाथा काव्य है, जो लोकमानस में बस गया है। यह वह प्रकाश है जिसके आलोक में गुलामी का अंधकार भाग रहा था। यह एक ओजपूर्ण, गतिशील और रागदीप्त काव्य है।

निज-भाषा राष्ट्रीयता का प्रमुख तत्व है। राष्ट्र के विकास के लिए अपनी भाषा ही सहायक होती है। सुभद्रा जी राष्ट्र के प्रत्येक कार्य के लिए विदेशी भाषा की अपेक्षा अपने देश की भाषा के प्रयोग में विश्वास रखती थी। उन्होंने 'मातृमंदिर कविता में लिखा था–

"तू हो आधार, देश को पार्लमेण्ट बन जाने में,
तो होगी सुख-सार, देश के उजड़े क्षेत्र बनाने में।"

सुभद्रा के गीतों में नारी आदर्श की पराकाष्ठा है। कहीं वह परिवार की धुरी है, कहीं चुनौती है, कहीं वात्सल्य रस का अजस्त्र निर्झरणी है, कहीं पुरुष के जीवन को आलोकित करने वाली प्रिया है और अवसर पड़ने पर रणचण्डी का रूप धारण कर शत्रु से लोहा लेने वाली, उस लोहे के चने चबवाने वाली वीर रसावतारी है, उसकी हुँकार में सिंहों की गर्जना है। विजय उत्सव की मयुर बेला में कवयित्री की हुँकार अर्थहीन नहीं है–

"सुनूँगी माता की आवाज, रहूँगी मरने को तैयार।"

सुभद्रा की नारी में प्रेम है, तप है, संयम और कर्त्तव्य-बोध है।

37

Women Political Leadership in India: A Study of Principal Alternative Paths to Power

Dr Khalid Hussain Siddiqui

Women political leadership in India in an otherwise masculine model of politics has been a fascinating subject for researchers in the fields of psychology, management, sociology and political science. The Chinese leader Mao Zedong said women hold half the sky. This is true demographically but politically this is not a fact. Women's numerical representation in legislatures and executive positions is very poor in India. But in the past two and half decades the breaking of the glass ceiling is occurring slowly but surely. Women have begun to assume important leadership positions. The main aim of this paper is a recognition and exploration of alternative accounts of female leadership in India, other than dynastic succession. The paper addresses dominant accounts of female political leadership in two ways. This paper will examine why female political leaders become popular and hold positions of power, other than as "martyrs wives and dynastic daughters". Equating female leadership with the dynastic account of leadership of females in South and Southeast Asia does not adequately explain the varied paths to power that many female political leaders in India have followed, at least in the past two and a half decades. It also does not reflect the changing political scene in India which has seen the growing importance of the state level parties, resulting in a regionalisation of politics, thus allowing regional or subnational leaders to become more influential at the national level. Therefore, this element of the paper is an attempt to rebalance an empirical oversight in the literature. The second element of the paper addresses *gender stereotypes* which emerge from essentialised accounts of behavioural styles of gendered leadership, such as the moral capital argument.

In order to address these two elements, the paper attempts to synthesise relevant literature on Indian politics and the politics of gender. The paper includes a brief contextualisation of the Indian political environment (women's political participation in the nationalist movement to present day) and the changing political institutional structure (the fragmentation and regionalisation of Indian electoral politics), a gendered analysis of sources of legitimacy in the Indian context, and a discussion of essentialised accounts of behavioural styles of gendered leadership. Prominent female politicians demonstrate the diverse manifestations of female political leadership in India. This paper will focus on the leadership of J. Jayalalithaa, Rabri Devi, Uma Bharti, and Mayawati.

The paper concludes that gender is an important factor of both the path to power as well as the exercise of leadership and the sources of legitimacy that leaders draw upon. Structural gender bias and gender-biased perceptions and expectations are understood to have a significant impact on assessments of behavioural style and performance. Yet these sources of gender power can be utilised by leaders, reinforcing and legitimising stereotypes in exchange for political power. Identity politics and political discourse play important roles in the exercise of leadership. However, the implications for women's political participation suggest little short-term benefits for women in politics. The changing political system has only worked to catapult a few women into positions of power. Nevertheless, female political participation and leadership in the local panchayats does have potential implications for the future generation of political leaders and the political participation of women.

Dynastic succession is the most frequently used explanation for women's rise to political (usually national) leadership in Asia. This consists largely of three elements relevant to this argument[1]. Firstly, twentieth century dynastic succession in Asia has taken place in times of transformational change, resulting in emergency dynastic succession (as a result of a coup d'etat or process of democratisation for example). Secondly, martyrdom often means a transferral of charisma onto the successor. Thirdly, the relatively high presence of women successors, it is argued, is due to the (perceived or actual) higher moral capital of women as opposed to men; the former as less corrupted or corruptible than men.

Comparative analyses of South and South-east Asian women leaders have frequently brought the dynastic succession account to the fore. Richter asserts "[i]n south and southeast Asia...the most important political posts open to women have been so because of *familial* ties to prominent male politicians - the opportunity for such women having been greatly enhanced by their husbands' deaths and often dramatic *martyrdom*[2]. Although Thompson concentrates more on female leaders of democratic transitions in South and Southeast Asia, his study offers insights into how gender structures the dynastic account of female leadership. He emphasises several features of dynastic succession including the symbolic representation of women as mothers healing the nation; women imbued with higher moral capital than men; and male chauvinism in the political sphere. However, Thompson's account of female political leadership is limited for three reasons. Firstly, as a large-scale comparative analysis of South and Southeast Asian women leaders, some contextual detail is lost, particularly in how the political context varies spatially, temporally, and discursively. This is crucial to understanding how female political leaders in India gain access to and sustain power in contemporary times. Secondly, Thompson's account has limited applicability to the Indian context and this is reflected in his limited discussion of Indian female leaders. He has included Indira Gandhi as his Indian example of dynastic succession, As Mitra argues, "[i]f we broaden the base of our enquiry and look at appointments to political office at all levels of the [Indian] system, succession by members from within the immediate kin will no doubt appear as the exception rather than the rule[3]." Thirdly, in concentrating on female leadership during democratic transitions (more representative of transformative leadership), Thompson does not touch on political leadership of career politicians (more representative of transactional leadership). A sustained professional career in politics is a more representative pattern and is thus becoming increasingly important for the study of female political leadership in India, not least so because of the recently enacted 73rd and 74th Amendments on panchayat reservations. Lastly, and this is not confined to Thompson's account of dynastic succession, arguments based around women's relatively higher moral capital compared to men rarely address their underlying essentialised assumptions.

The three criticisms of Thompson's work will be addressed in three ways. Firstly, to address the issue of contextual detail, an account of women's political role in India from the Independence struggle to the present day must be briefly outlined. This enables an understanding of the material and discursive *environment* in which female leadership in India is situated, the environment being a critical factor in the assessment of leadership. Secondly, a discussion of the changing structure of Indian electoral politics will demonstrate alternative opportunities for the emergence of women leaders, other than the dynastic route. This provides the institutional and environmental backdrop to the changing situational context of (female) political leadership in India. Thirdly, a discussion of the exercise of leadership will focus on a critique of accounts based on a gender-as-difference approach, such as the moral capital argument, and recognition of the structural gender bias that impedes women within institutional settings. A more contextualised understanding will be provided of how women leaders in India draw upon sources of legitimate authority and thus power. This situates leadership within a discursive context in which modern Indian women are perceived to act in a political dimension, which affects their perceived or actual style of leadership.

Alternative Paths to Power

Contemporary accounts differ somewhat in explaining a leader's path to power, but many accounts reproduce an insider/outsider dichotomy, which distinguishes between two sets of individuals. "Insiders" have risen through the ranks of the political institutional infrastructure whereas "outsiders", come to political leadership and/or formal political activity with little experience of the "rules of the game" yet may possess either popularity, expertise, ambition, or substantial interest in policy issues, or any combination of these. Gendered accounts of leadership highlight an additional category, the political 'surrogate', which, while similar to the concept of 'outsider', takes on its own unique significance in dynastic accounts of female leadership.

Hart outlines two features that are important in the accession to Indian leadership those of *winning mandates* and a leader's *pathway to power*. The importance of an individual's pathway to power in determining their legitimacy is especially relevant to the critique of the dynastic account of female leadership because "[t]he path taken to leadership in some part determines the power held by the leader, the legitimacy of his leadership, and, to some extent, support for his policies[4]". Therefore, a leader's route to the top determines in part the legitimacy that he or she commands and has implications for the success and sustainability of that leadership.

Hart also outlines the pathways to power offered by the Indian system as (1) the institutional ladder; (2) the move into politics of the "culture hero"; and (3) dynastic succession[5]. The third path of dynastic succession has been outlined above. Hart's account generally concurs with other accounts in the literature. If we recall, the main characteristics can include martyrdom followed by a transferral of charisma onto the dynastic successor, symbolic representation of women as mothers healing the nation, women imbued with higher moral capital than men, and male chauvinism in the political sphere.

I have attempted to synthesise some approaches to "paths to power" into a typology that is shown in Table 1 below. It is important to note the dynamic aspect of this typology is that different female leaders can represent different paths to power at different stages of their career. Also these categories are not fixed and their boundaries not impermeable but represent ideal types.

The "institutional ladder" path can be equated to that of the "insider" who climbs through the ranks often from the grassroots and develops leadership capability over time with acquired experience and expertise. Promotion is obtained through merit or otherwise and the individual gradually becomes more aware of the "rules of the game". The "institutional ladder" route–which provides long-term exposure to male-oriented political organisations-demonstrates how structural gender bias can impede the career progression of women, offering them limited strategic choices. They can conform to the rules of the game and thus internalise male, or more accurately, hegemonic masculine norms. This often means a woman has to "struggle to reconcile conflicting demands" to avoid violating gender norms and stereotypes - in short a woman has to "look like a lady, [and] act like a man[6]". The second path is that of the transfer to politics of the culture hero. In India this has been a marked phenomenon, particularly in the southern states of Andhra Pradesh and Tamil Nadu, where popular film stars have entered politics exploiting their mass popularity and cultural appeal, and have been successful as political leaders. While some have downplayed this as a phenomenon of Indian leadership, due to relatively few manifestations, others see this explicitly as the effect regional culture and populist politics can have on the appeal and legitimacy of political leaders.

To these three paths, I have added the concept of the "proxy" leader which in India is a scenario more visible at

Table 1
Typology of Paths to Power for Female Political Leaders

Paths to Power	*Represents*	*Characteristics*	*Examples of Prominent Female Politicians*
Dominant Account			
Dynastic succession	"Surrogate" of dead male kin/husband, "outsider", various "Dynastic succession" accounts	Successor takes mantle of predecessor, champions his cause; strives for justice, successor's political experience can vary relatively little to more substantial.	Indira Gandhi (contested), Sonia Gandhi
Alternative Path to Power			
Institutional	"Insider", or the "Institutional Ladder" (Hart, 1988)	Career politicians, learning the rules of the game over time. Structural gender bias may necessitate internalising the hegemonic masculine norms of the political institutional culture.	Mamta Banerjee; Uma Bharti Sheila Dixit, Jayalalitha, Mayawati (?)
Culture transfer	"Outsider" (but only political), "transfer to politics of the culture hero" (Hart, 1988)	Charismatic appeal, popularity gained through cultural profession such as acting, commonly becomes popular through populist policies or through cultural imagery, collapsing the real and the imaginary.	J.Jayalalitha, (early stages of career); Uma Bharti (early stages of career)

Contd.

Paths to Power	*Represents*	*Characteristics*	*Examples of Prominent Female Politicians*
Proxy	"Surrogate", "agent"	Acts as an agent on behalf of a *living* male realtive/husband. Ironically symbolises lack of agency and individual voice. Can mask real political participation by women. Increasingly significant to recognise reagrding women's participation at the panchayat level.	Rabri Devi (as proxy for Laloo Yadav).

the panchayat level but which has become symbolised by the leadership of Rabri Devi, former Chief Minister of Bihar, as a "proxy" for Rashtriya Janata Dal party leader Laloo Prasad Yadav[7]. In this sense, women are elected but act as an agent on behalf of their male relations, and exercise power in their interests. This has become more common and widespread due to the reservation policy enacted in the 73rd and 74th constitutional amendment reserving for women a third of all seats in the panchayat institutions. The "proxy" phenomenon has emerged as a source of criticism of the legitimacy of both participating women and the system itself. As a concept, the "proxy" agent is similar to the idea of the 'surrogate' or dynastic successor as power is conferred not on the basis of the proxy's own ability but on whom they are acting on behalf of. It is dissimilar in that the proxy is an agent for someone who is active in politics through them rather than as the predecessor whose mantle the surrogate takes on..

The Political and Social Environment

The political mobilisation of women during the fight for Independence has been identified as one of the key factors in determining women's political participation in contemporary times. Several accounts of the women's movement in India which accompanied the nationalist struggle for independence from British rule, note the lack of an emancipatory outcome and the enduring subservient nature of women's role in society. Women were welcome to join the resistance to British colonial rule, but their political activity was encouraged only insofar as to support the traditional gender hierarchy within Indian society. As long as their political activity supplemented but didn't sacrifice their traditional duties as wives, daughters and sisters, their political activism was encouraged. However, several male supporters of reform for women's issues supported women's franchise.

While the nationalist leader M.K. Gandhi supported the notion of female suffrage, he emphasised the need for unity and solidarity against the British Raj. Gandhi consistently mobilised the Hindu goddess of *Sita* as the supportive and sacrificing wife; in the process, "Gandhi was constructing a new ideal for Indian women that rewrote passivity and self-suffering as strength[8]". Demands of women for a place in the government of newly Independent India were legitimised by their involvement in the nationalist movement.

The role of Indian women in post-Independence and modern Indian politics is directly related to the lack of a significant outcome for the women's movement after the achievement of Independence from British rule by the nationalists. While a liberal discourse of equality ensued upon Independence in 1947, by 1974 the Committee on the Status of Women in India produced a commissioned report titled *Towards Equality* which evaluated and acknowledged the enduring plight of Indian women. Women's political participation was largely manifest through the women's movement, itself fragmented as a result of differing ideologies and issue-based protests, with only token numbers of women participating in "formal" politics, many of which were from higher class and caste backgrounds and had been supported by liberal progressive families. The women's movement has organised on diverse issues from dowry, arrack, violence (including rape), equal economic and employment opportunities (SEWA), ecofeminism, and anti-development protests opposed to displacement in the Narmada valley and similar state-sponsored developmental projects . In the last three decades, the Hindutva movement has also become a site of women's right-wing political mobilisation although with dubious potential for the empowerment of women, and has become particularly militant around communal issues.

Modern Indian politics has seen political parties appropriate women's issues, such as the concerns of the anti-arrack movement, and appear sympathetic towards them in order to capture the women's vote.. As a consequence of this appropriation, much of the women's movement has fragmented along ideological and political lines as women's organisations operate as an offspring of the major political parties.

Despite the movement-based nature of the women's political mobilisation, women are engaged in electoral politics with similar overall turnouts for men and women at assembly and Lok Sabha elections, with some regional variance. The Lok Sabha elections in May 2004 elected just over 8% of female candidates to the Lok Sabha, with proportions of contesting and elected women candidates varying considerably among political parties (see Table 2 below). As these figures show, the attitude and policy of the political party towards giving tickets to women to contest constituencies, and thus their symbolic manifestation for the participation of women in politics, is crucial in determining women's actual participation, especially with regards women's relatively lower economic independence and the financial resources required to run for political office.

The Changing Political Scene: Regionalisation and Fragmentation of Indian Electoral Politics

Many commentators have noted the rising importance of the state level parties in national politics in what many have called the "third phase of democratisation" in Indian politics. The last four Lok Sabha elections in India more than most have brought into sharp focus the importance of coalition-building and party alliances in order to win elections, so much so that it is recognised that they have 'become a central factor shaping politics in India". Some point to the changing political party system; others attribute this to India's vast diversity in terms of electoral demands, from the Dalit movement of Uttar Pradesh to the regional identity discourse of the southern states. Many see both as factors causing change. Secondly, populist politics in India is driven by discourse centred around a politics of identity, which fragments and destabilises the political agenda. Region-based politics as a result of India's vast diversity and the federal structure of the Indian polity have also contributed to this fragmentation of the political agenda and has given rise to the emergence of a fickle and unstable coalition politics sometimes based more on expediency than ideology or policy agenda.

Table 2
Results of the Lok Sabha Elections 2004 : National Parties

	Female Contestants			*Male Contestants*				
	Contested	*Won*	*Women Candidates Elected (%)*	*Contested*	*Won*	*Male Candidates Elected (%)*	*Proportion of Women in the Fray (%)*	*Presence of Women in Lok Sabha (%)*
Bharatiya Janata Party (BJP)	30	10	33.3	334	128	38.3	8.2	7.2
Bahujan Samaj Party (BSP)	20	1	5.0	415	18	4.3	4.6	5.3
Communist Party of India (CPI)	2	0	0.0	32	10	31.3	5.9	0.0
Communist Party of India Marxist (CPI) (M)	8	5	62.5	61	38	62.3	11.6	11.6
Indian National Congress (INC)	45	12	26.7	372	133	35.8	10.8	8.3
Nationalist Congress Party (NCP)	5	2	40.0	27	7	25.9	15.6	22.2
Totals for National parties	110	30	27.3	1241	334	26.9	8.1	8.2

Source : Election Commission of India, *www.eci.gov.in*

As a result, changes in party politics in India present alternative opportunities for women in India. Several prominent female political leaders have occupied the office of chief minister in different states simultaneously, some for a longer period than others.State level politics thus provides a wealth of experience for female political leaders, and recently five of India's states were governed by female chief ministers, totalling around half the population of India (The Hindu, 2003[9]). Thus changing Indian electoral politics has provided avenues for the emergence of women political leadership.

Essentialised Accounts of Gendered Leadership

There is a burgeoning literature in many fields of the social sciences on the contested issue of whether women and men lead differently. Some accounts rely on an *essentialised* conceptualisation of gender and leadership. Essentialised accounts attempt to explain (inflate) differences in leadership capabilities and style between men and women by arguing that women are *naturally* more caring and nurturing and men are *naturally* more aggressive because of differing hormone levels, the natural sexual division of childbearing, and female attributes bestowed upon them for use in motherhood. Fundamentally, these accounts conflate sex with gender. Their biologically reductionist outlook rejects accounts that attribute any purported difference in male and female leadership styles to processes of socialisation, which work to internalise socially constructed discourse on male/female difference. Other accounts argue that it is *gender*, a socially constructed, relational process, that constitutes (and is constituted by) the reinforced stereotypical roles of, and expectations about, men and women in society, and thus determines their likely leadership characteristics and relative strengths and weaknesses. Yet, employing the concept of gender still does not guard against essentialised accounts of how men and women lead. As the *gender-as-difference* approach demonstrates, many feminist advocates of the approach celebrate difference and the strengths and opportunities that gender difference provides, such as the skills with which one is equipped as part of the inherently gendered socialisation process.

Many assert there are real material differences between men and women because of gender differences in socialisation, and results in differentiated cognitive and emotional development. Others would argue that these professed differences are more symbolic than real and that difference exists more substantially *among* women than it does *between* women and men. The internalization of symbolic differences on an unconscious level has resulted in their materialization through the everyday "performativity" of gender stereotypical behaviour[10].

Whether the style of leadership among men and women is actually different or is simply constructed as so, the significance lies in the effect this perceived difference has on the leader-follower relationship. Astin and Leland assert that "while studies show no clear pattern of difference in behaviour between male and female leaders, subordinates react differently to similar behaviour according to whether the leader is a man or a woman[11]". Thus, the *perception* of a leader's behaviour is in part an outcome of gendered societal perceptions of men and women in leadership positions. This in turn feeds into the individual's self-reflexive understanding of their own ability to lead. In cases of political leadership, this produces a unbalanced situation which grants an advantage to the male leader. The issue of gender only becomes an issue for the woman politician; failure for the male politician is rarely attributed to gender. Nevertheless, studies show that "female leaders' style of governance [in India] is certainly not softer, less autocratic or more equal than that of male leaders...women's rule is not necessarily more democratic or less confrontational than that of male leaders[12]..." Behavioural traits may never embody the same meaning for a woman as they do for a man, and vice versa. Thus, male leadership behaviour will not be interpreted the same as female leadership behaviour, in part due to the institutionalisation of hegemonic masculine behaviour as the behavioural norm. Scholars like Sunder Rajan suggest that there is little difference between men's and women's style and performativity, professing that women leaders imbibe the male organisational norms[13]. This suggests that increasing numbers of women leaders may make little difference to institutional and political culture.

Women's Higher Moral Capital

In contrast, others arguing for the inclusion of more women into national and international political machinery, suggest that the presence of more women may have the effect of changing the style of governance within these institutions. This latter approach known as the *moral capital* argument argues that women are less corrupt than their male counterparts; they are less likely to act opportunistically with selfinterest, with the resulting benefits to democratic governance of society. This argument focuses on gender-as-difference, and therefore essentialises behavioural traits. This places constraints on efforts to destabilise existing gender norms and to bring about transformative change in gender relations. However, while the moral capital argument is theoretically problematic to some, the structural and gender bias that exists in many societies means that it is has proved to be a successful strategy for obtaining an initial advantage when attempting to acquire positions of power.

In sum, an individual's ability to lead and his or her corresponding behavioural style of leadership will be anticipated on the basis of gender-biased expectations, both in the form of observation by peers and the wider society, as well as through critical reflection of the leader on their own ability and performance. This will determine the efficacy and style of the individual in their role as leader, particularly in terms of adapting to the "rules of the game". The leader can however use these gender-biased expectations instrumentally to their advantage.

(Gendered) Conceptions of Legitimate Authority

As many studies of leadership note, the position of leader is intrinsically contingent on the position of follower (Hart, 1988;

Blondel, 1987; Duerst-Lahti and Kelly, 1995). The leader's position of authority is dependent on the willingness of followers' to grant power to the leader, to be exercised over the followers themselves. Therefore, followers' perception of the leader's legitimacy and authority is important. As women in Indian society have a significant lack of material and structural power relative to men, this is particularly relevant for the study of gender and leadership in India.

Weber's "three types of legitimate authority" (1947) is frequently quoted as a classic typology. Legitimate authority, according to Weber can be "traditional", what has always been will remain; "charismatic", based on an individual's appeal and personality; or "rational-legal", recognising the rational, legal authority of the ruler to govern over a subject population. These three categories are not mutually exclusive and each can manifest itself simultaneously to that of another, buttressing power derived from multiple sources of legitimate authority. The strong liberal democratic discourse in India suggests that the last of these three, "rational-legal" authority, is the most prevalent due to the vibrancy of democracy, the centrality of electoral politics in the political system, and high turnout levels of the electorate at polling time. Thus one of the central sources of legitimate authority of the Indian political leader is to win the mandate of the people.

While Weber's is an oft-cited classic typology, and is a good starting point, it does have its limitations. Most notably, Weber's analysis does not explicitly take account of how gender affects sources of legitimate authority. In the Indian case this has been analysed explicitly in terms of women leaders, and can be said to differ from some Western explanations. There are several interpretations of sources of authority for women in India, and a few contemporary accounts will be discussed here, namely roles of authority within the family, Hindu goddess imagery, and 'performative sustainability'.

Firstly, followers of women leaders in India, as in many places, frequently look to commonly understood roles of authority that women hold within the private sphere of the family. Most often she is referred to as the mother-figure, as the cultural reproducer of the nation and as the nurturing caretaker. These sources of authority, like any that draw upon socially established gender relations, can be said to embody *gender power*. In the case of women leaders in India, commonly understood gender roles for women are transposed from the private sphere of the household to the public sphere of politics, and with them, their sources of authority and social capital. Woman's symbolic (and/or material) sacrifice for the family is replaced by a symbolic (and/or material) sacrifice for the nation. Thus, as Sunder Rajan asserts, "the acceptable face of leadership is service; it denies [material] power, stresses sacrifice, and positions the hierarchy of public duty and private affections to give primacy to the first[14]". Their commonly understood sources of authority take on an altered form, providing them legitimacy in the political sphere. Women leaders in India become *didi* (elder sister), *behenji* (sister), and *amma* (mother). Many women leaders have capitalised on this imagery, such as Indira Gandhi who internalised and promo ted her image as *Bharat Mata* (Mother India). Many have used gender power to imbue themselves with legitimate authority and political capital.

Secondly, Hindu imagery is commonly invoked in India as a means to explain women's power. Goddess imagery mobilised in Hindu symbolism is linked to notions of *shakti* (women's power) and is common in Indian culture and philosophy. *Sita*, as the *pativrata* (model wife), is traditionally worshipped by girls and young women as the method of family institution to prepare and socialise daughters into positions of subservience for marriage . Kali and Durga, on the other hand, are the female goddesses that are feared for their potentially awesome rage summoned to take vengeance against demonic forces. As Madhu Kishwar asserts, "every woman has this roop, this aspect latent in her, that a woman is both gentle and nurturing, as well as capable of superhuman rage, which can destroy the world and hence needs to be feared".

Lastly, Weber's typology does not explicitly address the concept of credibility drawn from the performative aspect of leadership as a means of sustaining legitimacy. There are two interrelated aspects relating to performance, that of "efficacy" and that of "performativity". Regarding "efficacy", it can be argued that the institutional ladder route to power is based on the very premise of the rising leader's ability to prove he or she can deliver results while in office. For women leaders, winning a second mandate is a crucial element to becoming recognised and established, due to the perceived risk element to political parties of contesting women candidates and gendered perceptions of leadership ability based on behavioural expectations. However, regarding the "performative" aspect, some accounts of leadership posit that demonstrating efficacy in transactional politics is not a crucial factor to ensuring sustainability of leadership in an ostensibly democratic polity.

Thus, the performative aspect of leadership demonstrates the potential of a leader's source of legitimacy to change over time, and requires a longitudinal analysis as well as a focus on the perceived and actual performance of the politician's term in office as well as their performativity of leadership. As noted earlier, expectations are likely to be affected by gender-biased judgments of leadership performance.

Overview and Conclusions

Where J. Jayalalithaa, Mayawati and Uma Bharti have taken the institutional route, Rabri Devi represents the "proxy" route to power. All had a mentor who supported them when they first entered politics, although Rabri Devi's was more prescriptive towards her leadership performance. All except Mayawati draw upon Hindu goddess imagery as a means to muster legitimacy. Mayawati's exclusion is not surprising given that Dalits in general are less likely to mobilise Hindu imagery. All including Mayawati transpose sources of gender power from within the private family to the public sphere. All except Rabri Devi have renounced the prospect of being a mother and a wife and the same invoke notions of suffering for their service to their followers. All except Rabri Devi possess charismatic authority, some more in their own right, such as Mayawati and Uma Bharti, whereas Jayalalithaa draws some charismatic authority from her predecessor, M.G. Ramachandran. Rabri Devi draws upon Laloo's charismatic authority as his "proxy". As elected office-holders, all in theory possess strong rational-legal authority, yet in practice this authority may take second place to charismatic authority. Interestingly, Mayawati and Uma Bharti draw authority and legitimacy most from their (intersecting) identity(ies) which is situationally based within their respective movement-based politics. Both are low caste women but caste is a more salient factor for Mayawati as a *Dalit*. Uma Bharti draws legitimacy among *Hindutva* supporters as a *sadhvi* and her credibility as officeholder rather than mobiliser has increased over time. Yet both movement-based agendas offered little in the way of transformative potential for women; Mayawati's *Dalit* agenda obscures the voice of *Dalit* women, and the *Hindutva* communal agenda espoused by Bharti, although less vociferous now, is potentially violent, threatening and degrading to Muslim women and socially conservative for Hindu women.

The aim of this study is to provide an enriched and alternative account of female political leadership in India. Alternative paths to power, other than dynastic succession, were discussed. Four paths to power were outlined; that of "institutional", cultural transfer, "proxy", and dynastic succession. The first three, as alternative routes to power, were discussed in terms of their gender component. Addressing Thompson's (2002) lack of contextual detail in the Indian case, women's political participation in India was contextualised both within the political and social environment of Indian women's participation in politics, from the national movement to the present day. It was concluded that the alliance of the women's movement with the nationalist movement bore few emancipatory outcomes for women's political participation, as the latter was based on a strategy of solidarity by mobilising their commonly accepted subservient role in society to fight colonial domination. This provided an explanation towards understanding the disparity between women's improved legal status and the prevailing liberal political discourse compared with women's continuing poor status in Indian society and why women's political participation had not become more pervasive after independence.

Women political leadership was contextualised in terms of the changing scene of Indian politics i.e. of the regionalisation and fragmentation of electoral politics. While some female leaders have benefited from the changing political scene in terms of bargaining power within alliance formations with national parties, there is little to suggest that the fragmentation and regionalisation of Indian politics has increased the support of women candidates by political parties. Ultimately, the political parties have not lived up to the rhetorical support for women's participation in party structures. Thus, the changing political system has only worked to catapult a few women into positions of power. Thus, the presence of women in top positions has made little apparent difference to the allotment of tickets to women. In any case it appears to be an essentialised assumption that it would make a difference at all.

Women political leadership was further contextualised in terms of how legitimate authority is constructed in India, demonstrating how legitimacy in India is both a culturally-specific phenomenon, such as the mobilisation of Hindu goddess imagery and the transposing of sources of gender power from the private to the public sphere, as well as more general applications of Weber's classic typology. Lastly, underlying essentialised accounts of women's moral capital were challenged in a more general discussion of behavioural styles of leadership. One can conclude that while the moral capital and other similarly essentialised arguments are theoretically problematic and pose problems for destabilising constrictive gender norms, arguments like that of the higher moral capital of women tend to be accepted as a stereotypically gendered perception of leadership style, despite actual performative similarities between men and women. Thus structural gender bias and gendered-biased perceptions and expectations are understood to have a significant impact on assessments of behavioural style and performance. Yet these sources of gender power can be utilised by leaders, reinforcing and legitimising stereotypes. All except Rabri Devi have defied conventional behavioural styles of leadership expected by essentialised accounts of female political leadership. However in some cases the interest for more women in governance structures because they are perceived as less corrupt is a misguided but conscious effort and interest in increasing accountability and "good governance" in democratic institutions.

References

1. Hellmann-Rajanayagam, Dagmar (2004), "The Quick and the Dead: The Pioneers I: The Weeping Widow", Project Discussion Paper No. 8/2004, part of a series "Dynasties and Female Political Leaders in South Asia", edited by Claudia Derichs and Mark Thompson, p. 2
2. Richter, Linda K. (1990-1), "Exploring Theories of Female Leadership in South and Southeast Asia", *Pacific Affairs,* Vol. 63 Winter p. 528.
3. Mitra, Subrata (1988), "India: Dynastic Rule or the Democratisation of Power?", *Third World Quarterly,* Vol. 10 No. 1 January p. 159.
4. Hart, Henry C. (1988), "Political Leadership in India: Dimensions and Limits", Chapter 1, p. 20 in Kohli, A. (ed.) India's Democracy: An Analysis of Changing State-Society Relations, Princeton NJ: Princeton University Press,
5. *Ibid,* p. 51.
6. Stivers, Camilla (1993), Gender Images in Public Administration, London: Sage, p. 60.
7. BBC News Online (2001), "Laloo Prasad Sent to Jail", November 26.
8. Forbes, Geraldine (1998), Women in Modern India, (The New Cambridge History of India), New Delhi: Cambridge University Press, p. 132

9. Hindu, The (2003), "The Big Five", December 14.

   These five women chief ministers were Sheila Dixit (New Delhi), Jayalalithaa (Tamil Nadu), Uma Bharti (Madhya Pradesh), Scindia (Rajasthan), and Rabri Devi (Bihar). As The Hindu notes, "it would have been two-thirds of the country if Mayawati had not worked her way out of office in Uttar Pradesh recently" (2003).

10. Butler, Judith (1999), Gender Trouble: Feminism and the Subversion of Identity, (10th Anniversary Edition), London: Routledge, p. 35.

11. Stivers, Camilla (1993), Gender Images in Public Administration, London: Sage, p. 69.

12. Hellmann-Rajanayagam, Dagmar (2004), "The Quick and the Dead: The Pioneers I: The Weeping Widow", Project Discussion Paper No. 8/2004, part of a series "Dynasties and Female Political Leaders in South Asia", edited by Claudia Derichs and Mark Thompson, p. 3

13. Sunder Rajan, Rajeswari (1993), Real and Imagined Women: Gender, Culture and Postcolonialism, London: Routledge, p.108

14. *Ibid*, p. 110

38

राजनीतिक, सामाजिक एवं आर्थिक क्षेत्र में महिलाओं का नेतृत्व

डॉ॰ कुमारी मंजू

महिला अधिकार राजनीतिक कार्य सूची में सर्वोच्च स्थान पर है लेकिन खेद का विषय यह है कि महिला अधिकारिकता वास्तविक रूप में आज भी वह स्थान नहीं पा रही है जिसकी वह अधिकारिणी है। राजनीतिक क्षेत्र में जबतक महिलायें अपनी भागीदारी सत्ता के रूप में नहीं निभायेगी तबतक उनकी स्थिति सम्मानजनक नहीं हो सकती। डॉ॰ अम्बेदकर ने भी कहा था कि महिलाओं के संगठन के विकास के बिना राष्ट्र का विकास नहीं हो सकता। डॉ॰ अम्बेदकर के शब्दों में "I am a great believer in women's organisations. I know what they can do to improve the condition of the society if they are convinced."

यद्यपि भारतीय महिलायें राजनीतिक भागीदारी में पिछे रही है फिर भी अन्य विकसित देशों की तुलना में उनकी राजनीतिक भागीदारी अधिक ही रही है। जनसंख्या को ध्यान में रखकर देखा जाय तो भारतीय परिवेश के आम चुनाव में मतदान प्रक्रिया में पुरुषों की तुलना में वे काफी पिछे है साथ ही प्रत्याशियों के परिमाण में महिला प्रजातियों की भागीदारी अत्यन्त कम है। विभिन्न राजनैतिक दलों के चुनाव घोषणा पत्रों जनसभाओं, संगोष्ठियों और पत्र-पत्रिकाओं आदि में महिला अधिकारों पर बराबर चर्चा की जाती है।

सक्रिय राजनीति में उनकी भागीदारी पर सदा वाद-विवाद होता रहा है। वे देश की राजनैतिक व्यवस्था और अर्थव्यवस्था में उन्हें यथोचित स्थान दिये जाने की

बातें अक्सर की जाती है। लेकिन व्यवहार के रूप में देखा जाय तो महिलाओं की भागीदारी सक्रिय राजनीति में काफी कम है। चुनावी मैदान में यद्यपि महिला प्रत्याशियों की संख्या उत्तरोत्तर बढ़ती गई फिर भी उनका संगठनिक विकास नहीं हुआ। राजनीतिक दलों द्वारा महिला प्रत्याशियों को अधिक अवसर नहीं प्रदान किए गए है। इससे यह प्रतीत होता है कि वे संगठित राजनीति में अपनी भागीदारी नहीं बढ़ा रही है।

लेकिन महिला अधिकारिता को जब तक हम सिर्फ वैधनिक एवं संवैधनिक अधिकारों से जोड़कर देखते रहेंगे तब तक महिलाओं की स्थिति को सुदृढ़ता मिलना मुश्किल है। वैधनिक एवं संवैधनिक अधिकारों के साथ-साथ जब तक महिलाओं की शैक्षणिक स्थिति सुदृढ़ नहीं होगी तब तक महिला अधिकारिता का प्रश्न अधूरा रहेगा। शिक्षा का सीधा संबंध विकास से है, विशेषतः महिलाओं का विकास तब तक संभव नहीं जबतक वह शिक्षित न हो। क्योंकि महिला साक्षरता का सकारात्मक संबंध बाल विकास स्वास्थ्य के प्रति जागरूकता, निम्न जन्मदर एवं निम्न मृत्युदर से है।

निम्न रेखाचित्र से स्पष्ट है कि शिक्षा के स्तर में बढ़ोतरी के साथ-साथ शिशु मृत्युदर में गिरावट आई है।

शिक्षा, स्वास्थ्य एवं कल्याण, ये तीनों क्षेत्र जब तक आपस में एक-दूसरे से सहसंबंध स्थापित नहीं करेंगे तब तक महिला अधिकारिता संभव नहीं है।

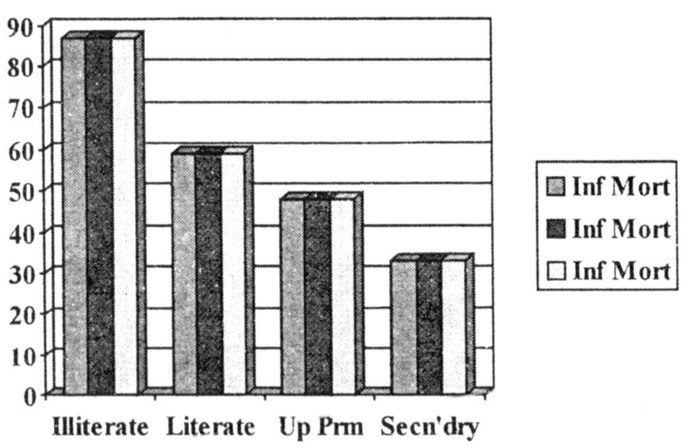

माताओं का शैक्षणिक स्तर एवं शिशु मृत्युदर

स्रोत इंडिया विजन 2020, योजना आयोग

विश्व की आधी आबादी अर्थात् महिलाएँ दोयम दर्जे की जिन्दगी जी रही है आज से नहीं बल्कि सदियों से। जीवन के विभिन्न क्षेत्रों में जैसे-आर्थिक सामाजिक एवं राजनीतिक क्षेत्रों में उनके समानता की बातें की जा रही है। महिला सशक्तिकरण के लिए भारत सहित विश्व के अनेक देशों में सरकारी एवं गैर सरकारी स्तर पर अनेक योजनाएँ चल रही है। समाज की इस महत्वपूर्ण धूरी को बिना सशक्त बनाए न तो समानता की बात संभव है और न सामाजिक न्याय की। स्पष्ट शब्दों में कहा जा सकता है कि पूरा नारी समाज की असमानता एवं पिछड़ेपन का शिकार है। महिला सामाजिक, आर्थिक एवं राजनीतिक रूप से काफी पिछड़ी हुई है।

यदि पूरे विश्व को विकसित, विकासशील और पिछड़े देशों में विभाजित किया जाय तो पूरी नारी समाज इससे भी अधिक हिस्सों में बंटी हुई है। जहां उनकी स्थिति काफी दयनीय है। मानवाधिकार के नियम कानून को पालन करने वाली विकसित राष्ट्र अमेरिका, ब्रिटेन, फ्रांस आदि देशों में भी महिलाओं का योगदान राजनीतिक आर्थिक एवं सामाजिक गतिविधियों में समान नहीं है। विश्व के हर समाज में स्त्री की दुर्दशा एक ही समान है। चीन में लोहे के जूते पहनाकर स्त्री के पांच छोटे कर दिए जाते थे। सिर्फ चीन ही नहीं विश्व के हर समाज में लोहे के सांचे में जकड़कर महिलाओं के व्यक्तित्व को बौना बना दिया गया। बाद में स्त्री बौनेपन को अपना गुण समझने लगी। इस मानसिकता से मुक्ति पाकर ही महिलाएं अपने को सशक्त कर सकती है।

अगर हम इतिहास के पन्ने पर नजर डालें तो हम पाते हैं कि भारतीय इतिहास के वैदिक युग में स्त्रियों की स्थिति सुदृढ़ थी। उन्हें कुल देवी का स्थान प्राप्त था। भारत में गार्गी मैत्रेयी जैसी प्रसिद्ध महिला दार्शनिक थी जो पुरुषों के समान ही भाषण प्रवचन तथा बहस गुबाहिशों में भाग लिया करती थी। स्वाधीनता संग्राम में भी महिलाओं का योगदान पुरुषों से कम नहीं था। स्वाधीनता आंदोलन में महात्मा गांधी के आह्वान पर महिलाओं ने ऐसे समय पर उसमें हिस्सा लिया जब सिर्फ 2 प्रतिशत महिलाएं शिक्षित थी। इससे यह अनुमान लगाया जा सकता है कि महिलाओं के लिए घर से बाहर निकलना कितना कठिन था, परन्तु तब भी वे बाहर निकली। आजादी के बाद भी संविधान सभा के सदस्य के रूप में महिलाओं ने स्वतंत्र भारत के लिए संविधान का मसौदा तैयार करने के काम में हिस्सा लिया।

सिर्फ हिन्दुओं में ही नहीं इतिहास का अध्ययन करने पर पता चलता है कि मुस्लिम महिलाएं भी अपने धर्म के विभिन्न पहलुओं में पारंगत थी। इसकी

शुरूआत पैगम्बर साहब की धर्म पत्नी हजरत खदिजा से हुई जो एक सफल महिला व्यापारी थी। वे धर्म को स्वीकार करने और मुस्लिम बनने वाली पहली इंसान थी। पैगम्बर साहब की एक मात्र पुत्री हजरत फातिमा इस्लाम धर्म के सभी पहलुओं में पारंगत थी और अपने आप में एक नेता थी। उनकी दो पुत्रियां जैनब और कुलपुत्र करबला के हादसे के बाद और इस्लाम के समाप्त करने की लौकिक शक्तियों की कोशिशों के मद्देनजर धर्म को सही रूप में पुर्नस्थापित करने के लिए उत्तरदायी थी। मुस्लिम महिलाएं न केवल विद्वान, इतिहासकार लड़ाईयों में भाग लेने वाली सेना प्रमुख और देखभाल करने वाली थी, वरन् इन सबसे बढ़कर कुशल हदीस की व्याख्याकार भी थी। इसके साथ ही मुस्लिम महिलाओं ने निकाह समारोहों में प्रमुख भूमिका निभाई।

इस प्रकार प्राचीन भारतीय ऐतिहासिक प्रमाणों से यह विदित होता है कि उस वक्त महिलाओं की स्थिति सम्मानजनक थी परन्तु विदेशी आक्रमणों ने भारतीय संस्कृति को प्रभावित किया पहले इस्लामाबाद में अंग्रेजों का प्रभाव भारतीय संस्कृति पर पड़ा। भवनों की कुदृष्टि से बचने के लिए पर्दा-प्रथा, सती प्रथा तथा जौहर प्रथा समाज का अंग बन गया। साथ ही बाल विवाह को बढ़ावा मिला इस प्रकार स्त्रियाँ शिक्षा से वंचित हो गयी।

भारत में इस्लाम का अभ्युदय व महिलाओं की गरिमा विपरित अनुपात में तेजी से बढ़ने लगी। लगभग सभी शासकों जमींदारों, सामंतों ने कमोवेश महिलाओं का शारीरिक, आर्थिक व सामाजिक शोषण किया। परिणामतः भारतीय स्त्रियों की राजनीतिक, आर्थिक एवं सामाजिक चेतना लुप्त हो गयी।

उन्नीसवीं शताब्दी के पूर्वाद्ध में भारतीय नारी की दशा अत्यंत निकृष्ट एवं शोचनीय थी। इसी काल में कन्या शिशु-वध, बाल-विवाह, बहु विवाह, आर्थिक कारणों से स्त्रियों का अनमेल विवाह, सती, देवदासी प्रथा, पर्दा प्रथा आदि खूब फली-फूली। 19वीं सदी के उत्तराद्ध में पाश्चात्य संस्कृति के आगमन एवं इस्लाम के पराभाव ने स्त्रियों के दशा में कुछ सुधार लाया। इस काल में बहुत सारे समाज सुधारक हुए जिन्होंने स्त्रियों की सम्मान के रक्षा के लिए अनेक सामाजिक कार्य किए जिनमें राजा राम मोहन राय सती प्रथा को नष्ट करने का संकल्प लिया। महर्षि देवेन्द्र नाथ ठाकुर, ईश्वर चन्द्र विद्यासागर ने ब्रह्म समाज से जुड़कर स्त्री विरोधी सामाजिक कुरीतियों को दूर करने का कार्य शुरू किया।

बीसवीं सदी में स्त्रियों के भावनाओं एवं आत्म-सम्मान को गांधी जी ने बल दिया। गांधी जी नारी को अबला कहना वे शक्ति का अपमान समझते थे। वे नारी

को अन्नपूर्णा समझते थे। गांधी जी ने महिलाओं के अतीत के कुंठाओं को तोड़ा और राजनीति में स्त्रियों का आह्वान किया। उसी के फलस्वरूप सत्याग्रह आंदोलन में सरोजनी नायडू, अरूणा आसफ अली, विजया लक्ष्मी पंडित, कमला नेहरू आदि प्रमुख स्त्रियां थी जिन्होंने 1919 में पहली बार राजनीतिक योगदान दिया।

इक्कीसवीं सदी इस क्रूर एवं भयावह सत्य की साक्षी है कि समाज का आधा हिस्सा महिलाएं अवांछित भेद-भाव और अन्यायपूर्ण व्यवस्था की शिकार है। आधुनिक सभ्यता के प्रसार के पहले यह पूरा भारतीय समाज स्त्रियों के एक विशाल कारागार की तरह थी। इस विषय में सारे धर्मो की स्थिति प्रायः एक ही समान थी। ईसाई मिशनरियों के पहले से स्त्रियों की स्थिति में बदलाव आया। मिशनरियों के द्वारा लड़कियों को अध्यापिका और परिचारिका के रूप में नियुक्त किया गया और स्त्रियों को सार्वजनिक जीवन में प्रवेश दिलाया। इस तरह भारतीय इतिहास में एक नया मोड़ आया। इसके पहले का भारत पुरूष प्रधान था।

विश्व की आधी आबादी अर्थात् महिलाएं दोयम दर्जे की जिन्दगी जी रही है। आज से नहीं, बल्कि सदियों से। जीवन के विभिन्न क्षेत्रों में जैसे आर्थिक, सामाजिक एवं राजनीतिक क्षेत्रों में उनके समानता की बातें की जा रही है। महिला सशक्तिकरण के लिए भारत सहित विश्व के अनेक देशों में सरकारी एवं गैर सरकारी स्तर पर अनेक योजनाएं चल रही है। समाज को इस महत्वपूर्ण धूरी को बिना सशक्त बनाए तो समानता की बात न तो संभव है और न सामाजिक न्याय की। स्पष्ट शब्दों में कहा जा सकता है कि पूरा नारी समाज ही असमानता एवं पिछड़ेपन का शिकार है। महिलाएं सामाजिक, आर्थिक एवं राजनीतिक रूप से काफी पिछड़ी हुई है। यदि पूरे विश्व को विकसित विकासशील और पिछड़े देशों में विभाजित किया जाता है तो पूरी नारी समाज इससे भी अधिक हिस्सों में बंटी हुई है। जहां उनकी स्थिति काफी दयनीय है।

मानवाधिकार के नियम कानून पालन करने वाले विकसित संयुक्त राष्ट्र अमेरिका, ब्रिटेन, फ्रांस आदि देशों में भी महिलाओं का योगदान राजनीतिक आर्थिक एवं सामाजिक गतिविधियों में समान नहीं है। महिलाओं के सशक्तिकरण के लिए उन पहलुओं को मजबूत बनाने की आवश्यकता है जिनका सीधा संबंध स्वावलम्बन और उत्थान से है। शैक्षिक, सामाजिक, आर्थिक और राजनीतिक क्षेत्र इनमें प्रमुख है। आम तौर पर इन सभी क्षेत्रों में महिलाएं काफी पीछे है। महिला सशक्तिकरण के लिए यह आवश्यक है कि सामाजिक एवं आर्थिक विकास के ग्रामों तक महिलाओं की पहुंच सुनिश्चित की जाय। महिलाओं के प्रति अन्याय के

दो क्षेत्र हैं पारिवारिक मामले और सामाजिक क्षेत्र। महिलाओं के लिए न्याय पाना कठिन अवश्य है लेकिन असंभव नहीं इस दिशा में महिलाओं के लिए अनेक स्वयंसेवी संस्थाओं की भूमिका उल्लेखनीय है जिसके प्रयास से बड़ी संख्या में महिलाओं को न्याय प्राप्त हुआ है।

राजनीतिक क्षेत्र में लम्बे समय से पुरूषों का वर्चस्व रहा। महिलाओं की स्थिति व्याख्या करने के लिए 1971 में एक समिति गठित की गई थी टुवर्ड इक्वालिटी शीर्षक से 1974 में प्रकाशित इस समिति की रिपोर्ट में कहा गया था कि संस्थागत तौर पर सबसे बड़ी अल्पसंख्यक होने के बावजूद राजनीति पर महिलाओं का असर नाम मात्र है।

महिलाओं के विकास और उनके अधिकारों की रक्षा के लिए संयुक्त राष्ट्र महासभा में 18 दिसम्बर 1979 को महिलाओं के विरूद्ध सभी प्रकार के भेद-भाव समाप्त करने के बारे में प्रस्ताव पारित किया गया जो 03 दिसम्बर, 1981 से पारित हुआ।

पूरे विश्व में महिलाएं कार्यकारी घरों में दो तिहाई का योगदान करती है, लेकिन उन्हें विश्व आय का मात्र दसवां हिस्सा प्राप्त हो पाता है और उन्हें विश्व सम्पत्ति में सौवें से भी कम हिस्सा प्राप्त है।

आजादी के बाद पंचवर्षीय योजना के दौरान विकास के मुद्दे पर महिलाओं के विकास पर भी जोर डाला गया। जिसमें पांचवी पंचवर्षीय योजना (1974-78) के दरम्यान महिलाओं से जुड़े मुद्दों के प्रति उल्लेखनीय परिवर्तन आया।

आठवीं योजना (1992-97) में पुनः महिलाओं के विकास पर जोर दिया। इसमें यह सुनिश्चित करने का प्रयास किया गया था कि विभिन्न क्षेत्रों से होने वाले लाभों से महिलाएं वंचित न रहें ।

नौंवी योजना (1992-97) में पुनः महिलाओं के विकास पर जोर दिया। इसमें यह सुनिश्चित करने का प्रयास किया गया था कि विभिन्न क्षेत्रों से होने वाले लाभों से महिलाएं वंचित न रहे।

नौवीं योजना (1997-2002) में महिलाओं के लिए नियोजन के धरणात्मक व्यूह रचना में दो उल्लेखनीय परिवर्तन किए गए। पहला महिलाओं के सशक्तिकरण ने नौवीं योजना के नौ प्राथमिक लक्ष्यों में से एक का रूप ले लिया। दूसरा, योजना ने महिला केन्द्रित और महिला संबंधित क्षेत्रों में विद्यमान सभी सेवाओं को एक धरा में मिलाने का प्रयास किया।

ग्यारहवीं योजना में महिलाओं के सशक्तिकरण की जो परिकल्पना की गई है उसमें समावेशी और समेकित विकास सामाजिक और राजनीतिक सशक्तिकरण के साथ-साथ स्त्री के लिए समान न्याय को प्रमुखता दी गई है।

पिछले कुछ वर्षों में महिलाओं के सशक्तिकरण को व्यापक समर्थन मिला है परन्तु यह प्रश्न अभी भी बना हुआ है कि हम इन उद्देश्यों और विभिन्न सामाजिक समूहों और क्षेत्रों की महिलाओं की आवश्यकताओं की प्राप्ति कहां तक कर सके हैं।

2001 की जनगणना के अनुसार महिलाओं की घरेलू कामों की गणना नहीं होती है। मारथा सी. नुसवाक के अनुसार महिलाएं दिनभर दूसरे कार्यभार में व्यस्त रहती है बच्चों व पति की देखभाल के कार्य में अपना समय व शक्ति लगाती है इसके बावजूद वे पौष्टिक भोजन, आर्थिक सुरक्षा व आराम से वंचित रहती है। नोबल पुरस्कार विजेता अर्मत्य सेन ने स्वीकार किया कि महिलाओं को घर से बाहर जो कार्य मिलते हैं वे निचले दर्जे के होते हैं तथा उन्हें वेतन भी पुरूषों से कम मिलता है। ये उनकी सामाजिक हैसियत व हक को विपरित रूप से प्रभावित करते हैं ।

यह बात गौर करने वाली है कि 80 प्रतिशत महिलाएं कृषि क्षेत्र में कार्यरत है जो एक असंगठित क्षेत्र है वे अपनी आर्थिक आमदनी के लिए 14 से 16 घंटे तक कार्य करती है और केवल 6 प्रतिशत ही औद्योगिक क्षेत्रों में कार्य करती है। यद्यपि रोजगार में महिलाओं की संख्या में वृद्धि हो रही है लेकिन उन्हें कम वेतन मिल रहा है। उनके कार्य की परिस्थितियां असंतोषजनक है। विश्व के 550 लाख कार्यरत गरीबों के 80 प्रतिशत महिलाएं हैं ।

इसमें संदेह नहीं कि महिलाएं काफी उन्नति कर चुकी हैं लेकिन फिर भी विचारों एवं संस्कारों में यथेष्ठ समकक्षता प्राप्त नहीं हो पाया है। इसका कारण यह है कि कालान्तर में जो अभ्यास कराया गया वह आज उसका संस्कार बन गया है। इस संस्कार के कारण वे स्वयं अपने भीतर दबी हुई है। आखिर इसी संस्कार के वजह से एक मां बेटी के जन्म पर दुःखी होती है और बेटे के जन्म पर खुश होती है।

अपने स्वास्थ्य के प्रति भी महिलाएं जागरूक नहीं है। राष्ट्रीय पारिवारिक स्वास्थ्य सर्वेक्षण के तीसरे चरण के आंकलन के मुताबिक 15 से 49 वर्ष की आयु वर्ग की 41 प्रतिशत महिलाएं औपचारिक शिक्षा से वंचित है। जबकि इसी आयु वर्ग के मात्र 18 प्रतिशत पुरूष औपचारिक शिक्षा से महरूम है। ग्यारहवीं योजना

में इसे बदलने की बात है। यह दस्तावेज कहता है कि यह एक महत्वपूर्ण विभाजन है जो हमें लिंग आधारित समस्याओं पर तत्काल ध्यान देने के लिए बाध्य करता है। समाज को इस विकृति से मुक्त करने के आर्थिक राजनीतिक एवं सामाजिक सशक्तिकरण के लिए उपयुक्त माहौल का निर्माण किया जायेगा। यह सुझाव स्वागत के लायक है। हालांकि पिछली सभी योजनाओं में इसी बात की चिंता की गई है।

1990 के आर्थिक सुधारों के बाद आर्थिक क्षेत्र के महिलाओं का योगदान धीरे-धीरे बढ़ रहा है। वह प्रत्येक क्षेत्र में कार्य कर रही है। चाहे व निजी क्षेत्र हो या सार्वजनिक क्षेत्र। संगठित क्षेत्र में महिलाओं का योगदान 2001 में बढ़कर 17.8 प्रतिशत हो गया। प्रमुख उद्योगों में महिला कर्मचारियों की संख्या विश्लेषण से पता चलता है कि अधिकतर महिलाएं सामाजिक और निजी सेवा क्षेत्र में कार्यरत है। आज महिलाएं राष्ट्रीय अर्थव्यवस्था में 60-80 प्रतिशत योगदान करती है।

भारतीय अर्थव्यवस्था को मजबूती प्रदान करने वाले सेवा क्षेत्र में विविध किस्म की दक्षता की मांग है। यदि लड़कियों एवं अबतक वंचित रही जातियों में उपयोगी साक्षरता के व्यापक विकास पर बल नहीं दिया गया तो निकट भविष्य में इन सभी क्षेत्रों को मानव संसाधन का भारी अभाव झेलना पड़ेगा।

स्वयं सिद्ध के कारण आज भारतीय महिला अपने आपको सशक्त समझने लगी है। स्वयं सिद्ध उन लड़कियों के मामले को लेते हैं जो कभी-कभी अनावश्यक है और अप्रसांगिक परिस्थितियों में छोड़ दी जाती है। स्वयं सिद्ध के माध्यम से उसे सशक्त बनाया जाता है।

लघु वित्त (Micro-Finance) के रूप में छोटे-मोटे कार्यो के लिए आर्थिक सहायता ने महिलाओं को काफी सशक्त किया है। इस सहायता के कारण आज महिलाएं घरेलू हिंसा की शिकार नहीं होती है अर्थात् महिलाएं जमीनी स्तर पर सशक्त हो रही है।

सामाजिक स्तर पर स्त्रियों में सुधार आया लेकिन राजनीति का परिदृश्य नहीं बदला है। भारत ही नहीं पूरे विश्व में महिला सशक्तिकरण की अवधारणा का प्रयोग हो रहा है। महिला सशक्तिकरण के संबंध में ऑफिस ऑफ द यूनाईटेड नेशंस हाई कमीश्नर, फॉर ह्यूमन राइट्स (Office of the United Nations High Commissioner for Human Rights) ने लिखा है "औरतों को शक्ति क्षमता तथा काबलियत देता है ताकि वह अपने जीवन स्तर को सुधार कर अपने जीवन दिशा को स्वयं निर्धारित कर सकें।"

भारत में किसी भी राजनीतिक दल में महिला आरक्षण के प्रति सकारात्मक दृष्टिकोण रखने के बावजूद इस दिशा में कोई कदम नहीं उठाया है। संसद में महिलाओं का प्रतिनिधित्व 8.3 प्रतिशत है। स्व. राजीव गांधी पहली बार संविधान संशोधन करते हुए पंचायती राज विधेयक में स्त्रियों के लिए 30 प्रतिशत आरक्षण का प्रावधान किया था।

वर्षों से अपनी लड़ाई औरत खुद लड़ते हुए इस 21वीं सदी में खुद अपनी ताकत बन गई आज महिलाएं प्रत्येक क्षेत्र में पुरुषों के साथ कदम से कदम मिलाकर आत्म विश्वास और साहस के साथ आगे बढ़ रही है। इसी आधार पर 21वीं सदी को महिलाओं की सदी की संज्ञा दी है।

योजना आयोग की सदस्या सैयदा हमीद 21वीं सदी में स्त्री सशक्तिकरण के रूप में एक मिशाल कायम की 12 अगस्त 2008 में नैश और इमरान का निकाह करवाकर एक नयी इतिहास की रचना कर डाली। सैयदा हमीद शायद पहली हिन्दुस्तानी मुस्लिम महिला थी जिन्होंने काजी का कर्तव्य निभाया और एक इस्लामी शादी करायी। मिडिया ने इसे वखूबी दुनिया के सामने पेश किया।

आज के दौर में महिलाएं कई प्रकार से अपनी कार्य क्षमता अपनी विद्वता से एवं आर्थिक नीति से भारतीय अर्थव्यवस्था को मजबूत कर रही है जैसे हमारे देश की इंदिरा नूई (C.E.O. Pepsico. India), सौन्दर्य एवं प्रसाधन के क्षेत्र में सहनाज का हर्बल उत्पादन, चन्द्रा कोचर (M.D. I.C.I.C.I. Bank), नयनालाल किदवई (H.S.B.C. Bank India Operations) मीडिया के क्षेत्र में महिलाओं की सहभागिता काफी रही है। जैसे शोभना भारतीया, Hindustan Times की Chair person बरखा दत्त आदि।

आज नेताओं के रूप में महिलाएं ग्राम पंचायत से लेकर विधानसभा एवं लोकसभा तक परिवर्तनकारी एवं रचनात्मक भूमिका बखूबी निभा रही है। राजनीति क्षेत्र में श्रीमती इंदिरा गांधी से लेकर सोनिया गांधी, श्रीमती शीला दीक्षित, सुषमा स्वराज, ममता बनर्जी, सुश्री मायावती एवं श्रीमती राबड़ी देवी इत्यादि ने भी अपने आपको सफल राजनीतिज्ञ साबित कर चुकी है।

अन्ततः इस मुट्ठीभर महिलाओं के विकास को हम न तो आर्थिक क्षेत्र में न तो सामाजिक क्षेत्र में और न तो राजनीतिक क्षेत्र में विकास का स्वरूप मान सकते हैं। क्योंकि जबतक हमारे देश के पिछड़े दलित एवं आर्थिक रूप से पिछड़े दलित एवं आर्थिक रूप से पिछड़े ग्रामीण महिलाओं का विकास न हो जाय तथा उन्हें देश

के पर्दे पर न लाया जाय। स्त्री सशक्तिकरण सौ प्रतिशत सफल तभी हो सकता है जब समानता एवं सद्भावना का विकास हो।

गांधी जी ने कहा है "सच्चा अर्थशास्त्र सामाजिक न्याय का हियायत करता है। वह समान भाव से सबकी भलाई का जिनमें कमजोर भी शामिल हैं, प्रयत्न करता है और सभ्य जनोचित सुंदर जीवन के लिए है।"

संदर्भ-सूची

1. हरिजन 09 अक्टूबर 1937
2. Chaturvedi S.K. : "Bhartiya Rajniti Mein Mahilaon Ka Yogdan", Loktantra Samiksha, Vol.24, No.1.4.1992.
3. Sen Agrawal, 2004

39

महिलाओं की राजनीतिक नेतृत्व-एक समीक्षा

संजीव कुमार

स्त्रियो को तो वही मिला जो पुरूष ने इच्छा से देना चाहा। इस स्थिति में भी पुरूष दाता के रूप में और औरत ग्रहित के रूप में सामने आई। इसका प्रमुख कारण औरतो के पास अपने आपको एक इकाई के रूप में संगठित करने के ठोस साधनों का अभाव है। उसका न तो कोई अतीत है और न इतिहास, न अपना कोई धर्म है और न ही सर्वहारा की तरह ठोस क्रिया-कलापों का एक संगठित जगत्। स्त्रियों के बीच सामूहिकता की भावना का अभाव है। ऐसी कोई जगह नही जहाँ वे झुंड बनाकर रहती हो यानि एक बड़े दल में अवस्थित हो, जैसा कि हम अमेरिकन नीगों को उनके 'घेटो' में पाते है या फिर सर्वहारा एकजुट होकर फैक्ट्रियो मे काम करता है तथा उसी स्थान पर उसकी चेतना विस्फोटक रूप लेती है। समूह के बदले औरत अकेली और पुरूषो के बीच बिखरी हुई है। वह पुरूष के घर में उसकी गृहस्थी मे काम करती है। वह पुरूष की दी हुई आर्थिक सुविधाओं को भोगती है उसी सामाजिक स्तर स अपना तादात्म्य स्थापित करती है पुरुष उसके आस-पास कभी पिता, कभी भाई, कभी पति, तो कभी पुत्र के रूप में रहता है। बुर्जुवा वर्ग की महिलाओ की समस्वरता अपने ही वर्ग के पुरूषो के साथ है, वह सर्वहारा वर्ग की स्त्रियो के साथ एक प्राण नही हो सकती। उच्च जाति की औरते निम्नजाति के औरते के साथ बहनापा स्थापित नहीं करती, जैसे-गोरी चमड़ी की औरते काली नीग्रो औरते के साथ। सर्वहारा-वर्ग सत्ताधारी-वर्ग के पूरे खात्मे का निर्णय ले सकता

है या अत्यंत पीड़ित नीग्रो अपनी दलित अवस्था मे पूरी मानव जाति को काले रंग देने के साधन की कल्पना कर सकता है, लेकिन औरत, पुरूष को खत्म करने की कल्पना नही कर सकती है। अतः अपने अत्याचारी और दमनकारी के साथ औरत के रिश्ते की तुलना किन्ही अन्य संबंधो के साथ नहीं की जा सकती है। स्त्री-पुरूष के सेक्स का विभेदीकरण वास्तव में एक जैविक तथ्य है, इतिहास की कोई घटना नहीं। मानव-दम्पति एक मौलिक इकाई है। अतः स्त्री-पुरूष में भेद की रेखा खीचकर समाज में दरार पैदा नहीं की जा सकती और यहीं पर हम औरत की मौलिक विशेषता पाते है, और सिद्ध होता है कि वह **"अन्या"** है।[1]

स्त्री को अमीर हो या गरीब, श्वेत हो या अश्वेत, अपनी लड़ाई खुद लड़नी होगी। यह दुनिया पुरूषो ने बनाई पर स्त्री से पूछकर नही। फ्रांस की राज्य क्रांति हो या विश्वयुद्ध, स्त्री से पुरूष सहारा लेता है और पुनः उसे घर लौट जाने को कहता है। वह सदियो से ठगी गई है। यदि उसने कुछ स्वतंत्रता हासिल भी की है तो उतनी ही जितनी की पुरूषो ने अपनी सुविधा के लिए देना चाहा।[2]

फ्रांस की जो स्थिति 1949 मे थी, पश्चिमी समाज उन दिनो जिस आर्थिक और सामाजिक परिवर्त्तन के दौर से गुजर रहा था, वह शायद हमारा आज का भारतीय समाज है, उसका मध्यंमवर्ग है, नगरो और महानगरो में बिखरी हुई स्त्रियाँ है जो संक्रमण के दौर से गुजर रही है।[3]

यदि कानून औरत को बराबरी का आधार दे भी दे तो समाजिकता नैतिकता और लोक व्यवहार उसके आड़े आ जाते है। दूसरी बातो के समान रहने पर भी आर्थिक क्षेत्र में औरत और मर्द बिल्कुल अलग-अलग जाति के रूप में प्रस्तुत होते है। पुरूषो को अच्छी नौकरी, बेहतर तनख्वाह और सफलता की ज्यादा सुविधाएँ मिलती है, उद्योग व्यवस्था और राजनीति में पुरूषो को ज्यादा ओहदे मिलते है महत्त्वपूर्ण पदो पर उनका एकाधिकार ही रहता है।[4]

वर्त्तमान समय में जब औरत जागतिक में रूचि लेना शुरू कर रही है, तब भी, वह वही जगत है जो पुरूष का है। पुरूष के मन मे इस जगत् के प्रति कोई संदेह नहीं, उसकी स्थिति असुरक्षित नहीं है। यह औरत की ही स्थिति है जो अपना विश्लेषण मांगती है। औरत यदि **'अन्या'** होना अस्वीकार करे, यदि वह समझौते से मुकरे तो इसका परिणाम होगा पुरूष जाति से जुड़ने की फलस्वरूप परम्परागत रूप से तमाम सुविधाओ का परित्याग।

औरत को केवल सेक्सुअल अवयवी नही समझा जा सकता। जैविक विशेषताओ का भी वही तक महत्त्व है, जहाँ तक वे सक्रिय रूप से ठोस मूल्यो के निर्माण में

सहायक होती है। औरत का आत्म-बोध केवल उसकी सेक्सुअलिटी से परिभाषित नहीं किया जा सकता। यह समाज की आर्थिक व्यवस्था द्वारा उत्पन्न परिस्थिति और मानव-समाज के तकनीकी-विकास के स्तर को परखने पर निर्भर करता है। हम देख चुके है कि जैविक रूप से औरत की मुख्यतयाः दो विशेषताएँ होती है। एक तो जगत् पर उसकी पुरूष की अपेक्षा कम होती है, और दूसरे वह अपनी जाति से अधिक स्थितिग्रस्त होती है, किन्तु ये तथ्य सामाजिक और आर्थिक संदर्भ में बिल्कूल ही दूसरे मूल्य बन जाते है। मानव-इतिहास में जगत् पर अधिकार प्राप्त करना मात्र शरीर द्वारा नहीं होता।

यह ठीक है कि आदिम काल में मनुष्य केवल वन्य-पशुओ को सामना करने और चट्टानो को तोड़कर रास्ता बनाने के लिए बाहुबल की जरूरत अधिक पड़ती थी, उस समय पुरूष की अदभ्य शक्ति की तुलना में औरत कमजोर सिद्ध होती थी, लेकिन आज तकनीकि विकास ने औरत और पुरूष के इस भेद को मिटा दिया। अब पुरूष की शारीरिक शक्ति की जरूरत पहले की तरह नहीं रही आज अनेक आधुनिक उर्जा सम्पन्न यंत्र केवल बटन दबाकर नियंत्रित किए जा सकते है अतः आधुनिक संसार मे कार्य व्यापारो के लिए शारीरिक शक्ति की जरूरत घटती जा रही है।[5]

अपनी पुस्तक 'परिवार, व्यक्तिगत-सम्पति और राज्य की उत्पति में एंगेल्स कहते है कि औरत का इतिहास वास्तव में तकनीक के इतिहास पर निर्भर करता है।

औरत का भाग्य और समाजवाद की स्थापना अनिवार्यतः परस्पर सम्बद्ध है, जैसा कि 'बेबल' ने लिखा है ''औरत और सर्वहारा दोनो ही दलित है और दोनो के सामाजिक जागरण की सम्भावना यांत्रिक सम्यता में अधिक पायी जाती है।'' औरत की समस्या उसकी श्रम की क्षमता के स्तर पर भी स्त्रियों को पुरूष के बराबर खड़ा कर दिया है। केवल पूँजीवादी पितृ-तंत्र ही अधिकांश देशो में औरत और पुरूष की एकता हो हासिल करने में बाधा देता है। पूंजीवादी अवरोधो की समाप्ति के साथ ही स्त्री और पुरूष समानाधिकार प्राप्त कर लेगे, जैसा कि हम सोवियत समाज मे देख रहे है। दुनिया में समाजवादी समाज की स्थापना हो जाने पर स्त्री और पुरूष में वर्ग-भेद नहीं होगा, बल्कि समानता के स्तर पर उत्पादन करते स्त्री-पुरूषो का एक ही वर्ग होगा श्रमिक वर्ग।[6]

स्वर्ग हो या नर्क, हर जगह स्त्री एक शक्ति बनी। पवित्रता का प्रतीक, क्योंकि उसके पास प्रजनन की जादूई शक्ति थी। उस शक्ति की पूजा की गई। ये

प्राचीन युग हमे कोई साहित्य नहीं देते, किन्तु महान पित्तृसत्तामक समाज अपने शिलालेखो और कालातीत परम्पराओ में उन स्मृतियो को संयोए हुए है, जब स्त्री को समाज में सर्वोपरि स्थान मिला हुआ था। ऋग्वेद के ऋचा-गीतो में स्त्री की जो वंदना है, उसमे ह्रास होता है ब्राह्मण-युग के साथ। वेदकालिन औरत को जो सत्ता मिली थी, कुरान में उसकी स्थिति हीन बना दी गई। गर्वीला मानव अपनी संतति के साथ धीरे-धीरे बाद की रोमन सम्यता के आगमन के साथ झुकता चला गया।[7]

बाल्जॉक के शब्दो में "औरत की नियति और सम्पूर्ण महत्ता इस बात में निहित है कि वह पुरूष के दिल की धड़कन बढ़ा सके। वह जंगम सम्पति है, जिसको पुरूष जहाँ चाहे, हॉक कर ले जा सकता है।"[8]

औधोगिक क्रांति के फलस्वरूप श्रामिक-वर्ग का विकास हुआ। कल-कारखानो में स्त्रियों की जरूरत पड़ी। अतः समाजवाद उनकी मुक्ति के लिए सहायक था। 1879 की 'समाजवादी कांग्रेस' ने घोषणा की कि स्त्री और पुरूष दोनो समान है, फिर भी नारी-मुक्ति का आह्वान एक गौण बनकर रह गया, क्योंकि पहला सवाल तो श्रमिक-संघर्ष और सर्वहारा की मुक्ति का था। उसके विपरीत बुर्जवा स्त्रियॉ सामाजिक संस्थाओं के चौरवटे पर स्थित होकर भी नए अधिकारो की मांग कर रही थी।

फ्रांसीसी महिलाओं को अंत में 1945 मे मतदान का अधिकार मिल गया। अंग्रेज स्त्रियों का काफी संघर्ष को बाद यह अधिकार 1928 मे मिला, क्योंकि उन्होंने प्रथम महायुद्ध में काफी सहयोग दिया था। अमेरीका में स्त्रियों को वोट कर अधिकार 1933 मे मिला।

सोवियत रूस में नारी-मुक्ति आंदोलन काफी जोरो से बढ़ा! महान नेता लेनिन ने स्त्री और मजदूर-वर्ग दोनो की मुक्ति का आह्वान किया, दोनो को एक बतलाया। 1936 के सोवियत संविधान की धारा 122 लिखती है, सोवियत रूस में स्त्री का आर्थिक, राजनीतिक, सांस्कृतिक और सार्वजनिक सारे अधिकार पुरूष के बराबर प्रदत किए जा रहे है।[9]

अंत में संयुक्त राष्ट्र संघ ने 1945 तक आते-आते दुनिया की सारी स्त्रियों और पुरूषो को समान अधिकार का ऐलान किया और अधिकत्तर देशों ने स्त्रियों को वोट का अधिकार देकर राजनीतिक जीवन में उनको प्रवेशाधिकार दिया।[10]

एक ही क्षेत्र है, जिसमे स्त्रियों ने आशातीत सफलता पाई है, वह है संस्कृति का। स्त्री हमेशा कला और साहित्य से जुड़ी रही। चूँकि औरत की जिन्दगी हमेशा सीमांत पर रहती है, इसलिए पुरूष ने इस जगत् के किनारे पार जाने के लिए

औरत का ही सहारा लिया। वह लेखको की प्रेरणा, मित्र और आलोचक हमेशा रही।[11]

यह ठीक है कि आज हम एक संक्रमण के दौर से गुजर रहे है। इस दुनिया में आज भी सारी सत्ता, सारे मूल्य और संस्थाएँ पुरूषो के हाथो में है। यदि स्त्रियो को कुछ अधिकार दिए भी गए है तो वे अमूर्त्त रह गए है। वे रूढ़ियो और पूर्वाग्रहो के कारण व्यावहारिक जगत् में लागू नहीं किए जा सकते। इसलिए अब भी स्त्री की पूरी पकड़ दूनिया पर नहीं है। कहने को तो स्त्री और पुरूष समान है, किन्तु वास्तव मे इन दोनो में बहुत बड़ा भेद कायम है।[12]

हमारी संवैधानिक आकांक्षाएँ राजनीति दलो के दल-दल में फँस गयी है, और इनते महान राष्ट्रीय कर्त्तव्य की दिशा मे भारत की सभी राजनीतिक पाटियों ने रोड़े खड़े कर दिए है। राजनीति में बाहुबलियों तक का वर्चस्व संवैधानिक लक्ष्य को प्राप्त करने में सबसे बड़ी बाधा है। इसका प्रमाण है महिला आरक्षण विधेयक 1998 ई0 का विरोध। इस समय लोक सभा मे महिलाओ का प्रतिनिधित्व मात्र 6.6% है। उस समय की संयुक्त मोर्च की सरकार ने भी लोकसभा, विधानसभाओं और राजकीय सेवाओ में 33% महिलाओ को आरक्षण देने की घोषणा की थी। इस उद्वेश्य को पूरा करने के लिए संविधान में आवश्यक संशोधन करने का भी आश्वासन दिया गया था, पर जब भी संविधान में संशोधन कर महिला आरक्षण बिल पारित करने की बात होती है तो सभी राजनैतिक पार्टीया उसमे कुछ न कुछ मिन-मेख निकाल कर जबरदस्त विरोध करती है, हंगामा कर संसद की कार्यवाही ठप कर देती है, फिर महिला आरक्षण विरोध करती है, हंगामा कर संसद की कार्यवाही ठप कर देती है, फिर महिला आरक्षण विधेयक को पुनः ठंडे बस्ते मे डाल दी जाती है, जो कि दुर्भाग्यवश महिलाओ के राजतीतिक नेतृत्व के लिए अभिशाप बन जाती है। अगर ये महिला आरक्षण बिल पारित हो जाए तो महिलाओ मे एक जुटतापूर्ण नेतृत्व का मार्ग प्रस्तुत करेगा।

जैसाकि बिहार में पंचायतो में महिला आरक्षण के लागू हो जाने से नारी के स्वरूप में तेजी से परिवर्त्तन आया है। ज़िस बिहार में नारी को घर की दहलीज से बाहर निकलने की आज्ञा न थी, आज उसी बिहार में नारी पुरूषो के साथ कंधे से कंधा मिलाकर काम कर रही हैं। वह घर की चार-दीवारी से निकलकर समाज के सर्वागीण विकास के लिए नीतियॉ तय कर रही है। महिला-आरक्षण के लागू हो जाने से पंचायते एक तुफानी सफर तय कर रहीं है, तो वही दूसरी तरफ उनकी बढ़ती हुई पहलकदमी से नौकरशाही और राजनीतिक हलका परेशान दिख रहा है।

महिलाओ को लग रहा है संविधान के तहत उन्हे जो अधिकार दिए गए है, वे मिलने चाहिए और सत्ता का सही विकेन्द्रीकरण होना चाहिए।[14]

संयुक्त राष्ट्र की एजेन्सी यू0 एन0 एफ0 पी0 ने अपनी ताजा रिपोट मे भारत में, पंचायत में आरक्षण के फलस्वरूप महिलाओ में उपजी चेतना की सराहना की है। आज सभी राज्यों में पंचायतो के माध्यम से महिलाएँ नये उत्साह और स्फूर्ति के साथ विकास गतिविधियों में योगदान दे रही है। आज देशभर में लगभग 10 लाख महिलाएँ मुखिया, सरपंच तथा अन्य पदो पर चुनाव जीत कर ग्रामीण शासन को दिशा दे रही है।

महिलाओ को अपनी क्षमताओ का एहसास हो गया है और वे कुछ कर दिखाने तथा अपनी पहचान बनाने के लिए अपनी इच्छा से चुनाव लड़ रही है। सत्ता में भागीदारी की यह मात्र केवल संख्या या अनुपात तक सीमित नहीं है। पंचायतो मे ग्रामीण महिलाओ की उपस्थिति से उनमे आत्म-विश्वास बढ़ा है और पहली बार एहसास हुआ है कि चुल्हा-चौका और बच्चे पालने के साथ-साथ वे अपने गॉव और समाज के लिए ऐसे काम भी कर सकती है जिनके लिए पुरूष शासित समाज ने कभी मौका नहीं दिया। यह देखने को मिल रहा है कि महिला प्रतिनिधि, पंचायतो का बजट तैयार करने की जिम्मेदारी सफलतापूर्वक निभा रही है। इसमे घरेलू-बजट तैयार करने का उनका अनुभव और सुझबुझ काम आ रहा है। बजट तैयार करते हुए वे उन कार्यो को अधिक महत्व देती है जो महिलाओ के उपयोग के है। यह भी देखने को मिल रहा है कि पंचायत की पदाधिकारी बनने से घर-परिवार में और आस-पास उनका समाज बढ़ गया है और जो मर्द पहले औरतो के सुझाव की अनदेखी करते थे, वे अब उनकी बातो को गंभीरता से लेते है और उनसे समानता का वर्त्ताव करते है। इस सम्मान और प्रतिष्ठा के चलते महिलाएँ गॉवो के छोटे-मोटे झगड़े और विवाद भी निपटाने लगी है। इस प्रकार महिलाओ के प्रति अभी तक चले आ रहे भेदभाव को दूर करने में मदद मिल रही है। पंचायती राज व्यवस्था में ज्यादातर महिलाएँ किसी की पत्नी या किसी की बहू बनकर चुनाव मे उतरती है। मौहरे के तौर पर ही सही, महिलाओ को चौखट लांधने की इजाजत तो पुरूष समाज से मिला।

महिला प्रतिनिधियो को जहाँ अवसर मिले है, वहाँ उनके सामने अनेक चुनौतियाँ भी है। उनके हर कदम पर आलोचनात्मक नजर रहती है। उनकी अपनी परम्परावादी सोच पुरूष सत्तावादी समाज भी उनके आगे बढ़ने में बाधक बन सकते है। इसलिए उन्हे सम्भल-सम्भल कर और पूरे आत्म विश्वास के साथ काम करना

होगा। उनसे कई अपेक्षाएँ है। सबसे पहला काम है गॉवो में महिला साक्षरता को बढ़ावा देना। प्राथमिक विद्यालयों की स्थिति ठीक हो, वहाॅ अध्यापको की नियुक्ति हो, दोपहर के भोजन की सही व्यवस्था हो, लड़कियो को स्कूल भेजने में माँ - बाप कोताही न करे, इन सब बातो पर महिला प्रतिनिधियों को विशेष ध्यान देना होगा। इसी तरह आंगनबाड़ी सही ढंग से चले, महिलाओ के लिए रोजगार परियोजनाओं तथा स्वरोजगार के प्रशिक्षण कार्यक्रमों का संचालन सही तरीके से हो, आपदाओ के समय सहायता वितरण में भ्रष्टाचार न हो, इन सब पहलुओ पर नजर रखनी होगी। पंचायतो के महिला प्रतिनिधियो का ग्रामीण भारत में दीप स्तम्भ की तरह चारो ओर चेतना और कार्यकुशलता की रोशनी फैलानी होगी। लड़कियो से भेदभाव और भ्रूण-हत्या जैसी नई पनप रही समस्याओं का मुकाबला भी उन्हे करना होगा। किसी ने कल्पना भी नहीं की थी कि पंचायतों में महिलाओं का आरक्षण उनके सशक्तिकरण और ग्रामीण समाज के चहुँमुखी विकास की संभावनाओ के इतने द्वार खोल देगा। इसमें कोई शक नहीं कि अपेक्षाएँ बहुत है किन्तु, महिलाओ में क्षमताओं और उर्जा का कोई अभाव नहीं है। आवश्यकता इस बात की है कि सरकार से प्रोत्साहन और मार्गदर्शन मिलता रहे। जैसे-जैसे महिला साक्षरता का प्रतिशत बढ़ेगा, वैसे-वैसे महिला मुखिया और सरपंच अधिक विश्वास व कार्यकुशलता के साथ गॉवो में सामाजिक, आर्थिक और सांस्कृतिक जीवन को बेहतर बनाने में अपनी भूमिका बढ़ायेंगी। यहीं नहीं, पंचायते उनके भावी राजनीतिक जीवन का 'पालना' सिद्ध होगी और यहीं के अनुभव के बल पर वे अपने आपको विधानसभाओं और लोक-सभा में जाने के लिए तैयार कर सकेंगी।[15]

आज 21वीं शताब्दी में प्रवेश करती हुई लाखों महिलाएं राष्ट्रीय जीवन के प्रत्येक क्षेत्र में कार्यरत है। कोई भी ऐसा क्षेत्र नहीं बचा है, जहाँ महिलाओं ने देश का नाम रोशन न किया हो। वह राष्ट्रपति, प्रधानमंत्री, मुख्यमंत्री, राज्यपाल, विधायक, सांसद, न्यायधीश बनकर राष्ट्र का संचालन कर रही है। इंदिरा गाँधी से लेकर तीजनबाई तक, अरूधती राय, कल्पना चावला, शुभामुद्गल, पी.टी. उषा, बरखादत्त, किरण बेदी, सानिया मिर्जा, कर्णम मलेश्वरी जैसी लाखो महिलाएँ जिनकी पहचान उनके पति या पिता से नही, बल्कि उनसे पिता या पति का पहचान है। महिलाओं ने इस पुरूष-प्रधान समाज में यह सिद्ध कर दिया है कि वे किसी भी तरह पुरूषों से कम नहीं है। वे हर क्षेत्र में आगे आई है, ये वे महिलाएँ हैं जिन्होंने वैसा मुकाम हासिल किया है जिसके लिए पुरूष भी तरसते हैं।

आवश्यकता तो इस बात की है कि पुरूष-प्रधान समाज अपनी अहंकारी सोच को त्यागकर महिलाओं को विशेष अवसर प्रदान करें।[16]

उपर्युक्त अध्ययन से यह निष्कर्ष निकलता है कि जहां तक भारतीय राजनीति का प्रश्न है आधी आबादी को सशक्त बनाएं बिना देश और समाज की तरक्की, (विकास) संभव नहीं है। संविधान में 73वाँ 74वाँ संशोधन करके महिलाओं को क्रमशः पंचायती राज संस्थाओं और नगर निकायों में एक-तिहाई आरक्षण दिया गया, जिसके फलस्वरूप महिलाओं को स्वतंत्र पहचान बनाने तथा अपना सामाजिक उत्थान करने का एक सबल मंच प्राप्त हुआ है। जिसके वजह उनमें व्यापक स्तर पर जागृति, शिक्षा, स्वास्थ्य और आर्थिक सशक्तिकरण का आभास हो रहा है।

लेकिन राज्य स्तर और केन्द्र स्तर पर महिला आरक्षण विधेयक 1996 से लोकसभा में पेश होकर आज भी पारित होने के लिए लंबित पड़ा है। जब तक राज्य और केन्द्र स्तर पर महिलाओं को समुचित भागीदारी नहीं मिलेगी, तब-तक महिलाओं के राजनैतिक नेतृत्व पर हमेशा ही प्रश्न-चिन्ह लगता रहेगा, जैसा कि हम देखते है कि आज आरक्षण के बल पर ही दलित राजनीतिक गतिविधियों मे पूरे आत्म-विश्वास के साथ कंधे से कंधा मिलाकर चल रहे हैं, जिसके फलस्वरूप भारतीय राजनीति में, दलित नेताओं के कदो में काफी इजाफा हुआ है, स्वालम्बी और ताकतवरकद का बनवाया है, दलितों के उत्थान के बारे में वे निःसंकोच अपना पक्ष संसद, विधान सभाओं में रखते हैं, जिसके कारण उनकी अपनी पहचान बनती है। ठीक उसी प्रकार जब-तक महिला आरक्षण विधेयक पारित नहीं होगा, तब तक **महिलाओं में राजनीतिक नेतृत्व** का सदा अभाव रहेगा और वे अपनी पहचान **'अन्या'** के रूप में ही बनाती रहेगी।

संदर्भ-सूची

1. स्त्रीः उपेक्षिता (सीमोन द बोउवार की विश्व चर्चित कृत्ति-सकेण्ड सेक्स का हिन्दी रूपान्तर) प्रस्तुति- डॉ0 प्रभा खेतान, पृष्ठ संख्या-25
2. स्त्रीः उपेक्षिता (सीमोन द बोउवार की विश्व चर्चित कृत्ति-सकेण्ड सेक्स का हिन्दी रूपान्तर) प्रस्तुति- डॉ0 प्रभा खेतान, पृष्ठ संख्या-19
3. स्त्रीः उपेक्षिता (सीमोन द बोउवार की विश्व चर्चित कृत्ति-सकेण्ड सेक्स का हिन्दी रूपान्तर) प्रस्तुति- डॉ0 प्रभा खेतान, पृष्ठ संख्या-16
4. स्त्रीः उपेक्षिता (सीमोन द बोउवार की विश्व चर्चित कृत्ति-सकेण्ड सेक्स का हिन्दी रूपान्तर) प्रस्तुति- डॉ0 प्रभा खेतान, पृष्ठ संख्या-25

5. स्त्रीः उपेक्षिता (सीमोन द बोउवार की विश्व चर्चित कृत्ति-सकेण्ड सेक्स का हिन्दी रूपान्तर) प्रस्तुति- डॉ0 प्रभा खेतान, पृष्ठ संख्या-44

6. स्त्रीः उपेक्षिता (सीमोन द बोउवार की विश्व चर्चित कृत्ति-सकेण्ड सेक्स का हिन्दी रूपान्तर) प्रस्तुति- डॉ0 प्रभा खेतान, पृष्ठ संख्या-45

7. स्त्रीः उपेक्षिता (सीमोन द बोउवार की विश्व चर्चित कृत्ति-सकेण्ड सेक्स का हिन्दी रूपान्तर) प्रस्तुति- डॉ0 प्रभा खेतान, पृष्ठ संख्या-54

8. स्त्रीः उपेक्षिता (सीमोन द बोउवार की विश्व चर्चित कृत्ति-सकेण्ड सेक्स का हिन्दी रूपान्तर) प्रस्तुति- डॉ0 प्रभा खेतान, पृष्ठ संख्या-66

9. स्त्रीः उपेक्षिता (सीमोन द बोउवार की विश्व चर्चित कृत्ति-सकेण्ड सेक्स का हिन्दी रूपान्तर) प्रस्तुति- डॉ0 प्रभा खेतान, पृष्ठ संख्या-67

10. स्त्रीः उपेक्षिता (सीमोन द बोउवार की विश्व चर्चित कृत्ति-सकेण्ड सेक्स का हिन्दी रूपान्तर) प्रस्तुति- डॉ0 प्रभा खेतान, पृष्ठ संख्या-68

11. स्त्रीः उपेक्षिता (सीमोन द बोउवार की विश्व चर्चित कृत्ति-सकेण्ड सेक्स का हिन्दी रूपान्तर) प्रस्तुति- डॉ0 प्रभा खेतान, पृष्ठ संख्या-70

12. स्त्रीः उपेक्षिता (सीमोन द बोउवार की विश्व चर्चित कृत्ति-सकेण्ड सेक्स का हिन्दी रूपान्तर) प्रस्तुति- डॉ0 प्रभा खेतान, पृष्ठ संख्या-71

13. खन्ना जी0वी0 उम0 उ0 वर्गीय- इंडियन वीमेन, विकास, नई दिल्ली

14. बिहार में पंचायती राज व्यवस्था- डॉ0 खगेन्द्व कुमार

15. अवस्थी, इंदिरा (1982)- रूरल वीमेंस इन इंडिया, सोशियो-इकोनॉमिक प्रोफाइल

16. खन्ना जी0वी0 उम0 उ0 वर्गीय- इंडियन वीमेन, विकास, नई दिल्ली

40

महिलाओं के सामाजिक एवं राजनैतिक नेतृत्व की दशायें एवं दिशायें

उषा चौधरी

किसी भी समाज का स्वरूप वहाँ की नारी की स्थिति पर निर्भर करती है। यदि उनकी स्थिति मजबूत और सम्मानजनक है तो समाज भी सशक्त और मजबूत होगा। यदि यही शक्ति शोषित और पीड़ित हो तो हम कैसे आगे बढ़ सकते हैं? यह विडम्बना ही है कि आज इक्कीसवीं सदी में भी महिलाओं को अपने अस्तित्व की रक्षा के लिए तथा अपने ही गर्भ में स्थान पाने के लिए संघर्ष करना पड़ रहा है, उन्हें वैचारिक आधार पर सबला के रूप में स्वीकारने और सामाजिक धरातल पर शोषण का प्रतिकार करने की ताकत जुटानी पड़ रही है। चारों ओर अँधेरा है- हम लड़कियाँ हैं, हम औरत है, क्या करें? कहाँ जाएँ? हमारा भविष्य क्या है? यहाँ तक कि स्त्रियों के प्रति नकारात्मक विचार धारा एक हिन्दी के प्रतिष्ठित कवि रघुवीर सहाय जी ने लिखा है कि,

''पढ़िए गीता बनिए सीता
फिर उन सबमें लगा पलीता
किसी मूर्ख की बन परिणीता,
निज घर-बार बसाइए।''

लोग कहते है कि स्त्रियों के प्रति अत्याचार की बातों को बहुत बढ़ा-चढ़ाकर कहा-लिखा जाता है। शायद हमारे न्यायकर्त्ताओं को भी यहीं सच लगता हो, तभी

तो आज तक हर दिन दहेज के लिए औरतें मारी जाती हैं और अपराधियों को सजा भी नही मिलती। भँवरीबाई, मैससेसे पुरस्कार पाने वालो के बलात्कारी, बाइज्जत रिहा कर दिया जाता है। आज भी गाँवों, छोटे कस्बों में उन पर होने वाले अत्याचारों की संख्या बढ़ रही है।

लेकिन क्या स्थिति सचमुच बहुत निराशाजनक है? नही! आज इक्कीसवीं सदी में हमारा देश भारत विकासशील देशों की श्रेणी में खड़ा है तथा इसकी हर क्षेत्रों में विकास करने की कोशिश भी जारी है। अपने देश द्वारा हर क्षेत्र में महिलाओं को विकास की ओर ले जाने का कार्य भी सराहनीय है। समाज में महिलाओं को प्राप्त स्थान सामाजिक विकास के स्तर को दर्शाता है। हाल ही की जनसंख्या रिपोर्ट में बताया गया है कि महिलाओं में साक्षरता बढ़ी है। ''नेशनल कमीशन फॉर वुमैन'' की रिर्पोट में कहा गया है कि नौकरी करने वाली स्त्रियों की संख्या लगातार बढ़ रही है। औरतों के विकास से सम्बंधित संयुक्त राष्ट्र के संगठन यूनिफेम ने दुनिया की स्त्रियों की प्रगति रिपोर्ट 2000 जारी की है। इसमें बताया गया है कि स्त्रियों की आर्थिक प्रगति की जानकारी, उनके निर्णयकारी पदों पर बैठे होने और पुरूषों के मुकाबले उनकी आय से भी जानी जा सकती है। जैसे कि कितनी स्त्रियाँ रोजगार पाने की क्षमता रखती हैं या स्वयं रोजगार कर रही है। सन् 1990 में नौकरी करने वाली स्त्रियों की संख्या 28 देशों में 30 प्रतिशत या इस से अधिक थी। सन् 1980 के मुताबिक 59 में से 51 देशों में प्रशासनिक और प्रबंधन के क्षेत्रों में स्त्रियों की संख्या बढ़ी है। सन् 1990 में ही 16 देशों में 30 प्रतिशत या इससे अधिक महिलाएँ उच्च पदों पर कार्य कर रही है।

अब स्त्रियों को यह समझ में आ गया है कि जब तक उनकी आर्थिक स्थिति नही सुधरती तब तक उनका विकास नहीं हो सकता। क्योंकि विश्व के 98 प्रतिशत संसाधनों पर पुरूषों का कब्जा है। इसलिए अब स्त्रियाँ वितीय बाजार में होने वाले परिवत्तनों में दिलचस्पी लेने लगी है। उन्हें अपने अनुकूल बनाने की कोशिश कर रही हैं। राष्ट्रीय अन्तराष्ट्रीय स्तर पर ऐसी आर्थिक नीतियाँ बनवाने में प्रमुख भूमिका अदा कर रही हैं जो स्त्री समर्थक हो। साथ ही ग्लोबलाइजेशन के इस दौर में अधिक मानवीय हो। बदलती तकनीक से स्त्रियाँ डरने के मुकाबले उसमें अधिक से अधिक दक्ष होने की कोशिश कर रही हैं।

सिंगापुर की ''यूनिफेम नेशनल कमेटी'' ने एक इक्विटी फंड बनाया है जो स्त्रियों के इस तरह ''एमपावरमेंट कार्यक्रमों'' के प्रचार में मदद करेगा। थोड़े ही समय में यह राशि 2 करोड़ डॉलर तक जा पहुँची ब्राजील सम्मेलन और हाल में ही

न्यूयॉर्क में हुए बीजिंग +5 सम्मेलन ने स्त्रियों को नई पहचान दी है। स्त्रियों को आत्मनिर्भर होना चाहिए। यह बात कम से कम अब महानगरों में सर्वमान्य हो चली है। महिला संगठनों, एन0 जी0 ओ0, नाटकों, पत्रकारिता ने स्त्री के पक्ष में माहौल बनाया है। जो फिल्में कभी कुटती-पिटती स्त्री को आदर्श रूप में प्रस्तुत करती थी वे "एमपावरमेंट ऑफ वुमेन" को सफलता का अचूक नुस्खा मानने लगी है। सारे दल स्त्रियों से तरह-तरह के वायदे करने लगे हैं। महिला आरक्षण के मुद्दे पर सभी दलों के सांसदों ने इस के समर्थन में जोरदार आवाज उठाई। यह एक महत्वपूर्ण पहल थी। दूसरी तरफ जो पुरूष नेता महिला सशक्तिकरण की बात कर रहे थे, उन्हें लगता है कि यदि वास्तव में 33 प्रतिशत स्त्रियाँ संसद में आ गई तो वे सब मिलकर सरकार बना लेगी। तब उनका क्या होगा? इसलिए वे आरक्षण की मांग का मजाक उड़ाने लगे।

राजनैतिक परिदृश्य में महिलाओं के भारतीय आजादी के आन्दोलन में क्रातिकारी वीरांगनाओं का इतिहास भी काफी समृद्ध रहा है। आजादी के संघर्ष में महिलाओं ने बढ़-चढ़कर हिस्सा लिया। मैडम भीकाजी कामा ने सन् 1907 में जर्मनी में हुए अन्र्तराष्ट्रीय समाजवादी सम्मेलन में भारत का प्रथम राष्ट्रध्वज फहराया/नोनबाला, सरला देवी चौधरी, प्रीतिलता, कल्पना दत्त, उज्जवला मजूमदार, दुर्गा भाभी, सुशीला देवी आदि न जाने कितनी महिलाएँ थी जिन्होंने, अंग्रेजों के विरूद्ध खुलकर संघर्ष किया। यही नहीं भारत भर की महिलाओं के लिए एक संगठन बनाने की पहल 1910-20 में ही होने लगी। सन् 1926 में अखिल भारतीय महिला सम्मेलन बना। सरोजनी नायडू महिला अधिकारों की प्रबल पक्षधर थीं। गाँधीजी भी समाज में महिलाओं के उच्च स्थान के पक्षधर थे। कस्तुरबा गाँधी, राजकुमारी अमृत कौर, कमला देवी चट्टोपाध्याय, अनसूया साराभाई, आदि भी महिलाओं के उत्थान के लिए कार्य करती रहीं। उत्तरं प्रदेश का "चिपको आन्दोलन" या कर्नाटक के "अपिक्को आन्दोलन" में महिलाओं ने बढ़ चढ़कर हिस्सेदारी की। नर्मदा बचाओं या शराब बंदी आन्दोलन भी महिलाओं की अगुआई में ही शुरू हुई। अम्मनबाई ने हिन्दु-मुस्लिम एकता की बात जोर-शोर से कही उनका कहना था कि हिन्दु-मुसलमानों के आपस में विवाह होने चाहिए तभी साम्प्रदायिकता की समस्या सुलझ सकती है। सन् 1942 के भारत छोड़ो आन्दोलन में मातंगिनी हाजरा को अंग्रेजों ने गोली से उड़ा दिया। सन् 1928-29 में शाखा बिल के समर्थन में बहुत सी महिलाएँ थी। कमला देवी चटटोपाध्याय का मानना था कि महिला संबंधी मुद्दों को निडरता से उठाया जाना चाहिए। आजादी के बाद हिन्दु कोड बिल पारित होने पर हिन्दु

समाज में बहुपत्नी प्रथा पर प्रतिबंध लगा दिया गया। बाल विवाह पर रोक लगा दी गई। विवाह की न्यूनतम उम्र बढ़ा दी गई। सन् 1961 में दहेज का लेना और देना रोक दिया गया।

अपनी इसी शक्ति को पहचान से वंचित और पिछड़े वर्ग से आने वाली महिलाओं ने जब शिक्षा की मशाल जलाई तो इसकी रोशनी ने महिला सशक्तीकरण की नई इबारत लिख दी।

"हटा दो सब बाधाएँ मेरे पथ की,
मिटा दो आशंकाए सब मन की,
जमाने को बदलने की शक्ति को समझो,
कदम से कदम मिला के चलने तो दो मुझको"

भारत के आन्दोलन की पड़ताल करते हुए सन् 1947 में पेशावर में वोट के अधिकार के लिए बड़ी संख्या में मुसलमान स्त्रियाँ जमा हो गयी थी। इन्हीं स्त्रियों ने संविधान में स्त्रियों को पुरूषों के बराबर अधिकार दिलवा दिए। महाराष्ट्र का मूल्य विरोधी आन्दोलन गुजरात का सेवा तथा नव निर्माण आन्दोलन और 60 के दशक के अंतिम दिनों में शुरू हुआ शाहदामील आन्दोलन के साथ स्त्री आन्दोलन को अधिक बल तब मिला जब स्त्री आन्दोलन एवं दलित आन्दोलन एक छतरी के नीचे आ गए। यह सब ऐतिहासिक घटनायें महिलाओं के सामाजिक एवं राजनैतिक नेतृत्व की दिशायें तय करती हुई आगे बढ़ती गई। पिछले कुछ दशक में महिलाओं में राजनैतिक चेतना का संचार ज्यादा हुआ है। आज यही वजह है कि वे चुनाव लड़ रही हैं और मतदान करने भी जा रही हैं।

महिलाओं में राजनैतिक चेतना लगातार बढ़ रही है बेशक महिलाओं के लिए संसद में 30 प्रतिशत आरक्षण की बात अभी पूरी न हुई हो, लेकिन महिलाएँ चुनाव लड़ रही हैं। उन्हें यह समझ में आ गया है कि महिलाओं को अपने वोट का सही इस्तेमाल करना चाहिए और उन्हें अपनी राजनीतिक भागीदारी क्रमशः बढ़ानी चाहिए। यह आकरण नही है कि चुनावों में खड़ी होने वाली महिलाओं को मिलने वाले वोटो में लगातार वृद्धि हुआ है। उनके वोट बटोरने का आकड़ा बढ़ा है। यह बात भी सामने आ रही है कि अब महिलाएँ स्वयं सत्ता में भागीदारी चाहती हैं। आँकडें भी इस बात की गवाही देते हैं। बिहार में हुए पंचायत चुनाव में बड़ी संख्या में महिलाओं की जीत भी यही दर्शाती है।

बिहार में 1999 के लोकसभा चुनाव में 20 महिलाएँ उम्मीदवार थी जिनमें 5 ने चुनाव जीता था। दूसरी ओर 2004 के चुनाव में 12 महिलाओं ने चुनाव लड़ा

था जिनमें तीन लोकसभा में पहुँच पायी थी। उधर दिल्ली में 1999 में 7 लोकसभा सीटो के लिए 7 महिलाओं ने चुनाव लड़ा था, जबकि 2004 में यह संख्या 15 तक पहुँच गई। यही चडीगढ़ में हुआ और 1999 के चुनाओं में एक महिला के लड़ने के मुकाबले 2004 में 3 महिलाओं ने चुनाव लड़ा। लेकिन अफसोस यही है कि मेट्रो शहरों जैसे चडीगढ़, मद्रास, मुंबई, कोलकता और दिल्ली में महिला उम्मीदवारों की जीत नहीं मिल पाई। लेकिन इसका एक सकारात्मक पक्ष यह है कि अब महिलाएँ घर की चाहरदीवारी से बाहर निकलकर राजनीतिक गलियारों में शिरकत करने की सोचने लगी हैं। 2004 और 1999 के आकड़ों पर नजर डाले तो दिल्ली में 7 सीटों के लिए 15 महिलाओं ने ताल ठोकी थी। लेकिन, जीती सिर्फ एक महिला। 2004 के आम चुनाव में कुल 35 महिलायें ही जीत कर संसद पहुँची, जबकि 1999 में 49 महिलाएं जीती थी। 2004 में महिलाएँ भले ही कम जीती हो लेकिन इसमें एक सकारात्मक बात यही रही है कि इनमें वोट देने वालों की संख्या में बहुत वृद्धि हुई है। इसका अर्थ यह है कि वोटर महिला उम्मीदवारों को पसंद कर रहे हैं। 1999 के मुकाबले 2004 में महिलाओं ने 50 लाख ज्यादा वोट बटोरे, जिसे आने वाले लोकसभा चुनावों में एक शुभ संकेत माना जा सकता है।

पंचायतों में महिलाओं की भागीदारी

कुल संख्या	-	*महिलाएँ*
मुखिया-8468		3784
ग्राम पंचायत-115876		54260
सरपंच-8463		4013
पंच-115878		54448
पंचायत समिति-11566		5371
प्रमुख-531		233
जिप सदस्य-1162		568
जिप अध्यक्ष-36		18

आज महिलाओं ने पंचायतों तक को भी बदल दिया है। आंगन की दहलीज पर जैसे ही उनके पांव पंचायत तक पहुँचे मानो, सब कुछ बदल गया। आज बिहार को आधी पंचायतों पर महिलाओं का कब्जा है। महिला मुखिया यदि बच्चियों के साथ होने वाले अन्याय के खिलाफ जागरूक है तो महिला सरपंच

पुलिस से भी भिड़ जा रही है। इसका असर ऐसा पड़ रहा है कि गाँवों का माहौल भी अब बदल रहा है। घुंघट में छिपी रहने वाली महिलाएँ अफसरों से नजर मिलाकर बात कर रही हैं तो अनपढ़ पंचायत प्रतिनिधि- बी0डी0ओ0 के ऑफिस में घूसकर विकास के कागज मांगती है। घरेलू हिंसा से लेकर शराब के खिलाफ उनकी आवाज गूँज रही है। बिहार के कुल 2 लाख 61 हजार 975 पंचायत जन प्रतिनिधियों में महिलाओं की संख्या 1 लाख 22 हजार 695 है। यह स्थिति पंचायत चुनावों में महिलाओं को मिले 50 प्रतिशत आरक्षण का ही असर है।

अपनी आजादी के लिए जागरूक महिलाएँ, बच्चों परिवारों और समुदायों की आजादी के लिए भी अपनी आवाज उठा रही है। इसलिए महिला आन्दोलन सिर्फ महिलाओं के लिए ही नहीं है। भारतीय महिला आन्दोलन ने तो दुनिया भर में अपनी खास पहचान बनाई है। दलित, श्रमिक, किसान, शहरी-ग्रामीण मध्यवर्गीय सभी तबकों की महिलाएँ इसमें शामिल है।

लोकसभा में स्त्रियों के प्रतिशत को लेकर आठ देशों- स्वीडन, डेनमार्क, फिनलैंड, नार्वे, आइसलैंड, नीदरलैंड, जर्मनी और दक्षिण अफ्रीका में 30 या उससे अधिक प्रतिशत का लक्ष्य प्राप्त कर लिया गया है। इन देशों में माध्यमिक स्कूलों में लड़कियों की शिक्षा और गैर कृर्षि क्षेत्रों में, उनके रोजगार में भी वृद्धि हुई है। जबकि यह प्रतिशत भारत में सिर्फ 8.9 प्रतिशत, पाकिस्तान और भूटान में 2 प्रतिशत, नेपाल में 6.8 प्रतिशत है। बंगला देश इसमें सबसे आगे है। वहाँ 9.1 प्रतिशत औरतें संसद में है। पिछले दिनों 33 प्रतिशत आरक्षण को लेकर हमारे राजनेताओं ने जो हाहाकर किया था उसे देखते हुए यह कहा नहीं जा सकता है कि हमारे यहाँ यह प्रतिशत कब पुरा होगा। हम चाहे खुद पर कितना भी गर्व करें लड़कियों की शिक्षा के क्षेत्र में श्रीलंका, और संसद में स्त्रियों की संख्या में बांग्लादेश सबसे आगे है।

भारत के संविधान में आज महिलाओं को बराबरी का दर्जा दिया गया है। आज महिलाएँ हर क्षेत्र में चाहे शिक्षा हो, राजनैतिक भागीदारी की बात हो, या अंतरिक्ष तक पहुँचने की बात हो चाहे प्रशासनिक प्रबंधन का क्षेत्र हो, यहाँ तक कि महिलाओं ने देश के सर्वोच्च राजनैतिक पद प्रधान मंत्री के पद पर "श्रीमती इंदिरा गाँधी" एवं कई राज्यों में मुख्यमंत्री पद पर जैसे दिल्ली में "श्रीमती शीला दीक्षित" तीन बार लगातार सत्ता संभालने में विजय पायी। त्रृणमूल कांग्रेस की सुश्री "ममता बैर्नजी", बिहार में श्रीमती "राबड़ी देवी" उत्तर प्रदेश में बहुजन समाज पार्टी से आन्दोलित "सुश्री मायावती" अपनी कर्त्तव्य को बखूबी निभायी

है। वर्त्तमान मे देश की प्रथम नागरिक यानी की राष्ट्रपति के पद पर भी "श्रीमती प्रतिभा पाटिल" अपना परचम लहरा रही है।

सन् 1975 में ही संयुक्त राष्ट्र में अन्तराष्ट्रीय महिला वर्ष या इंटरनेशनल वुमन ईयर मनाया गया था। महिला वर्ष की घोषणा के बाद भारत में पार्लियामेंट में उन्हें 33 प्रतिशत आरक्षण दिया जाए और वे पूर्ण बहुमत में हो इस पर लगभग सभी महिला संगठन, स्त्रियों के लिए काम करने वाली अन्य संस्थाएँ एकमत हैं। सन् 1971 में श्रीमती इंदिरा गाँधी के शासनकाल में पहली बार एक कमेटी का भी गठन किया गया था जिसे भारत की स्त्रियों के हालात का जायजा लेना था। इस रिर्पोट में बताया गया था कि स्त्रियों के विकास में यदि कोई बात सबसे अधिक बाधक है तो वे है हमारी रूढ़िया, परम्परा, रीति-रिवाज।

भारतीय राजनीति में महिलाएँ हमेशा से ही प्रभावशाली भूमिका में रही है। इन्दिरा गाँधी के रूप में देश को पहली महिला प्रधानमंत्री देने वाली भारतीय राजनीति में इस समय भी दर्जन भर महिलाएँ विभिन्न पार्टियों में महत्वपूर्ण मुकाम पर है। यह बात दुसरी है कि ये महिलाएँ शक्ति का प्रतीक या महिला सशक्तीकरण का जरिया नहीं बन सकी हैं। अभी वे राजनीतिक रूप से इतनी ताकतवर भी नहीं बन सकीं हैं कि संसद और विधायिकाओं में महिलाओं के लिए 33 प्रतिशत आरक्षण का विधेयक भी पारित करवा सके।

आज की राजनैतिक परिदृष्य में महिलाओं की स्थानीय निकायें त्रिस्तरीय पंचायतों में एक तिहाई आरक्षण मिलने से राजनैतिक सहभागिता में इनकी भागीदारी पुष्ट हुई है लेकिन ये प्रर्याप्त नहीं है। वर्तमान समय में भारतीय राजनैतिक व्यवस्था में महिलाओं की भागीदारी सुनिश्चित करने के लिए प्रयास तो किया जा रहा है परन्तु इस दिशा में ईमानदारी से कोई भी राजनैतिक दल आगे आने के लिए तैयार नहीं दिखती है। इसलिए राजनैतिक दृष्टिकोण से उनका सशक्तिकरण नही के बराबर हुआ है। पंचायती राज संस्थाओं में महिला आरक्षण के कारण बुनियादी स्तर पर महिलाओं की संख्या में वृद्धि तो हुई है लेकिन संसद, राज्य विधान सभाओं, केन्द्रीय एवं राज्यों के मंत्रिपरिषदों में उनकी संख्या अभी भी नगण्य है। अतः महिलाएँ राजनैतिक दृष्टिकोण से अभी भी 50 वर्ष पहले वाली स्थिति में ही है। इसलिए जरूरत है महिलाओं की राजनैतिक नेतृत्व की भागीदारी बढ़ाने की ताकि हमारे देश में नारी अपने बजूद के साथ-साथ देश की राजनैतिक दशा एवं दिशा को भी परिवर्त्तित कर सकें।

Brief Proceedings of the UGC National Seminar on "Dimensions of Women Political Leadership" held during 24-25 February, 2009 at R.N. College, Hajipur.

Brief Proceedings

The U.G.C. national seminar on "Dimensions of Women Political Leadership" was held during 24-25 February, 2009 at R.N. College, Hajipur. The entire proceedings of the seminar was split into 7 Sessions including inaugural and valedictory sessions. All the five technical sessions were divided on the basis of the sub themes of the seminar and concerned papers were presented there in, session wise proceedings are being noted hereunder in brief.

Day 1: 24 February, 2009

Time 11.30 A.M. - 12.30 P.M.

Inaugural Session 11.30 A.M.

The inaugural session was presided over by Dr. Nand Kumr Yadav, Pro-V.C., B.R.A. Bihar University, Muzaffarpur.

After inauguration by lighting lamp, Dr. S.P. Sinha, Principal of R.N.College, Hajipur welcomed the Chief Guest, Guests of Honour resource persons and participatants. In his welcome address, he highlighted the significance of the topic and said that it was high time to discuss various dimensions of women political leadership (WPL) in India in general and in Bihar in particular. He referred that Vaishali, being the birth place of democracy since ancient period, has also been famous for women's elegance. He further promised to render support to the teachers of the college to take up such kind of ventures.

The seminar was inaugurated by the Chief Guest Hon'ble Sri Ram Vilas Paswan, Minister Chemical & Fertilizers and Steel, Government of India, New Delhi. In his inaugural speech, Sri Paswan opined that a women have acquired top position more in Asian Countries than western world. But not proportionate with their population. He hoped that national consensus on women's reservation bill would be created by him and people in other political parties. He appealed women to become 'self assertive' for acquiring leadership in politics. He lamented that there has been changes in ideas, social beliefs and conditions but women's situation remains stagnant in terms of their political participation and leadership. He argued that there factors responsible for this situation are male's attitude, lack of education, lack of awareness among them and social inequality. He believed that if women become assertive men can not be hindrance or obstacle. Symbolic acquisition of power position as a few of women cannot be termed as 'empowered' – mass level participation was significant, he said –

In his inaugural address, Sri Paswan hailed the Indian democracy and said that women have been facilitated to acquire top political positions more in Asian countries than that of western world. On the issue of reservation of seats for women in national and state legislatures, he hoped that all the political parties will come to a consensus on the problem and women would be given reservation. He further suggested women to assert for the political leadership because he believed that women are initiated in politics for reasons like nations of patriarchal dominance, lack of education and awareness among them. He appealed women to be assertive, only then male bastion will be broken. He warned further that women of weaker sections like SC women can not be deprived of becoming part of decision making process of the country. They should not be contented with some elite women acquiring top positions in political power structure.

After inaugural address Dr. Archana Kumari the Organising Secretary introduced the topic and major hunches of the topic that prompted the organization of the Seminar. In her introductory address Dr. A. Kumari emphasized the assumption that the only way out for emancipation of women (from age old subjudation, deprivation and oppression) is their assured say and their share in decision making process and political power structure. In this context she referred western feminist scholars and views of National Commission for women of India. She further underlined that introduction of new arrangements of Panchayat Raj Institutions and Urban Local Bodies have opened the vista for women's entry into political leadership in a wide range. Introducing large number of women in one go will naturally lead to a lot of less active and less assertive nature of the women leadership. On the other hand voluntary organizations have made attempt to make women and other weaker sections aware of their political rights and their roles in administering the development at the local level.

She emphasized that there is need to sensitize women for self assertive roles in a sustained way. This would be only possible life the situation of social capital created or occurred among 'women actors'. In this process she underlined the tenets of concepts like political leadership, social capital, voluntarism and women political empowerment. Dr. Kumari pointed out that power (capacity to influence), formal position and support of the mass are the vital components of political leadership which can be efficiently achieved by practice of social capital. Social capital in turn as a situation in which actors have trust, network and shared objectives to act upon or to resist against the oppressor. She referred the works of Robert Putnam and some Indian scholars like Blomkvist Swain etc. She said that voluntarism does only not deliver in the development work but also in enhancing awareness and political participation among weaker sections, like women. To Dr. Kumari women empowerment has three basic components namely - freedom, enabling and control and political empowerment is necessarily concerned with those three components in political areas. She wished the seminar to discuss these conceptual issues for theorisation of various dimensions of women political leadership.

She enumerated the three major dimensions which need thread bare discussion namely - pattern of emergence and changing nature and expected as well as legitimate roles of women political leadership in both the micro and macro level perspectives. She said that expert views in more depth was to follow in the key note address.

Professor Sushma Yadav, Dr. Ambedkar Chair on social Justice, Indian Institute of Public Administration, New Delhi in her key note address dwelt upon the theoretical aspects of dimensions of women political leadership. On the basis of approaches to the leadership studies, she opined that leadership has three basic components-power position, legitimate roles and influenced followership. She urged that gender differences in effectivity of leadership was an important issue for discussion as there has been increasing presence of women in leadership roles in various walks of life. Referming a host of researches, she posited that women's styles tend to be more transformational. Discussing the various dimensions of women political leadership, she threw light on leadership effectiveness, glass ceiling for women leaders particularly in laddering up the rank owing to lack of human capital, gender-based differences and societal prejudices. She further discussed the issues related to breaking the 'glass ceiling'. She advocated that Indian women have abilities to overcome those hurdles. She further threw light on the historical perspectives of women political leaders and reasons of their rise. There has been trend of rising women leadership in the recent past at grassroots level but not in the legislatures. Finally she wished that issues regarding development of self-assertion among women for leadership roles in political sphere are seriously discussed. Women have been able enough to break the glass ceiling. She referred the dimensions mentioned by Organizing Secretary which were in her views, most urgent issues for discussion. Further she expressed her good wishes for successful discussion in the two-days long seminar.

Prof. Upendra Mishra of Deptt. of Pol. Sc., B.R.A.B.U. in his address as Guest of Honour, discussed the women political leadership at grassroots level. He mentioned that the new panchayat raj arrangements has instilled confidence among women in rural areas and coined it as a silent revolution in favour of women. He said that this new development has improved even SC/ST women to the level of the stake holders in the local governance. By rise of women leadership at grassroots level politics, the governance has becomes participatory, transparent, responsive and accountable which are the major components of good governance. In short, women political leadership working in active and effective way could make the governance 'good'.

Prof. Srivastava, the Registrar of the B.R.A. Bihar University, Muzaffarpur delivering his speech as Guest of Honour discussed about the attitude of males towards women empowerment and political leadership which according to him was hostile to women's rising roles. Though men, pointing out the dileman, he said that encourage women in general but discourage and check them at their formly level to take up roles in social domain. He thanked the organizing secretary for having taken up this venture of organizing national seminar. To him this was a sign of rising leadership qualities in women.

In his presidential address, Prof. Nand Kumar Yadav 'Indu' Pro-V.C., B.R.A. Bihar University congratulated the Principal Dr. S.P. Sinha and the organizing secretary for having organized U.G.C. national seminar for the first time in the College. He showed his agreement on the views of Hon'ble Ram Vilash Paswan on the hopes that weaker sections of women would assert themselves by their own in times to come. He said that time was ripe that women were able enough to take-up roles in political field. He further said that it was the men who started feminist movement and many Indian reformers and statesmen led women to prosperity and enabled them to take part in public affairs. Mahatma Gandhi brought the women out from walls though teaching in schools. Later he enumerated the issues discussed in inaugural session namely - self assertion, dismissing proxy leadership, social capital among women, fast evolution of women political leadership at grassroots level, glass ceiling owing to inadequate investment in human capital for women, gender biased differences and societal prejudices, breaking the glass ceiling and male's attitude towards women. He said that women teachers of his university have shown their capabilities of leadership. He said that university will render all possible help to the College for such academic activities.

Dr. Sanjeev Kumar Sharma, of CCS University, Meerut and Editor Indian Journal of Political Science, in his brief speech said that women leadership had not been a rare phenomenon in Indian Culture but a rich heritage of women were found in political roles. India have had brilliant women leaders. He suggested the participants to discuss knowledgeable and substantial which will enrich and develop Political Science in India. One should avoid repeating the oft said issues. He assured that he would discuss later the situation of Political Science in different parts of India in technical sessions.

Finally Dr. R.K. Verma of R.N. College, Hajipur delivered the vote of thanks. In his address Dr. Verma wished that women political leadership would be theorized in the discussions of the forth coming two days discussions.

Day-1: 24 February 2009

Technical Session-I (Theoretical Aspects)

Time: 12.30 PM - 2.15 PM

Eight papers were presented in the Technical Session - '1' which was presided over by Dr Sushma Yadav, Professor, Dr Ambedkar Chair of Social Justice, I I P A, New Delhi. Dr Vijay Kumar, University Professor, T M Bhagalpur University, Bhagalpur and Dr Sudhir Kumar Singh, Reader and Head, East and South East Asian Studies, Rajiv Gandhi University, Itanagar (Arunachal Pradesh) were the Discussants. Dr R K Verma was the Rapporteur of the session.

The paper on *"Omni-relevant but Dysfunctional Women Political Leadership at the Apex in Inida"* by **Dr L N Sharma,** University

Professor and Head Department of Political Science, Patna University (Retd) was received but he was not available for presentation for unavoidable reason.

First of all **Dr R K Verma** of R N College, Hajipur presented his paper on "*Social Capital, Voluntarism and Democratic Consolidation: A Review in Context of Women Political Leadership*". With a view to discuss women political leadership in its various dimensions, Dr Verma wished to review these concepts. Referring to Robert Putnam and some other Indian scholars, he briefly described 'social capital' as a situation in which women actors have to develop trust, networking and objectives interse where as voluntarism tends to compensate the deprivation, subjugation and oppression of a social class (women) by human impulse to serve the society. It aims at also creating awareness among weaker sections for political participation. Referring to Juan Linz, O'Donnel and Mainwaring, he described democratic consolidation as pattern of government. He enumerated the three basic components of democratic consolidation - (i) Legitimacy of practices and institutions, besides people's participation and liberties and acceptable modes of transfer of power with harmonious social order, (ii) democratic institutions reconciliatory to diverse societal interest and demands and (iii) people and political leaders use democratic methods in formation of stable government. Interlinking these concepts in context of treating women political leadership, Dr Verma summed up, "women's equal partnership in power sharing, decision making process and political participation is pre-requisite of democratic consolidation. This partnership can be assured only with creation of social capital among women themselves and in turn it can be achieved through voluntary efforts that will sensitize them into political roles from bottom up. The entire process will facilitate political recruitment and emergence of women political leadership from common category of women (mass women) and self-assertive participation among them." Finally, he wished women to join political leadership themselves neither by induction nor in proxy. **Certain clarifications** were sought from among the participants that were responded by Dr Verma. Dr Sanjeev Kumar Sharma of C C S University, Meerut (UP) **raised question** that the concepts of social capital and democratic consolidation were not exactly meant for women leadership in its emergence and role dimensions. Dr Verma responding to his query said that the spirit of these two concepts lies in the weaker sections of a given society and the women still fall in the category of weak and deprived section of a society. There is a need to make them assertive for their political rights and leadership roles for achieving the goal of consolidation of democracy.

Dr Manjari Verma presented the paper entitled *"Social Capital and Women's Political Leadership"* written by **Ms Sonal Shree**, Regional Manager, HR of HR Galaxy, Uttranchal and UP in her absence. It was posited that social capital encompasses the network fabric of social system and the credibility and norms of reciprocacity associated with it, which has two facets, one that could cover involvement with personal net work and the other, the professional and public one. The paper further argues that strong social networks can help advance women's careeer through their ability to exploit the system of contacts. Hence the impact of information technology (I T) will be friendly on the situation of social capital among women. The social capital makes women grow high in terms of political participation and roles of representation of constituents. She posits that despite low level of social capital among women, some women at macro level and a large number at micro level politics emerged as leader resulting into proxy leadership phenomenon. She however added that social capital is no guarantee of facilitating leadership emergence rather role of political parties and other societal organizations do have impact on it. She finally advocated that social capital is a kind of 'investment' that bridges the gaps between divergent interests. **Reacting** on the paper Dr Verma supported the position by his observation that social capital can be created not only 'intra-segment' rather 'inter-segment' and it is most suitable for a highly segmented society like India.

In his paper on *"The Myth of Gender Equity: Why are women Missing from Politics"* **Dr. N S Kotvi**, Research Officer and Editor, Vidhanmala (a quarterly journal of Himachal Pradesh Legislature, Shimla, HP) discussed the conceptual tenets of gender equity and argued that it was a matter of individuality vs. groupism. To him dilemma lies in the fact that 'though individual women have been participating essentially in all spheres of human activities, yet as a group they have been not so. They are identified with particular roles ascribed by society like mothering children, handling household affairs and serving their male counterparts. Responsibilities and power are two areas that men dominate in political sphere. Kotvi finds that all the hue and cry for gender equity is false and it is a myth in India so far political parties at macro level is concerned. The participants discussed the issue but they place factual arguments. Dr Archana Kumari **commented** that gender equality is a different connotation than the gender equity. She further argued that equity refers to both the equality and justice that Indian society denies in context of political leadership and roles especially at macro level.

Dr Subhash Chandra Roy, Assistant Professor, Chanakya National Law University, Patna in his paper on *"Gender Justice and Social Democracy"* dwelt upon the theoretical aspects of gender justice and opined that it is 'mantra' to protect women of their basic human rights in order to enable them to participate actively in family, society and nation. He enumerated the areas of gender justice namely, education, right to life, political rights and gender budgeting. They should be privileged as they interface the greatest risk in human reproductive system. Dr Verma added that equity combined the equality and justice, hence protective discrimination is essential for them.

Kumar Rakesh Ranjan, a research scholar of Patna University dwelt up on the qualities of a leader and significance of leadership for social and political change. His paper entitled, *"Rajnitik Netritva: Ek Sukshma Adhayayan"* centered on the concept of leadership in terms of salient features and significance. He termed leadership as an instrument of social and political change. Any society needs a disciplined power in order to achieve its goal which is provided by leadership. He enumerated sixteen qualities of a political leader that he should possess to sustain leadership. A great deal of discussions was held. Dr Verma **refuted** his position and said that these qualities are presented by psychologists mainly proponents of 'trait theory' of leadership, who never talked of political leadership. He further suggested consulting the work of Jean Blondel and R C Tucker for better understanding on the political leadership phenomenon.

Mona Tabassum of P G Department of Psychology, R N College, in her paper on *"Psychodynamics of Women Political Leadership"*, posited that women political leadership is a phenomenon related to mental makeup. She lamented that in societies having patriarchal dominance like India women are psychologically subjugated from very childhood and inhibited to take part in social domain. Despite having all qualities and positive attitude towards multiple roles, women are being deprived of taking part in decision-making process and political participation by the societal norms of patriarchal dominance. Hence the term 'women political leadership' should be discussed, revised and theorized under the backdrop of their psychological make up engrained in their mind. Many participants

opposed her position and arguments were placed that women are being made enable to take roles. Dr S P Sinha, Principal of R N College said that now males should not always be blamed for their psyche. Women have unique features and they have to bear greatest risks and responsibilities in the entire human reproductive system. So they are less enthused to take up political roles. Various politico-legal arrangements have been made in favour of women but they are themselves not willing to exploit them. In response, Dr Tabassum said that women should be given proper training of leadership roles, regarded in decision making both at family level and socio-political levels, facilitated to assert for exercising equal political and legal rights.

Professor N K P Singh, Head Department of Political Science, R N College, Hajipur in his paper entitled, "*Mahilaon Ke Rajnitik Netritwa Mein Badhayen*" enumerated the inhibiting factors of women political leadership in world. He pointed out that there is need to theorize the impediments of women political leadership. To him, international bodies propagate their rights through covenants on one hand and do not allow women to avail them on the other. The main cause of their backwardness in political arena is their invisibility in the economic order. Economic strength can make them enable to come into power positions. However, he quickly added that politico-legal arrangements especially the new panchayat raj and nagar panchayat arrangements have paved way for the women. He further suggested that these politico-legal arrangements should not only aim at providing equality but women should be considered as an effective instrument of development.

Dr K H Siddiqui, Department of Political Science, R N College, Hajipur in his paper entitled, "Women Political Leadership in India: An Analysis of Non-dynastic Paths to Power" hypothesized that women has begun to assume more leadership positions in last two decades. This development has brought a change in pattern of emergence of women political leadership i.e. from dynastic to alternative paths. The reason, to him, is the rise of regional parties and growing consciousness among the women, particularly in assuming roles in social and political domain. He argued that now women are acquiring power not from dynastic paths rather from alternative and legitimized paths. Theorisation on this line should be done in context of emergence of women political leadership. Clarifications were sought from the participants. Dr Sudhir Kumar Singh, **showed agreement** with the dogma but questioned the use of terminology. Referring the earlier studies, he said that the emergence of leadership in a democratic set up changes from kinship type to ascriptive or self-assertive types owing to rise of grassroots political leadership from compulsory provisions. Dynastic type of women leadership cannot be find in India as it has been experiencing democracy since 1930s. The paper of Dr C D Amar discussed gender discrimination in political leadership.

In her presidential address, **Prof Sushma Yadav** said that rigorous treatment towards theorization of women political leadership is still required. She further enumerated the issues emerged in the session. Those are (i) theorization of women political leadership in three dimensions namely emergence, nature and roles, (ii) social capital linked in a comprehensive way with recruitment and development of women political leadership, (iii) dealing consolidation of democracy in context of women political leadership and (iv) psychological aspects be made part and parcel of political leadership. She suggested the paper presenters to revise their write up in the light of the discussion before publication. She was of view that situations - political, legal, social and economic - have so emerged that women need only to assert their roles and exercise their political rights.

Dr Navanit Sinha of I I PA Bihar Regional Branch delivered the vote of thanks to the participants and resource persons for having come to the remotely situated College.

Day-1: 24 February 2009

Technical Session–II (Women Political Empowerment)

Time: 3.00 PM - 5.15 PM

Dr Sanjeev Kumar Sharma of Choudhary Charan Singh University, Merrut (UP), presided over the Technical Session II. Professor B P Singh of Vinoba Bhawe University, Hajaribagh (Jharkhand) and Dr Sudhir Kumar Singh of R G University, Itanagar (Arunachal Pradesh) were the Discussants. Dr. Indira Kumari of P G Department of Political Science, College of Commerce, Patna was the Rapporteur in the session. Large numbers of papers were received falling under this theme and several of presented papers had similar connotations. Thus, it is needless to discuss them all.

Dr Manjari Verma, Reader in Political Science, L S College, Muzaffarpur presenting her paper entitled, "Women and Political Empowerment" posited that the theme is on the global agenda evident from the fact that UN had taken the issue of Political Rights of Women in 1952 itself and World Plan of Action took up the issue in 1975. Later in 1980 in Copenhagen world leaders desired women's participation in promoting international cooperation and peace and in 1997 the UN Commission on Status of Women emphasized to assure equal share to women in decision-making process. Referring the steps taken in post independence period in India, she mentioned the setting up of the Committee on the status of women in India in 1971 was aimed at looking into the greater representation of women in political institutions. After lapse of two decades, the political actors ventured to bring the issue on political agenda in shape of bill of reservation of seats for women in Parliament and state legislatures in 1995 on one hand and flouted the passage of the bill on the other. She expressed happiness on the reservation of seats for women in local self-governments and hailed Nitish Kumar the CM of Bihar for having provided fifty per cent reservation for women in PRIs and ULBs. She opined that women political empowerment must be visible at macro level. Referring report of Rajasthan's Geeta Sharma, she posited that many underlying hurdles like male dominance from background in decision-making, failure to understand technical aspects of budget etc inhibit them to come up. Finally, she suggested creating a meaningful space for women in decentralized governance and access of women to all agencies, institutions and processes of governance. For this women should be given education and training in latest information technology as tool of political empowerment which would help them performing in social and political advocacy, strengthen their participation in political process, improving performance of elected women and enabling them to utilize indigenous knowledge for development of the society. Reacting on her paper **Dr Archana Kumari** raised the question as to who would give education and training to women. Is it government or voluntary organizations or political parties or pressure groups? This should be made clear. To her government has no business to educate and train them for political participation. She further observed that social capital should be created among women through voluntary efforts and civil society. She suggested that women political empowerment can be better assured if adolescent girls are trained and educated in the right unrest.

Dr Madhu Singh of RBBM College, Muzaffarpur in her paper entitled, "Women's Political Empowerment in India" discussed the sad plight of lesser participation of women and blamed the male dominance in different walks of life for flouting the women reservation bill in legislative houses. She further argued that women still cannot articulate strongly their views so to him political representation alone could not be sufficient mechanism for women to exercise their leadership. They needed knowledge, information, and influence on decision-making processes. She suggested strengthening women leadership by promoting opportunities for systematic learning to provide them a curriculum for political empowerment and self-development. She further suggested that women leadership and empowerment could be made more effective, if the male elected representatives, officials, family members as well as other elder women were made aware of gender issues. She advocated that reservation of women bill for legislative bodies should be passed as early as possible unless the situation would be more worsened. **Dr Mona Tabassum** of R N College expressed agreement with her position but raised doubt that all her suggestions were not feasible to be implemented some concrete suggestions should be given. The psychological aspects of women personality was very important to be considered for which no law, no government or international agencies might come to their rescue.

Dr Suman Sinha, Lecturer in English, R N College, Hajipur presented paper on "Political Awareness and Women Empowerment". She advocated that political awareness among women was essential for safeguarding their rights and promoting their status. She opined that despite several measures and constitutional provisions, they are still kept at bay. She said that women political leadership in India has proved their capability of quality leadership. She further emphasized that for political awareness and empowerment of women education should be universalizing among them. **Rupashree Jamuar,** Lecturer in Psychology of the same College in her paper on "Women Empowerment Through Education" said that empowerment refers to empowerment of women in the fields of education, economic and political activities, social and psychological status, this would enable them to break the shackles of male bastion. She suggested that recognizing women's contributions to the society, imparting knowledge and skill, instilling in them self-esteem and self-confidence, providing opportunities and making them able to have control over resources and ideas. The papers of **Dr Binda Kumari,** Reader and Head, Department of Political Science, Women's College, Samastipur entitled, "Mahila Shashaktikaran: Chunautiyan Evam Sambhawanayen" and **Dr Sita Sinha,** Lecturer in Political Science, S M D College Punpun, Patna entitled, "Mahila Shashaktikaran Evam Gramin Bharat" were received but they could not present.

In his paper entitled, "Mahila Shashktikaran: Ek Vaishwik Dristi", **Dr Pramod Kumar Dubey,** Head Department of Political Science, SMD College, Punpun presented the worldview of the situation of women political empowerment. He articulated that women empowerment refers to accruing benefits of authority and control on their life, awareness of rights, self-confidence, access to resources and control over the resources. He said that 20th century was characterized by growth of women empowerment and nearly 95% of countries have given equal political rights to women. But the situation of women in the political field have not been satisfactory evident from the fact that the number of women parliamentarians in all countries except Norway, Sweden, Denmark, Finland etc has been very low, however, he found that situation of women empowerment is better among democratic countries but political empowerment has not been satisfactory.

Prof H C Yadav, Head, Department of Political Science, Dr Ram Manohar Lohiya College, Muzaffarpur in his paper on "Mahilaon Mein Rajnitik Shashktikarn Evam Rajniti Mein Netritva Padon Par Unki Bhagidari" posited that women political empowerment has gained momentum owing to introduction of reservation of seats for them in Panchayati Raj Institutions and Urbal Local Bodies. This situation has mounted presser on leaders to introduce reservation for them in legislative houses. **Dr Shakil Ashraf** of SNSRKS College, Saharsa in his paper on "Rajniti aur Prashashan Mein Mahilayen" argued that despite several attempts women's enthusiasm, women have not been provided adequate share in politics and administration. He assessed the situation by the facts as lesser women provided space in important positions in politics and political institutions and less number of women given candidature by political parties in general elections. So far their share in administrative posts is concerned women have not been provided with chance to work as Chief Secretary, Principal Secretary, Home Secretary, Accountant General, Election Commissioner and Judges. He suggested providing 50% share in all formal positions at political and administrative levels. **Several of participants** refuted his position. It was largely argued that on the administrative posts, they are given chances as per seniority or tern. Besides several research scholars of different universities of Bihar presented their papers on the same theme.

Dr Prassanta, Education Product Manager, Mac Millan Publishers India Ltd, Patna in her paper, "Gender Biased Politics" on the thwarted women reservation bill, ironically commented, 'the ugly scenes and stalemate over tabling the Women's Reservation Bill in Parliament have had a very beneficial effect'. This has finally the grim truth into sharper focus that politics has proven to be very inhospitable form women in independent India evident from the fact that very thin percentage of women are found in Indian Politics. She concluded that the political empowerment of women not still has a long way to go but finally may not have to do with the periodic carnivals of India electoral democracy. Electoral representation of women needs to be both deeper and wider than its current manifestation in the fomr of the prominence of a few conspicuous women leaders.

Ms Bahalen Horo, Marwadi College (Boys Section), Ranchi University, Ranchi traced the model women political leaders in Indian history right from Rani Durgawati, Rani Lakshmibai to Sonia Gandhi. She said that Indian women are politically empowered evident from the fact that women political leaders have proved their leadership qualities inside and outside politics. She named a few prominent women politicians of today like Mayawati, Mamta Banerjee, Rabri Devi, Dayamani Barla, Medha Patekar and the Indian President Pratibha Devi Singh Patil who have inspired women from mass into political roles. She hoped that women would be empowered by their own consciousness.

In his presidential address lamented that the speakers repeated arguments, which inhibits discussions. He suggested to be substantial, brief and contributing a new thing. He enumerated the major issues emerged in the deliberations of the seminar. Those were - Gender biased role of male political actors at global level, Education and Training for political empowerment, Impact and Legitimacy of reservation for women, Impact of reservation at grassroots level political institutions, Psychological Factors, Social factors and share in administrative positions.

The Principal of the College, **Dr S P Sinha**, delivered vote of Thanks.

Day-1: 24 February 2009

Technical Session-III (WPL at Macro Level)

Time: 3.00 PM - 5.15 PM

The Technical Session - III was run simultaneously with Technical Session II. It was presided over by Professor Sushma Yadav of I I P A, New Delhi and Professor Vijay Kumar of T M Bhagalpur University, Bhagalpur and Professor N K P Singh of R N College,

Hajipur were the Discussants. Dr K H Siddiqui, R N College, Hajipur was the Rapporteur of the session.

More than a dozen of papers were presented in this session on the issue of macro level women political leadership in context of share in power structure and influencing factors. Some significant of them are illustrated hereunder. **Professor Baleshwar Prasad Singh** of Vinoba Bhawe University, Hajaribagh (Jharkhand) in his paper entitled, *"Social Texture and Women Political Leadership in India"* defined politics as inter-personal, inter-group and intra-group power relationship influencing decision making and their implementation. He advocated that women's participation in decision-making process is essential in view of the goal of fighting out gender-based discrimination and women's interest being taken into account by the entire polity. He lamented that despite tremendous democratic developments and introduction of information technology as well as globalization, women have still been put into the dockyard of the society due to severely hostile patriarchal values evident from the fact that they could never acquire even ten percent of the total strength of Parliament and any of the state Assemblies. He further lamented that none of the political parties in India have taken pain to press for reservation of thirty per cent of seats for women in the legislative bodies of India. Emphasizing the dearth of their presence in legislative bodies, he presented the worldview and said that merely 10.5 per cent of the seats in all parliaments of the world and 24 women so far have acquired headship of the government in the world. England and France have had only one woman as Prime Minister and U S has never paved way to any women to its presidential office in more than two hundred years. For this sad plight, he held that women empowerment was the pre-requisite for broadening the spectrum of women political leadership. He opined that women would gradually grow self assertive for political leadership roles. In course of time, they would come up from grassroots level for which the politico legal arrangements have already been made. Agreeing with the propositions of Prof Singh **Prof Vijay Kumar** of Bhagalpur University said that women have been struggling hard for power in India. He further observed that women have been fighting for right to franchise well before India became independent since 1930s. He asked, what long should we wait? We should not keep waiting rather allow women to break the shackles of patriarchal dominance, particularly in political sphere.

In his paper on, *"Women's Struggle for Power in India: Efforts and Achievements"* **Dr Vijay Kumar**, University Professor of T M Bhagalpur University argued that there has always been exceptional women in Indian politics since centuries but their real struggle began in 1930s. It was then the nationalists, British officials debated the women's right to vote, and as a result, four million women out of 30 million total voters exercised their right to vote in the provincial assembly elections. Since then women's presence were felt in the nationalist struggles like civil disobedience and other peaceful modes of struggle for independence. He opined that the notion of reservation for women has persisted constantly in overt and subtle way. To him this 'percent solutions' to women candidates in legislative contests mooted by the Congress party and in efforts to increase their participation in local government institutions points to the assertion of political power an struggle for space by the Indian women in political field. Assessing the struggle in last six decades, he concluded that male dominated Indian society has put them in existential arena.

In her paper entitled, "Women's Share in Power Structure: A Study of Macro Level Political Institutions" **Dr Henna Tabassum**, HOD Department of Sociology, A N College, Patna referred the poor representation of women in power structure at macro level political institutions and political party organizations and opined that they are kept limited to 'Women Cells'. She posited that the situation has improved in last two decades particularly in terms of quality of their participation in decision-making process despite quantitatively lesser strength. She suggested that it would be an urgent imperative to underline the changes taken place in situation of patterns of women political and mark the changes in social texture of women political leadership at macro level. She concluded that the women from lower strata of Indian society have entered substantially into power structure and macro level politics since 1990. She suggested that for making women deliver substantial roles there is need of improving their quality of life in terms of social, economic and educational development.

Dr Arjun Sharma, Department of Political Science, SMD College, Punpun, Patna (under Magadh University) in his paper entitled, *"Representation of Women in Indian Parliament: A Study of Changing Dimensions of Political Leadership"* opined that change in terms of education and employment opportunities would necessarily percolate into the political spheres. Discussing the poor representation of women from 1st to 14th Lok Sabhas, he said that the reservation of seats for women in local bodies would open opportunities for more women coming into fray for their presence in Indian Parliament and their effective participation. Discussing the recommendations of Geeta Mukherjee Committee formed in 1996 he hailed that it had recommended to include one woman nominated against two seats of Anglo Indian community in the Lok Sabha. He was very much optimistic about increase in women's share in Indian representative houses in times to come. The reason behind it has been the space created for them in the Panchayat Raj Institutions and Urban Local Bodies. He further argued that the reservation of seats for women in Indian legislatures could not be enacted due to ideological differences among various political parties. **Dr R K Verma** observed that Sharma's presentation did not underline the changing dimensions. The hypothetical propositions could not be considered as a researched finding. He further observed that discussion of Mukherjee committee recommendations do not support Sharma's position. Besides, the participants sought various clarifications. Sharma responded to the queries and hunches.

Dr Kumari Saroj of MDDM College Muzaffarpur in her paper entitled, *"Obstacles in the Path of Women Political Empowerment at Macro Level in India"* discussed the situation in which women's reservation bills brought with enthusiasm in Parliament since 12th Lok Sabha unsuccessfully as 81st, 84th, 85th and 108th constitutional amendments. She lamented those macro level politicians watered down the very purpose by sending it to Parliamentary Standing Committee. She also mentioned the arguments placed by different political parties justifying their respective stands. Finally, she concluded that no other measure had raised so many fundamental questions about the nature and composition of our society that hampered promotion of citizenship and equality. She lamented that the stalemate proves that gender has become legitimate as political category, it remained less legitimate than caste, class and tribe and the cross currents delineated above made it passage difficult.

The paper entitled "Swekshabad Tatha Mahilaon Ka Rajnitik Netritwa" written jointly by **Dr Sayed Shahnawaz Ajmeri and Irshad Ali** was presented by Ajmeri. He examined the macro-level women leadership in India in historical perspective and posited that women have been playing political roles and holding powerful positions in India. He gave the instance of Sonia Gandhi for having control over government of India as woman but lamented that very few (countable on finger tips) women make way to Parliament and state legislatures. In order to overcome this malady, he suggested that steps should be taken in regard to improve education, health, vibrant panchayat institutions and activeness of women at social level. He further suggested to mark the obstacles in the way of development of women political leadership.

The politico-legal arrangements in context of increasing the participation of women in political leadership were discussed by four presentations. Paper on "Mahila Netritwa Hetu Arakshan Ek Sashakt Madhayam" by **Dr Mukul Roy and A Hasan**, "Mahila Arakshan Ki Rajniti" by **Dr Prem Singh** and "Mahilaon Ke Liye Kanuni Prawdhan" by **Gita Sinha** were discussed in the session. Dr Mukul Roy advocated in favour of women reservation without which to him women political leadership at macro level will not grow. Dr Prem Singh favoured the arguments of political parties seeking quota within quota. Dr Gita Sinha argued that all the legal provisions in shape of laws in favour of women become ineffective owing to social taboos, inadequate education among women, hence reservation of seats for women in Indian legislatures required urgent attention. Other participants in their presentations presented similar views. **Gazanfar Alam,** Research Scholar of Patna Unvierstiy examined the politico-legal arrangement in favour of owmen's empowerment from sociological angle in his paper on *"Mahila Sashaktikaran-Rajnaitik-Vaidhanik Prawadhan: Ek Samajshastriye. Samiksha"*

Professor Sushma Yadav in her presidential address emphasized that women of lower strata of our society would definitely come into political arena at macro level and source would be the grassroots democracy. She, on the basis of discussion in the session, opined that women political leadership would more vibrant in the near future. She further enumerated the issues emerged in the session. Those were - gradual evolution of women leadership, efforts and achievements, enhancing quality of life for increased participation by women in political, positive changes in women political leadership at macro level, roles of political actors, legitimacy of gender considerations, historical inheritance, effectiveness of politico legal arrangements and reservation provisions.

Dr N K P Singh delivered the vote of thanks.

Day-2: 25th February 2009

Technical Session - IV ((WPL at Micro-Level)

Time: 10.00 AM - 12.15 PM

The Technical Session - IV was presided over by Professor Sushma Yadav of I I P A, New Delhi and Professor B P Singh of V B University, Hajaribagh (Jh) and Professor S. P. Sinha, Principal, R N College, Hajipur were the Discussants. Dr Shefali Roy, Department of Political Science, Patna Women's College, Patna University, Patna was the Rapporteur of the session.

In this session, the micro-level women political leadership was discussed. Women Political Leadership in panchayat raj institutions (PRIs), urban local bodies (ULBs), educational institutions, rural areas outside the political institutions and environmental movements were discussed in this session. Details of some representative papers are given hereunder.

The paper jointly written by **Dr Rajesh Kumar**, Asstt Professor and Anand Kumar, Lecturer of S D Institute of Technology and Management, Israna (Haryana) entitled, *"Women Leadership in Technical Institutions: A Case Study of S D I T M, Israna"* was presented by Dr Rajesh Kumar. He posited that teaching of science and technological subjects did not mean only crude learning of subject matter rather it involved various human activities also. These required leadership and women did play leadership roles. He added that concept of political leadership went with the assumption that leading activity necessarily include exercise of power and influence over the led. Based on examination of the cases of women leadership roles in extra-curricular and sports activities and imparting training in the studied technical Institute, Dr Kumar found that factors like age, experience and family background had very less impact on the leadership roles and exercise of power. It was the energy delivered and commitment to achieve the given objectives that had impact on performance of leading women in the Institute. He said that most of the leading women were form the young age group and service family background. They delivered leadership roles and exercised power over the students and the staff with firm commitment and showed deep interest in the tasks to be got performed from the led community (mainly students). It was found that commitment to the goal, mutual trust, networking and the shared objectives were the main factors of their successful leadership roles. Besides, personal qualities, working environment and power positions and support of the led community are influencing factors of leadership emergence. Various clarifications were sought from the participants. **Dr Shefali Roy** asked as to what was the link between women political leadership and roles delivered by the women faculty members leading students in sports and extra curricular activities. Dr Kumar responded that he was not a political scientist but he knew that power and influence constitute the political leadership. So the women faculty members exercising power and influence were the political leaders. He referred the introductory speech of the Organising Secretary Dr Archana Kumari delivered in the inaugural session.

Professor Upendra Mishra of B R A Bihar University, in his paper on "Emerging Pattern of Women's Political Leadership at Grassroots Level in India", posited that women after having been marginalized for a long period, they are given chances in PRIs and ULBs. They are now being brought to the forefront through their involvement in the decision-making process in local self-governments. But quickly lamented that the ideal of strong, truly representative and responsive PRIs was still a distant dream, however, on should be optimistic that silent revolution had already begun. He also hailed that politico-legal arrangements for women in local bodies have paved way for the women of the most downtrodden section of the society, the SC and ST women whose entrance have been assured. **Dr N K P Singh**, reacting on the paper, pined out the self-contradictory statement of Prof Mishra in his presentation including that of presented in inaugural session. The truly representative PRIs was said as a distant dream on one hand and raised high hopes from the same institutions. How can it be true? Prof Mishra said that what ever the situation of PRIs was, it was clear that these institutions have paved way to women political leadership and in due course the situation would improve.

Dr Kumari Manju, Department of Economics, R N College, Hajipur in her presentation on the topic, "Social Justice and Emergence of Women Political Leadership" posited that leadership is an evolutionary issue as advocated by Karl Marx. So the endeavours to establish social justice in India, particularly after 'Mandalization of Politics' have paved way for evolution of women political leadership. She referred the ideas of Ram Manohar Lohia and Dr B R Ambedkar and Seligman of Columbia. She emphasized that in the process of upheaval in social settings, legal suggestions, political and apolitical institutions and the circumstances created a crisis that gave rise to women political leadership. Dr Kumar Amrendra Narain of R N College, Hajipur raised questions and argued that the 'Mandalisation of Politics' was not a phenomenon of evolution of women political leadership but a phenomenon of rise of political leadership among the OBCs and Extremely Backward Castes, so far Bihar and UP were concerned. Women did not come on the forefront.

Dr Poonam Kumari of Patna Women's College, Patna in her presentation on *"Rajnitik Sahbhagita: Mahila Vikas Ki Kosishen"* said that if women could be self-assertive they could be in political leadership. She opined that three major components were necessary for women political empowerment - equality with men, development of their own abilities and right to decision making. Women political participation and their share in decision-making process have been facilitated by introduction of new arrangements of PRIs and ULBs, poverty alleviation programmes and programmes of food and health, to her, the improvement was not enough. So she said that there was need of emphasizing improvement in the situation of education, health, their substantial participation in local bodies. **Dr Anil Kumar Singh** of A B S College, Lalganj, in his paper, *"Panchayat Mein Netritwatmak Bhumika"* posited that women in macro level politics were found more effective but not at micro level. He referred the studies of Nelson and O R G Marg.who held the opinion that the participation of women particularly of BPL and SC /ST categories have been assured through local bodies and the influence of feudal and vested interests have been checked. Hence, women empowerment has been improving by their leadership roles in PRIs and ULBs. He argued that women cannot be empowered only with political empowerment rather they need to be empowered in social and economic fields.

Dr Naresh Kumar of Department of Political Science, B R A Bihar University, Muzaffarpur said in his paper, *"Bharat Mein Panchayati Raj Sansthaon Mein Mahila Ke Netritwa Ka Vikas: Mahila Shashktikaran Ka Ek Prayas"* that equal participation of men and women was the sign of a healthy society so they should have equal opportunity in educational, economic and political spheres. He posited that development of women leadership in local bodies could be taken as indicator of women political empowerment. Questions were raised by participants particularly by Dr K H Siddiqui on the issue that women political empowerment encompass two basic components–political participation and leadership roles - that refers to political empowerment as pre-requisite to political leadership whereas Dr Kumar had reverse proposition.

Dr Kumar Amrendra Narain of Economics Department, R N College, Hajipur in his paper entitled, *"Self Assertive Women Leadership Among Scheduled Castes: A Study of Jehanabad District, Bihar"* posited on the basis of empirical findings in Jehanabad district of Bihar that a new trend, in recent past, had emerged. In which the deprived sections came up to assert for their rights and reddressal of their grievances. The district's mainstay of economy is agriculture and most of the SC women are engaged in agricultural labour. To him, these women agriculture labourers were politically more assertive evident from the fact that in last eight years some SC women (case studies of few women political activists) joined panchayat election fray as candidates despite having been prevented by their family members and in one case one such woman did not care when her husband divorced her. He further informed that they participated well in the meetings of the panchayat bodies at village level. He concluded that their assertiveness was **not** attributed to education, awareness and democratization rather than it was **to resist** against the oppression and atrocities by the traditional dominants of the locality. The PRIs provided this opportunity to them to assert their roles and resistance. Dr S P Sinha reacting to the proposition said that if it was lack of education then it might be that their awareness level was high without which assertion and participation was not possible. He suggested Dr Narain to study the issue deeply and rigorously.

Dr Kamal Prasad Baudh, Principal Nalanda Teachers Training College, Nalanda, Biharsharif , in his paper "Bhartiye Mahilaon Ki Rajnaitik Sthiti Ke Vividh Ayam" enumerated the indicators of assessing the political situation of women namely their participation in elections, representation in state legislatures and organizations in political parties.

Those who presented paper on this theme were Dr Nutan Kumari, Research Scholar Magadh University, Bodh Gaya, Dr Mukesh Kumar Ray, PGT B N Collegiate School, Patna, Dr Sudhir Kumar, Department of Hindi, BRA Bihar Universtiy, Muzaffarpur, Priti Kumari PGT Baldeo Inter College, Dinapur and Kabita Kumari Rsearch Scholar, Sanskrit Department, Patna University, Patna and Amit Vikram, Research Scholar, Department of Political Science, Patna University, Patna

In her presidential address Prof Sushma Yadav summed up the views presented in the Session and said that it was micro level politics where women were found more visible, assertive, active and enthused. She said that women would asset to come up for leadership roles for their real say in politics. This would in turn make them visible at macro level politics. **Dr Kr Amrendra Narain of R N College** delivered the **vote of thanks**.

Day-2: 25th February 2009

Technical Session–V ((WPL in Bihar and Miscellaneous Issues)

Time: 12.30 PM - 2.30 PM

The Technical Session V was presided over by Professor Baleshwar Prasad Singh of V B University, Hajaribagh (Jharkhand). Dr Sushma Yadav of I I P A and Dr Manju Kumari of Department of Psycholgy, R N College, Hajipur were the Discussants and Dr Madhu Prabha Singh, Y N College, Dighwara (JPUniversity, Chapra) was the Rapporteur of the session.

Dr Shefali Roy, Department of Political Science, Patna Women's College, Patna University, Patna in her power point presentation on "Electoral Violence Hindering Women's Political Participation" dwelt up on the theoretical aspects of political participation and posited that political participation depends upon awareness, attitude and environment. Discussing the lesser degree of participation, she argued that causes were apathy, alienation, monopoly of masculine politics, weak and depended character of women and most important criminalisation of politics. She discussed the extent of electoral violence in Bihar with the help of data on violence and causalities during elections. She further presented the government's futile efforts of checking violence during polls and post election violence. To her the entire situation hindered women to encourage them into politics and the main reason behind it was the women's ignorance of political system and their political rights. She suggested that they should be made aware of politico-legal arrangements particularly laws made in their favour, society should come up to overcome the social evil like dowry, domestic violence, training programme should be arranged for specially women, mass and media should join the venture and of course the strict mechanism of conducting elections. Finally, she said that women should be instilled confidence and courage for political roles.

Dr Indira Sinha of College of Commerce, Patna in her paper on "Role of Women in Ecological Development" maintained that the environmental degradation affected women in tribal areas who depended on forests. Referring Himalayan hills of U P people collectively rose to defend local interest against the felling of trees.

In this context she mentioned the environmental movements like Chipko movement, Appiko movement etc which involved women. Women's involvement in these movements drew inspiration for others. Women are transforming the environmental issues into political ecology and pressing policy makers for the eco-friendly changes. **Dr Asha Rani** of G J College, Bihta, presented similar views.

Dr Pawan Kumar Yadav of R N College, Hajipur in his paper entitled, "women Political Leadership in Bihar: A Study of Inhibiting Factors and Prospects" lamenting on the poor plight of women's share in power structure and legislatures said that those women who got into politics were having little interest in legislative business. Discussing the reasons behind the sad plight of women in Bihar politics, he enumerated the inhibiting factors namely, their placement at weakest point in our society, over patronization of women by their male counterparts, electoral violence and malpractices, ineffective in political party organizations, socially backward women humiliated and abused and so on so forth. He went to suggest that dalit women are coming up fast for their rights but their livelihood requirements hinder them to do so. However, Dr yadav showed hopes that NGOs could play significant role in making them assertive for political roles in various ways and participatory governmental organizations have paved way for their improvement , establishment of increasing communication net works would come to their rescue.

Dr Manju Kumari of R N College Hajipur in her paper entitled, "Intergroup conflicts and inequality: Challenges For Women in Bihar" presented that inter group conflicts in our society had made women apathetic to the poltical roles. She mentioned various parameters of women empowerment in Bihar which was marred by the inter-group conflicts. She suggested further that free and compulsory education to women at least upto secondary levels, change in teachers' attitude, increasing the number of female teachers in schools, employers should apply fair and transparent methods of recruitment and women themselves would have to be self-assertive. **Monawwar Jahan**, Principal Women's Training College, Patna in her paper discussed the political empowerment of women in Bihar was encouraged by the reservation of seats for women in local bodies like PRIs and ULBs. **Dr Rakesh Ranjan** of Patna University depicted the challenges and prospects. Other participants discussed those. **Ambuj Kumar and Anju Sadhna** PGT B N Collegiate School (Bihar Mein Ubharata Mahila Netritwa),

Amrendra Kuamr Gond and Shashank Kumar both research scholars of Patna Unviersity (Bihar Mein Mahila Shashaktikaran Evam Panchayati Raj), **Bipin Chandra**, Research Scholar Department of History, PU, Patna Unviersity (Bihar Ki Panchayati Raj Vyawastha Mein Dalit Mahilaon ki Sahabhagita), **Sudhir Kumar** (Dimensions of Women Political Leadership) and many other also spoke on the issue.

Dr Usha Choudhary of Psychology Department, R N College, Hajipur presented paper on "Mahilaon Ke Rajnitik Netritwa Ki Dishayen" and traced the history of women's role in politics. She informed that women's organized movement was first started in 1920s and even Muslim women came out for political roles in 1947 in shape of agitating for voting rights. She lamented that the situation of women's political movement diminished after independence when democratic experiences were on peak. But again their entrance in to the local political institutions have paved way for them.

Many persons from the field of literature spoke on the issue of women political empowerment and leadership. **Mr Vinay Kumar**, Reader in English, R N College, Hajipur spoke on women's empowerment and referred the legends of English Literature. **Sudhir Kumar** of Hindi Department of BRABU, Muzaffarpur said that women had great role in creating history evident from the historical facts and Hindi literature. **Dr Kumar Rajani Kant Ranjan** Head, Department of Hindi R N College, Hajipur in his paper traced the marked the better and respectable situation of women in Jaishankar Prasad's literature. **Dr Kavita Kumari Singh** of the same Department found that women had to play roles in national political mainstream as revealed in literature of Subhadra Kumari Chauhan. She traced that women in her literature took part in agitations, resisting the oppressor ruler, foundation of parliament and dutifulness of citizens. **Dr Madhu Prabha Singh** of Y N College, Dighwara in her paper entitled, "Mahila Rajnitik Pratinidhitwa: Sahitya Ke Jharokhe Se" said that it was Hindi literature that painted the ugly picture of women getting into political arena by referring novel of Maitripusha. Besides she pointed out that terminology like petticoat government, jananaraj, lugairaj etc were being use in the literature that marginalize their enthusiasm and also that in Hindi literature proxy or patronized women leadership had been glorified not condemned. **Md Irshad Ali and Md Irshad Khan** both UGC NET research scholars of Patna University spoke on sociological aspects of killing of female foetus. **Dr Shailendra Mandal** of N I T, Patna presented his paper on "Modernisation, Uurbanization and Women's Political participation"

In his presidential address Prof B P Singh summarized the presentations and said that the session was full of variety of subject matters focusing Bihar. He further praised the participants for having presented mosaic views of women political roles and leadership drawn from and based on experiences and literature. Dr Suman Kumari of English Department of the College delivered the vote of thanks to the participants of the session.

Day-2: 25th February 2009

Valedictory Session

Time: 3.00 PM - 4.30 PM

Dr Sardar Deo Nandan Singh, retired Professor of Sociology, Patna University and former Chairman, Bihar State University Service Commission was the Chief Guest in the Valedictory Session which was presided over by Dr Ram Swari Devi, former Principal, Vaishali Mahila College, Hajipur.

Dr S P Sinha, Principal of R N College, Hajipur in his welcome address congratulated the Organising Secretary Dr Archana Kumari and other members of Organising Committee for having successfully conducted the two days long deliberations in the various sessions. He expressed gratitude to Dr Singh and Dr Devi for gracing their presence in the valedictory session. He further expressed hopes that the outcome of the seminar would be beneficial to the society especially women, teachers and the students. Dr Sinha accredited the learned participants and Resource Persons who had come across different parts of the country for the success of the seminar. He further thanked them for having traveled long and laboured hard for this venture.

After the welcome speech, **Dr K H Siddiqui, Dr Indira Sinha, Dr Shefali Roy, Dr Madhu Prabha Singh and Dr R K Verma** presented the Rapporteurs' reports of the technical sessions. Dr Verma emphasized the issues that emerged during the discussions. Those were - revision of concepts in male-female dichotomy, participation of elite women vs mass women, impact of patriarchal norms and psycho-physical texture, social classes, social capital and voluntarism and violence as inhibiting factor. He said these issues require rigorous treatment through researches.

The Chief Guest **Prof Singh**, in his address, dwelt upon the issues of women leadership from sociological angle. He opined that our social setting itself inhibited women entering into politics. He added that the phenomenon of 'proxy women leadership' was also the outcome of our societal and patriarchal norms, perpetuated through institutionalized methods. He pointed out that there has been graded inequality among the women themselves based on caste, class and social status. He gave various instances like women in family, society and politics hindered other women to play effective roles.

The President requested Dr Archana Kumari to present the recommendations of the Seminar for the approval of the House.

Recommendations of Seminar

Dr Archana Kumari in capacity of the Organising Secretary said although the conclusions were drawn in the respective technical sessions, it was essential to present them in capsule form:

Issues Emerged for Further Research Considerations

1. Theorisation of various dimensions of Women Political Leadership (herein after WPL) in context of Indian socio-political milieu
2. Interaction of theories like Social Capital, Voluntarism and Democratic Consolidation in context of WPL
3. Macro level WPL vs Micro level WPL
4. Self assertive vs Proxy WPL
5. Political Participation vs Political Empowerment
6. Kinship vs Ascriptive (laddering up through roles) modes of emergence of WPL
7. Roles in environmental protection breeds WPL
8. Actual impact of politico-legal arrangements on WPL
9. Violence and Structure of women's psyche as inhibiting factor

Strategies Recommended

She said that based on rigorous discussions in context of above issues in different sessions following strategies should be taken into considerations in right earnest:

(a) In context of theorization of the dimensions of WPL, following areas should be focused
   - (i) WPL in context of Democratic Consolidation
   - (ii) Self-assertive leadership in context of Social Capital
   - (iii) Voluntarism in context of Social Capital and Political Participation

(b) Political empowerment is the pre-requisite for political recruitment of women at grassroots level
(c) Education, feeling of dignity and interest in public affairs are the essential requirements for political empowerment and WPL
(d) Encouraging voluntary action and roles of civil society
(e) Environmental protection should be in the priority list of the political agenda
(f) Protective discrimination for women at levels of political institutions
(g) Strengthening psyche of women from childhood for equal status
(h) Instilling self-respect and self-confidence among women
(i) Reviewing the patriarchal norms in changing scenario like IT revolution, globalization, emergence of knowledge based society and new social movements
(j) Economic independence in all terms (earning, spending and saving)
(k) Women should be organized and take up action in groups like-women's organizations, voluntary organizations, pressure groups and political parties etc
(l) Women should resist violence instead of staying back out of fear

Dr Kumari sought the opinion of the House on the above issues and the recommendations. The House applauded and unanimously approved the recommendations.

In her presidential address, **Dr Ram Sawari Devi** congratulated the Organizing Secretary Dr Archana Kumari for having dared to organize a national seminar in a situation of patriarchal dominance and that too despite being a woman. She appreciated the issues emerged and recommendations made out of the discussions in the seminar. She said that the issues were of very high order and represent deep insight into the concepts and practice of the Women Political Leadership. She expressed thankfulness to the Principal of the College for being generous to invite her and supported a woman for such a kind of venture.

Dr Navanit Sinha, Hony Secretary of Indian Institute of Public Administration Bihar Regional Branch, Patna delivered the vote of thanks on behalf of the I I P A Branch. He expressed pleasure for the reason that he had very nice experience and time for last two days in the College and with the faculty members. He said that he was thankful to the Principal, College teachers, staff, and participants because the seminar served the cause and objectives of the I I P A. He also said he had the pride for having Dr Archana Kumari and Dr R K Verma as active office bearers of the Branch. He assured to render all kinds of cooperation in such kind of ventures of the College in future also.

Professor B N Jha of Chemistry Department, R N College, Hajipur delivered the vote of thanks on behalf of the Principal, teachers and office staff of the College.

Finally, the two days long seminar was declared over

Bibliography

Agarwal, Sushila (ed) (1988), *Status of Women,* Jaipur, Paintwell.

Agnew, Vijay (1979), *Elite Women in Indian Politics,* Vikash Publishing House, New Delhi.

Aiyar, Mani Shankar (2008), 'Status of Panchayats: The Journey Thus Far", *Inclusion,* March.

Andrew Stephen Reynolds (1999), "Women in the Legislatures of Executives of the World; Knocking of the Highest Glass Ceiling", *World Politics,* Vol. 51, No. 4, July, pp. 547-570.

Andrews, P. H. (1992), "Sex and Gender Differences in Group Communication: Impact on The Facilitation Process", *Small Group Research,* 23(I).

Asthana, P. (1974), *Women's Movement in India,* Vikas, Delhi.

Attekar, A. S., *The Position of Women in Hindu Civilization,* K. P. Jaisawal Research Institute, Patna.

Bartol, K. M. & Butterfiled, D. A. (1976), Sex Effects in Evaluating Leaders, *Journal of Applied Psychology,* 61, pp. 446-454.

Basu, D.D. (1997), *Introduction to Constitution of India,* Prentice Hall of Indian Pvt. Ltd., New Delhi.

Biernat, M. and Wortman,C. B. (1991), "Sharing of Home Responsibilities Between Professionally Employed Women and their Husbands", *Journal of Personality and Social Psychology,* 60, pp. 844-860.

Biyi, M. R. (2008), "Women's Political Empowerment: Imperatives and Imperilments", *South Asian Journal of Socio-Political Studies,* Jan.-June.

Book, E. W. (2000), *Why the Best Man for the Job is a Woman,* New Delhi, Harper Collins.

Bowman, G., Worthy, N. and Greyser, S. (1965), *Are Women Executives' People?* Harvard Business Review, 43(4), 14-28,164-178.

Browne, K. (2002), *Biology of Work: Rethinking Sexual Equality,* New Brunswick, Rutgers University Press, NJ.

Brysan, Valerie (1999), *Feminist Debater; Issue of Theory and Practice,* Macmillan, Hong Kond.

Burgess, D. and Borgida, E. (1999), "Who Women are who Women should be: Descriptive and Perceptive Gender Stereotying in Sex discrimination", *Psychology, Public Policy & Law,* 5, pp. 665-692.

Burnis, James Macgregor (1978), *Leadership,* Delhi Ambica Publication.

Burns, J. M. (1978), Leadership, New York: Plenum.

Carli, L. L. ((2001)), "Gender and Social Influence", *Journal of Social Issues,* 57, 725-741.

Catalyst, Women in U.S. *Corporate Leadership,* New York: Author, 2003.

Catalyst, Women "Take Care", Men "Take Charge", Stereotyping of U.S. Business Leaders Exposed, New York: Author, 2005.

Center for American Women and Politics; "Women in Elected Office 2006", *Retrieved* April 12, 2006, from *http://www.cawp.rutgers.edu/ Facts/Office holders/cawfps.html.*

Chandra, Bipin, A. Tripathi & B. De (2005), *Freedom Struggle,* National Book Trust, India, New Delhi.

Chaturvedi, S. K. (1992), "Bhartiya Rajniti Mein Mahilaon Ka Yogdan", *Loktantra Samiksha,* Vol. 24, No. 1.4.1992.

Chemers, M. M. (1997), *An Integrative Theory of Leadership,* Mahawa, New Jersy, Lawrence, Erlbaum.

Chemers, M. M. and Murphy, S. E. (1995), "Leadership and Diversity in Groups and Organizations", in M. M. Chemers, S. Oskamp, & M.A. Constanzo (Eds.), *Diversity in Organizations: New Perspectives for a Changing Workplace* 1997 (pp. 157-190) Thousand Oaks, CA.: Sage.

Chhatre, Ashwini, *Political Articulation and Accountability in Decentralisation: Theory and Experience from India,* Conservation & Society 6(1).

Dandvate, Pramila (ed) (1989), *Windows Abandoned and Destitute Women in India,* Radiant Publishers, New Delhi.

Dastoor, Aloo and Usha H. Mehta (1991), *Gandhi's Contribution to the Emancipation of Women,* Popular Prakashan, Mumbai.

Dastoor, Aloo J and Usha H. Mehta (1991), *Gandhi's Contribution to the Emancipation of Women*, Popular Prakashan, Mumbai.

Deshpande, Rajeshwari (2004), "How Gendered Was Women's Participation in Election 2004?" *Economic & Political Weekly*, Vol. xxxix, No. 51, December 18, p. 5431-5436.

Devi, Rathi (2006), "Gender Discrimination in Socialization", *Legal News & Views*, April, p.4.

Eagly, A., Makhijani, M. and Klonsky, B. (1992), "Gender and the Evaluation of Leaders: A Meta-analysis," *Psychological Bulletin*, 111, 3-22.

Eagly, A. H. and Johnson, B. T. (1990), Gender and Leadership Style: A Meta-analysis. *Psychological Bulletin*, 108(2), pp. 233-256.

Eagly, A. H. and Carli, L. L. (2003); "The Female Leadership Advantage: An Evaluation of the Evidence," *Leadership Quarterly*, 14, 807-834.

Eagly, A. H. and Carli, L.L. (2004), Women and Men as Leaders In J. Antonakis, R. J. Sternberg, & A.T. Cianciolo (Eds.), *The Nature of Learship*, Thousand Oaks, CA: Sage.

Economic & Political Weekly, May 19, 2001

Enloe, Cynthia Bananas (1990), *Beaches and Bases: Making Feminist Sense of International Politics*, University of California Press, Berkeley.

ESRC Research Group; *Women and Social Capital*, South Bank University, London, 2005.

Flectcher, J. K. (2001), *Disappearing Acts: Gender, Power, and Relational Practice at Work Boston:* MiT Press.

Fondas, N. (1997), 'Feminization Unveiled: Management Qualities in Contemporary Writings", *Academy of Management Review*, 22, 257-282.

Forsyth, D. R. (2006), *Group Dynamics* (4th ed.), Pacific Grove, CA : brokks/Cole.

Geary, D. C. (1998), *Male, Female: The Evolution of Human Sex Difference*, American Psychological Association Washington, DC.

Ghosh, Jayati (1999), "Women in Indian Politics", *Frontline*, October 8.

Government of India; *State of Panchayats*, Ministry of Panchayati Raj, New Delhi 2007-08 (Three Volumes).

Gupta, Shobha Kumari (2008), *Voluntarism, Social Capital and Women's Empowerment at Grassroots Level,* M P S Publishers Distributors, New Delhi.

Haq, Nisar-ul (2005), "The United Nations and the Elimination of Discrimination Against Women", *Indian Journal of Political Science,* Vol. 66, No. 1, Jan.-March.

Haq, Nisra-ul (2005),"The United Nations and the Elimination of Discrimination Against Women", *Indian Journal of Political Science,* Vol. 66, No. 1, Jan.-March.

Helgesen, S. (1990), *The Female Advantage : Women's Ways of Leadership,* New York: Doubleday.

Heptualla, Najama (ed) (1992), *Reforms for Women: Future Options,* Oxford & IBH Publishing Co. Pvt. Ltd., New Delhi.

Hoyt, C. and Blascovich, J. (2006), *Leadership Efficacy and Women Leaders' Responses to Stereotype Activation,* Manuscript Submitted for Publication.

Human Rights Watch, *Broken People of India: Caste Violence Against Untouchables,* HRW, New York, 1999.

http//www.thp.org/where_we_work/south_asia/India/map/bihar.

Inter-Parliamentary Union, "Women in National Parliaments", *Retrieved* June 30, 2006, from *http://www.ipu.org/wrnn-e/classif.htm.*

Jaggar and Rothenberg (ed) (1993), *Feminist Frame works : Alternative Theoretical Accounts of the Relations Between Women and Men,* McGraw Hill, New York.

Jan, L. (1991), "Participation as a Political Conceptualization", *The Journal of Politics,* Vol. 53, No. 1, 1991, p. 207.

Jha U.S. & P.L. Pujari (1996), *Indian Women Today : Tradition, Modernity and Challenge,* Kanishka Publishers, New Delhi.

Kapadia, K.M. (1966), *Marriage and Family in India,* Oxford University Press, Calcutta.

Kapoor, Promila (2001), *Empowering the Indian Women,* Publication Division, Ministry of Information and Broadcasting, Govt. of India.

Kasturi, Leela, Development, Patriarchy and Politics : Indian Women in the Political Process, 1947-1992 , 1998

Kaviraj, S. (1986), "Indira Gandhian Indian Politics", *Economics and Political Weekly,* Sept. 20-27, 1986, p. 1697.

Kumar Abhay (1999), *Electoral Violence,* Kanishka Publishers, New Delhi.

Kumari, Archana (2008), Nepal Rajniti: Samvidhanwad Evam Prajatantra ki Vikash, M P S Publishers Distributors, New Delhi.

Kumari, A., & Kidwai, S. (1998), Crossing the Sacred Line : Women's Search for Political Power, Orient Longman, India.

Lassweli H.D. (1951), *Political Writing of Harold D. Lasswell,* Illinois: The Free Press.

Latneihzori (2007), *Women's Development in India,* Mittal.

Madhu, K. (1996), "Women and Politics", *Economic and Political Weekly,* Oct. 26.

Madhuanand, S. and R.C. Majumdar (ed) (1953), *Great Women of India,* Almora, Advaita Ashrama.

Mahatma Gandhi, *Young Indian,* Feb. 26, 1918.

Majumdar, D. N. (1961), *Races and Cultures in India,* Asia Publishing House, Bombay.

Majumdar, Veena (1993), *Women and the Political Process,* Durgabhai Deshmukh Memorial Lecture, Council for Social Development, New Delhi.

Manu: *The Laws of Manu,* Vol. viii, p. 416.

Mathew, George (2008), "A New Deal for Panchayats", *Panchayat Raj Update,* April.

Mehrotra, Nirlika, S. M. Patnjali (2008), "Culture Versus Coercion, Other side of Nirmal Gram Yojna", *Economic and Political Weekly,* October 25.

Mehta, R. (1978), *The Western Educated Hindu Women,* Asia Publishing Home, Bombay.

Menon, L. D. (1975), "India and the International Women's Year", *India Quarterly,* Vol. 31, No. 3, July-September p. 278.

Michael Keran (1988), "Moses as a Visionary Realist", *International Political Science Review,* Vol. 9, No. 1, pp. 71-84.

Mishra, Jugal Kishore (2006), "Empowerment of Women in India", *The Indian Journal of Political Science,* Vol. LXVII, No. 4, Oct.-Dec.

Mishra, Subhesh (2008), "Apatriyashit Badhotri," *India Today,* November 19, p. 20 (in Hindi).

Mohanty, Manoranjan (Ed.) (2004), *Class, Caste, Gender,* Sage Publication.

Mukherjee, Ila (1972), *Social Status of North Indian Women,* 1526-1707 A.D., Shivial Agarwal and Company.

N. Wold; *Fire with Fire, The New Female Power and How it will change the 21st Century,* Chattu and Windus, London, 1993.

Nandy, Ashis (1976), *At the Edge of Psychology : Essays in Political and Culture,* Delhi: Oxford University Press, 1980, p. 114; and Stanley A. Kochanexla, Mrs. Gandhi's Pyramid; The New Congress: in Henry C. Harf (ed.) Indira Gandhi's India, Colorads : Westview Press, pp. 93-124.

Narayan, Usha (1999), "Women and Political Participation: Twenty First Century Challenges, " *Mainstream,* Vol.-xxvii, No. 16, April 10.

Nath, Vikas, "Digital Governance: Building and Sustaining Democratic and Accountble Governance Structures Using Its", p. 9, *http; ://www, edd e.vt edu/cligital gov./gov – Meny.ht ml.*

Newton Juclith L. (1983), *Sex and Class in women's History: Essays from Feminist Studies,* Routledge and Kegan Paul, London.

Nieva, V. E. and Gutek, B. A. (1981), Women and Work: A Psychological Perspective, New York.

P. Thomas (1964), *Indian Women Through the Ages,* Asia Publishing House, Bombay.

Palanithurai, G. (2005), *Dynamics of New Panchayati Raj System in India,* Vol. IV Concept Publishing Company, New Delhi.

Pam, Rajput; *Women's Political Participation in India : An Agenda for Empowerment.*

Panicker, K. M. (1955), *Hindu Society and the Cross-Road,* Asia Publishing House, Bombay.

Peterson, V. Spike and Anne Sisson Runyon (1999), *Global Gender Issues* (2nd ed.), : Westview Press, Oxford.

Peterson, V. Spike and Anne Sisson Runyon (1999), *Global Gender Issues* (2nd ed), Oxford: West view Press.

Phadanwis, Urmilla (ed) (1978), *Women of the World,* New Delhi.

Pintu, M. (2005), 'Development Through Empowerment of Women in India', The *Kurukshetra,* Aug..

Political Empowerment of Women: High level Intergovernmental meeting of Review Regional Implementation of Baijing platform for Action, 26-29 Oct. 1997.

Powell, G. N. (1999), "Reflections on the Glass Ceiling : Recent Trends and Future Prospects", In G.N. Powell (ed.), *Handbook of ?Gender and Work* (pp. 325-345), Thousand Oaks, CA : Sage.

Powell, G. N. and Graves, L. M. (2003), *Women and Men in Management* (3rd ed.), Thousand Oaks, CA : Sage.

Putnam, Robert ((2001)), "Social Capital: Measurement and Consequences." Isumia : *Canadian Journal of Policy Research*, 2, (2001): 41.

Putnam, Robert; *Making the Democracy Work : Civic Traditions in Modern Italy*, Princeton University Press, Princeton

Rajpurohit and Bela Rani Sharma (1965), *Trends in Women's Studies*, Annual Publication Pvt. Ltd., New Delhi.

Ranganathan, Saraa (1998), *Women and Social Order: A profile of Major Elicitors and Determinants*, Kanishka Pub., New Delhi.

Ranjana Kumari (1994), *Women Parliamentarians*, Har Anand Publication, New Delhi.

Reynolds, Andrew Stephen (1999), "Women in the Legislature and Executives of the World: Know King at the Highest Glass Ceiling" *World Politics*, Vol. 51, No. 4 (July 1999).

Rose, E.D. (1973), *The Hindu Family in Its Urban Setting*, Oxford University Press, Delhi.

Roy, Anapurna (2008), "Empowerment For Change", *Yojana* October.

S.T. Fiske and G. Lindzey (Eds.), *The Handbook of Social Psychology* (Vol. 2, pp. 982-1026), McGraw-Hill, Boston

Saxena, S. K., Vaishali Singh (2000), *Human Rights Indicators: Some Issues*, Anamika Publishers, New Delhi.

Sengupta, Padmini (1974), *The Story a Women of India*, Indian Book Company, New Delhi.

Sethi, Renu (1988), "Determinants of Women's Active Political Participation", the *Indian Journal of Political Science*, Vol. 49, No. 4, Oct.-Dec. 1988, p. 565.

Shah, Mihir (2008), "The Real Radicalism of NREGA", *The Hindu*, 22 May.

Shalini; *Women Empowerment*, Novelty and Co., Patna, p. 1997.

Sharma, Arjun (2007), "Rising Roles of Nirdaliyas", A Case Study of the 14th Lok Sabha General Election, 2004". *The Indian Journal of Political Science*, Vol. LXVIII, No. 2, April-June, 2007, pp. 373-389.

Sharma, Kumud (1998), *Power vs. Representation: Feminist Dilemmas, Ambivalent State and the Debate on Reservation for Women in India*, Occasional Paper No. 28, Centre for Women Development Sudies (CWDS).

Sharma, Priyanka (2008), *Women Empowerment and Working Women*, Book Enclave, Jaipur.

Sinha, Niroj (1989), *Women as Marginals in Politics*, in Pramila Dandvate (ed.)*: Destitute Women in India*, Radian Publishers, New Delhi.

Srinivas, M. N., *The Changing Position of Indian Women*, University Press, Madras.

Subramanian, Malathi (2002), "Women in Indian Politics; Participation and Representation" in Lal, Malashri, & Paul Kumar, Sukrita, Eds., *Women Studies in India : Contours of Changes*, Indian Institute of Advanced Studies, Shimla UNIFEM (2000) Progress of South Asian Women (2000), New Delhi.

Swamy, K. Kuppu (1987), "Women and Political Awakening", *Roshni*, July Sept..

Batliwala, S. (1994), *The Meaning of Women's Empowerment;* Harvard Series on Population and International Health.

The Times of India; 22 January, 1991.

The Times of Indian, Patna Edition, May – 7, 2004, p.1.

Twenge, J. M. (2001), "Change in Women's Assertiveness in Response to Status and Roles : A Cross-Temporal Meta-Analysis 1931-1993", *Journal of Personality and Social Psychology*, 18, 2001, pp. 133-145.

UNDP; *Gender and Governance*, Human Development Research Centre (UNDP), New Delhi. 2003

UNDP, "Women Political Participation and Good Governance: 21st Century, Challenges, *UNDP Report*, 2000.

United Nations: 'Women and Decision – Making', *Women–2000;* New York.

Verma, R. K. and G. K. Yadav (1996), "Women in Bihar Politics", *Economic & Political Weekly,* 14 April.

Verma, R.K. and M. Singh (2001), "Voluntarism and Panchayat Elections in Bihar 2001: A Study ", *Indian Journal of Public Administration,* Oct.-Dec..

Verma, R. K. and M. Singh (2001), "Women Political Empowerment at Grassroots in Bihar: Role of Voluntarism", *Vidhanmala,* Annual No.

Verma, R. K. (1996), "Political Leadership: Issues in Concept and Approches", *Journal of Social and Economic Studies,* Combined Issue.

Verma, R. K. (1991), *Rural Political Leadership: A Study of Social Structure and People's Perception,* Amar Prakashan, Delhi.

Verma, R. K. (2007), *Panchayat Raj Elections in Bihar A Study of the People, Parties and Electoral Process* (Mimco), Report submitted to ICSSR, New Delhi.

Weiner, Myron (1976), "Plitical Participation : Crisis Political Process", in N.D. Palmer, *Elections and Political Development : The South Asian Experiences,* Vikash Publishing House, New Delhi.

Women's Movement, Advancement of Women in India, 1995-1999, A draft report, August, 1999.

Yhosh, Gopi Nath (2008), "Transparency and Accountability", *Yojna,* August.

इण्टर पार्लियामेन्ट्री यूनियन : राजनीति में महिलायें (1995-2005)

अन्नान कॉफी (2006), वीमेन इन डिसिजन मेकिंग. *www.un.org/events.*

महाजन सुमित्रा (2001), 'महिला सशक्तिकरण– दर्शन लक्ष्य और उपलब्धियाँ, *योजना,* अगस्त।

पाण्डेय, जितेन्द्र कुमार (2006), महिला सशक्तिकरण में पंचायत राज की भूमिका, *कुरूक्षेत्र,* अगस्त।

शर्मा, निशिथ राकेश (2006), पंचायती राज संस्थान में महिलाओं की बढ़ती भूमिका, *कुरूक्षेत्र,* अगस्त।

पाण्डेय, जितेन्द्र कुमार (अगस्त 2006 *कुरूक्षेत्र*), महिला सशक्तिकरण में पंचायती राज की भूमिका, पृ. सं. 30-31

शोध यात्रा : शोध एवं शिक्षण परिषद् ग्वालियर (म.प्र.)

शोध विधिका : पंचायत राज एवं ग्रामीण विकास शासन, महाराजा स्वशासी महाविद्यालय छतरपुर (म.प्र.)

पाठक, इन्दू (2007), 'राजनीतिक सहभागिता एवं महिला सशक्तिकरण', *कुरूक्षेत्र,* मार्च।

राजाराम, कल्पना (2008), भारत का संविधान और भारतीय राजनीति व्यवस्था, स्पेक्ट्रम बुक्स प्रा.लि., जनकपुरी, पृ. 419-422।

गुप्ता, सरोजकुमार (2007), भारतीय नारी, कल, आज और कल, प्रकाशन संस्थान, नई दिल्ली, पृ. 330-361।

के. एम. मात्यु (2001), मनोरमा ईयर बुक।

गुप्ता, अरूण कुमार (2005), 'वीमेन इम्पावरमेंट एण्ड सोशल जस्टिस‍, द मेरठ जरनल ऑफ पॉलिटिकल साइन्स एण्ड पब्लिक एडमिनिस्ट्रेशन, वर्ष-8, क्रम 1 और 2, जनवरी-दिसम्बर।

जॉन, मेरी, आल्टरनेट मॉर्डरनीटिज रिजर्वेशन्स एण्ड वीमेन्स मूवमेंट इन 20वीं सेंचूरी इंडिया।

जोशी, आर.पी. एवं रूपा मंगलानी, सम्पादक, भारत में पंचायती राज, राजस्थान हिन्दी ग्रन्थ अकादमी, जयपुर।

निशा, उल-हक (2005), 'द यूनाईटेड नेशन्स एण्ड द एलीमीनेशन ऑफ डीस्क्रीमिनेशन अगेन्सट वीमेन', द इण्डियन जरनल ऑफ पॉलिटिकल साइन्स, वर्ष-66, क्रम-1, जनवरी-मार्च।

पाण्डेय जितेन्द्र कुमार (2006), महिला सशक्तिकरण में पंचायती राज की भूमिका, अगस्त, पृ. सं. 30, 31।

पाठक, इन्दू (2007), राजनीतिक सहभागिता एवं महिला सशक्तिकरण, कुमायूँ विश्वविद्यालय, नैनीताल, *कुरूक्षेत्र,* मार्च, पृ. सं. 26-30।

मित्तल, ए. के., भारत का राजनीतिक एवं सांस्क तिक इतिहास, साहित्य भवन पब्लिकेशन्स, आगरा ।

शर्मा, निशिथ राकेश (2006), पंचायती राज संस्थाओं में महिलाओं की बढ़ती भूमिका, *कुरूक्षेत्र,* अगस्त।

साधना आर्य, निवेदित मेनन, जिनी लोकनीता, सम्पा. नारीवादी राजनीति, संघर्ष एवं मुद्दे, हिन्दी माध्यम कार्यान्वयन निदेशालय, दिल्ली विश्वविद्यालय, नई दिल्ली।

सुहेली (2006), 'सोसियो-इकोनोमिक स्टेटस ऑफ वीमेन इन इण्डिया', रिभ्यू ऑफ पॉलिटिक्स, वर्ष-14, क्रम-1, जनवरी-जून।

स्वप्निल सारस्वत, डॉ. निशांत सिंह, समाज, राजनीति और महिलाएं, दशा और दिशा, नमन प्रकाशन, नई दिल्ली।